Lecture Notes in Computer S

Commenced Publication in 1973
Founding and Former Series Editors:
Gerhard Goos, Juris Hartmanis, and Jan van Le

T0238147

Juhnyoung Lee   Junho Shim
Sang-goo Lee   Christoph Bussler
Simon Shim (Eds.)

Data Engineering Issues
in E-Commerce and Services

Second International Workshop, DEECS 2006
San Francisco, CA, USA, June 26, 2006
Proceedings

 Springer

Volume Editors

Juhnyoung Lee
IBM T. J. Watson Research Center, USA
E-mail: jyl@us.ibm.com

Junho Shim
Sookmyung Women's University, Seoul, Korea
E-mail: jshim@sookmyung.ac.kr

Sang-goo Lee
Seoul National University, Seoul, Korea
E-mail: sglee@europa.snu.ac.kr

Christoph Bussler
Cisco Systems, Inc., USA
E-mail: ch.bussler@aol.com

Simon Shim
San Jose State University, USA
E-mail: sishim@e-mail.sjsu.edu

Library of Congress Control Number: 2006927371

CR Subject Classification (1998): H.4, K.4.4, J.1, H.3, H.2, K.5

LNCS Sublibrary: SL 3 – Information Systems and Application, incl. Internet/Web
and HCI

ISSN   0302-9743
ISBN-10   3-540-35440-9 Springer Berlin Heidelberg New York
ISBN-13   978-3-540-35440-6 Springer Berlin Heidelberg New York

Springer is a part of Springer Science+Business Media

springer.com

© Springer-Verlag Berlin Heidelberg 2006
Printed in Germany

Typesetting: Camera-ready by author, data conversion by Scientific Publishing Services, Chennai, India
Printed on acid-free paper   SPIN: 11780397   06/3142   5 4 3 2 1 0

Preface

Welcome to the second International Workshop on Data Engineering Issues in E-Commerce and Services (DEECS 2006) in conjunction with the 8th IEEE Conference on E-Commerce Technology and the third IEEE Conference on Enterprise Computing, E-Commerce and E-Services. The purpose of the DEECS workshop is to provide an annual forum for exchange of state-of-the-art research and development in e-commerce and services. Since the increasing demand on e-commerce and services, we are witnessing a continuing growth of interest in the workshop.

The increased number of submissions this year includes a record number from Asia. We received 47 papers: 6 from North/South America, 9 from Europe, and 32 from Asia. Of these, 15 regular papers and 8 short papers were accepted. The technical program reflects an increasing development of principles in service engineering, service-oriented architecture, data and knowledge engineering, and business models and analysis. It also reflects an increased emphasis on system and tool implementation, and applications to service practices, evidencing a maturation of the underlying principles.

Many people worked hard to make this year's workshop a success. The Program Committee members carefully reviewed and discussed every paper, and made difficult decisions. The expert opinions of many outside reviewers were invaluable in making the selections and ensuring the high quality of accepted papers. We also thank authors for their interest and contribution. We thank members of the workshop committee for helping to ensure that the workshop ran smoothly. We also thank organizers of the 8th IEEE Conference on E-Commerce Technology and the third IEEE Conference on Enterprise Computing, E-Commerce and E-Services, for their support and help for the workshop. Without these efforts, this workshop would not have been possible, and we are truly grateful.

June 2006

Sang-goo Lee   Juhnyoung Lee   Junho Shim
Christoph Bussler   *Program Chair*   *Publication Chair*
Simon Shim
General Co-chairs

Organization

General Chairs

Sang-goo Lee, Seoul National University, Korea
Christoph Bussler, Cisco Systems, Inc., USA
Simon Shim, San Jose State University, USA

Program Chair

Juhnyoung Lee, IBM Research, USA

Proceedings and Web Chair

Junho Shim, Sookmyung Women's University, Korea

Program Committee

Marco Aiello, University of Trento, Italy
Cristiana Amza, University of Toronto, Canada
Luciano Baresi, Politecnico di Milano, Italy
Carlo Batini, Milano - Bicocca, Italy
Boualem Benatallah, University of South Wales, Australia
Michael Berger, Siemens, Germany
Martin Bichler, University of Munich, Germany
Bernard Burg, Panasonic, USA
Ron Cao, IBM China Research Lab, China
Malu Castellanos, Hewlett-Packard, USA
Juno Chang, Sangmyung University, Korea
Yuan-chi Chang, IBM T.J. Watson Research Center, USA
Rada Chirkova, North Carolina State University, USA
Jonghoon Chun, Myungji University, Korea
Chin-Wan Chung, KAIST, Korea
Jen-Yao Chung, IBM T.J. Watson Research Center, USA
Vivian Ding, IBM China Research Lab, China
Ernst-Erich Doberkat, University of Dortmund, Germany
Asuman Dogac, Middle East Technical University, Turkey
Schahram Dustdar, Vienna University of Technology, Austria
Johann Eder, Technical University of Vienna, Austria
Dennis Fetterly, Microsoft, USA
Claude Godart, INRIA, France
Richard Goodwin, IBM T.J. Watson Research Center, USA
Paul Grefen, Eindhoven University of Technology, Netherlands
Mohand-Said Hacid, University Lyon 1, France

Chun Hua Tian, IBM China Research Lab, China
Susan Urban, Arizona State University, USA
Vassilios Verykios, University of Thessaly, Greece
Roel Wieringa, University of Twente, Netherlands
Andreas Wombacher, University of Twente, Netherlands

Center for E-Business Technology, Seoul, Korea

Table of Contents

Business Models and Analysis

Web Services

E-Commerce Systems

An Approach to Detecting Shill-Biddable Allocations in Combinatorial Auctions

Tokuro Matsuo[1], Takayuki Ito[2], and Toramatsu Shintani[2]

[1] School of Project Design,
Miyagi University,
Gakuen, Taiwa, Kurokawa-gun, Miyagi, 981–3298, Japan
matsuo@myu.ac.jp
[2] Department of Information Science and Engineering,
Nagoya Institute of Technology,
Gokiso-cho, Showa-ku, Nagoya,
Aichi, 466–8555, Japan
{itota, tora}@ics.nitech.ac.jp
http://www-toralab.ics.nitech.ac.jp/~{itota, tora}

Abstract. This paper presents a method for discovering and detecting shill bids in combinatorial auctions. Combinatorial auctions have been studied very widely. The Generalized Vickrey Auction (GVA) is one of the most important combinatorial auctions because it can satisfy the strategy-proof property and Pareto efficiency. As Yokoo et al. pointed out, false-name bids and shill bids pose an emerging problem for auctions, since on the Internet it is easy to establish different e-mail addresses and accounts for auction sites. Yokoo et al. proved that GVA cannot satisfy the false-name-proof property. Moreover, they proved that there is no auction protocol that can satisfy all three of the above major properties. Their approach concentrates on designing new mechanisms. As a new approach against shill-bids, in this paper, we propose a method for finding shill bids with the GVA in order to avoid them. Our algorithm can judge whether there might be a shill bid from the results of the GVA's procedure. However, a straightforward way to detect shill bids requires an exponential amount of computing power because we need to check all possible combinations of bidders. Therefore, in this paper we propose an improved method for finding a shill bidder. The method is based on winning bidders, which can dramatically reduce the computational cost. The results demonstrate that the proposed method successfully reduces the computational cost needed to find shill bids. The contribution of our work is in the integration of the theory and detecting fraud in combinatorial auctions.

1 Introduction

This paper presents a method for detecting shill bids in combinatorial auctions. Auction theory has received much attention from computer scientists and economic scientists in recent years. One reason for this interest is the fact that Internet auctions such as Yahoo Auction and eBay have developed very quickly and widely. Also, auctions in B2B trades are increasing rapidly. Moreover, there is growing interest in using auction

J. Lee et al. (Eds.): DEECS 2006, LNCS 4055, pp. 1–12, 2006.
© Springer-Verlag Berlin Heidelberg 2006

mechanisms to solve distributed resource allocation problems in the field of AI and multi-agent systems.

Combinatorial auctions have been studied very widely as one of most important auction formats. In a combinatorial auction, bidders can make bids on bundles of multiple different items. The main issue in a combinatorial auction is its winner determination problem. The computation for winner determination is an NP-complete problem, since there can be exponential numbers of bundles of items and an auctioneer needs to find a bundle combination that maximizes revenue. Many studies have approached this problem by investigating a variety of search algorithms.

The Generalized Vickrey Auction (GVA) is one of the combinatorial auctions that are strategy-proof, i.e., the dominant strategy is for bidders to declare their true evaluation value for a good, and its allocation is Pareto efficient. Many scientists in the field of auction theory have focused on GVA because of its strategy-proof property. The details of GVA are described in Section 2.

As Yokoo et al. pointed out, false-name bids and shill bids are an emerging problem for auctions, since on the Internet it is easy to establish different e-mail addresses and accounts for auction sites. Bidders who make false-name bids and shill bids can benefit if the auction is not robust against false-name bids. A method to avoid false-name bids and shill bids is a major issue that auction theorists need to resolve.

Yokoo et al. proved that GVA cannot satisfy the false-name-proof property. Moreover, they proved that there is no auction protocol that can satisfy all of the three major properties, i.e., false-name-proof property, Pareto efficiency, and strategy-proof property. Thus, they have developed several other auction protocols that can satisfy at least the false-name-proof property. However, satisfying the false-name proof property prevents them from developing Pareto efficient and strategy-proof protocols.

On the contrary, in this paper we propose a method for detecting shill bids with GVA in order to avoid them. Our algorithm can judge whether there might be a shill bid from the results of the GVA's procedure. If there is the possibility of a shill bid, the auctioneer can make the decision of whether to stop allocation of items based on the results. Namely, we build an algorithm to find shill bids in order to avoid them. This differs from the approach of Yokoo et al., which builds mechanisms to avoid shill bids.

A shill bid is defined as two or more bids created by a single person, who can unfairly gain a benefit from creating such bids. Therefore, the straightforward way to find shill bids is to find a bidder whose utility becomes negative when his/her bids and those of another bidder are merged. The merging method is described in Section 3. However, this straightforward method requires an exponential amount of computing power, since we need to check all of combinations of bidders. Thus, in this paper, we propose an improved method for finding a shill bidder. The method is based on the brute force algorithm, and it can dramatically reduce the computational cost.

The rest of this paper consists of the following six parts. In Section 2, we show preliminaries on several terms and concepts of auctions. In Section 3, shill-biddable allocations are defined and discussed. In Section 4, the brute force algorithm used in this paper is introduced. In Section 5, we explain how we handle a massive number of bidders. Finally, we present our concluding remarks and future work.

2   Related Work

Milgrom analyzed the shill-biddable feature in VCG [6]. Bidders in GVA can profitably use shill bidders, intentionally increasing competition in order to generate a lower price. Thus, the Vickrey auction provides opportunities and incentives for collusion among the low-value, losing bidders. However, this work does not refer to the method of detecting shill bidding in combinatorial auctions.

Yokoo et al. reported the effect of false-name bids in combinatorial auctions [13]. To solve the problem, Yokoo, Sakurai and Matsubara proposed novel auction protocols that are robust against false-name bids [11]. The protocol is called the Leveled Division Set (LDS) protocol, which is a modification of the GVA and it utilizes reservation prices of auctioned goods for making decisions on whether to sell goods in a bundle or separately. Furthermore, they also proposed an erative Reducing(IR) protocol that is robust against false-name bids in multi-unit auctions [12]. The IR protocol is easier to use than the LDS, since the combination of bundles is automatically determined in a flexible manner according to the declared evaluation values of agents. They concentrate on designing mechanisms that can be an alternative of GVA. Due to our fundamentally different purpose, we do not simply adopt off-the-shelf methods for mechanism design.

Some studies[2][7][9] proposed methods for computing and calculating the optimal solution in combinatorial auctions. These analyses contributed to the pursuit of a computational algorithm for winner determination in combinatorial auctions, but they did not deal with shill bidding and are fundamentally different approaches from our work. However, some of these algorithms can be incorporated in our work. Combinatorial auctions have a computationally hard problem in which the number of combinations increases when the number of participants/items increases in an auction, since agents can bid their evaluation values as a set of bundled items.

Sandholm[7] propose a fast winner determination algorithm for combinatorial auctions. Also, Sandholm[9] showed how different features of a combinatorial market affect the complexity of determining the winners. They studied auctions, reverse auctions, and exchanges, with one or multiple units of each item, with and without free disposal. We theoretically analyzed the complexity of finding a feasible, approximate, or optimal solution.

Fujishima et al. proposed two algorithms to mitigate the computational complexity of combinatorial auctions [2]. Their proposed Combinatorial Auction Structured Search (CASS) algorithm determines optimal allocations very quickly and also provides good "any-time" performance. Their second algorithm, called VSA, is based on a simulation technique. CASS considers fewer partial allocations than the brute force method because it structures the search space to avoid considering allocations containing conflicting bids. It also caches the results of partial searches and prunes the search tree. On the other hand, their second algorithm, called Virtual Simultaneous Auction (VSA), generates a virtual simultaneous auction from the bids submitted in a real combinatorial auction and then carries out simulation in the virtual auction to find a good allocation of goods for the real auction. In our work, to determine optimal allocations quickly in each GVA, we employ the CASS method. However, Fujishima's paper does not focus on shill bids.

Leyton-Brown et al. proposed an algorithm for computing the optimal winning bids in a multiple units combinatorial auction [5]. This paper describes the general problem in which each good may have multiple units and each bid specifies an unrestricted number of units desired for each good. The paper proves the correctness of our branch-and-bound algorithm based on a dynamic programming procedure. Lehmann et al. proposed a particular greedy optimization method for computing solutions of combinatorial auctions [4]. The GVA payment scheme does not provide for a truth-revealing mechanism. Therefore, they introduced another scheme that guarantees truthfulness for a restricted class of players.

3   Preliminaries

3.1   Model

Here, we describe a model and definitions needed for our work. The participants of trading consist of a manager and bidders. The manager prepares multiple items, and bidders bid evaluation values for what they want to purchase.

- In an auction, we define that a set of bidders/agents is $N = \{1, 2, \ldots, i, \ldots, n\}$ and a set of items is $G = \{a_1, a_2, \ldots, a_k, \ldots, a_m\}$.
- $v_i^{a_k}$ is bidder i's evaluation value at which the ith bidder bids for the kth item $(1 \leq i \leq n, 1 \leq k \leq m)$.
- $v_i(B_i^{a_k,a_l})$ is bidder i's evaluation value at which the ith bidder bids for the bundle including the kth and lth items $(1 \leq i \leq n, 1 \leq k,l \leq m)$. The form of this description is used when the bidder evaluates more than two items.
- $p_i^{a_k}$ is the payment when agent i can purchase an item a_k. When the bidder i purchases the set of bundles of items, the payment is shown as $p_i(B_i^{a_k,a_l})$.
- The set of choices is $G = \{(G_1, \ldots, G_n) : G_i \cap G_j = \phi, G_i \subseteq G\}$.
- G_i is an allocation of a bundle of items to agent i.

Assumption 1 (Quasi-linear utility). *Agent i's utility u_i is defined as the difference between the evaluation value v_i of the allocated good and the monetary transfer p_i for the allocated good. $u_i = v_i - p_i$. Such a utility is called a quasi-linear utility, and we assume the quasi-linear utility.*

Assumption 2 (Free disposal). *Regarding the true evaluation values of any bidder, for bundles B and B', if $B \subset B'$, $B \neq B'$, $v_i(B, \theta_i) \leq v_i(B', \theta_i)$ holds.*

Namely, in this paper, when the number of items in a bundle increases, the total evaluation values for the bundle decrease. This means that free disposal is assumed.

Each bidder i has preferences for the subset $G_i \subseteq G$ of goods, which here is considered a bundle. Formally, each bidder has type θ_i, that is, in a type's set Θ. Based on the type, we show that the bidder's utility is $v_i(G_i, \theta_i) - p_i^{G_i}$ when the bidder purchases item G_i for $p_i^{G_i}$. Note that $(v_i(G_i, \theta_i))$ is bidder i's evaluation value of bundle $G_i \subseteq G$.

3.2   GVA: Generalized Vickrey Auction

GVA was developed from the Vickrey-Clarke-Groves mechanism [10][1][3], which is strategy-proof and Pareto efficient if there exists no false-name bid. We say an auction protocol is Pareto efficient when the sum of all participants' utilities (including that of the auctioneer), i.e., the social surplus, is maximized. If the number of goods is one, in a Pareto efficient allocation, the good is awarded to the bidder having the highest evaluation value corresponding the quality of the good.

In the GVA, first each agent tells his/her evaluation value $v_i(G_i, \theta_i)$ to the seller. We omit the "type" notation and simply write $v_i(G_i, \theta_i) = v_i(G_i)$. The efficient allocation is calculated as an allocation to maximize the total value:

$$G^* = arg \max_{G=(G_1,...,G_n)} \sum_{i \in N} v_i(G_i).$$

The auctioneer informs the payment amount to the bidders. Agent i's payment p_i is defined as follows.

$$p_i = \sum_{i \neq j} v_j(G^*_{\sim i}) - \sum_{i \neq j} v_j(G^*).$$

Here, $G^*_{\sim i}$ is the allocation that maximizes the sum of all agents' evaluation values other than agent i's value. Except for agent i, it is the allocation in which the total evaluation value is maximum when all agents bid their evaluation values:

$$G^*_{\sim i} = arg \max_{G \backslash G_i} \sum_{N-i} v_j(G_j).$$

3.3   Example of Shill Bids

In auction research, some papers have reported the influence of false name bids in combinatorial auctions, such as GVA[13]. These are called "shill bids." Here, we show an example of shill bids.

Assume there are two bidders and two items. Each agent bids for a bundle, that is, $\{a_1, a_2, (a_1, a_2)\}$.

Agent 1's evaluation value $v_1(B_1^{a_1,a_2})$: $\{\$6, \$6, \$12\}$
Agent 2's evaluation value $v_2(B_2^{a_1,a_2})$: $\{\$0, \$0, \$8\}$

In this case, both items are allocated to agent 1 for 8 dollars. Agent 1's utility is calculated as $12 - 8 = 4$.

If agent 1 creates a false agent 3, his/her utility increases.

Agent 1's evaluation value $v_1(B_1^{a_1,a_2})$: $\{\$6, \$0, \$6\}$
Agent 2's evaluation value $v_2(B_2^{a_1,a_2})$: $\{\$0, \$0, \$8\}$
Agent 3's evaluation value $v_3(B_3^{a_1,a_2})$: $\{\$0, \$6, \$6\}$

Agent 1 can purchase item a_1 and agent 3 can purchase item a_2. Each agent's payment amount is $8 - 6 = 2$ and each agent's utility is calculated as $6 - 2 = 4$. Namely, agent 1's utility is 8 dollars (because agent 3 is the same as agent 1).

3.4   Impossibility Theorem

Yokoo et al. examined the effect of false-name bids on combinatorial auction protocols[13]. False-name bids are bids submitted by a single bidder using multiple identifiers such as multiple e-mail addresses. They showed a formal model of combinatorial auction protocols in which false-name bids are possible. The obtained results are summarized as follows: (1) the Vickrey-Clarke-Groves (VCG) mechanism, which is strategy-proof and Pareto efficient when there exists no false-name bid, is not falsename-proof; (2) there exists no false-name-proof combinatorial auction protocol that satisfies Pareto efficiency; (3) one sufficient condition where the VCG mechanism is false-name-proof is identified, i.e., the concavity of a surplus function over bidders.

4   Shill-Biddable Allocation

4.1   Definition

We define a shill-biddable allocation as an allocation where an agent can increase his/her utility by creating shill bidders The word "shill bid" has generally multiple meanings. In our paper, "shill bid" is used as same meaning with false-name bid, that is a sheme agent produces false-agents. In our work, we use a term of the "shill bidding", that is an extended conception of false-name bid. Then, how can we judge and know that the allocation is shill-biddable In general, shill bidders are produced by a bidder who is up to increasing his/her utility. We propose a method for judging and discovering allocations that may be susceptible to shill bids ("shill-biddable allocation"). When shill bidders are created, the number of agents increases in the situation where no shill bidder is created. When the number of real bidders is n and the total number of bids is $n + n'$, we find that the number of shill bidders is n'. However, we can know what kind auctions have shill biddable possibility.

Definition 1 (Shill-biddable allocation). *A shill biddable allocation is an allocation where agents who create shill bidders can increase their utility over that of an agent who does not create shill bidders in an auction.*

When agents create shill bidders in the auction, the agents' utilities increase. For example, we assume that winner agent i's utility is $u_i(B_i^{a_1,\ldots,a_k,\ldots,a_m})$ in an auction. $u_i(B_i^{a_1,\ldots,a_m})$ is agent i's total utilities including a set of bundled items $(a_1,\ldots,a_m)$, where agent i does not create shill bidders in the auction.

Here, we consider the situation where the agent creates shill bidder u'_i. The original agent bids a set of bundled items $(a_1,\ldots,a_k)$ and the shill agent bids another set of bundled items $(a_{k+1},\ldots,a_m)$. We assume that each agent can purchase items for which he/she bids. The original agent's utility is $u_i(B_i^{a_1,\ldots,a_k})$ and the shill agent's utility is $u'_i(B_i^{a_{k+1},\ldots,a_m})$, where agent i makes a shill bidder in the auction. A shill-biddable allocation is defined when the following equation holds. $u_i(B_i^{a_1,\ldots,a_k,\ldots,a_m}) \le F(u_i(B_i^{a_1,\ldots,a_k}), u'_i(B_i^{a_{k+1},\ldots,a_m}))$.

In the above equation, $F(\cdot)$ means a kind of merge function, e.g. summation or maximization, etc. In this paper, we assume that the merge function is a maximizing function because maximum values are the evaluation values at which the agent can pay for the item.

Under the **Assumption 1**, we can show the concrete merge equation as follows: $F(u_i(B_i^{a_1,\ldots,a_k}), u'_i(B_i^{a_{k+1},\ldots,a_m}))=\{\max\{u_i(B_i^{a_1,\ldots,a_k,\ldots,a_m}), u'_i(B_i^{a_1,\ldots,a_k,\ldots,a_m})\}\}$. For example, we consider a merge investment by using the following two agents' values, that is, $v_1(B_1^{a_1,a_2,a_3})$ is $\{2,6,5,8,7,11,13\}$ and $v_2(B_2^{a_1,a_2,a_3})$ is $\{5,4,6,7,10,9,15\}$. In this case, merge investment $v_{1,2}(B_{1,2}^{a_1,a_2,a_3})$ is $\{5,6,6,8,10,11,15\}$.

4.2 Hardness of Naive Computation

A feature of shill bids is that the scheming agent can increase his/her utility when he/she bids the evaluation values divided into multiple bids. We can determine the possibility of shill bidders by comparing the utilities between a calculation using an individual agent's evaluation value and one using the merged values. Here, we consider an auction in which agents $\{1, 2, \ldots, i, \ldots, n\}$ participate. The number of merged investments is calculated as $2^n - n - 1$, namely the computational cost is $O(2^n)$. Furthermore, in the GVA, the Vickrey-Groves-Clarke pricing mechanism is known computational complexity [8]. It is the hardness of naive computation when the existence of possibility of shill bidders are enumerated using all bidders' values. Furthermore, when we determine the payments for winners in VCG, we need a computational cost of $O(2^n)$ for each winner. Therefore, a huge computational cost is required to judge whether an allocation is shill-biddable. Consequently, we propose a cost-cutting method for finding shill-biddable allocations and a heuristic method for auctions involving a massive number of bidders.

5 Brute Force Algorithm

5.1 Shill-Bidders Must Be Winners

Agents who create shill bidders basically cannot increase their utilities without the shill bidder winning in an auction. We can show this feature through the following theorem.

Theorem 1 (Shill-bidders must be winners). *An agent who creates shill bidders can not increase his/her utility unless a shill bidder wins.*

Proof. We prove that bidder agent i's utility u_i does not decrease when the agent's shill bidder does not win in an auction. When bidder i does not create any shill bidders, bidder i's payment p_i can be illustrated by using the following equation. $p_i = \sum_{i \neq j} v_j(G^*_{\sim i}) - \sum_{i \neq j} v_j(G^*)$. When the bidder agent creates shill bidders, bidder i's payment p'_i is $p'_i = \sum_{i \neq j} v_j(G'^*_{\sim i}) - \sum_{i \neq j} v_j(G'^*)$.

Here, we show $p'_i \geq p_i$ in the following proof. We assume bidder i's shill bidders do not win in the auction. Also, the set of allocations in the auction does not change. Namely, $G' = G \not\ni s$ holds. The difference between p'_i and p_i is shown as follows. $p'_i - p_i = \sum_{i \neq j} v_j(G'_{\sim i}) - \sum_{i \neq j} v_j(G') - (\sum_{i \neq j} v_j(G_{\sim i}) - \sum_{i \neq j} v_j(G)) = \sum_{i \neq j} v_j(G'_{\sim i}) - \sum_{i \neq j} v_j(G_{\sim i})$. Next, we show $\sum_{i \neq j} v_j(G'_{\sim i}) \geq \sum_{i \neq j} v_j(G_{\sim i})$.

We assume that the number of items is m, where these include an a item's set $M = \{a_1, a_2, \ldots, a_m\}$. A set of bids is assumed to be $B=\{B_1, \ldots, B_{i-1}, B_{i+1}, \ldots, B_n\} \in$

$G_{\sim i}$. However, the set of bids is shown as $B' = B \cup \{B'_1, \ldots, B'_{n'}\} \in G'_{\sim i}$. The set $\{B'_1, \ldots, B'_{n'}\}$ is the subset of the shill bid.

Allocations $G_{\sim i}$ and $G'_{\sim i}$ can be shown as $G_{\sim i} = \max \sum_{x=1}^{n} p_x y_x$, $s.t. \sum_{x|z \in G_{\sim i}}$ $y_x \geq 1, \forall z \in \{1, \ldots, m\}, y_x \in \{0, 1\}$. and $G'_{\sim i} = \max \sum_{x=1}^{n+n'} p_x y_x$, $s.t. \sum_{x|z \in G'_{\sim i}}$ $y_x \geq 1, \forall z \in \{1, \ldots, m\}, y_x \in \{0, 1\}$. Then, $\max \sum_{x=1}^{n} p_x y_x \leq \max \sum_{x=1}^{n+n'} p_x y_x$. Namely, the following inequality holds. $\sum_{i \neq j} v_j(G'_{\sim i}) \geq \sum_{i \neq j} v_j(G_{\sim i})$. Thus, $p'_i \geq p_i$. Suppose that $u_i = v_i - p_i$, $u_i \geq u'_i$ holds.

5.2   Winner-Based Algorithm

Based on the above theorem1, we propose a method to determine the possibility of shill bidding by using the winners' evaluation values in a combinatorial auction. In this paper, we assume the case where there is one agent who is engaging in shill bidding, because the analysis is complicated when there are multiple agents who create shill bidders. Shill bidders are created by separating the bids of an original agent. Namely, the original agent can increase the utility by dividing his/her bidding actions. When the original bidder and his/her shill bidders are winners of an auction, we can determine how much the agent increases the utility by comparing the utilities of divided bidding and merged investment bidding. Intuitively, we propose a winner-based algorithm, which is based on a comparison of utilities between bidding in real auctions and bidding based on our method. We describe our proposed algorithm in detail.

Input: evaluation values of bundles for each player.
Output: True if there is a shill bid.
　　　　　False if there is no shill bid.

Function Detecting a Shill bid
begin
　　Determining winners and calculating payments based on GVA.
　　Creating a power set S for a set of players.
　　for each $s \in S$
　　　　Merging players' evaluation values in s by merge function $f(s)$.
　　　　Determining winners and calculating payments based on merged evaluation values by GVA.
　　　　$u_{f(s)} :=$ the utility of s after merged. $u_{sum_s} :=$ sum of the utilities in s before merged.
　　　　if $u_{f(s)} < u_{sum_s}$
　　　　　　return True
　　return False
end.

Here, we define a merge function f and show the merged agents' evaluation values and payment from a set of agents. We assume that the set of agents who are merged is $\{i, i+1, \ldots, j\} \in N$.

Definition 2 (Merge function). *f is the merge function, which is defined as $f(i, i+1, \ldots, j)$ when a set of agents $\{i, i+1, \ldots, j\}$ are merged.*

To compare bidder's utilities between the case in the real auction and the case based on merged investment, merged agents' evaluation values v, payments p, and utilities u is defined as follows.

$v_{f(i,i+1,...,j)}$ is merged evaluation values based on agents $\{i, i+1, \ldots, j\}$s' evaluation values. $p_{f(i,i+1,...,j)}$ is agents $\{i, i+1, \ldots, j\}$s' payment amount under merged investment. $u_{f(i,i+1,...,j)}$ is agents $\{i, i+1, \ldots, j\}$s' utilities under merged investment.

In this section, we assume that $v_{f(i,i+1,...,j)}$ is the following maximum function among agents' evaluation values for each item.

Maximum selection method. The maximum selection method is shown that $v_{f(i,i+1,...,j)}$ is shown as $(\max_{i,i+1,...,j}\{v_i^{a_1}\}, \quad \max_{i,i+1,...,j}\{v_i^{a_2}\}, \ldots, \max_{i,i+1,...,j}\{v_i(B_i^{a_1,...,a_m})\})$ for agent i's evaluation value $(v_i^{a_1}, v_i^{a_2}, \ldots, v_i(B_i^{a_1,...,a_m}))$.

If there is the possibility of shill bidders, the following equation holds.

$$\sum_{i,i+1,...,j} u_{i,i+1,...,j} > u_{f(i,i+1,...,j)}$$

$\sum_{i,i+1,...,j} u_{i,i+1,...,j}$ is the total sum of the agents' $\{i, i+1, \ldots, j\}$ utilities in the case of divided bidding in the allocation of the same items.

Here, we show an example of merge valuations by using the maximum selection function. For example, assume there are four agents and three items $M = (a_1, a_2, a_3)$ in an auction. Each agent bids for a bundle, that is, $\{(a_1), (a_2), (a_3), (a_1, a_2), (a_1, a_3), (a_2, a_3), (a_1, a_2, a_3)\}$.

> Agent 1's value $v_1(B_1^{a_1,a_2,a_3}) : \{7, 0, 0, 7, 7, 0, 7\}$
> Agent 2's value $v_2(B_2^{a_1,a_2,a_3}) : \{0, 0, 0, 0, 0, 0, 16\}$
> Agent 3's value $v_3(B_3^{a_1,a_2,a_3}) : \{0, 6, 0, 6, 0, 6, 6\}$
> Agent 4's value $v_4(B_4^{a_1,a_2,a_3}) : \{0, 0, 8, 0, 8, 8, 8\}$

In GVA, winners are decided as the combination in which social surplus is maximum, that is, \$21 when agents 1, 3 and 4 are selected. Agent 1 can purchase item a_1 for \$2, agent 3 can purchase item a_3 for \$1, and agent 4 can purchase item a_4 for \$3. Each agent's utility is calculated for \$5.

Here, to detect a shill bidder, our algorithm merges the agents' evaluation values. When agent 1's and agent 3's evaluation values are merged, the merged value $v_{f(1,3)}$ is shown as $\{7, 6, 0, 7, 7, 6, 13\}$.

The merged payment of agents 1 and 3, $p_{f(1,3)}$, is \$8, which is calculated as $16 - 8 = 8$. Agent 4's payment p_4 is \$3. $u_{f(1,3)}$ is calculated as $13 - 8 = 5$. This shows that agent 1 and 3 can increase their utilities by dividing their evaluation values if agents 1 and 3 are identical. Namely, this situation indicates the possibility of a shill bidder.

The combination of merged evaluation values is $\{v_{f(1,2)}, v_{f(1,3)}, v_{f(1,4)}, v_{f(2,3)}, v_{f(2,4)}, v_{f(3,4)}, v_{f(1,2,3)}, v_{f(1,2,4)}, v_{f(1,3,4)}, v_{f(2,3,4)}, v_{f(1,2,3,4)}\}$. When all possible outcomes are enumerated, we can determine which agent might be a shill bidder. However, the combinations of merged investment increase exponentially when the number of agents and items increase. To solve this problem, we propose a greedy algorithm in the next section.

6 Handling a Massive Number of Bidders

The combination of merged evaluation values can be computed as $\sum_{l=2}^{m} {}_mC_l$. For example, when the number of agents is 10, the combination is calculated to be $\sum_{l=2}^{10} {}_{10}C_l = 1003$. Naturally, winner determination using GVA is an NP-hard problem. Namely, in the above example, the calculation of GVA's method is conducted 1003 times.

Here, to solve the computational cost problem in a massive number of bidders, we propose an algorithm to find shill bidders. We assume the following condition.

Assumption 3 (Possibility of shill bids). *When one of the bidders' evaluation values involves a bundle's evaluation value that is more than the sum of all items' evaluation values, shill bids can be successful. Namely, $v_i(B_i^{k,k+1,\ldots,l}) \leq \sum_k^l v_i^k$.*

We show the algorithm as follows. The feature of our algorithm is searching for agents who might be shill bidders. To decrease the search space, our algorithm searches for agents, who might be shill bidders, based on pruning of searching candidate.

[Algorithm]. (**Step 1**) Winners are determined based on bidders' evaluation values. The winners' utilities u_i are reserved. (**Step 2**) Our system reserves winners' evaluation values and agents' evaluation values, which determine the winners' payments. (**Step 3**) Evaluation values as described in the above assumption are searched for. Based on the search, the set of evaluation values is judged to fall into one of the following two cases. (1) The type of evaluation value shown in the above assumption does not exist. (2) The type of evaluation value shown in the above assumption does exist. (**Step 4**) In the former case (1), winners' payment amounts are calculated. In the latter case (2), the process moves to (**step5**). (**Step 5**) Our system finds bidders whose payments are determined based on the evaluation value of an agent who bids according to the above assumption. (**Step 6**) Winners' evaluation values are merged based on the method shown in Section 4. Winners' utilities $u_{f(\cdot)}$ in each merged investment are reserved. Agents' utilities u_i are compared with the merged agents' utilities $u_{f(\cdot)}$. (**Step 7**) Based on the comparison made in (**step 5**), when there are cases in which the difference between u_i and $u_{f(\cdot)}$ is not equal, a list of agents who take part in these cases is shown to the auction operator.

7 Experiments

We conducted a experiment to show the efficiency of the winner-based algorithm shown in Section 4.2. In the experiment, we measured the average elapsed time to judge whether the given bids can include shill bids or not. Figure 1 shows a result where the number of items is 3. We varied the number of bidders from 3 to 17. If there is no possibility of shill bids, for simplicity, the elapsed time is defined as the elapsed time to search all combinations of bidders. We created 1,000 different problems for each number of bidders.

The evaluation values for player i is determined as follows: First, the evaluation values for each single item are determined for each bidder based on uniform distribution.

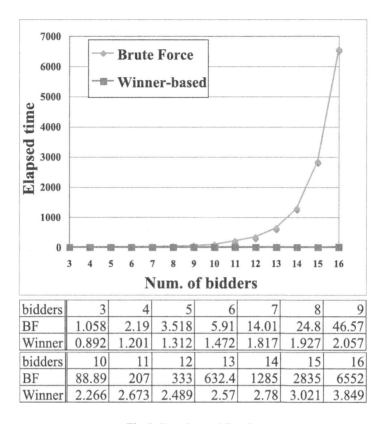

bidders	3	4	5	6	7	8	9
BF	1.058	2.19	3.518	5.91	14.01	24.8	46.57
Winner	0.892	1.201	1.312	1.472	1.817	1.927	2.057
bidders	10	11	12	13	14	15	16
BF	88.89	207	333	632.4	1285	2835	6552
Winner	2.266	2.673	2.489	2.57	2.78	3.021	3.849

Fig. 1. Experimental Results

Second, we determined whether items in a bundle is substitute or compliment at the probability of 0.5. Third, if the items in a bundle are compliment, the evaluation value of the bundle is defined as sum of evaluation values for the items in the bundle. If the items are substitute, the evaluation value of the bundle is defined as maximum of evaluation values for the items in the bundle.

In the both algorithms, we need to compute combinatorial optimization problems in GVA. Thus, in this experimentation, we utilize the BIN and the other improving methods in the CASS algorithm[2]. The experimental environment is Java SDK 1.4.2, Mac OS X 10.3, Power PC G5 2Ghz dual, and 1.5 GB memory.

Figure 1 shows an experimental result where the number of items is 3. We created 1,000 different problems and show the averages of the elapsed time to detect shill biddable allocation. The vertical axis shows the elapsed time (msec). The horizontal axis shows the number of bidders.

In terms of the heuristic algorithm shown in Section 5, the computation cost is clearly similar to or less than that of the winner-based algorithm. Thus, we focus on the winner-based algorithm shown in Section 4.2. In the worst case, the brute force algorithm(BF) clearly needs an exponential time to judge whether a shill bid is included or not. Thus, in the figure 1, the elapsed time of the brute force algorithm increased exponentially. On the contrary, the winner-based algorithm we proposed needs a linear time. The reason of the efficiency of the winner-based algorithm can be described as follows: Even the number of bidders increases, the number of winners must be lower than the number of items. Thus, in the winner-based algorithm, we do not need exponential number of combinations of bidders. The number of combinations are always lower then the number of items.

8   Conclusions

This paper proposed a method for detecting shill bids in combinatorial auctions. Our algorithm can judge whether there might be a shill bid from the results of GVA's procedure. However, a straightforward way to detect shill bids requires an exponential amount of computing power because we need to check all possible combinations of bidders. Therefore, in this paper we proposed an improved method for finding shill bidders. The method is based on winning bidders. The results demonstrated that the proposed method succeeds in reducing the computational cost of finding shill bids.

References

1. E. H. Clarke. Multipart pricing of public goods. *Public Choice*, 11:17–33, 1971.
2. Y. Fujishima, K. Leyton-Brown, and Y. Shoham. Taming the computational complexity of combinatorial auctions: Optimal and approximate approaches. In *Proc. of the 16th International Joint Conference on Artificial Intelligence (IJCAI99)*, pages 548–553, 1999.
3. T. Groves. Incentives in teams. *Econometrica*, 41:617–631, 1973.
4. D. Lehmann, L. I. O'Callaghan, and Y. Shoham. Truth revelation in approximately efficient combinatorial auctions. *Journal of the ACM*, 49(5):577–602, 2002.
5. K. Leyton-Brown, M. Tennenholtz, and Y. Shoham. An algorithm for multi-unit combinatorial auctions. In *Proc. of 17th National Conference on Artificial Intelligence (AAAI2000)*, 2000.
6. P. Milgrom. *Putting Auction Theory to Work*. Cambridge University Press, 2004.
7. T. Sandholm. An algorithm for optimal winnr determination in combinatorial auctions. In *Proc. of the 16th International Joint Conference on Artificial Intelligence(IJCAI'99)*, pages 542–547, 1999.
8. T. Sandholm. Issues in computational vickrey auctions. *International Journal of Electronic Commerce*, 4(3):107–129, 2000.
9. T. Sandholm, S. Suri, A. Gilpin, and D. Levine. Winner determination in combinatorial auction generalizations. In *Proc. of the 1st International Joint Conference on Autonomous Agents and Multi-Agent Systems (AAMAS02)*, pages 69–76, 2002.
10. W. Vickrey. Counterspeculation, auctions, and competitive sealed tenders. *Journal of Finance*, XVI:8–37, 1961.
11. M. Yokoo, Y. Sakurai, and S. Matsubara. Bundle design in robust combinatorial auction protocol against false-name bids. In *Proceedings of the 17th International Joint Conference on Artificial Intelligence (IJCAI-2001)*, pages 1095–1101, 2001.
12. M. Yokoo, Y. Sakurai, and S. Matsubara. Robust multi-unit auction protocol against false-name bids. In *Proceedings of the 17th International Joint Conference on Artificial Intelligence (IJCAI-2001)*, pages 1089–1094, 2001.
13. M. Yokoo, Y. Sakurai, and S. Matsubara. The effect of false-name bids in combinatorial auctions: New fraud in Internet auctions. *Games and Economic Behavior*, 46(1):174–188, 2004.

Explanation Services and Request Refinement in User Friendly Semantic-Enabled B2C E-Marketplaces

Simona Colucci[1], Tommaso Di Noia[1], Eugenio Di Sciascio[1],
Francesco M. Donini[2], Azzurra Ragone[1], and Raffaele Rizzi[1]

[1] Politecnico di Bari, Via Re David, 200, I-70125, Bari, Italy
{s.colucci, t.dinoia, disciascio, a.ragone}@poliba.it,
raffaele@raffaelerizzi.com
[2] Università della Tuscia, via San Carlo, 32, I-01100, Viterbo, Italy
donini@unitus.it

Abstract. This paper presents an approach aimed at fully exploiting semantics of supply/demand descriptions in B2C and C2C e-marketplaces. Distinguishing aspects include logic-based explanation of request results, semantic ranking of matchmaking results, logic-based request refinement. The user interface has been designed and implemented to be immediate and simple, and it requires no knowledge of any logic principle to be fully used.

1 Introduction

Do we really need semantics in e-marketplaces? "Where's the beef" after requesting the annotation effort needed to take advantage of semantic-enriched descriptions? As it is well-known the currently most prominent e-commerce application on the web, EBay, does not use semantics, neither does Google, and both work –fine, you may add. As a matter of fact semantic web technologies open extremely interesting new scenarios, including: formalization of annotated descriptions that are machine understandable and interoperable, without being biased by usual drawbacks of natural language expressions; the possibility to reason on descriptions and infer new knowledge; the validity of the Open World Assumption, overcoming limits of structured-data models. Nevertheless there are seriuos issues that should not be underestimated: the annotation effort is considerable, though promising results are being obtained on automated extraction and ontology mapping and merging [21]; computational complexity is often demanding also for simple reasoning tasks; interaction with semantic-based systems is often cumbersome and requires skills that most end users do not have –and are not willing to learn. Moreover we believe that the effort of annotation should be rewarded with inferences smarter than purely deductive services such as classification and satisfiability, which, although extremely useful show their limits in approximate searches (see Section 3).

J. Lee et al. (Eds.): DEECS 2006, LNCS 4055, pp. 13–27, 2006.

In this paper we show that a semantic-enabled marketplace can provide valued-added services in terms of explanations to users requests, ranking of offers and request refinement, and that use of such systems can be made easy and immediate. Main contributions of this paper include: full exploitation of nonstandard inferences for explanation services in the query-retrieval-refinement loop; semantic-based ranking in the request answering; design and implementation of a completely graphical and usable interface, which requires no prior knowledge of any logic principles, though fully exploiting it in the back-office.

2   The Need for Semantics in the Matchmaking Process

We start revisiting the rationale of knowledge-based approaches to the matchmaking process between demand and supplies. Let us observe that in a generic marketplace where supplies and demands are multiattribute descriptions, all the attributes identifying the supplies as well as describing the demand, should be considered related with each other at least via some implication and disjointness relations. Considering a simple example, if a requester is looking for *a room for two persons* and in the marketplace there is an advertisement for a *double room; use of mini-bar included*, then the user should be fully satisfied by the advertisement. From the previous example we can observe that:

– Both the demand and the supply follow a product-centric structure. There is a product to be searched / advertised with some features describing it.
– The match and classification process are not simply based on features comparison after the identification of the product category[1]. If we grouped supplies (and demands) with respect to product categories Bedroom and DoubleRoom then we would not identify the equivalence between a double room and a bedroom for two persons. Also features must be taken into account during the classification process as they characterize the semantics of classification items.

If we model products and related features in an ontology $\mathcal{T}$ using a logical language, we can exploit its formal semantics during the classification and matching processes. In particular we can identify the compatibility of a supply with respect to a demand checking the satisfiability of their logical conjunction. If it is satisfiable then they are compatible. On the other hand if the information modeling a supply imply (are classified by) the one of the demand, then the latter is completely satisfied by the former. Formally, a request R (conversely a resource O) is satisfiable w.r.t. $\mathcal{T}$ if there is at least one interpretation in all the interpretations for $\mathcal{T}$ which is also an interpretation for R (conversely for O). For what concerns classification, given R and O both satisfiable w.r.t. $\mathcal{T}$, we say that O is classified by R if all the interpretations for O are also interpretations for R.

Formally, let $\mathcal{M}$ be the interpretations set for $\mathcal{T}$ and $\mathcal{M}_R$ the set of interpretations in $\mathcal{M}$ that satisfy the request R (respectively $\mathcal{M}_O$ for the resource O). We have R (conversely O) is satisfiable if $\mathcal{M}_R \not\equiv \emptyset$ and R classifies O if $\mathcal{M}_O \subseteq \mathcal{M}_R$.

---

[1] This is a typical approach in current marketplaces – see eBay among others.

Given R and O both satisfiable w.r.t. an ontology, logic based approaches to matchmaking proposed in the literature [20, 18, 19] use classification/implication and satisfiability to grade match results in five categories. We recall such a classification list:

1. Exact. $\mathcal{M_R} = \mathcal{M_O}$ – The demand is semantically equivalent to the supply. All the interpretations for R are also interpretations for O.
2. Full - Subsumption. The information within the supply semantically implies the one within the demand. $\mathcal{M_O} \subseteq \mathcal{M_R}$ – All the interpretations for O are also interpretations for R.
3. Plug-In. The information within the demand semantically imply the one within the supply. $\mathcal{M_R} \subseteq \mathcal{M_O}$ – All the interpretations for R are also interpretations for O.
4. Potential - Intersection. The information within the supply are semantically compatible with the one in the demand. $\mathcal{M_R} \cap \mathcal{M_O} \neq \emptyset$ – Some interpretations for R are also interpretations for O.
5. Partial - Disjoint. The information within the supply are semantically incompatible with the one in the demand. $\mathcal{M_R} \cap \mathcal{M_O} = \emptyset$ – No interpretation for R is also an interpretation for O.

2.1 Fully Exploiting Semantics

Largest part of logic-based approaches only allow, as shown before, a categorization within match types. But while exact and full matches can be rare (and basically equivalent), a user may get several potential and partial matches. Then a useful logic-based matchmaker should provide a –logic– ranking of available resources vs. the request, but what we get using classification and satisfiability is a boolean answer. Also partial matches, as pointed out in [19], might be just "near miss", *e.g.*, maybe just one requirement is in conflict, but a pure satisfiability check returns a hopeless *false* result, while it could be interesting to order "not so bad" offers according to their similarity to the request.

One may be tempted to revert to classical and well assessed Information Retrieval (IR) algorithms to get a rank for approximate matches (*e.g.*, so-called Hybrid approaches [17]), but regardless of well-known limits of unstructured text retrieval, there is something IR algorithms cannot do, while a logic approach can: provide explanations for match results and suggest revision of requests. We illustrate the rationale of such an approach by computing what is needed in order to "climb the classification list" presented above and reach a **Full** or an **Exact** match.

In particular, if we get a Partial match we could revise R relaxing some restrictions, in order to reach a Potential match. Once we get a Potential match we can hypothesize what is not specified in O in order to reach a Full match and subsequently we can suggest to the user what is not specified in the relaxed R but it is in O. The ideal match sequence should be then:

$$\text{Partial} \rightarrow \text{Potential} \rightarrow \text{Full} (\rightarrow \text{Exact})$$

Now consider a demand and a supply as depicted in Figure 1(b) and the ontology in Figure 1(a) representing the knowledge domain related to pictures content. Because of the disjoint relations between daffodils and tulips we have a

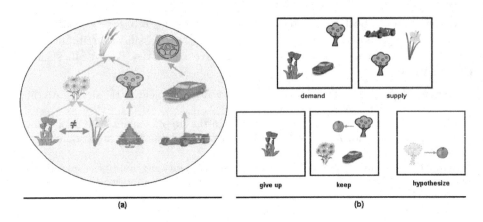

Fig. 1. (a) The reference Ontology – (b) A *demand* and a *supply* in the pictures marketplace; the contracted demand (*keep*) and the information to be given up (*give up*); features to be hypothesized in O in order to have a Full match with K(*hypothesize*)

Partial match between the demand and the supply. A contraction of the demand is needed in order to continue the matchmaking process. Notice that we have to contract less information as possible. Then in the contracted request we maintain the information about flowers and we give up only the one on tulips (see Figure 1(b)). After the contraction, a Potential match occurs between the contracted demand and the supply. We call the new contracted demand K (for Keep). With respect to O now we have $\mathcal{M}_K \cap \mathcal{M}_O \neq \emptyset$.

Now to reach a Full match we should reduce $\mathcal{M}_O$. This is possible hypothesizing some unspecified characteristic H (for Hypothesis) in O such that $\mathcal{M}_O \cap \mathcal{M}_H \subseteq \mathcal{M}_R$. If we hypothesize H as depicted in Figure 1(b) we obtain that the conjunction of O and H implies K, producing a Full match.

The previous example shows that some revision and hypotheses are needed in order to perform an extended matchmaking process and go through match classes.

– **Partial → Potential.** Contract R to K, giving up elements G conflicting with O: extend $\mathcal{M}_R$ to $\mathcal{M}_K$.
– **Potential → Full.** Make hypotheses on O adding missing characteristics H with respect to K: reduce $\mathcal{M}_O$.

Observe that we are not asking the requester to actually go through the whole process. Yet our approach has a twofold advantage: the requester can use provided information to actually revise her request and moreover the information we extract is also all what is needed to compute a semantic distance between R and O. Once we know what has to be contracted and hypothesized it is possible to compute a match degree based on K, H, G and $\mathcal{T}$, that is what is needed in order to reach a Full match taking into account the semantics modeled in the ontology $\mathcal{T}$. In case of multiple resources, we can use this match degree as a score to rank such resources according to R. With respect to the previous example, the match degree is a function $\varphi(G, K, H, \mathcal{T})$ combining all the causes for a non-Full match. Notice that φ needs also $\mathcal{T}$ to compute the *match_degree*; in fact in $\mathcal{T}$ the semantics of K, H, R and O are modeled, which should be taken into account when evaluating how to weigh them with respect to O and R. Before making the final step beyond, moving from a Full to an Exact match, some considerations are needed. In an *Open World* semantics, what is not specified in a formula has not to be interpreted as a constraint of absence. It is a "don't care" specifications. This can be due to basically two reasons:

– the user really does not care about the unspecified information.
– the user does not own that knowledge. She is not aware that it is possible to specify some other characteristics in the request, or she simply did not consider further possible specifications. She is not necessarily an expert of the marketplace knowledge domain.

In the second case a further refinement makes sense. A way to do this is to present to the user all the knowledge modeled in $\mathcal{T}$ and ask her to refine the query, adding characteristics found in $\mathcal{T}$. This approach has at least two main drawbacks:

1. The user must be bored browsing all $\mathcal{T}$ in order to find something interesting to be added to the request.
2. She can choose something in $\mathcal{T}$ which is not in any offer in the marketplace. Then after the query refinement she is not able to see any change in the list ranked using $\varphi(\mathsf{G}, \mathsf{K}, \mathsf{H}, \mathcal{T})$.

To avoid the above drawbacks, we might suggest to the requester *only* those characteristics able to change the ranked list of offers within the marketplace.

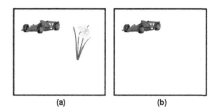

(a)   (b)

Fig. 2. Fake bonuses (a) and real bonuses (b)

Then (in an ideal marketplace where the only offer is O) we could suggest to the user to refine the contracted request adding features represented in Figure 2(a) showing B' (for Bonus) *i.e.*, what is specified in O but is not in K. But notice that in B' we have *daffodils*, that is the source of inconsistency of the original request R with the original O. Then it would be very strange if the user refined her request by adding something which is in conflict with her initial preferences. We call B' *fake bonuses* because of the above observation. The user is likely to refine adding at most $B = sportCar$ (see Figure 2(b)) specification. Adding B to K the "distance" from a Full match is reduced but we do not reach an Exact match.

Full → quasi-Exact. Suggest to the requester what should be added to K looking at non requested features B (for bonus) in O –Reduce $\mathcal{M}_\mathsf{K}$.

In the following we will refer to Description Logics (DL) and model a DL-based framework to cope with the issues introduced here.

3   Non-standard Reasoning Services

Description Logics (DLs) are a family of logic formalisms for Knowledge Representation [2] whose basic syntax elements are *concept names, role names, individuals*.

In the following, we assume the reader be familiar with DLs syntax and semantics. DL-based systems usually provide at least two basic reasoning services:

1. *Concept Satisfiability*: $\mathcal{T} \models R \not\equiv \bot$ –Given a TBox $\mathcal{T}$ and a concept R, does there exist at least one model of $\mathcal{T}$ assigning a non-empty extension to R?
2. *Subsumption*: $\mathcal{T} \models R \sqsubseteq O$ –Given a TBox $\mathcal{T}$ and two concepts R and O, is R more general than O in any model of $\mathcal{T}$?

Matchmaking services outlined in the previous section call for other non-standard inferences we briefly recall hereafter. Let us consider concepts O and R, if their conjunction $O \sqcap R$ is unsatisfiable in the TBox $\mathcal{T}$ representing the ontology, *i.e.*, they are not compatible, one may want to retract specifications in R, G (for *Give up*), to obtain a concept K (for *Keep*) such that $K \sqcap O$ is satisfiable in $\mathcal{T}$. In [10] the Concept Contraction problem was defined as follows:

Definition 1. *Let $\mathcal{L}$ be a DL, O, R, be two concepts in $\mathcal{L}$ and $\mathcal{T}$ be a set of axioms in $\mathcal{L}$, where both O and R are satisfiable in $\mathcal{T}$. A Concept Contraction Problem (CCP), identified by $\langle \mathcal{L}, O, R, \mathcal{T} \rangle$, is finding a pair of concepts $\langle G, K \rangle \in \mathcal{L} \times \mathcal{L}$ such that $\mathcal{T} \models R \equiv G \sqcap K$, and $K \sqcap O$ is satisfiable in $\mathcal{T}$. Then K is a contraction of R according to O and $\mathcal{T}$.*

Obviously, there is always the trivial solution $\langle G, K \rangle = \langle R, \top \rangle$ to a CCP, that is give up everything of R. On the other hand, when $R \sqcap O$ is satisfiable in $\mathcal{T}$, the "best" possible solution is $\langle \top, R \rangle$, that is, give up nothing — if possible. Hence, a Concept Contraction problem amounts to an extension of a satisfiable one. Since usually one wants to give up as few things as possible, some minimality in the contraction must be defined [15].

If the offered resource O and the request R are compatible with each other, *i.e.*, they *potentially match*, the partial specifications problem still holds, that is, it could be the case that O — though compatible — does not imply R. Then, it is necessary to assess what should be hypothesized (H) in O in order to completely satisfy R. In [10] the Concept Abduction problem was defined as follows:

Definition 2. *Let $\mathcal{L}$ be a DL, O, R, be two concepts in $\mathcal{L}$, and $\mathcal{T}$ be a set of axioms in $\mathcal{L}$, where both O and R are satisfiable in $\mathcal{T}$. A Concept Abduction Problem (CAP), identified by $\langle \mathcal{L}, R, O, \mathcal{T} \rangle$, is finding a concept $H \in \mathcal{L}$ such that $\mathcal{T} \models O \sqcap H \sqsubseteq R$, and moreover $O \sqcap H$ is satisfiable in $\mathcal{T}$. We call H a hypothesis about O according to R and $\mathcal{T}$.*

Obviously the definition refers to satisfiable O and R, since R unsatisfiable implies that the CAP has no solution at all, while O unsatisfiable leads to counterintuitive results ($\neg R$ would be a solution in that case). If $O \sqsubseteq R$ then we have

$H = \top$ as a solution to the related CAP. Hence, Concept Abduction amounts to extending subsumption. On the other hand, if $O \equiv \top$ then $H \sqsubseteq R$.

Intuitively, Concept Abduction and Concept Contraction can be used for respectively subsumption and satisfiability explanation. For Concept Contraction, having two concepts whose conjunction is unsatisfiable, in the solution $\langle G, K \rangle$ to the CCP $\langle \mathcal{L}, R, O, \mathcal{T} \rangle$, G represents "why" $R \sqcap O$ are not compatible. For Concept Abduction , having R and O such that $O \not\sqsubseteq R$, the solution H to the CAP $\langle \mathcal{L}, R, O, \mathcal{T} \rangle$ represents "why" the subsumption relation does not hold. H can be interpreted as *what is specified in R and not in O*. It is intuitive that adding new constructors increases DL languages expressiveness. Nevertheless, it is a well known result [6] that this usually leads to an explosion in computational complexity of inference services. Hence a trade-off is necessary. Here we refer to the $\mathcal{ALN}$ (**A**ttributive **L**anguage with unqualified **N**umber restrictions) subset of OWL-DL.

Ontologies are usually designed as *simple-TBox* in order to express the relations among objects in the domain. With a *simple-TBox* the left side is represented by a concept name in all the axioms (for both inclusion and definition). Notice that as in $\mathcal{ALN}$ only *unqualified existential restriction* is allowed, the restriction on the *ObjectProperty* must be `<owl:Thing/>`. For $\mathcal{ALN}$ algorithms have been implemented to solve Concept Abduction and Concept Contraction Problems [8] and MaMaS (**Ma**tch **Ma**ker **S**ervice) reasoner[2] supports such inference services. In [19] polynomial algorithms were introduced to provide a semantic-based score for, respectively, potential and partial matches. In particular, the `rank potential` algorithm (from now on `rp` for compactness), which will be used later on, computes, given a set of $\mathcal{ALN}$ axioms $\mathcal{T}$ and two $\mathcal{ALN}$ concepts O and R both satisfiable in $\mathcal{T}$, a *semantic distance* of O from R with respect to the ontology $\mathcal{T}$. Notice that we write *the distance of R from O* rather then *the distance between O and R* because of the non-symmetric behavior of `rp` (see [19] for further details). Recalling the definition, $\text{rp}(O, R)$ corresponds to a numerical measure of what is still missing in O w.r.t. R. If $O = \top$ we have the maximum value for $\text{rp}(O, R)$, that is the maximum (potential) mismatch of O from R. The value returned by $\text{rp}(\top, R)$ hence amounts to how specific is a complex concept expression R with respect to an ontology $\mathcal{T}$, what we call the *depth* of R: $\text{depth}(R)$. Such a measure is not trivially the depth of a node in a tree for at least two main reasons:

1. An $\mathcal{ALN}$ ontology, typically, is not a simple terms taxonomy tree, *i.e.*, its structure is not limited to simple IS-A relations between two atomic concepts[3].
2. An $\mathcal{ALN}$ complex concept is generally the conjunction of both atomic concepts and role expressions.

We remark that even though $\mathcal{ALN}$ is less expressive than the $\mathcal{SHOIN}(D+)$ supported by OWL DL, it allows the minimum set of operators needed to model requests and offers in a marketplace, in order to deal with concept taxonomy, disjoint groups, role restrictions ($\mathcal{AL}$), and number restriction ($\mathcal{N}$) to represent quantity.

---

[2] http://sisinflab.poliba.it/MAMAS-tng/DIG

[3] It can be better represented as a labeled oriented graph.

4   Algorithms and Their Rationale

With respect to the match classification presented in Section 2 we show how it is possible to exploit both standard and non-standard inference services for DL in order to identify match classes and go from a Partial match to a Full (or Exact) match, and use the obtained information to provide a semantic-based score measuring similarity w.r.t. the request.

Using Subsumption and Concept Satisfiability we can rewrite match classes in terms of Description Logics. Given an ontology $\mathcal{T}$ and a request R and an offer O, expressed as DL complex concepts, both satisfiable w.r.t. $\mathcal{T}$, we have:

$$\textbf{Exact: } \mathcal{T} \models R \equiv O - \textbf{Full: } \mathcal{T} \models O \sqsubseteq R - \textbf{Plug-In: } \mathcal{T} \models R \sqsubseteq O$$
$$\textbf{Potential: } \mathcal{T} \models R \sqcap O \not\equiv \bot - \textbf{Partial: } \mathcal{T} \models R \sqcap O \equiv \bot$$

Both Concept Abduction and Concept Contractioncan be used to suggest guidelines on what, given O, has to be revised and/or hypothesized to obtain a Full match with R.

[**Partial→Potential**] If $R \sqcap O \equiv \bot$ – Partial match – then solving the related Concept ContractionProblem we have $R \equiv G_R \sqcap K_R$ such that $K_R \sqcap O \not\equiv \bot$ w.r.t. $\mathcal{T}$. That is, we contract R to K_R such that there is a Potential match between the contracted request and O.

[**Potential→Full**] Once we are in a Potential match, we can formulate hypotheses on what should be hypothesized in O in order to completely satisfy the contracted R. If we solve the related Concept Abduction Problem, we can compute an hypothesis H such that $O \sqcap H \sqsubseteq K_R$ and reach a Full match with the contracted request.

The above concepts can be formalized in the following simple algorithm:

Algorithm. $retrieve(R, O, \mathcal{T})$
input $O, R \equiv K \sqcap G$ concepts satisfiable w.r.t. $\mathcal{T}$
output $\langle G, H \rangle$, *i.e.*, the part in R that should be retracted
and the part in O that should be hypothesized to have a
full match between O and K (the contracted R)
begin algorithm
1:   **if** $\mathcal{T} \models R \sqcap O \equiv \bot$ **then**
2:       $\langle G, K \rangle = contract(O, R, \mathcal{T})$;
3:       $H_K = abduce(O, K, \mathcal{T})$;
4:       **return** $\langle G, H \rangle$;
5:   **else**
6:       $H = abduce(O, R, \mathcal{T})$;
7:       **return** $\langle \top, H \rangle$;
end algorithm

Notice that $H = abduce(O, R, \mathcal{T})$ [rows 3,6] determines a concept H such that $O \sqcap H \sqsubseteq R$, $\langle G, K \rangle = contract(O, R, \mathcal{T})$ [row 2] determines two concepts G and K such that $R \equiv G \sqcap K$ and $\mathcal{T} \models K \sqcap O \not\equiv \bot$ following minimality criteria as suggested in [10, 8]. The information extracted by **retrieve** algorithm are what is needed to compute a similarity score between R and each supply. We refer here to a match degree function with values in [0..1].

$$\varphi = \left(1 - \frac{m}{N_R}\right) \cdot \left(1 - \frac{n}{N_K}\right) \tag{1}$$

where $N_R = \mathrm{rp}(\top, R)$, $m = \mathrm{rp}(K, R)$, $n = \mathrm{rp}(O, K)$ and $N_K = \mathrm{rp}(\top, R)$. The first factor in the previous formula represents how much of the original R has to be contracted with respect to its length and then compute a score for G; the second one gives an estimation of how many information required in K is underspecified in O.

[**Full→quasi-Exact**] Now we can try to get as close as possible to an Exact match, suggesting to the user, in a request refinement stage, what is specified in O and has not been originally requested by the user. In order to overcome the suggestion of "fake bonuses", we have to identify which part of O generated the inconsistency with R before contracting. We can solve a Concept Contraction-Problem between O and R contracting O. That is we have $O \equiv G_O \sqcap K_O$ such that $K_O \sqcap R \not\sqsubseteq \bot$ w.r.t. $\mathcal{T}$. In [10], among others, the conjunction minimal solution to a CAP is proposed for DLs admitting a normal form with conjunctions of concepts. A solution belonging to such solution is in the form $B = \sqcap_{j=1..k}C_j$, where C_j are DL concepts and is **irreducible**, *i.e.*, B is such that for each $h \in 1, ..., k$, $\sqcap_{j=1..h-1,h+1..k}C_j$ is not a solution for the CAP. The algorithm presented in [10] and implemented in MaMaS, allows to compute an irreducible solution.

In the following the algorithm $computeBonus(O, R, \mathcal{T})$ is presented, able to compute what should be hypothesized in the requester preferences in order to get a better match result, and –if possible– an Exact match (see 2). It takes as input an offer O, a request R and the ontology $\mathcal{T}$ they refer to.

Algorithm. $computeBonus(O, R, \mathcal{T})$
input O and R DL concepts both satisfiable w.r.t. $\mathcal{T}$ reference ontology
output B_{irr} a set of DL concepts representing bonuses
begin algorithm
1:    $B = \emptyset$;
2:    $B_{irr} = \emptyset$;
3:    $\langle G_R, K_R \rangle = contract(O, R, \mathcal{T})$;
4:    $\langle G_O, K_O \rangle = contract(R, O, \mathcal{T})$;
5:    $B = abduce(K_R, K_O, \mathcal{T})$;
6:    **for each** $C_j \in B$
7:        $B_{irr} = B_{irr} \cup \{C_j\}$;
8:    **return** B_{irr};
end algorithm

The problem of **fake bonuses** is taken into account in rows 3-5 of *compute-Bonus*. In row 3, a Concept ContractionProblem is solved, contracting R in K_R and identifying in G_R the source of inconsistency with O. In row 4 the same is performed for O identifying in K_O the part of the offer which is compatible with R and in G_O the incompatible one and then likely to contain the **fake bonuses**. In row 5 we compute B, solution of Concept Abduction Problem such that $K_R \sqcap B \sqsubseteq K_O$. Notice that adding B to K_R we are neither in a Plug-In match nor in an Exact one with respect to the contracted request K_R. In fact, we would have a Plug-In match if $K_R \sqcap B \sqsubseteq O$ rather than K_O and we could have an Exact match adding also **fake bonuses** which are isolated now in G_O. We notice here that an obvious improvement in the definition of users preferences and query results can be obtained explicitly determining features that are mandatory to satisfy user's request and features that she considers less stringent. We hence implemented the possibility to define explicitly strict and negotiable constraints, following the approach presented in [9]. For the sake of conciseness we do not report here the modifications to the algorithms, but refer the reader to that paper.

4.1 Illustrative Example

In order to better clarify our approach we propose a simple illustrative example. Let us consider the a demand and two supplies as depicted in Figure 3[4]. Computing $retrieve(Demand, Mercedes, \mathcal{T})$ and

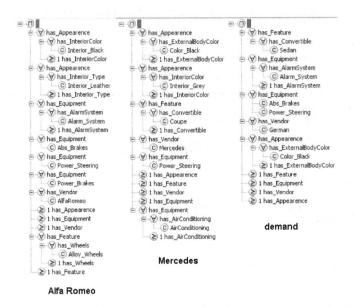

Fig. 3. The demand an supplies description used for the example

$computeBonus(Mercedes, Demand, \mathcal{T})$ we obtain results as shown in Figure 4(a) and a match $\varphi = 70\%$.

Computing $retrieve(Demand, Alfa, \mathcal{T})$ and $computeBonus(Alfa, Demand, \mathcal{T})$ we obtain results as shown in Figure 4(b) and a match degree $\varphi = 60\%$. If we refine the request adding *Power_Brakes* and *Interior_Leather* taken from the bonus of $Alfa$, we have the rank in the results list changes with a match degree of 70% for $Alfa$ and 60% for $Mercedes$.

---

[4] In Figure 4 and 5 the logic-based representation of the descriptions is depicted only for illustrative purpose. The GUI of the tool we present in Section 5 uses a more user friendly approach to composition and visualization of descriptions.

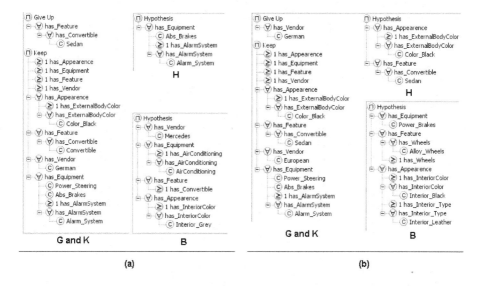

Fig. 4. (a) Matchmaking results for Mercedes - (b) Matchmaking results for Alfa

5   Prototype System

Based on the theoretical framework presented in the previous sections we developed an application fully exploiting semantic-based matchmaking procedures. The information presented within the system interface is ontology independent, *i.e.*, it is built on the fly once the reference ontology –hence the chosen marketplace domain– has been specified. Then, if the marketplace changes, the new ontology can be loaded to dynamically present to the user the new domain knowledge available and ready to be used. The GUI is divided in three main sections: in the first one (see Figure 5) the user is guided through the browsing of the ontology in order to select characteristics of the good to be searched (in other words to compose the request); in the second one (Figure 5(b)) the set of desired/undesired characteristics is shown; in the third one, a list of the offers within the marketplace is presented (see Figure 6(a)), ranked with respect to the match degree with the request. For each supply a graphical representation is presented both of the match explanation (see Figure 6(b)) and of the bonuses the user can select and add to refine the request. As shown in Figure 5(a), in order to browse the ontology an approach different from the classical tree-view is used. In the left side of the browsing panel root classes are presented. Those classes (this is the only configuration information to be provided to the tool) are the starting point for the navigation and features search. Double-clicking on a Class name, only its Subclasses are shown (in the right side of the panel). The classes navigation path is visible in the upper side of the panel. Then the user is able, whenever she wants, to go back to any level she visited previously and continue the navigation exploring other branches of the classes hierarchy. Once the user finds the characteristics she was looking for, she can drag them

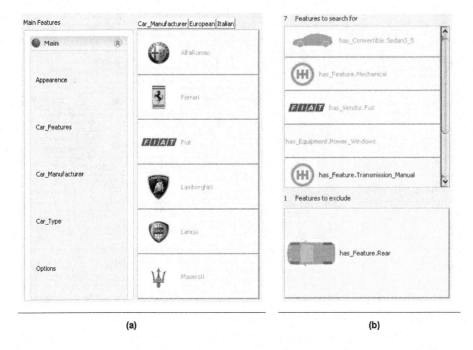

(a)   (b)

Fig. 5. (a) Ontology Browser - (b) Query Panel

in the query panel. Exploiting the domain/range relations, the query is formulated using also the ObjectProperties defined within the ontology. In the query panel, the user can express preferences both positive and negative. The panel is divided in two areas (see Figure 5(b)). In the upper one the user collects characteristics she would like to find in the resource to be matched; in the lower one characteristics explicitly not required are set. Both in the navigation and query panel, ancillary information are associated to the ontology classes and visualized ,e.g., an image icon associated to each class, in order to improve the interface usability. Using `<rdfs:comment/>` it is possible to specify the image to be shown as an icon for the class. If no ancillary information are present, then only the class name, and the ObjectProperty having the class as range, are displayed (see Figure 5(b)).

The results panel (see Figure 6) is structured as a ranked list. Each item in the list represents a supply in the marketplace whose match degree is computed with respect to the demand. Each supply is visualized as a list of sub-panels, where the user is able to see:

- **Not Satisfiable Features:** what are the causes of inconsistency. In this panel both K_R and K_O (see Section 4) are shown. Then the user is able to see what in her request is in conflict with the supply (Requested) and why the conflict arises (Proposed).
- **Uncertain Features** H: what is specified in the contracted request K and is not in the supply O.

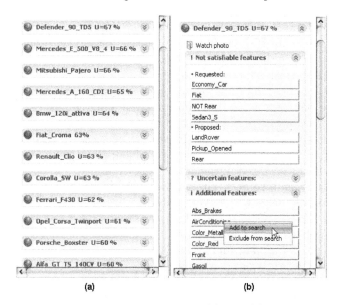

Fig. 6. System Results (a) and (b)

  – **Additional Features:** what is over-specified in the supply but is not requested, in other words the bonuses. This sub-panel offers an additional feature with respect to the previous two. For each bonus presented the user is able to add it to the "features to search for" or to the "features to exclude" and refine the query.

The reasoner is not embedded within the tool. This one communicates with the inference engine via a DIG 1.1 interface over HTTP. Since the tool exploits both standard and non-standard inference services as presented in Section 4, we use MaMaS reasoner system, which exposes a standard DIG 1.1 interface enhanced with additional tags to support the above mentioned services.

6   Related Work

Studies on matchmaking system go a long way back. For a detailed report on general matchmaking issues and systems we refer the interested reader to [19]. Here we concentrate only on relevant work in semantic matchmaking. In [13, 16] subsumption based matchmaking was initially introduced. In [20] a language, LARKS, was proposed specifically designed for agent advertisement. The matching process was carried out through five progressive stages, going from classical IR analysis of text to semantic match via Θ-subsumption. The notion, inspired by Software Engineering, of *plug-in* match was introduced to overcome in some way the limitations of a matching approach based on exact match. No ranking was devised but for what is called relaxed match, which basically reverts again to a IR free-text similarity measure. So a basic service of a semantic approach, such as inconsistency check, seems unavailable with this type of match. In [23] a matchmaking framework was proposed, which operated on service descriptions in

DAML+OIL and was based on the FaCT reasoner. An extension to the approach in [20] was proposed in [18] where two new levels for service profiles matching are introduced. Notice that there, the *intersection satisfiable* level is introduced, whose definition corresponds to the one of *potential matching* proposed in [19]. The approach presented does not introduce a ranking method to measure proximity of service descriptions. In [19] properties that a matchmaker should have in a DL based framework, were described and motivated, and algorithms to classify and rank matches into classes were presented, *i.e.*, *Full match:* all requested characteristics are available in the description examined; *Potential match:* some part of the request is not specified in the description examined; *Partial match:* some part of the request is in conflict with the description examined. The algorithms compute a semantic distance between each description w.r.t. a request in each class. In [3] the Difference Operator in DLs was proposed for matchmaking in the framework of web services The approach uses the Concept Difference, followed by a set covering operation optimized using hypergraph techniques. A DL-based system, which allows the treatment of negotiable and strict constraints has been proposed in [9]. That approach is complementary to the one proposed here, as we can extend preferences selection while maintaining a separation between strict and negotiable constraints. The need to overcome simple deductive based semantic-matchmaking is now increasingly acknowledged. Recent approaches try to tackle this isssue adopting fuzzy-DLs as in Smart [1] or hybrid approaches, as in the OWLS-MX matchmaker [17]. Such approaches, anyway, relaxing the logical constraints, do not allow any explanation or automated revision service.

7   Conclusion and Future Work

In this contribution we have presented a formal approach and a system that –in our opinion– clearly show the benefits of semantic markup of descriptions in an e-marketplace. We have presented algorithms to provide logic-based explanation services, semantic ranking of matchmaking results, and request refinement, and shown that semantic-based techniques, with their inherent advantages, can be implemented in a usable way, which does not require specific expertise to be used to their full power.

We are carrying out preliminary tests on the system, with the aid of human volunteers. The domain we selected was one of used cars. Experiments are related to evaluate both the theoretical approach and the usability of the tool. The evaluation of different match degree functions is also under investigation.

References

1. S. Agarwal and S. Lamparter. smart - a semantic matchmaking portal for electronic markets. In *Proceedings of International IEEE Conference on E-Commerce Technology*, 2005.
2. F. Baader et al. editors. *The Description Logic Handbook*. Cambridge University Press, 2002.

3. B. Benatallah et al. Request Rewriting-Based Web Service Discovery. In *Proceedings of ISWC'03*, 2003.
4. B. Benatallah et al. Semantic Reasoning for Web Services Discovery. In *Proc. of Workshop on E-Services and the Semantic Web at WWW'03*, 2003.
5. A. Borgida. Description Logics in Data Management. *IEEE Transactions on Knowledge and Data Engineering*, 7(5):671–682, 1995.
6. R.J. Brachman and H.J. Levesque. The tractability of subsumption in frame-based description languages. In *Proceedings of the Fourth National Conference on Artificial Intelligence (AAAI-84)*, 1984.
7. S. Colucci et al. Concept Abduction and Contraction in Description Logics. In *Proceedings DL'03*, 2003.
8. S. Colucci et al. Uniform Tableaux-Based Approach to Concept Abductiona and Contraction in ALN DL. In *Proceedings of DL'04*, 2004.
9. S. Colucci et al. Concept Abduction and Contraction for Semantic-based Discovery of Matches and Negotiation Spaces in an E-Marketplace. *Electronic Commerce Research and Applications*, 4(4):345–361, 2005.
10. T. Di Noia et al. Abductive matchmaking using description logics. In *Proceedings of IJCAI 2003*, 2003.
11. T. Di Noia et al. Semantic matchmaking in a P-2-P electronic marketplace. In *Proceedings of SAC '03*, 2003.
12. T. Di Noia et al. A system for principled Matchmaking in an electronic marketplace. In *Proceedings of WWW '03*, 2003.
13. E. Di Sciascio et al. A Knowledge-Based System for Person-to-Person E-Commerce. In *Proceedings of ADL-2001*, 2001.
14. F. M. Donini et al. Reasoning in Description Logics. In Gerhard Brewka, editor, *Principles of Knowledge Representation*, Studies in Logic, Language and Information, pages 193–238. CSLI Publications, 1996.
15. P. Gärdenfors. *Knowledge in Flux: Modeling the Dynamics of Epistemic States*. Bradford Books, MIT Press, Cambridge, MA, 1988.
16. J. Gonzales-Castillo et al. Description Logics for Matchmaking of Services. In *Proceedings of ADL'01*, 2001.
17. M. Klusch et al. Owls-mx: Hybrid owl-s service matchmaking. In *Proceedings of AAAI Fall Symposium on Agents and the Semantic Web*, 2005.
18. L. Li and I. Horrocks. A Software Framework for Matchmaking Based on Semantic Web Technology. In *Proceedings of WWW '03*, 2003.
19. T. Di Noia et al. A system for principled Matchmaking in an electronic marketplace. *International Journal of Electronic Commerce*, 8(4):9–37, 2004.
20. M. Paolucci et al. Semantic Matching of Web Services Capabilities. In *Proccedings of ISWC'02*, 2002.
21. P. Shvaiko and J. Euzenat. A Survey of Schema-based Matching Approaches. *Journal on Data Semantics*, 4, 2005.
22. K. Sycara et al. LARKS: Dynamic Matchmaking Among Heterogeneus Software Agents in Cyberspace. *Autonomous agents and multi-agent systems*, 5:173–203, 2002.
23. D. Trastour et al. Semantic Web Support for the Business-to-Business E-Commerce Lifecycle. In *Proceedings of WWW'02*, 2002.

Customer Future Profitability Assessment:
A Data-Driven Segmentation Function Approach

Chunhua Tian[1], Wei Ding[1], Rongzeng Cao[1], and Michelle Wang[2]

[1] IBM China Research Lab
Beijing, China
{chtian, dingw, caorongz}@cn.ibm.com
[2] IBM Business Consulting Services
Beijing, China
wangmkh@cn.ibm.com

Abstract. One of the important tasks in customer relationship management is to find out the future profitability of individual and/or groups of customers. Data mining-based approaches only provide coarse-grained customer segmentation. It is also hard to obtain a high-precision structure model purely by using regression methods. This paper proposes a data-driven segmentation function that provides a precise regression model on top of the segmentation from a data mining approach. For a new customer, a structure model constructed from profit contribution data of current customers is adopted to assess the profitability. For an existing customer, external information such as stock value performance is taken into the regression model as well as historical trend prediction on the profit contribution. In addition, this paper shows how the proposed approach works and how it improves the customer profitability analysis through experiments on the sample data.

1 Introduction

In today's market, the importance of effective customer service management becomes widely recognized. While customers are the primary source of revenue, efficient customer management also improves the operational efficiency and reduces risks exposed to enterprises. An excellent customer service often becomes a real differentiator and is hard to copy as an element of brand (unlike commoditized products). It prevents the products and services from being commoditized and from falling into mere price competition eventually.

However, an excellent service does not necessarily mean the same service for all the customers; instead, it should satisfy diversified requirements of various customers in an efficient and effective way. Thus, it is essential for an enterprise to understand its customers to provide personalized services to individual customers to maximize the value [1]. CRM (Customer Relationship Management) introduced useful ideas to address such concerns, including customer orientation, customer centricity, customer insight, and customer segmentation, to name a few. The notion of customer orientation and customer centricity focuses on managerial guidance to help an enterprise to plan and practice from a customer perspective. The notion of customer insight yields an integrated and structured approach to managing a client's financial matters and

J. Lee et al. (Eds.): DEECS 2006, LNCS 4055, pp. 28–39, 2006.

relationships and typically involves a high-touch, enabling, and consultative relationship with targeted customers. The idea of customer segmentation requires to partitioning the universe of customers into a number of target groups. Each group of customers shows similar needs and/or characteristics, and the members of a group are likely to exhibit similar purchasing behaviour.

The notion of customer value is often a key criterion in customer segmentation [2]. The goal of a customer value assessment is to find the profitability of an individual customer or a group of customers [3]. There have certain practices on the customer profit contribution calculation, which take into account factors such as purchased products/services, and the profitability of the products/service in [4] and [5]. Customer profit contribution can provide an understanding of what has happened. However, the practices cannot say much about the future profitability. For example, in a banking RM (Relationship Manager) allocation, a senior RM is usually a scarce resource, who is desired to be allocated to high-value customers. For a new customer such as an enterprise or a high-value individual, there is no historical transaction data, but the profitability information will be needed for the RM allocation. Also, periodical adjustments to the RM allocation to existing customers will require information on the future profitability of customers. The paper discusses methods and techniques for assessing the future profitability of customers.

The rest of this paper is structured as follows: Section 2 presents a mixed approach combing data mining and regression analyses for the profitability estimation. The feasibility of the proposed approach is discussed through an experiment in Section 3. Concluding remarks and future research topics are outlined in Section 4.

2   Customer Future Profitability Assessment

2.1   Data-Driven Segmentation Function Approach

Prediction is not a new problem. Structural models (such as a time series model) and regression methods are often adopted in solving prediction and forecasting problems. For customer profitability analyses, techniques based on data mining have been used to identify key factors and estimate the profitability. The data mining-based techniques often provide categorical results, such as one or more groups of high value customers, and groups of low value customers. A structural model can provide a more precise value, if certain parameters are precisely estimated. Unfortunately, however, it is not straightforward to have precise estimates for a single model having the same set of parameters in a global space. We argue that data mining and regression approaches can be combined to improve parameter estimation precision. Using a data mining-based method, customers are divided into several groups. Then, a regression technique can be utilized for parameter estimation for each group.

The procedure of this data-driven segmentation function approach is stated as follows:

1) Segment customers $\{C_k : k = 1, \cdots, N\}$ with m customer attributes (or information) to several groups $\{G_i : i = 1, \cdots, n\}$. The attribute set of customer k is expressed as $X_k = (x_{k,1}, x_{k,2}, \cdots, x_{k,m})$.

2) Establish an explicit group criteria according customer attributes (or information) by a decision tree algorithm, expressed as $G_i \overset{\Delta}{=} \{C_k : l_{ij} \leq x_j \leq u_{ij}\}$.

3) For each group G_i, establish a profitability function f_i with parameter set A_i, that is, the profitability $P(C_k)$ of a customer C_k from group G_i is defined as

$$P(C_k) = f_i(X_k; A_i) \text{ if } C_k \in G_i.$$

4) Estimate the parameter A_i for each group i by a regression model.

Once the model is constructed, it is necessary to verify the feasibility of the model and improve its adaptation. There could be two alternatives.

1) Sample-based testing: Split the data set into two groups, group A (larger percentage) for an analysis, and group B for testing. In group A, a cluster analysis, regression, and other methods can be used to set up models and estimate model parameters. Group B's data is used to test the precision of the models.

2) Back testing: A tracking mechanism is developed to monitor the real values in certain periods and compare them with the initial estimation. Also, it adjusts the model or segmentation approach over time in an evolving way.

2.2 Customer Information

There are a number of customer classification methods. For example, based on the potential transaction volume, customers can be grouped into wholesale clients (e.g., enterprise customers for the banking industry) and retail clients (e.g., individual customers in the banking industry). However, many of the classification algorithms require data or information that is not readily available. Without requiring any data, one easy way to classify customers is to group them into two classes: new customers and existing customers.

Based on the availability, customer information can be divided into four categories:

1) Public information, such as an enterprise's business model, stock price, and market share. Such information is readily available or obtainable from media and other public channels even without any business relationship with the customer.

2) Demography information, such as individual's income, the enterprise's financial state, which usually becomes available once a business relationship is formed.

3) Transaction information, such as products purchased, and service consuming history which is available only when there are transactions with customers.

4) Hidden information, such as private information, and trade secret which may be useful for understanding customer behavior, but unavailable or illegal to obtain.

The distinction between new customers and existing customers is that new customers have no transaction information, which is the source of the traditional profit contribution calculation. This fact requires that new customers and existing customers need to be treated differently in the profitability assessment methods, as described in the following sections.

while the current market information is an important indicator of business operations which are key determinants of the future transaction behavior. Thus, it requires certain external customer information to augment the information space. Finally, an enterprise's performance will also have significant impact on its customers' future profitability. Thus, these three kinds of information should be taken into account in the model which is shown in Fig. 3. The entire method is shown in Fig. 4.

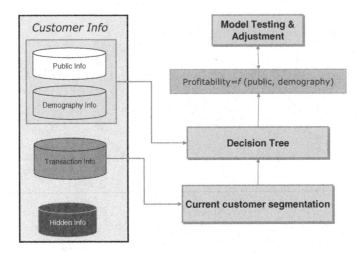

Fig. 2. Profitability Assessment Method for New Customer

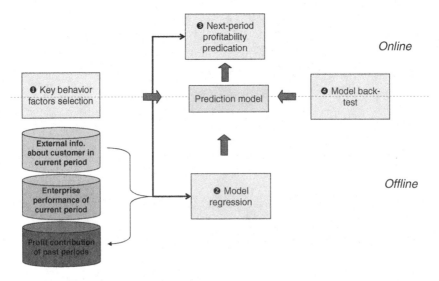

Fig. 3. Profitability Prediction Model for Current Customers

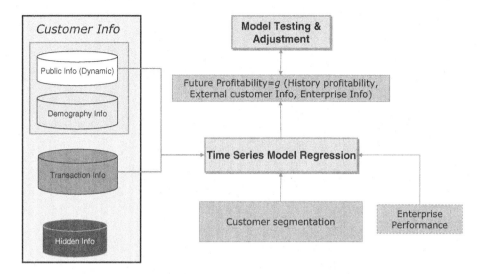

Fig. 4. Profitability Prediction Method for Current Customers

3   Experiment

Actual enterprise data would be an ideal way to verify the proposed approach. Unfortunately, such information is not readily available. We used a set of fabricated data in this experiment by adopting part of the methods proposed in a data mining tool - DB2 IM (Intelligent Miner) for Data [6].

3.1   New Customer Profitability Assessment

3.1.1   Data Preparation and Preprocessing
Original data comes from the America Census Bureau Data, 1996 [7] with 32560 records and 15 attributes for each record. The dataset contains demographic, salary, gain or loss from investment and other critical information that can be used to categorize and predict variables.

Field 'Fnlwgt', 'Capital_gain', 'Capital_loss' and 'Native_Country' are deleted because they have little impact on profitability. A field "Newcustomer" which denotes whether a customer is new was added, and the values were stochastically assigned. For the purpose of this, another 3 fields were added. "Profit" denotes customer profit contribution of the present year. "Tenure" is the duration of partnership. "CreditScore" denotes the customer credit level. For a new customer, these 3 attributes are empty. For an existing customer, these field values are generated according to the following procedure.

1) Create customer clusters based on demography attributes by a demographic clustering algorithm, and 5 clusters are obtained.
2) For each existing customer,
```
Random=RAND();
If ClusterID=0
```

```
      If Random <0.7
              ProfitAll_P=70;
      Else
              ProfitAll_P=30;
Elseif ClusterID=1
      ProfitAll_P=15;
Elseif ClusterID=2
      ProfitAll_P=50;
Elseif ClusterID=3
      ProfitAll_P=20;
Else
      ProfitAll_P=30;
If Random <0.5
      ProfitAll= ProfitAll_P +RAND()*10;
Else
      ProfitAll= ProfitAll_P-RAND()*10;
Profit=ProfitAll*(1-RAND()*0.3);
Tenure= ProfitAll /12*(1+RAND());
If Profit<50
      CreditScore= Random/2;
Else
      CreditScore= Random*4;
```

For cleaning data, 996 records were discarded due to incomplete attributes. For reducing data, attribute 'Education' and 'Hours_Per_Week' were removed due to high correlation with the attribute 'Education_num'. Attribute 'Profit' and 'CreditScore' were transformed to a log form. Attribute 'Age', 'Education_num' were discretized based on range or quartile.

Because the data is not real, it is impossible to verify whether the proposed approach is meaningful to a new customer. So we just compare the profitability prediction from a decision tree model with real profit to show the precision of the proposed approach. So only "current customer" records are adopted in the following analysis, which are 26896 records.

3.1.2 Customer Segmentation

For simplification, customer value is defined just as (Customer Profit of the present year, Credit Score), i.e., field "Profit" and "CreditScore". To ensure the quality of the segmentation, a clustering method and NN (Neural Network) method are adopted separately.

According to the demographic clustering method [8] provided by DB2 IM with parameter maximum iteration as 5, maximum number of clusters as 9 and precision improvement factor as 2, customers are classified into 5 segments as shown in Fig. 5. Cluster 0 is HH (High profit, High credit) group. Cluster 1 is MH (Medium Profit, High credit) group. Cluster 2 is LH (Low profit, High credit) group. Cluster 3 is HL (High profit, Low credit) group. Cluster 4 is MM (Medium profit, Medium credit) group.

NN method gives a more precise classification with 9 segments. With parameter maximum iteration as 5, and maximum number of clusters as 9, the clustering results are shown in Fig. 6.

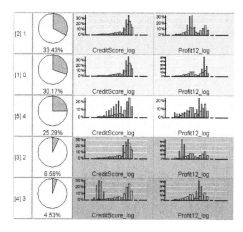

Fig. 5. Customer Segmentation according to a Clustering Method (Gray histograms show the overall distribution, and color ones are the cluster distribution.)

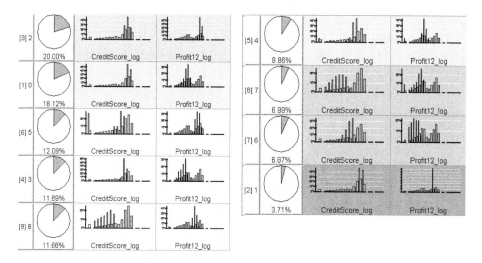

Fig. 6. Customer Segmentation according to NN Method (Gray histograms show the overall distribution, and color ones are the cluster distribution.)

The relationship between these two sets of clusters is shown in Table 1. The groups by NN method are also labeled according to the same denotation as those groups by the clustering method, where M^+ denotes strong medium and M^- means weak medium. Suppose that

Group 0 (clustering method) = group 1 and 2 (NN method)
Group 1 (clustering method) = group 0 and 4 (NN method)
Group 2 (clustering method) = group 3 (NN method)
Group 3 (clustering method) = group 5 (NN method)
Group 4 (clustering method) = group 6, 7 and 8 (NN method)

The precision is above 70%. So in the following, the segmentation from the clustering algorithm is adopted for simplification.

Table 1. Comparison of customer segmentation from demographic clustering (row) and NN method (column)

Neural Clustering	0(HH)	1(MH)	2(LH)	3(HL)	4(MM)	Total
0(M⁻H)		4402	472			4874
1(M⁺H)	997					997
2(HH)	5380					5380
3(LH)		2334	1211			3145
4(M⁻M⁺)		1982		164	238	2384
5(HM)	1737			897	616	3250
6(M⁻M)		256	72		1120	1848
7(M⁻M⁻)		17	15	20	1829	1881
8(MM⁻)				137	3000	3137
Total	8114	8991	1770	1218	6803	26896

3.1.3 Profitability Assessment

Based on the segmentation by the clustering algorithm, the decision tree shown in Fig. 7 is constructed.

Fig. 7. Decision Tree

The prediction value from the decision tree is shown in Table 2, where the row title denotes the real group label, while the column title denotes the predicted group label according to the decision tree. It shows that group 0 and 4 can be well predicted, there is significant error in group 1, and group 2 and 3 cannot be predicted at all. The percentage of correct prediction is 75%.

Table 2. Real value vs. prediction value by decision tree (Original Dataset)

	0	1	4	2	3	Total
0 (Real)	**8,111**	0	3	0	0	8,114
1 (Real)	3,413	**5,185**	393	0	0	8,991
4 (Real)	1	13	**6,789**	0	0	6,803
2 (Real)	0	1,579	191	**0**	0	1,770
3 (Real)	0	6	1,212	0	**0**	1,218
Total	11,525	6,783	8,588	0	0	16,896

It may be due to the size of group 2 and 3 are too small compared with other groups according to the analysis of [9]. So a stochastic sampling to group 0, 1 and 4 is carried out to make the 5 groups approximately equal in size. Based on the sample data, the decision tree is re-constructed and the comparison of new decision tree is shown in Table 3. Compared with original data, group 2 and 3 can be clearly identified. However, the precision of group 1 drops significantly.

Table 3. Real value vs. prediction value by decision tree (Unbiased Dataset)

	0	1	4	2	3	Total
0 (Real)	**343**	602	51	503	0	1,499
1 (Real)	0	**1,621**	0	0	1	1,622
4 (Real)	15	1	**860**	5	820	1,701
2 (Real)	0	0	191	**1,579**	0	1,770
3 (Real)	12	0	93	6	**1,107**	1,218
Total	370	2,224	1,195	2,093	1,928	7,810

These two datasets show that demography features cannot entirely reveal customers' real profitability. However, most of the prediction errors occur between groups with adjacent level in profit or credit level. The errors can be kept at an acceptable level if the demography factors are well selected.

3.2 Profitability Prediction for Existing Customers

As for existing customers, 2 more fields are added. Field "Profitex" denotes customer profit contribution in the last year. Another field "Market" is added to denote customers' market status, which will have impact on the profitability in the next period.

112 records are stochastically selected from Group 0 according to the clustering algorithm described in Section 3.1. Field "Profitex" is generated according to a normal distribution with field "Profit" value as its mean value and 20% of field "Profit" value as its variance. Field "Market" is selected among 21, 24, 27, 29 according to discretion of $Profit\text{-}0.8*Profitex$.

A linear regression analysis results with both variables and only "Profitex1", as shown in Fig. 8, illustrate that using both time series variables and corresponding market status index is more accurate than using single variables. Similar results are also depicted by RBF (Radical Basis Function) and NN(Neural Network) based prediction methods.

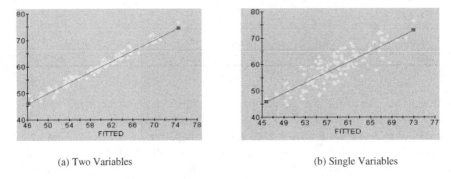

(a) Two Variables   (b) Single Variables

Fig. 8. Profitability Prediction Result (2-variables vs. single variable)

4 Conclusion

In customer management, the future profitability of customers is an important factor for a number of operation decisions such as RM allocation, service provided, etc. Most of current practices approach the problem through customer profit contribution calculation based on historical data. The approach provides little insight into the future profit contribution of existing customers and potential profit contribution of new customers. This paper proposed a data -driven segmentation function approach which improves estimation precision by using customer segmentation from a clustering algorithm. New customer profitability is estimated based on the segmented model constructed from existing customers. For an existing customer, external information in the present period is taken into account along with a pure time-series analysis on the profit contribution in the past periods. An experiment is designed to illustrate the feasibility of the proposed approach. One limitation of the proposed approach is that it does not consider customer lifecycle stage. In fact, the customer lifecycle is a key factor [10] [11] and can be another dimension in segmentation or the structural model. We plan to address this topic in the future work by extending the proposed model.

References

1. Thomas, J., Reinartz W., Kumar, V.: Getting The Most out of All Your Customers. Harvard Business Review (2004) 117-123
2. Zeithaml,V.A., Roland, T.R., et al.: The Customer Pyramid: Creating and Serving Profitable Customers. California Management Review. Vol. 42 No.4 (2001) 118-142
3. Kaplan, R. S., Narayanan, V.G.: Measuring and Managing Customer Profitability. Journal of Cost Management (September/October 2001) 5-15
4. Sherman, G. : How to Unlock Customer Profitability http://www.crm2day.com/library/EEpkyZukEkLmhoVtRi.php

5. Pfeier, P.E., Bang, H.: Non-parametric Estimation of Mean Customer Lifetime Value. Journal of Interactive Marketing Vol. 19 No.4 (2005) 48-66

6. Cabena, P., Choi, H.H., Kim, I. S., Otsuka, S., Reinschmidt J., Saarenvirta G.: Intelligent Miner for Data Applications Guide. IBM Redbook SG24-5252-00 (1999)

7. Newman, D.J., Hettich, S., Blake, C.L., Merz, C.J.: UCI Repository of Machine Learning Databases (http://www.ics.uci.edu/~mlearn/MLRepository.html). Irvine, CA: University of California, Department of Information and Computer Science. (1998)

8. Michaud, P.: Clustering techniques. Future Generation Computer Systems. Vol. 13 No.2 (1997) 135-147

9. Huang, Y.M., Hung, C.M., Jiau, H.C.: Evaluation of Neural Networks and Data Mining Methods on a Credit Assessment Task for Class Imbalance Problem. Nonlinear Analysis: Real World Applications (to be published)

10. Venkatesan, R., Kumar V.: A Customer Lifetime Value Framework for Customer Selection and Resource Allocation Strategy. Journal of Marketing 68 (2004) 105-125.

11. Pfeifer, P.E., Haskins, M.E., Conroy, R.M.: Customer Lifetime Value, Customer Profitability, and the Treatment of Acquisition Spending. Journal of Managerial Issues, Vol. XVII No. 1 (2005) 11-25

Optimization of Automatic Navigation to Hidden Web Pages by Ranking-Based Browser Preloading

Justo Hidalgo[1], José Losada[1], Manuel Álvarez[2], and Alberto Pan[2,*]

[1] Denodo Technologies, Inc.
Madrid, Spain
{jhidalgo, jlosada}@denodo.com
[2] Department of Information and Communications Technologies.
University of A Coruña, Spain
{apan, mad}@udc.es

Abstract. Web applications have become an invaluable source of information for many different vertical solutions, but their complex navigation and semistructured format make their information difficult to retrieve. Web Automation and Extraction systems are able to navigate through web links and to fill web forms automatically in order to get information not directly accessible by a URL. In these systems, the main optimization parameter is the time required to navigate through the intermediate pages which lead to the desired final pages. This paper proposes a series of techniques and algorithms that improves this parameter by basically storing historical information from previous queries, and using it to make the browser manager preload an adequate subset of the whole navigational sequence on a specific browser, before the following query is executed. These techniques also handle which sequences are the most common, thus being the ones which are preloaded more often.

1 Introduction

The world wide web has become the most important source of information for all kinds of knowledge areas, such as competitive intelligence, product comparison, operational business intelligence, and so on. Most of the information stored in the web is hidden behind forms (authentication, information-filling, etc.), navigational links with JavaScript, session maintenance, and so on. These web sites, generically known as Deep Web or Hidden Web, are estimated to keep more than five hundred times the information which resides in web pages accessible through a static URL [2].

In the last years some research groups and industrial companies have been focusing on automatic browsing and extraction of information from Deep Web sources. Basically, obtaining information from web sources is divided into two main steps: firstly, being able to browse through the access pages up to the first page of results; secondly, extracting information from the result web pages, in either a structured or unstructured way. Some of the research groups (p.e. [11]) deepen into how to browse through the different access pages for the system to get to the result page. Other works center

---

* Alberto Pan's work was partially supported by the "Ramón y Cajal" programme of the Spanish Ministry of Education and Science.

J. Lee et al. (Eds.): DEECS 2006, LNCS 4055, pp. 40–49, 2006.

on the extraction step ([1], [6], [7] and [8] for a survey) and how to obtain structured or indexed information from the web. Both steps (browsing and structuring) are intertwined since after browsing to the first result page, it must be parsed so to know its internal structure, and how to access possible detail and "more result" pages.

When building web automation systems or information integration applications with access to web sources, it is critical to optimize the web access efficiency. Web sources are slower than traditional corporate and local sources, such as relational databases, because of: (1) their inherent distributed structure, (2) http, WWW's communication protocol, and (3) the way web sources structure their information in pages, so that a "virtual table" might imply browsing through tenths, hundreds or even thousands of web pages (mainly "more results" pages and "detail" pages).

There are complex web sources which require long navigation sequences before arriving at the real query form, due to session maintenance. For example, in many real sources it is necessary to introduce login/password information, after what the user must navigate through one or more pages until arriving at a certain query form. This fact can cause that a query take a very long time to execute.

The different flows of navigation of several queries have "common denominators", that is, sequence elements that are repeated such as the login/password access, or the different options by which the site can be browsed before arriving at a concrete page. Much processing time is lost because the system does not consider that from a query to another, it would only be necessary one step back and a new selection; instead, it repeats the complete navigation access path from the beginning.

The optimization of the process flow can provide many considerable improvements as far as the access time to each source is concerned, sometimes in orders of magnitude - mainly in sources which reside in servers with small bandwidth, or in sources with many intermediate steps -. This work describes a series of techniques which allow to optimize access to web sources in a mediator-wrapper architecture [13], even though this approach is valid for a stand-alone web extraction system.

This paper shows a novel approach regarding to web source browsing optimization, based on browser reutilization and use of a cost repository. The structure of this work is as follows: Section 2 and Section 3 introduce the web browsing optimization challenge by characterizing its main components. Section 4 shows the Cost Repository Parameters, while Section 5 describes how to obtain an adequate sequence prefix; Section 6 explains how the browser pool can select which sequences must be preloaded at execution time. Section 7 explains the two sequence ranking algorithms proposed. Finally, Section 8 takes care or other important issues, and Section 9 summarizes on conclusions. A previous phase of this work was presented in [4].

2   Using a Browser Pool to Browse Web Sources

The web automation system proposed in this work uses browsers as basic elements able to access information stored or dynamically generated by web applications, and that might require prior authentication, and/or link traversing. The use of a browser instead of an HTTP client improves the quality and quantity of web applications which can be browsed since it emulates a user's behaviour, so many issues such as session maintenance, javascript, etc., are taken care by the browser internals.

The approach followed in this paper is focused on the component known as Browser Pool. This module is responsible for receiving the requests, each of which is associated with a specific web navigation, and selecting one of its set of browsers for the request to be executed. This request is called "Navigational Sequence", and it is composed of a set of actions which must be performed by the browser. The language to describe these sequences is known as NSEQL –Navigational Sequence Language, thoroughly described in [9]-, and has been designed for executing them on the Internet browser interface (Microsoft Internet Explorer and Netscape Firefox). Table 1 shows an example of an NSEQL program, which guides a browser from the home page of a hypothetical electronic bookshop to a query result page, after the user is authenticated, the search terms are inserted and the query form is submitted.

The first line commands the browser to access the initial page. Lines 2 to 5 show how the browser must fill the authentication form and click on a button in order to submit the information. "@LOGIN" and "@PASSWORD" are attributes used to parameterize the sequence. Finally, after the browser receives the page after the authentication process, lines 6 to 9 are executed so that the page's "searchBrick" form is found and its search field "field-keywords" is filled with information provided by attribute "@QUERY". Finally, the form information is submitted, and the result page is returned. The browser will return information about the status of each of the sequence steps, plus the HTML code of the last page.

When this query must be executed several times with the same of different attributes, one can observe that the most important optimization parameter is the "browse time" spent by the system to access the information stored in the pages hidden behind links, authentication and query forms. How the Browser Pool decides which browser is assigned to a specific request, and how to optimize the execution of these sequences, are the main purposes and value propositions of this paper.

3   Optimizing Navigational Sequences

The proposed solution in this article is an extension of the pool of browsers, so that for each browser, the sequence of navigation actions which took it to its current state is stored. When a new sequence is to be executed, it is verified whether there is any browser that it has some sequence with a common prefix with the recently received sequence. In that case, the system will evaluate whether it is better to reuse the browser's current state or to start from the beginning. Thus, in the previously commented case, when the new sequence arrives, the pool realizes that there is a browser which is a single step from the desired state, and reuses it.

In addition, to avoid the problem of the initialization cost –time required to start the browser, and navigate through different pages until arriving at a specific result page-, the pool of browsers starts up a preconfigured number of browsers pointing to the pages which, according to the cost repository, are more suitable to respond to the queries, previewing the future needs. This is obtained by means of a historical ranking of sources and states. The browser pool must make use of both status information and cost statistics –or, more precisely, access cost statistics-.

Table 1. NSEQL Description

```
1. Navigate(http://www.ebookshop.com,0)
2. FindFormByName(implogin,0)
3. SetInputValue(imapuser,0,^EncodeSeq(@LOGIN))
4. SetInputValue(pass,0,^EncodeSeq(@PASSWORD))
5. ClickOnElement(button,INPUT,0)
6. FindFormByName(searchBrick,0)
7. SetInputValue(field-keywords,0,^EncodeSeq(@QUERY))
8. FindElementByAttribute(INPUT,NAME,Go,0,true)
9. ClickOnSelectedElement()
```

Status information will be used by the pool to control where its browsers are in each moment. Currently, information managed is the set of navigational sequences, where the path followed by each browser is defined sequentially. This information is required by the pool to determine, when a new query arrives, which of its elements has a minor distance with respect to the target –the element of the new sequence to execute-.

Access information will allow the pool to initialize its browsers so that, statistically, the following sequences' starting nodes are as close to the first ones' finishing nodes as possible. The associated cost will be lower when sequences are closer.

In the case that the browser selected for the following sequence had previously executed that same one, the system must decide whether the browser's current state is the optimal, or whether it must browse to a later or earlier state. When the optimal state is at a previous step, a "back sequence" must be executed. This special sequence has a series of implications that will be commented in section 8.

4   Web Automation Optimization Cost Parameters

A cost repository is used to store information about the browsers, such as the complete access route for parameterised query (query type) to a web source and the utilization ranking, which will allow for the pool of browsers to select the appropriate access route to initialize the new navigators.

An important characteristic in the cost repository is the storage of information by each access route and time section. In our preliminary studies we have observed great existing differences of web source performance in different time sections. The use of a navigational sequence or another also depends on the time section in which the request is made.

The required general parameters for an adequate physical access optimization are the following for each query type:

a)   information about its related navigational sequence (the one which allows the browser to access the desired results), written in NSEQL.

b)   each query will increase by one the number of queries per time section on this query type. This will be used to generate the sequence ranking.

c)   finally, the last attribute stored is the route subset, the navigational sequence prefix that the browser should navigate automatically so that the user query is optimized regarding the access to the web source. Initially, it is assigned the complete NSEQL sequence. The browser reuse algorithm can be used so that when it finds the "back sequence", that prefix (the difference between the whole NSEQL sequence and the back sequence) is the value stored at the cost repository.

An aggregate method will compute the number of ocurrences per time section for each navigation sequence, thus obtaining a relative ordering with respect to their frequence of utilization.

On a frequency basis (so as not to disturb the runtime execution of the optimizer), an update thread will take care of taking these occurrences and generating the relative ordering of each query type per time section with respect to the rest of them, according to their frequency of utilization. This processing can make use of a typical mean average ($M(k) = \Sigma \eta_i(k)v_i$, i=1..k, where $\eta_i(k) = 1/k$), or more appropriate probability functions. This ordering will be stored in a "position" attribute on the cost repository, for every query type and time section.

5   Selecting a Reutilization Prefix for a Specific Sequence

One of the optimization techniques described in this work is related to selecting the most appropriate subset of the NSEQL navigational sequence (a "prefix") to preload a browser so that, when a web automation query is executed on the system, the browser is already positioned on the best possible sequence element. This way, web browsing performance can improve even orders of magnitude, since HTTP connection is the parameter which affects the most to efficiency overall. A conservative approach takes as prefix the sequence elements counting from the home page to the first page with variables. For example, the sequence elements required to access the authentication or the query form. This technique is not error-prone, but might not be optimal in the case there are more than one form, and the changing variables between queries do not take part on the first n-m forms (where m=0 would mean the worst case possible, in which no variable changes among queries, so that the browser could just stay at the first result list page).

In our case we propose the following: for every query type and time section (in case the behaviour differs depending on the time), we keep information about whether there are any value changes in each attribute of the sequence. These changes take the last "m" sample queries. This way, the system can choose at runtime whether the prefix should "stop" at the first query form, or, in case its variables have not changed, it can use some more sequence elements. This is implemented with a 2xN matrix, where n is the number of attributes per query type and time section, in the following way: {{attribute$_1$, boolean$_1$}, {attribute$_2$, boolean$_2$}, ..., {attribute$_n$, boolean$_n$}}, where boolean$_i$ indicates whether that attribute has changed in the previous i executions.

This method, although more computationally intensive (requiring $O(N*m)$), it is very flexible with regards to the use of the variables. For example, the prefix will take into account whether an attribute used in an authentication form stores always the same values or not; in the first case, it will be considered that the attribute has, actually, a constant value.

As an example we will use the NSEQL program from Table 1, in which a book-shop web application access is automated. We can observe that there are two pages in which attributes are used: the authentication page and the query page. A conservative optimization technique would select the sequence prefix defined from the home page to the authentication page (that is, the sequence `Navigate(http:// www.ebookshop.com,0); WaitPages(1)`), and would use it from then on.

However, the technique proposed in this work does not create a prefix *a priori*. Instead, it will depend on the queries performed by the system on that specific query type. Let us take a look at a set of sample queries for the previously mentioned electronic bookshop in Table 2. Let us also imagine that the configuration attribute "m" equals to 3, which is the number of sample queries checked for each attribute in order to find any change of values.

Table 2. Sample Queries for the Electronic Bookshop Web Application

N	LOGIN	PASSWD	QUERY	N	LOGIN	PASSWD	QUERY
1	Joe	Joe	Java	8	Joe	Joe	CORBA communications
2	Joe	Joe	Java	9	Christie	Christie	Java
3	Joe	Joe	Relational Databases	10	Christie	Christie	Java
4	Joe	Joe	UML	11	Christie	Christie	Java
5	Christie	Christie	UML	12	Christie	Christie	Java
6	Christie	Christie	Mediators Web	13	Joe	Joe	Java
7	Joe	Joe	ActiveX				

Using the information on that table, the system generates the sequence prefix before each query. For the first query, as there is no previous information, the conservative technique is used in which the browser is positioned in the first page in which any attribute is required –in this case, the authentication page-. Since "m" equals to 3, the first three queries use this technique strictly. In the fourth query, since the login and password values have kept the same value in the last "m" queries, the prefix is modified so that it positions the browser in the query form page. This allows this fourth query to save a few page browsings. Again, for the fifth query the browser is position in the query form page, but a different pair login/password is provided. In this case, if a "back page" sequence is provided by the user, the appropriate subset of this sequence is provided in order to go back to the authentication page; if no sequence is given, it is very dangerous to try the Back button in session maintenance web applications, so, if it is not explicitly configured to try it –because the administrator has decided that this web application behaves correctly with the Back option-, it is better to open a new browser (in order to clean any session information) or reuse an existing one, and perform the whole sequence. As the sample queries are being executed, this technique works as depicted. The last issue we want to show here is that, before executing the twelfth query, since both the pair login/password and query attributes have not changed in the previous "m" queries, then the prefix used is actually the whole sequence, so that, since the twelfth query repeats all the attributes, the response will be the same as in the previous query.

This last behaviour must be described a little bit more carefully. In some cases, re-using the browser results absolutely can be a better-than-good idea, since web data might have been updated since the last query (p.e. in highly-variable values in finan-cial web applications, or because the last query was executed a long time ago). There-fore, in these cases it might be better that, even if all attribute values have not changed, to repeat the last query form so that the browser is forced to query the server for new results. This, too, can be configured.

The value of the "m" attribute can be chosen heuristically, but must be carefully se-lected. If we choose a very low "m" (e.g. 1), this means that the algorithm will react by taking only the last query executed. When attributes vary in a frequent way, the prefix will not be very useful, and "back page" sequences will have to be executed many ways. If m takes a big value, this means that the conservative technique will be used unless fixed attribute values are used most of the times.

6   Browser Pool Run-Time Optimization

The previous technique allows the system to choose a promising prefix sequence which avoids automatic browsing of the whole web flow. This section complements it by allowing the browser pool to preload the most promising sequences, that is, the ones which will be executed with the most probability.

Every time a query is executed with a predefined navigational sequence, the cost repository must store that fact, so that a "sequence ranking" per time frame is created. Thus, the browser pool will start up the preconfigured number of browsers. Each one of these browsers will directly access, without a query having been made, the set of better positioned sequences in the ranking –this does not mean one sequence per browser: if one sequence is much better positioned than the rest, this could mean than two or more browsers navigate to it-. These browsers will stop right in the state of the sequence in which it is necessary to insert execution-time data –user data, login, password, etc.- by using the technique from section 5; thus, the system is optimizing their utilization.

When a new browser is launched, the optimizer must take into account two types of information: the one provided by the cost repository, plus that provided by the pool about the rest of the browsers which are already active –so that, for instance, if the active browsers are already coping with the first two sequences in the ranking, the new browser is taken to the third one-.

If a new query arrives which implies the use of a browser, the pool will check whether there are already some of the already active-but-idle ones with the same se-quence required. If more than one browser responds, the pool will decide which one to use by measuring which one has to use a lesser number of navigational events to get to the step in which execution-time data must be inserted. This is achieved by using the concept of "distance".

The other possibility is that no active-but-idle browser is in that required sequence (i.e. no browser is currently in any page belonging to that sequence). This situation can lead to the following choices: (1) If the probability that this sequence is invoked again in a future query is much lower –a configurable parameter- than the probability of the sequences already involved in the current executable queries, a new browser can be started even if some of the rest are not in use, in order to avoid that arriving queries which make use of the more typical sequences can not take advantage of the optimizer, because they have to either wait for a browser to finish, or start up another browser. (2) It also can happen that the pool does not accept the creation of a new browser –p.e. there is a maximum number of allowed instances-. In this case, the pool will use the active-but-idle browser with owns the sequence with the lowest ranking number.

The following section explains the ranking algorithm in more detail.

7 Ranking Phase

The browser pool is responsible for creating a ranking with the set of navigational sequences used by the system in real time. The issue in creating this ranking relates to how will the topmost sequences be mapped to the browsers which are currently available (NUM_BROWSERS).

We offer two possibilities: the first one is to map these browsers with the top x%, while the second one is to use the NUM_BROWSERS/n top sequences. Let us see one example for each choice.

Table 3 shows the sample query type utilization used in the following examples. We have nine sources (from "A" to "F"), each of which has a percentage value of use as shown in the table. This value has been obtained as described in sections 4 and 6.

Table 3. Sequence Utilization Example

SEQUENCE	%	SEQUENCE	%
A	8%	F	2%
B	6%	G	2%
C	6%	H	1%
D	4%	I	1%
E	2%		

Let us suppose that the user desires to map browsers with query types in the top X%, with NUM_BROWSERS = 10, and X%=20 (that is, the user wants to map the topmost 20% of the sequences to the browsers), 20% is achieved by the first three sequences: A, B and C (8% + 6% + 6%); for sequence A, 8%*10 browsers / 20% = 4 browsers; and finally, 6%*10 browsers / 20% = 3 browsers for sequences B and C.

This means that the first four browsers will be started and preloaded with sequence A's prefix, other three will have B's prefix, and the other three, C's prefix.

Otherwise, the user might want to map browsers with a maximum number of query types. A parameter n = 5 means that the user wishes the first five sequences to be adequately distributed along the available browsers. In the previous table, this means that sequences A, B, C, D and E will be used, which stands for 8% + 6% + 6% + 4% + 2% = 26%. For sequence A, there will be 8%*10 browsers/26% = 40/13 = 3 browsers; for sequences B and C, 6%*10 browsers/26% = 30/13 = 2.5 browsers (3 and 2); 4%*10 browsers/26% = 20/13 = 1 browser for sequence D; and finally, 2%*10 browsers/26% = 20/26 = 1 browser for sequence E.

8 Other Issues

Some issues must be taken into consideration when considering the implementation of these techniques. First of all, if a browser can be reused so that the same sequence previously executed is called again, one would wish that it would navigate back to the most adequate sequence element (i.e. web page) so that this new query does not have to take the whole path back from the beginning; unluckily, this is not possible in most of the times: (1) in some occasions, this is due to web redirections which do not allows us to exactly know how many "back steps" the system must perform; (2) in other ones, when a web application does not allow to open more than one session with the same login/password values, the system might not be able to find the correct back sequence; (3) finally, in some stateful web applications, the back sequence does not work (this is also true in some AJAX-based web applications [3]). Therefore, the system will not browse back, but will start from the beginning of the sequence to achieve the correct state. This is not always a feasible solution. When session maintenance is kept by the browser, the navigational sequence might change (usually because this second time, the authentication form page is not shown, leading the user from the home page directly to the search form page, thus disabling the usefulness of the sequence). In those cases, the user should explicitly provide a "back sequence" to lead the browser to the correct sequence element (for example, by pressing the "Disconnect" button and browsing to the most interesting page in terms of optimization).

Another challenge to be taken into account is that the browser session can expire before an appropriate query arrives. In order to avoid the error produced if this browser is tried to be used, there are a few options: one is to make browsers navigate randomly through a link and repeating this same sequence at certain intervals. Another one is to restart the sequence whenever it fails. The chosen option is the configuration of session timeout for each source - with a default value -, so that the pool of browsers acts before the session expires.

This approach can be expensive if a pay is realized per access, since the system will automatically access web sources which might not be actually used. Thus, in these cases, this optimization must not be taken into account.

9 Conclusions

This paper has described a set of techniques and algorithms which optimize how web automation and extraction systems access transactional web applications. These systems are critical in mediator applications which make use of web data for solutions such as Competitive Intelligence or Single Customer View, and, thus, must behave with a high performance and efficiency. Use of cache is not always the best solution, since web application usually store real-time, highly changing information. We show an innovative way of accessing data from Hidden Web, by storing historical information from previous queries to the different query types, and applying a set of techniques to obtain the best sequence element that each browser should point to. These techniques have been implemented as part of the physical layer optimization of a mediator/wrapper environment for web sources [5][10].

References

1. Arasu, A. and Garcia-Molina, H. Extracting Structured Data from Web Pages. Proceedings of the ACM SIGMOD international conference on Management of data. 2003.
2. Bergman M.K. The Deep Web. Surfacing Hidden Value. http://www.brightplanet.com/technology/deepweb.asp
3. Garret, J. J. Ajax: A New Approach to Web Applications. http://www.adaptivepath.com/publications/essays/archives/000385print.php
4. Hidalgo, J., Pan, A., Losada, J., Álvarez, M. Adding Physical Optimization to Cost Models in Information Mediators. 2005 IEEE Conference on e-Business Engineering. 2005.
5. Hidalgo, J., Pan, A., Losada, J., Álvarez, M., Viña, A. Building the Architecture of a Statistics-based Query Optimization Solution for Heterogeneous Mediators. 6th International Conference on Information Integration and Web-based Applications & Services. 2004.1.
6. Knoblock, C.A., Lerman, K., Minton, S. and Muslea, I. Accurately and Reliably Extracting Data from the Web: A Machine Learning Approach. Bulletin of the IEEE Computer Society Technical Committee on Data Enginnering. 1999.
7. Kushmerick, N., Weld, D.S. and Doorembos, R. Wrapper induction for information extraction. Proceedings of the fifteenth International Joint Conference on Artificial Intelligence. 1997.
8. Laender, A. H. F., Ribeiro-Neto, B. A., Soares da Silva, A. and Teixeira, J. S. A Brief Survey of Web Data Extraction Tools. ACM SIGMOD Record 31(2). 2002.
9. Pan A., et al, 2002. Semi-Automatic Wrapper Generation for Commercial Web Sources. Proceedings of IFIP WG8.1 Working Conference on Engineering Information Systems in the Internet Context. 2002.
10. Pan, A., Raposo, J., Álvarez, M., Montoto, P., Orjales, V., Hidalgo, J., Ardao, L., Molano, A., Viña, A. The DENODO Data Integration Platform. 28th International Conference on Very Large Databases. 2002.
11. Raghavan S. and García-Molina H., Crawling the Hidden Web. Proceedings of the 27th International Conference on Very Large Databases. 2001.
12. Wiederhold, G. Mediators in the Architecture of Future Information Systems. IEEE Computer, March 1992.

Transforming Collaborative Business Process Models into Web Services Choreography Specifications

Pablo David Villarreal[1], Enrique Salomone[1,2], and Omar Chiotti[1,2]

[1] CIDISI, Universidad Tecnológica Nacional - Facultad Regional Santa Fe,
Lavaisse 610, 3000, Santa Fe, Argentina
pvillarr@frsf.utn.edu.ar
[2] INGAR-CONICET, Avellaneda 3657, 3000, Santa Fe, Argentina
{salomone, chiotti}@ceride.gov.ar

Abstract. Languages for web services choreography are becoming more and more important for B2B integration. However, the development of web services-based systems is complex and time-consuming. Enterprises have to agree on collaborative business processes and then derive their respective web services choreographies in order to implement B2B collaboration. To support it, this paper presents a MDA approach for collaborative processes. We describe the components and techniques of this approach. We show how collaborative process models defined with the UP-ColBPIP language can be used as the main development artifact in order to derive choreography specifications based on WS-CDL. The transformations to be carried out are also discussed. The main advantage of this MDA approach is that it guarantees that the generated web services choreographies fulfill the collaborative processes agreed between the partners in a business level.

1 Introduction

Web services are having more and more interest to implement B2B information systems for carrying out inter-enterprise collaborations. The need to specify these collaborations based on this technology has led to the requirement of web services choreography languages. There are several standards proposed to describe web services-based business processes (also known as web services composition). They can be classified according to three types of web services composition that can be defined [3]: Choreography, Behavioral Interface and Orchestration.

Choreography describes collaborative processes involving multiples services, i.e. it describes the global view of the interactions between the services of the partners without considering private details of processing required by the partners. The languages ebXML Business Process Specification Schema (BPSS) [14] and Web Services Choreography Description Language (WS-CDL) [9] support the definition of choreographies. BPSS is not oriented to web services. It allows defining business transactions into binary collaborations. WS-CDL is focused on web services and supports multi-party collaboration. *Behavioral Interface* describes collaborative processes from the point of view of one partner, i.e. the order in which a partner sends messages to and receives messages from its partners, and hence it describes the public aspects of a web service including its observable behavior. It is also known as

J. Lee et al. (Eds.): DEECS 2006, LNCS 4055, pp. 50–65, 2006.
© Springer-Verlag Berlin Heidelberg 2006

conversation protocol [2], business protocol or abstract process [4]. In B2B collaborations, behavioral interfaces of the partners should be derived from choreographies or collaborative processes agreed between them. *Orchestration* describes both public aspects (derived from the behavioral interface) and private aspects of the web services, i.e. the service business logic (e.g. internal rules) that supports the partner's behavior in the interaction with other partners.

In this paper we focus on the generation of web services choreographies in order to define the logic of the collaborative processes in a technological level. Currently, web services choreographies can be specified using the language WS-CDL. However, as it has been recognized by other authors, choreographies are more a design that an implementation artifact [3]. They are not intended to be directly executed. Therefore, for design purposes, the use of an XML-based language to specify choreographies is less useful than a graphical modeling language. Moreover, business aspects cannot be captured with WS-CDL. A WS-CDL choreography is defined as one that describes a collaboration between services in order to achieve a common goal. But support is not provided to define common goals or other business aspects. In this way, a graphical modeling language should be provided as well as a procedure for generating automatically choreographies in a technical language such as WS-CDL.

Due to the fact that choreographies describe interactions as part of the collaborative processes that partners agree to achieve common goals, they should be derived from collaborative business process models. These models are designed in a business level by business engineers and system designers, who are not acquainted with the technical details of the collaboration. Hence, collaborative process models should be independent of the technology to enable their implementation by using different B2B standards according to the technological requirements of the partners [1].

To support the above issues, the Model-Driven Architecture (MDA) Initiative [12] has been identified as a key enabler to support the modeling and specification of collaborative processes [17, 18]. A MDA approach enables both the design of collaborative processes independent of the idiosyncrasies of particular B2B standards, and the automatic generation of B2B specifications based on a B2B standard from conceptual collaborative process models. As part of this approach, the UML Profile for Collaborative Business Processes based on Interaction Protocols (UP-ColBPIP) has been defined [15,18]. This language allows business engineers to define several views of the collaboration, from the definition of the partners, their roles and the common goals, up to the definition of the interaction protocols that realize the collaborative processes and the provided and required business interfaces of the roles.

In a previous work, we described the generation of technological solutions based on ebXML BPSS using a MDA approach [17]. We showed how most of the concepts used by BPSS can be derived from the conceptual elements provided by UP-ColBPIP. In another previous work, we described the generation of technological solutions based on web services composition using a MDA approach [19]. In this case we show how, for each partner involved in a B2B collaboration, BPEL abstract processes can be derived from collaborative process models defined with UP-ColBPIP. In this way, we had applied a MDA approach to generate B2B specifications and we also have validated the UP-ColBPIP language against standard languages. The conclusions were most of the UP-ColBPIP concepts can be represented in BPSS or BPEL.

This paper discusses the application of a MDA approach for collaborative processes to derive WS-CDL specifications. The purpose is to validate that UP-ColBPIP provides the required conceptual modeling elements to generate specifications based on web services choreographies. We do not aim to provide a standard language but to study suitable conceptual elements a collaborative process modeling language should provide, in order to support the modeling in a business level and enable the automatic generation of specifications based on standard languages in a technological level.

This paper is organized as follows. Section 2 describes the MDA approach we propose for collaborative processes. Section 3 describes the transformation of UP-ColBPIP models into WS-CDL and WSDL specifications. A brief description of the conceptual elements provided by UP-ColBPIP is also provided. Section 4 discusses related work. Section 5 presents conclusions and outlines future research directions.

2 MDA Approach for Collaborative Business Processes

The OMG's MDA initiative proposes a conceptual framework along with a set of standards (UML, MOF, XMI, etc.) to build model-driven development methods. In MDA, the development process consists of: defining platform or technology-independent models (PIMs), selecting the platform-specific models (PSMs) and executing the transformations that generate PSMs from PIMs, and finally generating the code from the PSMs. In MDA, the concept of system can refer to software, an enterprise, a set of enterprises and so on. In the domain of collaborative processes, the system to be built includes the specifications of: collaborative processes and partners' interfaces, both defined with a technology-specific language.

Figure 1 shows the corresponding components of the MDA approach we are proposing along with the techniques we provide to build the components:

- **Collaborative Business Process Models based on UP-ColBPIP.** They are the technology-independent process models and are built through the modeling language UML Profile for Collaborative Business Processes based on Interaction Protocols (UP-ColBPIP) [15, 17, 18]. This UML Profile is based on UML 2.
- **WS-CDL and WSDL models.** WS-CDL models represent the technology-specific collaborative process models. Web services composition standards are based on the Web Service Description Language (WSDL), which is used to define the web services of the partners. WSDL models represent the technology-specific partners' interfaces. To build WS-CDL and WSDL models we define their corresponding metamodels, which can be derived from the XML schemas provided by these standards. Thus, a model corresponds to a XML document. Although the XML code may be directly generated from UP-ColBPIP models, this intermediate representation allows the transformation be more modular and maintainable.
- **Transformations of UP-ColBPIP models into WS-CDL and WSDL models.** These transformations define a set of transformation rules to allow the generation of WS-CDL models from UP-ColBPIP models. They define the correspondence between UP-ColBPIP concepts and WS-CDL and WSDL concepts. These transformation rules are implemented through a method and a tool for model transformations, which support the definition and automatic execution of the rules.

- **WS-CDL and WSDL Specifications.** The final outputs of the transformations are the XML files of the WS-CDL process specifications and the WSDL partners' interfaces specifications. The transformation of technology-specific models into the corresponding specifications is almost direct. This can be supported through XML production rules that convert a UML class models into a XML version.

In this work, we focus on UP-ColBPIP models and the definition, in a conceptual way, of the transformations of UP-ColBPIP into WS-CDL. Transformations of UP-ColBPIP into WSDL were described in [19]. The other techniques and components are also out of the scope of this paper. They can be found in [15].

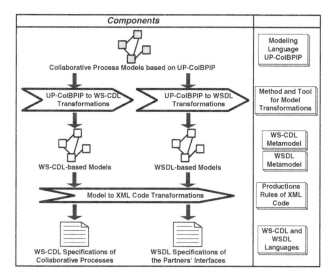

Fig. 1. MDA Approach for Collaborative Processes

3 The Modeling Language UP-ColBPIP

UP-ColBPIP is a modeling language to design technology-independent collaborative processes. It encourages a top-down approach and provides the conceptual elements to support the modeling of four views:

- *B2B Collaboration View*, which defines the partners, the roles they fulfill, their relationships, the collaborative agreement parameters and the hierarchy of common business goals to be fulfilled by the partners in a B2B collaboration.
- *Collaborative Processes View*, which defines the processes partners have to perform. They are defined informally extending the semantics of use cases.
- *Interaction Protocols View*, which defines the interaction protocols that realize the collaborative processes.
- *Business Interfaces View*, which defines the business interfaces required by the partners to support the exchange of messages of the interaction protocols.

The first and second views correspond to the analysis stage, in which the requirements of collaborative processes are defined. The last views correspond to the design stage of collaborative processes. From these last views, technological solutions can be generated. Following we describe the Interaction Protocols View.

3.1   The Interaction Protocols View

This view focuses on the design of interaction protocols that realize the behavior of the collaborative processes. In the B2B collaborations domain, an *interaction protocol* describes a high-level communication pattern through a choreography of business messages between partners playing different roles [16]. The purpose of modeling collaborative processes based on interaction protocols is to fulfill the requirements of B2B collaborations [15,16]: enterprise autonomy, decentralization, peer-to-peer interactions, global view of the collaboration and support for negotiations.

In contrast to activity-oriented processes, interaction protocols focus on the exchange of business messages representing interactions between partners. Activities each partner performs for processing the information to be received or producing the information to be sent are not defined in the interaction protocols.

In addition, B2B interactions cannot be restricted to mere information transfer [7]. They also have to express the communication of actions between the partners. Communicative aspects can be represented in interaction protocols through the use of speech acts [13]. In an interaction protocol, a business message has a speech act associated, which represents the intention that a partner has with respect to an exchanged business document through the message. Furthermore, decisions and commitments done by the partners can be known from the speech acts. This enables the definition of complex negotiations in collaborative processes.

UP-ColBPIP extends the semantics of UML2 Interactions to model interaction protocols. Hence, they are defined using UML2 Sequence Diagrams. Following we describe the main conceptual elements used to define interaction protocols.

As an example, we describe the interaction protocol *Demand Forecast Request*, which realizes a simplified process to manage collaborative demand forecasts. Figure 2 shows the sequence diagram of this protocol, in which partner "A" plays the role *supplier* and partner "B" plays the role *customer*. They are defined by lifelines.

The basic building block in an interaction protocol is a *business message*. It defines an interaction between two roles, a sender and a receiver. A business message contains a *business document* and its semantics is defined by its *speech act* associated. In this way, a business message expresses the sender has done an action, which generates the communication of a speech act representing the sender's intention with respect to the exchanged business document. Also, the message indicates the sender's expectative that the receiver then acts according to the semantics of the speech act. For example, in the message *request(DemandForecast)*, its associated speech act indicates the supplier's intention of requesting a demand forecast to the customer. It also implies the customer has to respond with a suitable speech act, such as *agree* or *refuse*. The suitable speech acts to be used depend on the speech act library selected.

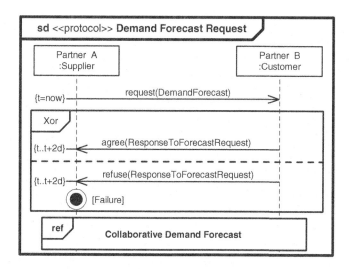

Fig. 2. Sequence Diagram of the Interaction Protocol *Demand Forecast Request*

A business message is a one-way asynchronous communication and is managed by the receptor just as a signal to be interpreted for activating its internal behaviors. This feature is essential in B2B interactions because the sender's internal control should not be subordinated to the receiver's response.

In addition, a business message may require the sending of a receipt and/or a read acknowledgment by the receiver towards the sender, for indicating to the sender that the message has been received and/or understood by the recipient. It is defined in the atributes *isReceiptAcknowledgementRequired* and *isReadAcknowledgementRequired*.

A *business document* represents the information conveyed by the message. In the example, the business document *DemandForecast* contains details about the period, products and time horizon required for the forecast.

A *Control Flow Segment* represents complex message sequences in the interaction protocol's choreography. It contains a control flow operator and one or more interaction paths. An *interaction path* can contain any protocol element: messages, terminations, interaction occurrences, and nested control flow segments. The stereotype *control flow segment* extends the semantics of the *combined fragment* of UML2 to provide suitable control flow operators for defining collaborative processes.

The semantics of a control flow segment depends on the operator used: Xor, Or, And, If, Loop, Transaction, Exception, Stop and Cancel. The *And* operator represents the execution of parallel interaction paths in any order. The *Xor* operator represents that only one path, of a set of alternative paths, can be executed in case its condition is evaluated to true. The *Or* operator represents the selection of several paths from several alternatives. Each path is executed in case its condition is evaluated to true. The *If* operator represents a path that is executed when its condition is true, or nothing is executed. This can also have an *else* path, which is executed when the condition of the first path is false. The *Loop* operator represents a path that can be executed while its condition is satisfied. Two types of *Loop* segments can be defined: a loop "For" with the condition "(1,n)", where its path must be executed at least one time; and a loop "While" with the condition "(0,n)", where its path can be executed zero or *n* times. The *Transaction* operator indicates messages and paths of the segment have to be done atomically, and messages cannot be interleaved with messages of other paths. The *Exception* operator represents a path to be followed if an exception occurs according to the path's condition. The *Stop* operator represents paths that manage exceptions and require the abrupt termination of the protocol. The *Cancel* operator represents paths to be followed to manage exceptions. Different to *Stop* and *Exception* operators, the exception to be managed can occur in any point of the interaction protocol. A segment with this operator has to be defined at the end of the protocol.

The protocol of Figure 2 has a control flow segment with the operator *Xor* and two paths. This segments indicates the *customer* can respond in two way: it accepts the supplier's request and commits to carry out the demand forecast in the future (message *agree*); or it rejects the supplier's request and then the protocol ends.

Conditions represent logical expressions that constraint the execution of a message or a path in a control flow segment. They are defined in natural language or using OCL (Object Constraint Language) expressions.

Duration and Time constraints are used to define duration and deadlines on messages or protocols. They can be defined using relative or absolute dates. In Figure 2, the last two messages have a relative time constraint, which indicates the messages have to be sent before two days, after the occurrence of the first message.

An *Interaction Occurrence* represents the invocation of another interaction protocol referred as the nested protocol. In Figure 2, if the *customer* agrees on the *supplier's* request, then the nested protocol *Collaborative Demand Forecast* is invoked, in which the customer and the supplier agree on a common forecast.

Finally, an interaction protocol can have implicit or explicit *terminations*. Explicit termination events are: *success* and *failure*. *Success* implies the protocol ends in a successful way. Failure implies the protocol ends in an unexpected way, but from the point of view of the business logic. In Figure 2, if the customer rejects the supplier's request, the protocol ends with a failure. Else, after invocating to the nested protocol, the protocol finishes successfully in an implicit way.

4 Generation of WS-CDL Specifications from UP-ColBPIP Models

In this section we discuss the generation of WS-CDL specifications from models of collaborative processes defined with UP-ColBPIP. First, we describe the generation of type definitions of a WS-CDL document. Then, we describe the transformation of UP-ColBPIP elements into WS-CDL elements required to generate choreographies from the protocols defined in a UP-ColBPIP model. We describe the output of the transformations using the protocol defined in the above section. Figure 3 shows some parts of the WS-CDL document that is generated from this interaction protocol.

4.1 Generation of the Package and Type Definitions of a WS-CDL Document

The root element of a WS-CDL document is the *package*, which contains type definitions. In UP-ColBPIP, the root element is the B2B collaboration. Therefore, a B2B Collaboration is mapped into a package in WS-CDL (see line 1 in Figure 3).

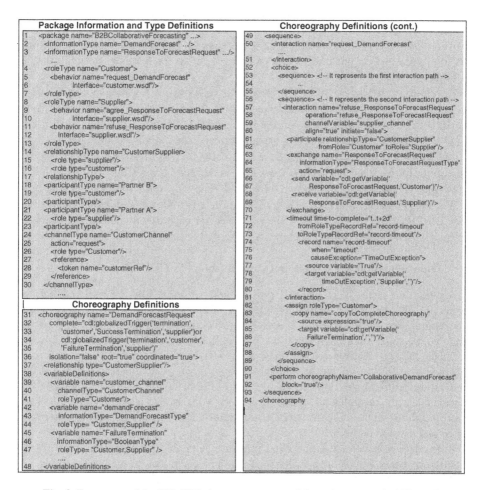

Package Information and Type Definitions		Choreography Definitions (cont.)	
1	`<package name="B2BCollaborativeForecasting" ...>`	49	`<sequence>`
2	`<informationType name="DemandForecast" .../>`	50	`<interaction name="request_DemandForecast"`
3	`<informationType name="ResponseToForecastRequest" .../>`	51	`</interaction>`
	`...`	52	`<choice>`
4	`<roleType name="Customer">`	53	`<sequence> <!-- It represents the first interaction path -->`
5	`<behavior name="request_DemandForecast"`	54	`..`
6	`Interface="customer.wsdl"/>`	55	`</sequence>`
7	`</roleType>`	56	`<sequence> <!-- It represents the second interaction path -->`
8	`<roleType name="Supplier">`	57	`<interaction name="refuse_ResponseToForecastRequest"`
9	`<behavior name="agree_ResponseToForecastRequest"`	58	`operation="refuse_ResponseToForecastRequest"`
10	`Interface="supplier.wsdl"/>`	59	`channelVariable="supplier_channel"`
11	`<behavior name="refuse_ResponseToForecastRequest"`	60	`align="true" initiate="false">`
12	`Interface="supplier.wsdl"/>`	61	`<participate relationshipType="CustomerSupplier"`
13	`</roleType>`	62	`fromRole="Customer" toRole="Supplier"/>`
14	`<relationshipType name="CustomerSupplier>`	63	`<exchange name="ResponseToForecastRequest"`
15	`<role type="supplier"/>`	64	`informationType="ResponseToForecastRequestType"`
16	`<role type="customer"/>`	65	`action="request">`
17	`<relationshipType>`	66	`<send variable="cdl:getVariable('`
18	`<participantType name="Partner B">`	67	`ResponseToForecastRequest,'Customer')"/>`
19	`<role type="customer"/>`	68	`<receive variable="cdl:getVariable('`
20	`<participantType/>`	69	`ResponseToForecastRequest,'Supplier')"/>`
21	`<participantType name="Partner A">`	70	`</exchange>`
22	`<role type="supplier"/>`	71	`<timeout time-to-complete="t..t+2d"`
23	`<participantType/>`	72	`fromRoleTypeRecordRef="record-timeout"`
24	`<channelType name="CustomerChannel"`	73	`toRoleTypeRecordRef="record-timeout">`
25	`action="request">`	74	`<record name="record-timeout"`
26	`<role type="Customer"/>`	75	`when="timeout"`
27	`<reference>`	76	`causeException="TimeOutException">`
28	`<token name="customerRef"/>`	77	`<source variable="True"/>`
29	`</reference>`	78	`<target variable="cdl:getVariable('`
30	`</channelType>`	79	`timeOutException','Supplier','')"/>`
	`....`	80	`</record>`
Choreography Definitions		81	`</interaction>`
31	`<choreography name="DemandForecastRequest"`	82	`<assign roleType="Customer">`
32	`complete="cdl:globalizedTrigger('termination',`	83	`<copy name="copyToCompleteChoreography"`
33	`'customer','SuccessTermination')or`	84	`<source expression="true"/>`
34	`cdl:globalizedTrigger('termination','customer',`	85	`<target variable="cdl:getVariable('`
35	`'FailureTermination','supplier')"`	86	`FailureTermination','','')"/>`
36	`isolation="false" root="true" coordinated="true">`	87	`</copy>`
37	`<relationship type="CustomerSupplier"/>`	88	`</assign>`
38	`<variableDefinitions>`	89	`</sequence>`
39	`<variable name="customer_channel"`	90	`</choice>`
40	`channelType="CustomerChannel"`	91	`<perform choreographyName="CollaborativeDemandForecast"`
41	`roleType="Customer"/>`	92	`block="true"/>`
42	`<variable name="demandForecast"`	93	`</sequence>`
43	`informationType="DemandForecastType"`	94	`</choreography>`
44	`roleType= "Customer,Supplier" />`		
45	`<variable name="FailureTermination"`		
46	`informationType="BooleanType"`		
47	`roleType="Customer,Supplier" />`		
	`....`		
48	`</variableDefinitions>`		

Fig. 3. Fragments of the WS-CDL document generated from the protocol of Figure 2

WS-CDL *informationType* definitions are derived from the *business document types* defined in the collaborative processes view of the UP-ColBPIP model. They represent a business document type from a content B2B standard and contain a reference to the XML Schema provided by the standard. They are used to indicate the type of the business documents exchanged in collaborative processes. In Figure 3, lines 2-3 define the business document types to be used for the protocol of Figure 2. Furthermore, general information types, such as *boolean*, can also be generated.

A *role* defined in a B2B collaboration is mapped into a *roleType* in the WS-CDL document. A roleType enumerates observable behavior a participant can exhibit in order to interact. This behavior is defined according to the operations provided by a WSDL interface of the participant. In the business interfaces view of a UP-ColBPIP model, *business services* of the *required and provided interfaces* of a role indicates the business messages that roles can send and receive, respectively. Hence, a *behavior* is generated in a roleType for each business service defined in the *provided business interface* of the role. For example, in Figure 3, lines 4-13 define the role types and its behaviors corresponding to the roles involved in the protocol of Figure 2.

A *relationshipType* in WS-CDL defines a relationship between two roles and optionally the subset of the behavior they exhibit. A relationshipType is derived from the B2B relationship connector defined in the B2B collaboration, which specifies a static relationship between two roles. As an example, see lines 14-17 in Figure 3.

A *partner* can play several roles in a B2B collaboration of a UP-ColBPIP model. Therefore, for each partner a *participantType* is defined in WS-CDL with the roles it has to play. For example, in Figure 3, lines 18-23 show the participants generated.

The last type definitions are *channelTypes*. There is not a corresponding element in UP-ColBPIP. However, a channelType is defined for each role to indicate the channel through which the role will receive messages (e.g.: see lines 24-30 in Figure 3).

4.2 Transformation of Interaction Protocols into WS-CDL Choreographies

An interaction protocol is mapped into a *choreography*. For the root interaction protocol of the UP-ColBPIP model, a root choreography is generated. Choreographies derived from interaction protocols are generated in the same package, because it corresponds to the B2B collaboration where the protocols were defined. Several attributes describes a WS-CDL choreography. The *isolation* attribute is set to "false" because variables (e.g.: business documents) defined in an interaction protocol can only be visible within the protocol. However, they can be correlated with variables of nested protocols as it is explained further on. The *coordination* attribute is set to "true" since an interaction protocol assumes the roles agree on how it is ended.

References to relationships between roles are generated matching the roles of the relationship types and the roles of the interaction protocol that is being transformed.

Then, choreography's *variables* are defined. Business documents used in the interaction protocol are mapped into variables with the corresponding information type. A variable used in a condition of a control flow segment is also mapped into a variable in the choreography. Channel variables are generated for each channel type defined. Variables generated are made available to each role.

In Figure 3, lines 31-48 show the choreography generated from the interaction protocol of Figure 2. Some of the variables generated are also showed.

Once the choreography has been defined, its activities are derived from the elements that make up the interaction protocol's choreography, as it is described below.

4.2.1   Transformation of Business Messages

A business message of an interaction protocol is transformed into an *interaction*. Both elements are the basic building block in their respective languages. An interaction in WS-CDL can be: a request, a response or a request-response (i.e a synchronous interaction). To represent the asynchronous communication of a business message, it is mapped into a request interaction.

Acknowledgements in a business message are used to assure the state synchronization between two roles when they exchange a message. WS-CDL does not support the definition of acknowledgments in an interaction. However, state synchronization can be achieved in WS-CDL defining an interaction as aligned, i.e. setting to "true" the *align* attribute. Another solution is to generate a request-response interaction where the response exchanges correspond to the acknowledgements.

The *operation* attribute of an interaction, which specifies what the recipient of a WS-CDL message should do when it is received, is derived from the signature of the business message, because it corresponds to one of the business services defined in the provided business interface of the receiver role. The *channelVariable* of the interaction is generated according to the channel in which the role is the target of the interaction. The *initiate* attribute is true if the business message represents the first interaction in the interaction protocol. The *participants* of the interaction are derived from the lifelines representing the receiver and sender role of the business message.

A business document conveyed in a business message is mapped into an *exchange*, which defines the information to be exchanged during the interaction. The *action* attribute is set to "request" to represent the asynchronous communication of the business message. In addition, the *send* and *receive* variables of the exchange are also generated from the business document of the business messages, in order to both roles save the exchanged business document.

If a business message has a duration or time constraint associated, a *timeout* is generated. If it has a duration constraint, the *time-to-complete* attribute contains the timeframe within which an interaction must complete after it was initiated. If the message has a time constraint, the *time-to-complete* attribute contains the deadline within which an interaction must complete after it was initiated. The duration and time constraints are those provided by UML. They can be defined in relative or absolute time and using intervals. However, in WS-CDL a timeframe or a deadline has to be defined in absolute time. Hence, the *time-to-complete* attribute is generated with the same value (in relative or absolute time) defined in the duration or time constraint of the business message. Then, the developers have to redefine the value of this attribute in case a relative time has been used. The *fromRoleTypeRecordRef* and *toRoleTypeRecordRef* attributes are also generated with a reference to a *record* of the interaction, which is used to notify both roles when a timeout exception occurs. In this case, the *when* attribute is set to "timeout".

Finally, a business message of an interaction protocol can have multiple instances. However, multiple instances of an interaction are not supported in WS-CDL.

In Figure 3, lines 57-81 define the interaction generated from the business message *refuse(ResponseToForecastRequest)* of the protocol of Figure 2.

4.2.2 Transformation of Control Flow Segments

They are transformed into WS-CDL control flow activities according to the operator used (summarized in Table 1). WS-CDL control flow activities are: *sequence*, *parallel*, *choice* and *workunit*. They capture the basic control flow constructs.

A control flow segment (CFS) with the operator *Xor* is mapped into a *choice* activity. This type of CFS can represent an event-driven choice or a data-driven choice, such as the choice activity of WS-CDL. A CFS without conditions represents an event-driven choice, meaning that the choice depends on the occurrence of the first element defined in one of the interaction paths. Else, a CFS with conditions represents a data-driven choice. The first type of CFS is mapped into a choice activity, and a sequence activity is generated for each interaction path. The second type of CFS is mapped into a choice activity and a workunit activity is generated for each interaction path. The condition of the path is transformed into a XPath expression defined in the *guard* attribute of the workunit. Its *repeat* attribute is set to "false". Its *block* attribute is also set to "false" because variables used in the conditions of CFSs can be different in each interaction path and it is assumed that the variable information is available at the moment of the evaluation.

Table 1. Transformation of control flow segments into WS-CDL control flow activities

Control Flow Segment	WS-CDL Control Flow Activity
Xor (data-driven choice)	A Choice and a Sequence activity for each interaction path
Xor (event-driven choice)	A Choice and a WorkUnit activity for each interaction path
Or	A Parallel activity and a Choice for each alternative interaction path. In the Choice activities, two WorkUnits are defined.
And	Parallel activity
Loop (0,n)	WorkUnit. Guard="Repetition condition". Repeat="True"
Loop (1,n)	WorkUnit. Guard="True". Repeat="Repetition condition"
If	WorkUnit. If it contains two paths, it is mapped as a Xor
Stop	Exception WorkUnit
Cancel	Exception WorkUnit

A CFS with the operator *And* is mapped into a *parallel* activity and a *sequence* activity is generated for each interaction path.

A CFS with the operator *Or* cannot be mapped into a direct way in WS-CDL. Like BPEL, it does not support a construct representing several activities can be executed and at least one must be executed. However, this CFS can be represented in WS-CDL in the following way. A parallel activity is generated and within this activity a choice activity is generated for each alternative interaction path. Within the choice activity, two workunit activities are defined, one representing the activities to be carried out in case of the condition is evaluated to true and another one to represent the opposite case. This last activity is generated to guarantee the termination of the parallel activity because it completes successfully when the enclosed activities complete successfully.

A CFS with the operator *If* is mapped into a *workunit* if it has only one interaction path. The *block* and *repeat* attributes are set to "false" and the *guard* attribute contains the CFS's condition. If the CFS has two interaction paths, it is transformed into the same way that a CFS with the operator *Xor* and two interaction paths.

WS-CDL does not distinguish between loop "For" and loop "While". Loops can be defined with a *workunit*. To represent a CFS with a loop "For", a workunit activity is generated with the *guard* attribute settled to "true" and the *repeat* attribute with the repetition condition. To represent a CFS with a loop "While", a workunit is generated with the *repeat* attribute settled to "true" and the *guard* attribute with the repetition condition. In both cases repetition condition is derived from the CFS's condition.

A CFS with the operator *Transaction* cannot be mapped into any construct of WS-CDL. It does not support the definition of transactions for interactions, such as in ebXML BPSS. A CFS with the operator *Exception* cannot also be mapped into any construct of WS-CDL. It does not support the definition of exception blocks in a specific point of the interaction and that does not require the end of the choreography.

A CFS with the operator *Stop* or *Cancel* is mapped into an exception workunit defined within the *exceptionBlock* of the choreography. Although WS-CDL does not support the definition of exception blocks in specific points of the choreography, the CFS with the *Stop* operator can be transformed into an exception workunit, where its *guard* attribute contains the exception condition derived from the path's condition of the CFS. If a CFS with the operator *Cancel* has an interaction path with the condition "TimeException", an exception workunit is generated with a *guard* using the WS-CDL function *hasExceptionOccurred*. The parameter *exceptionType* of this function contains the name of the caused exception according to the defined in the timeout elements of the generated interactions. In the other cases, for each interaction path defined in the CFS with the operator *Cancel*, an exception workunit is generated with the *guard* attribute containing the exception condition defined in that path. The above transformation indicates that the *Stop* or *Cancel* CFSs have the same semantics, except that a Stop CFS can be defined in a specific point of the protocol.

In Figure 3, lines 52-56 and 89-90 show the activities generated from the CFS with the operator *Xor* of the protocol of Figure 2.

4.2.3 Transformation of Terminations

An interaction protocol can have an implicit termination, such as the WS-CDL choreographies. Hence, it is not necessary to generate any WS-CDL element if the protocol has an implicit termination. Also, an interaction protocol can have explicit terminations: *success* or *failure*. However, there is not a corresponding construct in WS-CDL that represents the semantics of these terminations. Moreover, WS-CDL does not provide a construct to define terminations in a specific point of the choreography, such as the used in ebXML BPSS (*success* and *failure* states) and BPEL (*terminate* activity). To represent an explicit termination in WS-CDL, we have to add a condition in the *complete* attribute of the choreography. A termination variable is added to the choreography and available to both roles. After the activity where the termination should occur, an *assign* activity is added to set to "true" the value of the termination variable in order to the expression of the choreography's *complete* attribute evaluates to true and the choreography completes. A termination variable can be added to the choreography to represent a success termination and another one to represent a failure termination. In Figure 3, lines 32-35 and lines 82-88 show an example.

In addition, a WS-CDL *finalizerBlock* does not have a correspondence with any modeling element of UP-ColBPIP, therefore it cannot be derived from interaction protocols. However, this construct can only be used in non-root choreographies and it is not clear when a successfully completed choreography can require further action. Due to finalizer blocks cannot be generated, *finalize* activities are also not used. Furthermore, since in an interaction protocol the roles agree on whether it completes successfully, with a failure or with an exception occurrence (like in a WS-CDL coordinated choreography), finalizer blocks are not required.

4.2.4 Transformation of Interaction Occurrences

An interaction occurrence is transformed into a *perform* activity, which allows the definition of nested choreographies. If the interaction occurrence is defined within a CFS, an expression should be generated for the *choreographyInstanceId* attribute of the perform activity representing the interaction occurrence. The *block* attribute always is set to "true", because in UP-ColBPIP a protocol must wait for the termination of its nested protocols in order to continue after their execution. The business documents of an interaction protocol can be correlated with the business documents defined into the nested protocol. Correlations are defined with a comment stereotyped *Correlation* associated to the interaction occurrence. Correlations are mapped into bindings between the variables (representing the business documents) of the enclosing choreography (the protocol) and the enclosed choreography (the nested protocol). In WS-CDL, correlations are called binding and they are defined with the *bind* element.

For example, in Figure 3, lines 91-92 show the perform activity representing the interaction occurrence *Collaborative Demand Forecast* of the protocol of Figure 2.

4 Related Work

There are several Model-Driven Development (MDD) approaches proposed to generate technological solutions based on web services composition [2,6,10]. They focus on the modeling and automatic code generation of behavioral interfaces. Hence, they support the modeling and specification of the behavior of collaborative processes but only from the point of view of one partner. As a result they do not support the global view of the interactions, which is required in the modeling of collaborative processes and the specification of web services choreographies.

In [11], transformation of WS-CDL choreographies into BPEL abstract processes is defined. This approach starts from WS-CDL choreography definitions and it does not consider the use of a graphical modeling language to define choreographies or collaborative processes. However, according to MDA principles, a language to define technology-independent models should be provided, as it is proposed in this paper.

In [8, 17], choreographies are generated from collaborative process models. They focus on the generation of choreographies based on the language ebXML BPSS, which is based on business transactions instead of using web services. In [8], the language UN/CEFACT Modeling Methodology (UMM) has been used and validated to generate ebXML BPSS specifications. In [17], we used and validated UP-CoLBPIP to generate ebXML BPSS specifications. The implementation of transformation rules were carried out by using a model transformation tool we are developing. However, the transformations presented in this work have not been implemented yet in that tool.

Furthermore, other approaches focus on the generation of the behavioral interfaces of partners from collaborative process models [5] [19]. The target language used is BPEL. These approaches focus on the definition of behavioral interfaces in the technological level while in the business level the focus is on the collaborative process models. Hence, the use of choreographies in the technological level is not considered. This is possible because a web service choreography cannot be implemented in a direct way but it is implemented through the definition of behavioral interfaces and orchestrations for each partner. This is one of the arguments against the use of a XML syntax to define choreographies [3] because they are more useful as design artifact than an implementation artifact. However, collaborative process models and choreographies can be used as design artifact. The former should capture the business aspects and the later should capture the technical aspects according to the target technology.

Finally, we are not aware of other MDA approaches that focus on the generation of WS-CDL choreographies from collaborative process models. In the MDA approach proposed in this paper, the objective is to support the definition of technology-independent collaborative processes in a high abstraction level. This is different to the idea of generating graphical notations for technology-specific languages such as WS-CDL. We consider that the main artifacts of the development in B2B collaboration should be the collaborative process models. However, the use of standards is required in order to partners' systems can interoperate and implement collaborative processes. Currently there are different standards, new versions of them can appear and new standards can be proposed. Therefore a technology-independent modeling language for collaborative processes is required and should provide the main conceptual elements to define theses processes in a business level and to generate processes specifications based on the different standards.

5   Conclusions and Future Work

In this paper we have described how web services choreographies based on WS-CDL can be generated from collaborative process models defined with the modeling language UP-ColBPIP, according to the principles of a MDA approach for collaborative processes. The main advantage of using this MDA approach is that it guarantees that web services choreographies generated in the technological level fulfill the collaborative processes defined in a business level. The transformation rules proposed in this paper reduce the risk of inconsistence between collaborative process models and their corresponding web services choreographies based on WS-CDL.

The use of a UML Profile for modeling collaborative processes in a business level allows partners focus mainly on the business aspects of the B2B collaboration. Also, the use of interaction protocols to model collaborative processes supports the requirements of enterprise autonomy, decentralization and peer-to-peer interactions, as well as it supports business aspects such as the definition of negotiations and commitments through the use of speech acts. These business aspects are not captured in standards such as WS-CDL, which focus mainly on the technical aspects of the collaborative processes based on web services technology. However, WS-CDL could be enriched with conceptual elements more oriented to business aspects such as speech acts. Also, UP-ColBPIP could also be enriched with several characteristics provided by WS-CDL, such as the concepts of channel, tokens and finalizer blocks.

As result of the transformation rules of a UP-ColBPIP model into a WS-CDL specification, most of the conceptual elements provided by UP-ColBPIP can be represented in WS-CDL. Although WS-CDL only provides the basic control flow activities, most of the control flow operators used in UP-ColBPIP can be represented in WS-CDL. However, multiple instances of interactions and explicit terminations of the choreography are not supported in WS-CDL.

An open issue is to determine if WS-CDL specifications generated from UP-ColBPIP models are well-formed. But we cannot to determine if a WS-CDL specification is well-formed, as well as it is not possible to determine yet this with UP-ColBPIP models. To guarantee correctness of these models and specifications a formalized model has to be generated. We are working on the formalization of UP-ColBPIP models using Petri Nets. The purpose is to enable the verification of collaborative processes, previous to the generation of B2B specifications.

References

1. Baghdadi, Y.: ABBA: An architecture for deploying business-to-business electronic commerce applications. Electronic Commerce Research and Applications, 3(2004) 190-212
2. Baïna, K, Benatallah, B., Cassati, F., Toumani, F.: Model-Driven Web Service Development. CaiSE'04, Springer (2004) 290-306.
3. Barros, A., Dumas, M., Oaks, P.: A Critical Overview of the Web Service Choreography Description Language (WS-CDL). BPTrends Newsletter 3 (2005).
4. BEA, IBM, Microsoft, SAP, Siebel: Business Process Execution Language for Web Services. http://www-106.ibm.com/developerworks/library/ws-bpel/, 2003.
5. Bruno, G. and La Rosa, M.: From Collaboration Models to BPEL processes through service models. BPM Workshops 2005, WSCOBPM 2005, 75-88, 2005.
6. Gardner, T.: UML Modelling of Automated Business Processes with a Mapping to BPEL4WS, 17th ECOOP, Darmstadt, Germany (2003).
7. Goldkuhl, G., Lind,M.: Developing E-Interactions – a Framework for Business Capabilities and Exchanges. Proceedings of the ECIS-2004, Finland, 2004.
8. Hofreiter B., Huemer C.: ebXML Business Processes - Defined both in UMM and BPSS. Proc. of the 1st GI-Workshop XML Interchange Formats for Business Process Management, Modellierung 2004, Germany, 81-102, 2004.
9. Kavantzas, N., Burdett, D., Ritzinger, G., Fletcher, T., Lafon, Y.: Web Services Choreography Description Language Version 1.0. W3C Candidate Recommendation (2005), W3C.
10. Koehler, J., Hauser, R., Kaporr, S., Wu, F., Kurmaran, S.: A Model-Driven Transformation Method. 7th International Enterprise Distributed Object Computing, 2003.
11. Mendling, J. and Hafner, M.: From Inter-Organizational Workflows to Process Execution: Generating BPEL from WS-CDL. OTM 2005 Workshops. LNCS 3762,506-515, 2005.
12. Object Management Group: MDA Guide V1.0.1, 2003. http://www.omg.org/mda.
13. Searle, J.R.: Speech Acts, an Essay in the Philosophy of Language, Cambridge University Press, Cambridge, 1969.
14. UN/CEFACT and OASIS: ebXML Business Specification Schema Version 1.10, http://www.untmg.org/downloads/General/approved/ebBPSS-v1pt10.zip (2001)

15. Villarreal, P.: Method for the Modeling and Specification of Collaborative Business Processes. PhD Thesis. Universidad Tecnológica Nacional, Santa Fe, Argentina (2005).
16. Villarreal, P., Salomone, H.E. and Chiotti, O.: B2B Relationships: Defining Public Business Processes using Interaction Protocols. Journal of the Chilean Society of Computer Science, Special issue on the Best Papers of the JCC 2003, Vol. 4(1) (2003).
17. Villarreal, P., Salomone, H.E. and Chiotti, O.: Applying Model-Driven Development to Collaborative Business Processes. Proceedings of the 8th Ibero-American Workshop of Requirements Engineering and Software Environments, Chile, 2005.
18. Villarreal, P., Salomone, H.E. and Chiotti, O.: Modeling and Specifications of Collaborative Business Processes using a MDA Approach and a UML Profile. In: Rittgen, P. (eds): Enterprise Modeling and Computing with UML. Idea Group Inc, (in press).
19. Villarreal, P., Salomone, H.E. and Chiotti, O.: MDA Approach for Collaborative Business Processes: Generating Technological Solutions based on Web Services Composition. Proceedings of the 9th Ibero-American Workshop of Requirements Engineering and Software Environments, Argentine, 2006, in press.

Evaluation of IT Portfolio Options by Linking to Business Services

Vijay Iyengar, David Flaxer, Anil Nigam, and John Vergo

IBM Research, T.J. Watson Research Center, Yorktown Heights, NY 10598, USA
{vsi, flaxer, anigam, jvergo}@us.ibm.com

Abstract. The management of IT portfolios in most enterprises is a complex and challenging ongoing process. IT portfolios typically contain large numbers of inter-related elements. In this paper, we present a model and a method for determining and evaluating IT portfolio options for use as a decision aid in the ongoing management of the portfolio. Business benefits of the portfolio options are articulated by linking IT portfolio elements to componentized business services. Characteristics of the IT portfolio elements are abstracted to a level of granularity suited for portfolio analysis. Our model allows various forms of uncertainty that are utilized in the evaluation. Our evaluation method determines a set of portfolio options with the associated cost/benefits tradeoffs. Business constraints and pruning methods are used to present only the relevant and available options and their tradeoffs to the IT portfolio manager.

1 Introduction

The management of IT (Information Technologies) portfolios is a complex ongoing process in many enterprises. One aspect of this complexity is that enterprises typically have a large portfolio of IT assets like applications, projects that transform existing applications and install new ones, and system platforms supporting the operation of the applications. In addition, there are important relationships between portfolio elements (e.g., functional dependencies) that need to be considered during portfolio management. McFarlan suggested managing these IT assets as a portfolio using a value and risk-based approach in 1981 [1]. Portfolios in equities markets have used and benefited from portfolio management approaches that systematically consider risks and returns [2]. However, there are important differences between financial portfolios and IT portfolios. Some of the differentiating characteristics are: the granularity of the portfolio elements, their inter-relationships, the temporal attributes of portfolio elements (e.g., time taken by transformational IT projects before delivering value), business constraints that need to be considered in IT portfolios (e.g., complex resource constraints) and the multi-dimensional nature of metrics to evaluate IT portfolio elements. The success of multi-dimensional metrics like the Balanced Scorecard validates the view that many organizations consider dimensions like customers, internal processes, learning and growth in addition to the financial performance metrics [3].

Another aspect of complexity is the need to improve the business benefits delivered by the IT portfolio and this issue is referred to in the literature as "business

J. Lee et al. (Eds.): DEECS 2006, LNCS 4055, pp. 66–80, 2006.
© Springer-Verlag Berlin Heidelberg 2006

alignment of IT" and "business/IT gap" [4, 5, 6]. It has been suggested that improvement of business/IT alignment is the most important problem for many enterprises [7]. This problem is addressed in [7] by focusing on the alignment between the IT portfolio's objectives and enterprise strategy, by analyzing relationships between projects leading to their optimization, and by organizing the portfolio to deal with the uncertainties of the environment. In a more recent work [8], the authors articulate the value of service orientation at the business level to allow companies to transform themselves to respond to changing market conditions. They discuss the role of componentization and business services orientation to enable an adaptive enterprise to operate in a value net [8].

An important aspect of the IT investment and portfolio management process is the evaluation of portfolio options in terms of costs, benefits and risks [6]. The main contribution of this paper is to leverage the ideas of componentization and service orientation presented in [8] to articulate business benefits by linking these componentized services to the IT portfolio elements. The fine grain characterization of business benefits enabled by this linkage provides a level of transparency that can be valuable in the evaluation of portfolio options. This analysis supplements the extensive work that has been done in the financial valuation of IT portfolios [9, 10]. We hypothesize that our fine grain benefits characterization is particularly valuable for analyzing tradeoffs between portfolio elements that have significant overlap in functionalities (e.g., they impact the same componentized business service in the enterprise [8]). Also, the business services oriented metrics used in our analysis can be especially useful in providing insights into some of the non-financial strategic factors considered by an enterprise [8, 9].

We present a model to represent IT portfolio elements and componentized business services and their relationships. Our model captures key attributes of the IT portfolio elements and represents the portfolio at a level of granularity suitable for analysis and decision making by a portfolio manager (not an individual project manager). Examples of attributes include project phases, costs, schedules, deliverables and dependencies between portfolio elements. Examples of the uncertainties modeled include variability in estimated costs, schedules and business benefits [11]. We use Monte Carlo simulation to determine the impact of these uncertainties [12]. This approach has been shown to have the flexibility to handle realistic aspects of risk including dependencies [13]. Business constraints can also be represented in our model and are used to filter out portfolio options that need not be considered in the evaluation. Our evaluation determines the cost / benefit tradeoffs for the portfolio options taking into account the uncertainty model. The multi-dimensional nature of the costs and benefits [14] are taken into account in the pruning of options so that only the relevant tradeoffs are presented to the decision maker.

We will use a running example that was motivated by an actual portfolio management case. Even though we use a small example in terms of the portfolio size for the sake of illustration, its characteristics are rich enough to discuss the features of our model and method. The example will have applications and transformational projects as elements of the IT portfolio. Extensions to other types of portfolio elements are outside the scope of this paper (e.g., systems, human resources).

2 The Example

The running example we use in this paper is from the production monitoring domain that is applicable in various industries (e.g., semiconductor, petroleum, automotive). We consider business services supporting real-time production monitoring and control. In particular, we focus on monitoring for abnormalities in the production process that can result in production stoppage. We will use two metrics to quantify the business benefits to this business service (BS1): 1) Timeliness of abnormality alerts generated by the monitoring and 2) Skilled resource needs and related productivity gains. Evaluation of activity monitoring techniques typically requires a more complex framework that factors in granularity and accuracy of alerts, value of multiple alerts, and timeliness [15]. For illustration, we choose a simplified view with a single timeliness metric that assumes other factors like accuracy are normalized across all options. The diversity of the types of benefits measured by these two metrics indicates the typical heterogeneity in the benefit dimensions. Decision makers may choose not to translate all the benefits to homogeneous monetary terms. In such cases, the decision aid tool must allow for multi-dimensional evaluation results.

Portfolio management is an ongoing process. In our example, we will assume being at a decision point at which the functionality for the business service BS1 is provided by the manual analyses of production data periodically collected by a legacy application (denoted LA). Two new applications are being considered. An SOA-based application for collecting real-time data from the production facility (denoted as II) and an application (denoted EW) that will automatically analyze data from II to generate abnormality alerts. The motivation for application II is that it can provide real-time data on a SOA platform. Application EW has the promise (though with some significant uncertainty) of providing both earlier alerts and productivity gains by reducing manual analyses.

Three transformational projects are being considered with respect to the above applications. The first project (P1) would upgrade the legacy application LA to provide real-time data. The second project (P2) would develop the application II in two phases and the third project (P3) would similarly develop application EW in two phases.

Further details of the applications and transformational projects in this example will be discussed while illustrating our model in the following sections.

3 Our Model

In this section we will introduce our model and illustrate its usage with the example that was introduced in the previous section. Conceptually, the model stitches together two pieces of Enterprise Portfolio Management viz. Projects and Componentized Business Services (Figure 1). A Project is made up of Phases and each Phase in turn can have Deliverables associated with it. Since our current example has to do with Applications, each Deliverable transforms an Application-Version to a new Application-Version. A more general model of course need not be limited to Applications; it should be able to address transformation of systems, processes, organizations etc. On the other hand, a Business Service can have a number of Realization Choices. These choices are modeled as disjunctions where each disjunct can be made up of a number of conjunctions i.e. a specific business service can be realized through A2 or (A1 and

B2) or (A1 and C2) where the Ai, Bi and Ci are specific application versions. Costs can come in many flavors – we demonstrate this by associating completion cost with project Phase and operating cost with Application-Version. Similarly, business benefits are modeled in the Realization Choices. Lastly the model allows for dependencies between project Phases as well as between Application-Versions. Costs and Benefits can be modeled as arbitrarily complex structures to meet the needs of the business situation. The model also allows representation of uncertainty in various quantities like phase duration, costs, and benefits realization. We will now introduce details of our model in stages using the running example for illustration.

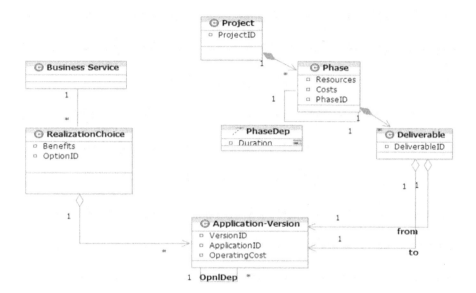

Fig. 1. Our model linking IT elements (e.g., projects, applications) to Business Services

3.1 Applications and Projects

Applications in the portfolio are allowed to have versions that represent differing levels of support for various functionalities. Similarly, the projects can be composed of a linear sequence of project phases. Details from finer grain project elements like tasks are rolled up to the granularity of phases for our analysis. The levels of granularity chosen for applications and projects should be commensurate with frequency at which the portfolio decisions are made. Applications and projects are linked by allowing the specification of application upgrades as possible deliverables of project phases. An application upgrade deliverable specifies the starting and ending application versions of the upgrade. The application version can be upgraded when the project phase(s) providing the corresponding upgrade deliverable completes. This linkage is illustrated in Table 1 for the running example. The legacy application LA can be upgraded as discussed earlier by phase 1 of project P1. The two new applications II and EW are developed in two phases (1, 2) of the projects P2 and P3, respectively. The starting points for these applications are II.1 (shorthand notation for application II at version 1) and EW.1, respectively. The first phase of projects P2 and P3 delivers the upgrade of these applications to II.2 and EW.2. This corresponds to a pilot deployment. The second phase of projects P2 and P3 completes the development of II and EW to the operational versions, II.3 and EW.3, respectively.

Table 1. Project to Application Linkage

Project	Phase	Application Upgrade Deliverable		
		App.	From version	To version
P1	1	LA	1	2
P2	1	II	1	2
P2	2	II	2	3
P3	1	EW	1	2
P3	2	EW	2	3

A project phase can have dependencies not on just the previous phase but on phases of other projects. Table 2 illustrates the dependencies in our example. For example, the first phase of project P1 does not have any dependencies and the 'Time' column for this phase specifies it can take in the range of 10 to 12 months to complete. The second phase of project P3, on the other hand, depends on its previous phase (phase 1) needing time in the range of 10 to 12 months after the previous phase completes. It also depends on phase 2 of project P2 and needs 2 months after its completion. These project phase dependencies and times can be rolled up from more detailed project plans or estimated directly. The model for uncertainty in the time durations will be discussed later in Section 3.4.

Operational dependencies between applications are also represented in our model. In our example, application EW has a dependency on application II to provide the data. Table 3 captures this dependency at the application versions granularity. For example, version 2 of application EW can operate if either version 2 or 3 of application II is operational.

Table 2. Project Phase Dependencies

Project	Phase	Dependencies		
		Project	Phase	Time (months)
P1	1	-	-	[10,12]
P2	1	-	-	[6, 8]
P2	2	P2	1	[12, 14]
P3	1	-	-	[4, 6]
		P2	1	[1, 1]
P3	2	P3	1	[10,12]
		P2	2	[2, 2]

Table 3. Operational Dependencies between Applications

Application	Version	Dependencies	
		Application	Version
EW	2	II	2
		II	3
EW	3	II	3

3.2 Costs

Our model allows representation of the typical costs associated with projects and applications. These include one time costs like the cost of completing a project phase and recurring costs like the monthly cost of operating an application. Factoring in all the costs is critical to the success of the portfolio management task. For example, if we are considering retiring some current applications we need to model any contractual penalties incurred due to their early retirement. Tables 4 and 5 present the cost structure for the running example.

3.3 Linkage to Business Benefits

The application and project attributes discussed above are typically obtained by a bottoms-up approach. Business benefits on the other hand require a top-down approach where we start with the business services and link them up with IT portfolio elements. Our model allows the specification of one or more choices for the realization of a business service. Each realization choice (RC) can specify one or more applications (at specified versions) as being necessary to provide the functionality for the business service being considered. For each choice RC we allow further specification of how well this choice performs in the realization. The most straightforward way of specifying this is to assess and estimate the business benefits achieved by each choice (using the list of benefit types for the corresponding business service).

Table 4. Operating Costs for Applications

Application	Versions	Operating Costs ($ per month)
LA	1, 2	5000, 5000
II	1, 2, 3	100, 100, 2000
EW	1, 2, 3	100, 100, 1000

Table 5. Completion Costs for Project Phases

Project	Phases	Completion Costs ($x1000)
P1	1	200
P2	1, 2	50, 100
P3	1, 2	25, 50

Clearly, this estimation step is critical to the analyses of the portfolio and the challenges in benefits estimation have been discussed in the literature [16, 17]. Some of the lessons learned in the field from similar quantifications of business value are important to consider and address [17]. The choice of the granularity, namely business service, at which we choose to perform the benefits assessment, is an important factor to consider. At this level of granularity it is possible to specify metrics for measuring benefits that have intuitive meaning to the stakeholders. In our example, the use of metrics like timeliness and productivity improvement leads to more transparency than if we had used an aggregate monetary benefit metric. Increased transparency can reduce the possibility that stakeholders will game the system [17]. In addition, processes for getting consensus estimates will have to be implemented to get the buy-in from the stakeholders. Most importantly, if an enterprise uses the componentized business services as its operational model [8], the business service becomes a natural point for linking the IT portfolio elements to the business.

Table 6 lists the four realization choices for our business service example BS1. The first realization choice RC1 is to use the legacy application in its current version LA.1. The lack of real time data results in a loss of the timeliness benefit as indicated in Table 6 (benefits are specified by the minimum and maximum over the range of possible values). The second realization choice RC2 is the upgraded legacy application LA.2. The real-time capability of this version improves the timeliness benefit over the first choice RC1. The third choice RC3 is to use version 3 of the application II (II.3). The benefits provided by this choice are identical to that of RC2 (i.e., due to real-time data collection). The last choice RC4 is to realize the business service using the combination of applications II and EW at versions II.3 and EW.3, respectively. For this choice, the potential improvements in both timeliness and productivity with the associated uncertainties are indicated in Table 6.

Table 6. Realization choices for the business service BS1

Realization Choice	Application Versions	Timeliness Benefit (minutes)	Productivity Benefit (%)
RC1	LA.1	[-15,-15]	[0, 0]
RC2	LA.2	[0 , 0]	[0, 0]
RC3	II.3	[0, 0]	[0, 0]
RC4	II.3 & EW.3	[0, 15]	[0, 50]

3.4 Uncertainties

Portfolio management involves looking ahead at project plans and estimating project phase completion dates, costs, and benefits. Clearly, any model for these quantities needs to represent the uncertainties in their estimates. We allow a range of models for uncertainties in these estimates in which the user can specify the underlying statistical distribution for the values and the corresponding parameters [11]. In our running example, we illustrate this by specifying uncertainties for the durations of project phases and for the business service benefits. We use the simplifying independence assumption for the uncertainties in project durations in the example. The two business service benefits represent orthogonal aspects (timeliness, productivity) and so their associated uncertainties are treated as being independent. As mentioned earlier, the Monte Carlo approach used can model dependence between uncertainties [13]. In our example we use the uniform distribution for modeling the uncertain quantities and Tables 2 and 6 specified the minimum and maximum values for their ranges. The next section details how the uncertainty model is used in the analysis.

3.5 Business Constraints

We allow certain types of business constraints to be specified as a part of the model. These are important to ensure that the analysis and its results are realistic and actionable. An important type of constraint is the specification of the minimum functionality that the portfolio has to achieve at all times while it is undergoing transformation. In our example, the corresponding constraint is that business service BS1 has to be realized by any one of the specified choices at all times. This is the only business constraint specified for our running example.

Another type of constraint would be to further specify minimum values for the benefits metrics that have to be achieved. Upper bound on total cost reflecting budgetary constraints is another type of constraint. Constraints can also specify groupings of IT portfolio elements that need to be bundled together for development or retirement.

4 Analysis Method

The earlier section specified the model for specifying elements of the IT portfolio, their relevant attributes and relationships between them and to business services. In a typical usage scenario we expect the portfolio manager to select a subset of business services for the analysis to focus on. If the business services are part of a componentized view of the enterprise [8], then the components may provide a natural way of selecting the subset of services for analysis. Selecting a subset of business services for the analysis implies that only the subset of the IT portfolio linked to them (as specified in our model) is analyzed. The analysis uses the information in our model and returns a pruned set of portfolio options for enabling the selected business services along with their tradeoffs in terms of costs and benefits. Each portfolio option uniquely specifies the completed project phases and the final state of the application in the linked IT portfolio subset.

Our portfolio evaluation technique (PET) is sketched out in Figure 2. Next, we will describe the algorithm in some detail using references to step numbers in Figure 2. In addition to the model, input to PET includes the state of the IT portfolio at the current decision point. It also includes analysis parameters like the selected subset of business services and the time horizon for computing costs and benefits.

Algorithm PET:
Input: (Model M containing {Business Services S, Projects P, Applications A, Constraints C}, Current decision point X, Analysis Parameters Q contains {Sq = Subset of S, Time horizon T})
Output: (Pruned list of Portfolio Options O with {costs, benefits})

Determine sets of services, projects, applications that need to be analyzed together
1a. Construct graph R {S, P, A} with nodes corresponding to elements of S, P and A. Edges of R represent relationships due to realization choices, project phase deliverables or dependencies.
1b. Create a subgraph Rq {Sq, Pq, Aq} from R by selecting nodes connected to the services in Sq.
1c. Partition the services Sq, projects Pq, applications Aq into connected groups G by computing connected components of Rq. The elements of a connected group g in G will be referred to as Sg, Pg, and Ag, respectively.

Translate project phase dependencies, application operational dependencies and project application linkage into inconsistency maps P2P, A2A and P2A, respectively. Used to prune portfolio options.
2. Create inconsistency maps between phases of distinct projects (P2P), versions of distinct applications (A2A) and between project phases and application versions (P2A).

Exhaustively enumerate list of portfolio options Og for each connected group g in G.
3a. For each connected group g in G
   3b. Og is initially empty
   3c. For each project p in Pg
      Validity check in step 3d uses the inconsistency map P2P.
      3d. For each valid phase pp of p that is consistent with the current decision point X
         3e. Choose pp as an option for the last phase completed in project p.
         3f. Create a new list Og by using this project p choice to each option in the original list.
      End for
   End for
   3g. For each application z in Ag
      Validity check in the step 3h uses the inconsistency maps A2A and P2A.
      3h. For each valid version v of application z that is consistent with the current decision point X
         3i. Choose v as the final version for application z.
         3j. Create a new list Og by using this final version choice for z to each original option.
      End for
   End for
   pruning is possible at this stage since options can be checked against some business constraints
   3k. Prune options list O by discarding options that do not satisfy constraints C
End for

4a. Set up scenarios N by randomly choosing values in model based on uncertainty distributions.
4b. For each scenario n in N
   4c. For each connected group g in G
      4d. For each portfolio option o in Og
         4e. Compute times for project phase completions and application version changes
         4f. Compute costs and benefits for this scenario for the time horizon T
      End for
      4g. Update dominance relationships based on current scenario
   End for
End for

5. Aggregate results {costs, benefits} over all the scenarios in N

Compute partial order over the portfolio options using dominance across all costs and benefits
6. Compute results as the pruned list of portfolio options (organized by connected groups) by keeping only the dominant ones

Fig. 2. Sketch of Portfolio Evaluation Technique – PET (comments are in italics)

The algorithm first determines the subset of the IT portfolio that is relevant to subset of business services selected for analysis (step 1b). This is done by determining the IT portfolio elements connected to the selected services by the relationships in our model. We can then group the business services and IT portfolio elements into connected components [18] in the graph that models relationships between portfolio elements (step 1c). Each of these groups (called a *connected group*) represents related elements that have to be analyzed together and is closely related to the concept of *Programme* in the Val IT Framework [6]. Note that our definition of a connected group factors in linkages to business services. This allows us to group together IT elements (e.g., projects) that may not have functional dependencies but are still related by impacting the same business service. Grouping together such IT elements is critical to modeling possible business level synergies and redundancies between them.

The project phase dependencies, application operational dependencies and the project to application linkage represent constraints specifying which portfolio options are valid. Step 2 of the algorithm represents these constraints in structures called inconsistency maps suitable for checking and pruning later in the algorithm.

Step 3 of the algorithm creates the list of portfolio options that have to be considered in the analysis. The list is created by exhaustively forming the combinations of options for each portfolio element in the group. Checks against the inconsistency maps are performed as the list is created to exclude invalid options. The options list creation is organized by first considering the valid options for the project phases that are completed (Steps 3c to 3f). Then, steps 3g to 3j consider the valid options for the final application versions. Note that a possible final state for an application could be that it is retired. Some of the business constraints can be used to prune the portfolio options list at this stage (Step 3k). In our example, we can discard any option if corresponding final states of applications do not satisfy the constraint that the business service has to be realized by one of the specified choices at all times.

Uncertainties in various model quantities are handled by Monte Carlo simulation of a number of scenarios based on the specified distributions. The number of scenarios is an analysis parameter that is provided as input to PET. Steps 4a and 4b-4f perform the set up of all scenarios and the analysis of each scenario, respectively. The computation of times for completion of project phases and application version changes is done on an earliest possible time basis taking into account the relevant constraints (step 4e). In our example, retirement times for applications reflect the need for the business service to be realized by one of the specified choices at all times. We track and update the dominance relationships based on all the costs and benefits dimensions for each scenario (Step 4g). An option dominates another in a scenario if it improves in one or more dimensions of the evaluation (costs, benefits) and is no worse in the rest.

Step 5 aggregates the costs and benefits over all the scenarios. This step computes the partial order over the portfolio options using dominance relationships collected for all the scenarios. We use a probabilistic notion of dominance to determine the partial order. The user can specify the probability thresholds to be used with respect to the scenarios to declare an option to be dominated by another. In our example, we use a strict notion of dominance that requires that an option O1 be dominated by another option O2 in all the scenarios before it (O1) can be discarded from consideration. The dominated options in the partial order are discarded and the remaining pruned set of portfolio options with the aggregated costs and benefits tradeoffs are returned as the results of the analysis (step 6). The resulting options are organized using the connected groups computed earlier in Step 1. This facilitates a hierarchical approach to considering the portfolio options: within the connected group and across multiple groups.

5   Results for the Running Example

We will present the results of applying our model and method to the running example to illustrate how our approach supports the decision process in portfolio management. We perform the analysis corresponding to the decision point where none of the project phases have been performed and the three applications are at versions LA.1, II.1 and EW.1, respectively. We also specify that the analysis evaluate the tradeoffs with 1000 scenarios using the uncertainty distributions specified.

The analysis considered 84 valid portfolio options of which 59 satisfy the functionality constraint. Our analysis then computes the costs and benefits for this list of 59 options and automatically prunes the list using the dominance relationship to produce results containing only 5 portfolio options for consideration by the portfolio manager. Table 7 lists these portfolio options and their defining characteristics: completed project phases and final application states. The cost/ benefits tradeoffs for these options are listed in Table 8 and shown graphically in Figure 3. Table 8 lists (and Figure 3 displays), for each quantity, the mean value on top and the [1st quartile, 3rd quartile] values below (across all scenarios). We will briefly discuss these 5 options in order of increasing expected cost.

The first and lowest cost option is to not perform any of the projects and continue operating with application LA at version 1. The cost of $240K is basically the operating cost for LA.1 of $5K per month over the time horizon of 48 months. The lack of real time data leads to the poor timeliness benefit (-15) and there is no improvement beyond the baseline productivity (0).

The second option is to replace the legacy application LA by developing the II application to version II.3. This is accomplished by completing phases 1 and 2 for project P2 and then retiring the application LA.1 and replacing it with the operational application II.3. The cost for this option includes the cost of project P2 and the operating costs for application LA.1 followed by II.3. The uncertainty in the schedules is reflected in the variability in cost. The timeliness benefit reflects the improvement due to real time data when II.3 replaces LA.1.

Table 7. Results: Portfolio Option Definitions

Portfolio	Project phases completed			Final application versions		
Option	P1	P2	P3	LA	II	EW
1	-	-	-	1	-	-
2	-	2	-	-	3	-
3	-	2	2	-	3	3
4	1	-	-	2	-	-
5	1	2	2	-	3	3

Table 8. Results: Costs and Benefits for Portfolio Options

Portfolio Option	Cost $ (x1000)	Timeliness Benefit (minutes)	Productivity Benefit (%)
1	240 [240, 240]	-15 [-15, -15]	0 [0, 0]
2	308.1 [306.3, 309.9]	-6.3 [-6.4, -6.1]	0 [0, 0]
3	411.2 [410, 412.6]	-2.1 [-4.1, 0]	13.7 [7, 20.2]
4	440 [440, 440]	-3.4 [-3.6, -3.3]	0 [0, 0]
5	611.3 [610, 612.6]	0.8 [-1.2, 2.9]	13.7 [7, 20.2]

The third option is to complete phases 1 and 2 of projects, P2 and P3. The increased expected cost of $411.2K reflects the added project completion costs. Application LA is retired when application II.3 is delivered by project P2. At this point the realization of the business service BS1 is provided by II.3 instead of by LA.1. When project P3 delivers EW.3, the realization is again changed to be provided by the combination of II.3 and EW.3. The improvement in expected values for both benefits reflects the sequence of more valued realizations for the business service BS1. The higher variability in both benefits reflects the higher uncertainty in the value provided by application EW.

The fourth option is to upgrade the legacy application LA to version 2 by completing phase 1 of project P1. The high cost of this upgrade is reflected in the total cost of $440K. Only the timeliness benefit is improved by the real time data from the upgraded application. The improvement in timeliness is a little better than what option 2 delivered due to the quicker delivery of LA.2 when compared to II.3.

The last option is to complete all the project phases. The motivation for this option is that it is typically faster to upgrade the application LA than to get II.3 fully developed and operational. However, this comes at a high expected cost of $611.3K. There is a small improvement in the timeliness benefit when compared to what is achieved by option 3.

The portfolio manager can compare these tradeoffs and consider any other extraneous factors to make the decision on which option to pursue. For example, a conservative decision maker interested in achieving some benefit improvement but averse to uncertainty might choose option 2. A more aggressive decision maker might pick option 3 which has the potential for higher benefits with maybe an acceptable increase in cost. The goal of our analysis is to have the decision maker to focus on a relatively small set of options and consider the tradeoff summary to make the portfolio transformation decisions. This is more likely if the dimensionality of the space of tradeoffs is kept relatively small. Limiting the number of dimensions is also important to make the tradeoffs more comprehensible to the decision makers.

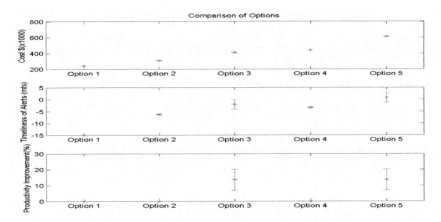

Fig. 3. Graphical comparison of portfolio options

6 Discussion

Our model and method for determining portfolio options organizes the available options using the notion of connected groups defined in Section 4. As mentioned earlier, this allows a natural hierarchical decomposition of the portfolio management process. Within a connected group we can compare the business benefits provided by the available options using the linkages to business services. Prioritization across the entire enterprise (and multiple connected groups) is likely to utilize global metrics. Examples of such metrics include homogeneous measures of financial benefits and assessments of strategic alignment [19].

The running example illustrated the set of portfolio options generated for one connected group. In the worst case, if we ignore all constraints, the number of options that can be considered is given by $2^{|applications|} \times \prod_{projects} (1+|\ phases\ |)$, where projects and applications correspond to those within each connected group. For our example, this worst case count of options is 144. However, if we factor in the dependencies within and between projects and applications, only 84 of these have to be considered. Considering the functionality constraints further reduces this number to 59. Analysis of these 59 options and filtering out the dominant ones shrinks the set of options presented to the decision maker to the set of five discussed in Section 5. The scalability of our exhaustive approach can be an issue when we have large connected groups. Choosing the right level of granularity for project phases is an important way of controlling the complexity. Project phases should reflect the abstraction that is appropriate for major portfolio decision checkpoints. Beyond this, one can design heuristics that further restrict the set of options considered but do not cause a significant degradation in the quality of decisions made by the portfolio manager. The design of these heuristics based on the nature of the costs and benefits functions is a candidate for future work.

7 Conclusions

We have presented an approach to evaluate enterprise IT portfolio options by linking portfolio elements to business services. The linkage of portfolio elements to business services in our model allows intuitive and fine grained representation of the business benefits from various realizations. Our model represents the characteristics of the IT portfolio at a level of granularity appropriate for portfolio level decision making. The model allows representation of dependencies between portfolio elements and rolled up information on schedules and costs. Our model includes a flexible way to specify uncertainties in various estimated quantities. We have also presented an exhaustive enumeration algorithm that uses this model to determine a pruned set of portfolio options with their cost/benefit tradeoffs using metrics based on the linked business services. We believe that the transparency in benefits provided by this approach supplements evaluations based purely on financial metrics and result in better portfolio management decisions.

References

1. F.W. McFarlan, "Portfolio Approach to Information Systems", *Harvard Business Review*, 59(5), September 1981, pp. 142-150.
2. H.M. Markowitz, "Portfolio Selection", *Journal of Finance*, 7 (1), 1952, pp. 77-91.
3. R.S. Kaplan, D.P. Norton, *The balanced scorecard: translating strategy into action*, Harvard Business School Press, 1996.
4. P.A. Strassmann, *The Squandered Computer: Evaluating the Business Alignment of Information Technologies*, Information Economic Press, April 1997.
5. Harvard Business Review, *Collection of articles on the Business Value of IT*, Harvard Business School Press, 1999.
6. IT Governance Institute, *Enterprise Value of IT Investments – The Val IT Framework*, USA, 2006, *www.itgi.org*.
7. C. Benko, F.W. McFarlan, *Connecting the Dots: Aligning Projects with Objectives in Unpredictable Times*, Harvard Business School Press, 2003.
8. L. Cherbakov, G. Galambos, R. Harishanker, S. Kalyana, and G. Rackam, "Impact of Service Orientation at the Business Level", *IBM System Journal*, Vol. 44, No. 4, December 2005, pp. 653-668.
9. P.P. Tallon, R.J. Kauffman, H.C. Lucas, A.B. Winston, and K. Zhu, "Using Real Options Analysis for evaluating uncertain investments in Information Technology", *Communications of the Association for Information Systems*, vol. 9, 2003, pp. 136-167.
10. I. Bardhan, S. Bagchi, and R. Sougstad, "A real options approach for prioritization of a portfolio of information technology projects: A case study of a utility company", *Proc. 37th Hawaii International Conference on System Sciences*, 2004.
11. J.P. Kindinger, J.L. Darby, "Risk Factor Analysis – A new Qualitative Risk Management Tool", *Proceedings of the Project Management Institute Annual Seminars & Symposium*, September 2000.
12. D. Vose, *Quantitative Risk Analysis, A guide to Monte Carlo Simulation Modeling*, Wiley, 1996.
13. J.R. van Dorp, M.R. Duffey, "Statistical dependence in risk analysis for project networks using Monte Carlo methods", *Int. J. Production Economics*, 58 (1999), pp. 17-29.

14. P. Tallon, K. Kraemer, and V. Gurbaxani, "Executives' Perceptions of the Business Value of Information Technology: A Process-Oriented Approach", *Journal of Management Information Systems*, Vol. 16, No. 4, Spring 2000, pp. 145-173.

15. T. Fawcett and F. Provost, "Activity Monitoring: Noticing Interesting Changes in Behavior", *Proceedings of the Fifth ACM SIGKDD International Conference on Knowledge Discovery and Data Mining*, 1999, pp. 53-62.

16. B. Boehm and K. Sullivan, "Software Economics: A Roadmap", *The Future of Software Economics*, ACM Press, 2000, pp. 319-343.

17. M. Moore, R. Kazman, M. Klein, and J. Asundi, "Quantifying the value of architecture design decisions", *Proceedings of the Twenty fifth International Conference on Software Engineering*, 2003, pp. 557-562.

18. A.V. Aho, J.E. Hopcroft, and J.D. Ullman, *Data Structures and Algorithms*, Addison Wesley, 1983.

19. IT Governance Institute, *Enterprise Value of IT Investments – The Business Case*, USA, 2006, *www.itgi.org*.

Process Driven Data Access Component Generation

Guanqun Zhang[1], Xianghua Fu[2], Shenli Song[2], Ming Zhu[3], and Ming Zhang[2]

[1] IBM China Research Laboratory, Beijing 100094, China
zhanggq@cn.ibm.com
[2] Department of Computer Science, Xi'an Jiaotong University, Xi'an 710049, China
[3] School of Software Engineering, Xi'an Jiaotong University, Xi'an 710049, China

Abstract. Process and data are two key perspectives of an SOA solution. They are usually designed relatively independently by different roles with different tools, and then linked together during the implementation phase to produce a runnable solution. It follows the separation of concerns principle to reduce development complexity, but it results in an integration gap for data access in processes, including both functional and non-functional aspects. Currently the gap is manually bridged, so that the development quality and efficiency highly depend on developers' capability. This paper proposes a novel approach to automatically bridge the gap by generating data access components whose granularity and performance are optimized according to process models. Firstly we build a platform independent process data relationship model (PDRM) based on process and data models, and then generate data access components with proper granularity by analyzing the PDRM. Furthermore, indexing technology is applied to optimize performance of data access components.

Keywords: Process, Data Access Component, Granularity, Index, SOA.

1 Introduction

SOA[1] is today's premier approach to implement 'On Demand' [2] solutions, and BPEL4WS[3] is a dominating technology in SOA to design and implement processes that manipulate data and provide functions[4,5]. Fig. 1 illustrates an SOA based solution architecture that separates business processes, software components and enterprise data in different layers. Following the separation of concerns principle, process modeling and data modeling are performed by different roles with different tools in the solution design phase, and then in the implementation phase they will be integrated together to produce a runnable solution. This paradigm leads to an integration gap of data access in processes, including both functional and non-functional aspects, which is now bridged mostly by manual work. At the same time, many enterprise solutions are data intensive[6], the relationships among process and data models are very complex; and furthermore, non-functional requirements of data access, like throughput, response time, etc, should also be satisfied. The above factors show that it is hard to develop high quality code for data access in processes; it demands the staff to have deep understanding of both process and data models, as well as their inter-relationships. The

J. Lee et al. (Eds.): DEECS 2006, LNCS 4055, pp. 81–89, 2006.

manual integration approach inhibits development efficiency, and the development quality depends on the staff's capability.

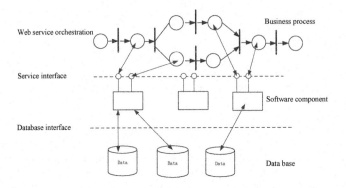

Fig. 1. SOA based Solution Architecture Overview

There are some existing technologies to facilitate process and data integration. Sybase PowerDesigner[8] supports reusing data models during process model design, but it does not support process data integration in the implementation phase. ORM technology[9] enables to generate code to access relational databases in an object oriented way, and data persistence design[10] and SDO[11] support unified data access. Although the code generation reduces development work, but the generated codes are simply mapped with tables in database and are not optimized from process perspective.

This paper proposes a novel method to integrate process and data in an SOA solution. It focuses on the solution implementation phase, and takes process models and data models as inputs, then automatically generates data access components whose granularity and performance are optimized according to processes. It can reduce cost and improve efficiency of the development effort for data access components in a solution. Section 2 proposes a base Process Data Relationship Model (PDRM) to enable further analysis for automatic code generation and optimization. Section 3 then introduces the approach to generate data access components whose granularity is optimized by analyzing components' data and path similarity from process aspect. Section 4 presents the method to identify candidate database columns that should be indexed to improve data access performance. Section 5 shows a case study to validate the method. Finally the conclusion and future work are discussed in Section 6.

2   Process Data Relationship Model

In SOA solution, a process manipulates data by calling corresponding services that are implemented as data access components. The data flows from variables in processes to messages of service call, and then to data entities in database. Logically these variables, messages and data entities are linked together, but actually in the design phase they are modeled by different roles using different tools, and then integrated together in the implementation phase. There are complicated many-to-many relationships among these data. Currently most of the integration work is done manually by data access component developers, who need to understand process models, data models and their relationships very well in order to develop high quality code. To automate the integration work and reduce efforts, we build a new Process Data Relationship Model (PDRM) to specify the relationships and data access flows derived from process models. It is the base for further analysis to enable automatic data access component code generation and optimization.

2.1   Data Mapping Between Process and Data Models

A process includes a set of activities $A = \{a_1, a_2, ..., a_n\}$, the input data items of activity a_i are $\{d_{i,k}^{(i)}\}_{k \in I}$, and its output data items are $\{d_{i,k}^{(o)}\}_{k \in I}$. The data items have mapping relationships with data entities defined in database.

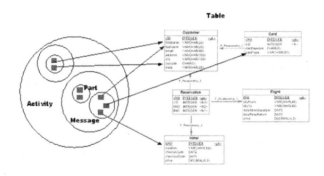

Fig. 2. Data Mapping between Process and Data Models

Fig. 2 illustrates sample mapping relationships between data items in a process and data entities in a data model. Messages have complex hierarchical structure, and their leaf elements can be mapped to table columns. We can see that the mappings between messages and tables are complex many-to-many relationships. We define the relationships based on process activities with data operations:

Definition 1 <Data Access Node - DAN>. If an activity a_i in a process contains data access operations, this activity is defined as "Data Access Node (DAN)". It is represented as $a_i = \{< D_i, t_i, n_i, R_i >\}_{i \in I}$, where D_i is the NDS (see definition 2) of a DAN, $t_i \in \{select, delete, update, insert\}$ is the type of data operation, n_i specifies how many times the node will be executed since there is loop in processes, and R_i is the non-functional requirements, like response time, etc.

Definition 2 <Node Data Set - NDS>. The above D_i is defined as the set of I/O data items: $D_i = \{\{d_{i,k}^{(i)}\}, \{d_{i,k}^{(o)}\}\}_{k \in I}$. $|D_i|$ is the number of items in the set.

Definition 3 <Process Data Mapping - PDM>. If a data item d_i in NDS maps to a column c_j in a data entity, we say that there is a mapping relationship between d_i and c_j The "Process Data Mapping (PDM)" is the set of all these mapping relationships, which is expressed as $M = \{< d_i, c_j >_{i \in I, j \in J}\}$.

2.2 Data Access Flow

In general, there are two types of activities in a process[2]: basic function activities and structured activities. We focus on the function activities that possibly have data operations. Existing Web services composition languages, including BPEL4WS, are weak on data access specification. We define the Data Access Flow (DAF) to specify the data operations based on BPEL process model. The DAF is represented as a weighted direct graph $G = \{\{A, B\}, E\}$, in which A is the set of Data Access Nodes, B is the set of control nodes (typical control nodes are {C,CE, P,PE}, which represent the start and end of choice and concurrency), and E is the weight of nodes and edges. The node weight is defined as how many times the node will be executed in a process instance, and the edge weight is defined as its execution probability: the weight of concurrency or sequence edge is 1, and the weight of choice edge is the probability that the edge will be executed. Fig. 3 is a sample data access flow.

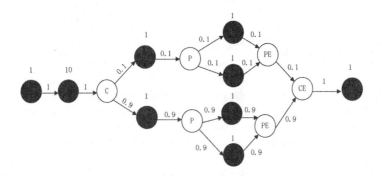

Fig. 3. Data Access Flow

3 Data Access Component Generation Based on Cluster Analysis

In this paper, we propose a new method to automatically generate data access components based on Process Data Relationship Model. Object-Relational Mapping[9, 10] technology already supports data access code generation for existing tables. It will be used when you want to take advantage of transparent persistence and use of a relational database. But basically it maps relational table definitions to object classes directly, and does not address the issue of data access component granularity. Because a service call usually manipulates data from multiple tables, so it will be bound with multiple fine grain components generated by ORM framework. A component with too fine granularity is an inhibitor of system performance[6]. Based on the Process Data Relationship Model built in section 2, we generate data access components and optimize their granularity by consolidating those components handling similar data and adjacent in process.

To generate components with proper granularity, we develop an algorithm based on clustering analysis[14, 15]. The Distance, a key variable in clustering algorithm, is calculated according to two dimensions: (1) The data similarity between nodes; and (2) the path similarity between nodes. Dimension 1 is to ensure that the data items handled in a component have maximum relativity, so that the component is high data cohesion. Dimension 2 is to reduce database connections times by merging components that are executed in sequence.

Definition 4 <Data Similarity - DS>. Given two nodes a_i and a_j, and their data set D_i and D_j, then their Data Similarity is defined as:

$$SIM_D(a_i, a_j) = \frac{|D_i \cap D_j|}{|D_i \cup D_j|}$$

Definition 5 <Path Similarity - PS>. If $Dist(a_i, a_j)$ is the shortest distance between node a_i and a_j, then Path Similarity is defined as:

$$SIM_P(a_i, a_j) = \frac{1}{Dist(a_i, a_j)}$$

Definition 6 <Data Access Node Similarity - DANS>. The similarity of two nodes a_i and a_j is defined as:

$$SIM(a_i, a_j) = w_1 SIM_D(a_i, a_j) + w_2 SIM_P(a_i, a_j)$$

After data access node similarities have been calculated, clustering analysis method is adopted to determine granularity by consolidating those components whose Data Access Node Similarity is higher than a threshold value R_{min} which is manually defined. The basic algorithm is described as follows:

Input: Threshold R_{min}, weight w_1, w_2, data access node set
Step1: Initially set each Node Data Set as a cluster.
Step2: Calculate node similarity $SIM(a_i, a_j)$ between a_i and a_j, and fill-in to the data access node similarity matrix R as R_{ij}.
Step3: Scan matrix R, for each R_{ij}, if $R_{ij} > R_{min}$, then consolidate the two nodes a_i and a_j into a cluster.

Step4: Go back to Step 2, until there is no $R_{ij} > R_{min}$.

Step5: Generate one data access component for each cluster.

Output: Data access components

4 Index Creation

Section 3 generates data access components based on static relationship between process and data models. Furthermore, we can leverage dynamic information of processes to optimize performance of data access components. This paper focuses on optimize query performance by adopting index technology, how to optimize write/update operations will be studied in future. Indexing will significantly improve query performance. Current database systems like DB2 have already provided supporting tools to create indexes for specified columns. The challenge is to determine which columns should be indexed. There are some methods to automatically create indexes based on statistics information collected in runtime environment[17]. What we proposed is to analyze process dynamic information in design time[16], which will significantly reduce runtime maintenance cost. The basic idea is to create indexes for those frequent accessed columns in tables by simulating and analyzing processes.

Definition 7 < Activity Frequency in a process - AF >. If a node a_k is executed n_k

times in a process instance, and then its AF in the process is $AF_k = n_k / \sum_{k \in I} n_k$.

Indexing improves query performance but inhibits write/update performance, so we need to balance the query and update factors. For a specific column L in database, we identify the process activities that manipulate it through the process data relationship model. And then its query factor QF_l and update factor UF_l will be calculated according to related activities' AF and data access types. As to the balance between query and update factors, currently we use manual parameters configuration: R_Ratio for the benefit of indexing for query, and W_Ratio for the inhibition to update. Therefore, for the specific column L, its weighted value for indexing is defined as $Index_l = QF_l * R\_Ratio - UF_l * W\_Ratio$. The columns with higher value have more requirements for indexing, so that we create indexes for columns whose values are higher than a specified threshold value.

5 Case Study

To verify our approach and prototype, we take the typical travel agency scenario as a sample case, in which a travel agency called NiceJourney will provide its travel arrangement services, including user registration, flight reservation and hotel reservation, etc. There are 10 activities in the BPEL model and 5 tables in the data model.

Traditional ORM technologies will produce 5 components for 5 tables, but we generate only three components: *LoadFlight* to access flight data, *LoadHotel* to access hotel data, and *MakeReservation* to make reservation. Because load flight data and load hotel data are two parallel query tasks, they are implemented as two separated components. And since the tasks for making reservation are tightly coupled, there is only one component even though it will handle data across two tables.

Indexes are created for frequently queried columns by consolidating their read/write operations based on data access flow. Fig. 4 shows that there are total 8 indexes (1 cluster index and 7 non-cluster indexes) generated for corresponding columns from various tables. And we compared the performance between with-index and no-index for the same process, with same database configuration, using same data access components. 1340 random data records were appended into the database, and 20 flows were constructed as test cases, each flow was executed for 500 times. The total response time for with-index is 0.359s, while the response time for no-index is 0.719s. We can see in Fig. 5 that for more execution times, indexing has more significant improvement on response time.

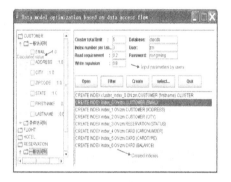
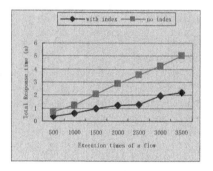

Fig. 4. Identify Index   **Fig. 5.** Compare Response Time

6 Conclusion

Web services and Service Oriented Architecture provide the premier approach for on demand enterprise solutions, in which process and data are two key perspectives. But currently there is no effective mechanism to integrate process and data in implementation phase. This paper proposes a new method by analyzing the relationships between process models and data models and then automatically generating data access components that are in proper granularity and optimized against processes. A set of Eclipse based tools has been implemented to support the new method. The main contributions of this paper include:

(1) Propose a new Process Data Relationship Model (PDRM) to specify the complex relationships among process model and data models, and also corresponding data access flows. It enables further data access component generation and optimization.

(2) Enable automatic data access component generation by analyzing PDRM, whose granularity and performance have been optimized from process point of view. Components with high data and path similarity are consolidated as a larger component based on clustering analysis, and frequent accessed columns are identified to create indexes based on dynamic information in processes to improve performance.

(3) Implement a set of tools to enable process data orchestrated development, effectively bridged the integration gap between process and data in implementation phase, development time and cost is reduced, and solution quality is ensured.

This paper addressed some problems in process and data integration domain. Based on this we will continue to focus on the following three topics in the future to better facilitate process data orchestrated solution development. 1) Non-functional requirements are usually identified in solution level, a big challenge is how to decompose these high level non-functional requirements to process activity level so that to better facilitate data access component generation and optimization. 2) This paper proposes a new Process Data Relationship Model, but how to automatically or semi-automatically create the model is an important and critical issue. 3) This paper focuses on how to optimize data access from process point of view; on the other hand, it is very interesting to optimize processes based on data models, especially for transactions in processes.

References

1. C. H. Crawford, G. P. Bate, L. Cerbakov, K. Holley, C. Tsocanos. Toward an on demand service-oriented architecture. IBM System Journal. 2005, 44(1):81-107.
2. On Demand, http://www.ibm.com/ondemand
3. BPEL4WS. http://www-128.ibm.com/developerworks/library/specification/ws-bpel/
4. Pasley, J. How BPEL and SOA are changing Web services development, Internet Computing,2005, 9(3):60 – 67.
5. Jim Rivera, Building SOA-based Applications Using Process-Driven Development, BEA.
6. Martin Fowler. Patterns of Enterprise Application Architecture. Addison-Wesley, 2002.
7. Bart Orriëns, Jian Yang, Mike P. Papazoglou. A Framework for Business Rule Driven Web Service Composition. ER 2003 Workshops, LNCS 2814, 2003: 52–64.
8. PowerDesigner, http://www.sybase.com/products/developmentintegration/powerdesigner
9. Scott W. Ambler. Mapping Objects To Relational Databases. Senior Consultant, Ambysoft Inc. http://www.ambysoft.com/essays/mappingObjects.html
10. Christian Bauer, Gavin King. Hibernate in Action. Manning publication Company. 2004. http://www.hibernate.org
11. Castro P., Giraud F., Konuru R., et al. A Programming Framework for Mobilizing Enterprise Applications. Proceedings of the Sixth IEEE Workshop on Mobile Computing Systems and Applications (WMCSA 2004). 2004: 196 – 205.
12. DAO, http://java.sun.com/blueprints/corej2eepatterns/Patterns/DataAccessObject.html
13. Martin Keen, Jonathan Cavell, Sarah Hill, et al. BPEL4WS Business Processes with WebSphere Business Integration: Understanding, Modeling, Migrating. IBM RedBook SG24-6381-00,2004.
14. Jiawei Han, Micheline Kamber. Data Mining: Concept and Techniques. China Machine Press. 2001:223-261.

15. Lee JK, Jung SJ, Kim SD, Jang WH, Ham DH. Component identification method with coupling and cohesion. Proceedings of the 8th Asia-Pacific Software Engineering Conference,2001.79~88.
16. Kerim Tumay. Business Process Simulation. Proceedings of the 1996 Winter Simulation Conference.
17. Kai-Uwe Sattler, Eike Schallehn, Ingolf Geist. Autonomous Query-Driven Index Tuning. IDEAS 2004: 439-448.

Using Naming Tendencies to Syntactically Link Web Service Messages

Michael F. Nowlan, Daniel R. Kahan, and M. Brian Blake

Department of Computer Science, Georgetown University,
234 Reiss Science Building, Washington, DC 20057-1232
{mfn3, drk8, mb7}@georgetown.edu

Abstract. Service-oriented computing (SOC) enables organizations and individual users to discover openly-accessible capabilities realized as services over the Internet. An important issue is the management of the messages that flow into and out of these services to ultimately compose higher-level functions. A significant problem occurs when service providers loosely define these messages resulting into many services that in effect cannot be easily integrated. State of the art research explores semantic methods for dealing with this notion of data integration. The assumption is that service providers will define messages in an unpredictable manner. In our work, we investigate the nature of message definitions by analyzing real, fully-operational web services currently available on the Internet (i.e. from the wild). As a result, we have discovered insights into how real web services messages are defined as affected by the tendencies of the web services developers. Using these insights we propose an enhanced syntactical method that can facilitate semantic processing by classifying web services by their message names as a first step.

1 Introduction

Web services are at the core of service-oriented architectures (SOA) and the SOC paradigm [15]. Web services can be defined as networked capabilities with openly accessible interfaces such that they can be discovered and executed by other machines, in real-time. Web service composition involves putting together a *chain* of multiple, related services. If, for example, an intelligent software component or software agent uses a Web service to purchase airline tickets, then the agent likely has enough information to submit queries to other applicable services such as hotels, rental cars, and entertainment events.

One of the aims of the WS-Challenge 2005 [21] was to demonstrate how such chains can be constructed by agents looking only at syntactical elements of Web Service Description Language (WSDL) documents and foregoing the semantic capabilities included with such technologies as DAML [5], OWL-S [8] , and BPEL4WS [5]. The work presented in this paper further investigates that aim by analyzing real services in order to understand the actual *tendencies* of service providers when creating message names. By integrating these tendencies captured from real web services with straightforward syntactical approaches, we introduce a quick, *just-in-time* message management approach that effectively facilitates service discovery and composition without the processing overhead and many specifications required by full semantic

J. Lee et al. (Eds.): DEECS 2006, LNCS 4055, pp. 90–99, 2006.

techniques. This approach *does not completely replace semantic approaches*, but can help to speed the overall discovery and composition process by filtering and aggregating services by their message names prior to semantic processing.

This paper proceeds in the next section with a discussion of related work in the area of service composition from both a syntactic and semantic point of view. The subsequent section describes the web services repository consisting of open services from the Internet. Section 4 describes the enhanced syntactical approach that we devised to help correlate messages and Section 5 describes an extension of those approaches to service composition. Finally in Section 6, we experiment with discovering services based on user documents to evaluate if our approaches can help suggest relevant services in the context of a user's daily routine.

2   Related Work

Techniques for the discovery and composition of web services are the target of many related projects for service-oriented computing. Srivastava and Koehler [8] and Rao [17] detailed the progress that has been made in the field of service composition and detailed the two competing approaches, *semantic* and *syntactic* techniques. Semantic approaches generally support the integration of web services by exploiting the semantic description of their functionality using ontological approaches [1] [19] [19] [10]. Conversely, syntactic projects tend to concentrate on string manipulation and thesauri approaches to correlate services [15]. Our approach is not related to the semantics approaches to discovery/composition but more closely related to the syntactic projects. Rocco [18] uses rigorous string manipulation software to help equate web services messages while Pu [15] uses an eXtensible Markup Language (XML) type-oriented rule-based approach.

The innovation in our work differs from related projects in that we attempt to capture the tendencies of the software designers/developers that create the web services. By using these tendencies, we create lightweight approaches that combine the nature of message naming (as selected by software designers in operational environments) with standard string manipulation approaches. Unlike projects that evaluate their approaches through performance, our work uses perhaps the largest repository of functional web services to qualitatively determine the effectiveness of our approach to correlate web services messages on the open Internet.

3   Message Naming Tendencies

In developing an algorithm that is capable of equating the messages of multiple web services, we took an applied, bottom-up approach. The first step was to understand the tendencies of the software developers that name the web services. In order to get an understanding of these tendencies, we manually downloaded and verified the functionality of as many services as we could identify on the Internet. Web services came from a number of web services repositories [21], Amazon Corporation [1], and random Internet searches. Two students spent approximately 40 hours downloading and verifying service functionality using Mindreef's Soapscope application [12]. From this effort, we collected 490 WSDL documents. After 40 hours of investigation, it became difficult to find new services. Consequently, we believe that our repository is perhaps one of the biggest of its type (i.e containing published functional services).

The 490 service descriptions can be decomposed into 12,187 total part names (i.e. part names are the independent parameter strings that comprise a web service message). 2490 part names remain once duplicate entries (i.e. part names occurring multiple times in the same WSDL file) are removed. Finally, once all duplicates are removed, there are 957 unique part names across all services in the repository. Intuitively there are more input part names than output part names. Another interesting result is that only 27% of output part names (after removing duplicates) are unique across services, while the inputs are 43.9% unique (i.e. the outputs are more homogeneous than the inputs). Since the developers are more likely to use the same or similar part names for output messages, this suggests that, when accessing the Universal Description, Discovery and Integration (UDDI) registries, a user should first search by web services outputs then by inputs in order to increase search speed. Table 1 lists the quantitative details of the repository.

Table 1. Detailed Information about the Repository

Statistic Description	Inputs	Outputs	Total
Number of Web Services			490
Gross Number of Part Names			12,187
-------------------------------------	----------	-------------	--------
Number of Part Names (Unique within each WSDL)	1816	674	2,490
Overall Unique Part Names (23 names overlap inputs and outputs)	798	182	957

3.1 Common Message Names

In order to scope our experiment we decided to focus on the top 30 most common part names, because 30 best reflected the names with the number of similar names over 5 occurrences although range was from 536 occurrences to 5 occurrences of a particular part name. We loosely classified the top 30 part names as *ambiguous*, *descriptive*, or *more descriptive*. The part names are listed in Table 2. The authors recognize that these classifications are subjective and use them in an attempt to stratify the results.

Table 2. Top 30 Most Common Part Names

Ambiguous	Descriptive	More Descriptive
Parameters, Body, LicenseInfo, ResponseInfo, SubscriptionInfo, Header, Result, Return, Symbol, Password, Identifier, Fault, IdentifierType, Text, Type	LicenseKey, Username, Name, Height, Width, Style	StartDate, EndDate, Year, AsOfDate, City, Email, Country State, Month

3.2 Ambiguous and Descriptive Message Names

We have found that the most ambiguous part names in messages are those that use the actual section names of the SOAP message (i.e. *parameters, body, header, fault*, etc.). Even using semantics, these types of strings would be difficult to correlate as they could be related to almost anything. We, however, later found that some of the ambiguous names have specialized meanings within certain web services development environments that depart from the WSDL standards. After analyzing the repository, we found that 15 of the top 30 most common part names are ambiguous strings as shown in Figure 1. There are 1200 occurrences of the most common part names out of 2490 possible part names (unique per service). In other words, almost 50% of the input/output messages use only 3.1% (i.e. 30 of the 957) of the unique names whereas 82% of the common part names are ambiguous. The percentage of common part names by type considering all occurrences is illustrated in Figure 2.

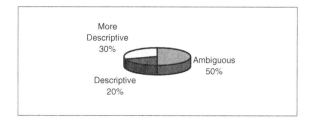

Fig. 1. Percentage of Common Names by Type

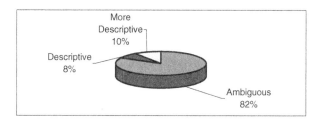

Fig. 2. Percentage of Common Names by Type and by Occurrence (1200 out of 2400)

Ambiguous part names, which are shown to be a common practice among web services developers, are counter-productive to automated approaches to both service discovery and composition. Developers use ambiguous names perhaps based on shortsightedness. Although their services are openly available, the developers still build their services as if the services were only internal to their intranet. Machine-to-machine interactions are either not considered, or perhaps our analysis suggests that the service-oriented paradigms are not thoroughly adopted by those developers that are building the services. However, the immaturity of the tools to support web services development may also play a part. In the remaining experiments, we focus on the more descriptive message names in developing matching algorithms. Experimentation results with ambiguous names are shown for comparison.

4   Correlating Message Names to Enhance Syntactic Processing

The size of our web services repository unfortunately is not adequate for performing significant composition experiments. However, we attempt to provide insight into composition by understanding the similarity of message names across all services. In other words, even if two services do not naturally integrate sequentially, it is important to our experimentation to discover that some subset of their messages have the same meaning. We conducted this experimentation by using a specific text similarity algorithm coupled with the naming tendencies perceived in the repository. Naming tendencies were extracted from the more descriptive part name strings that were occurred most frequently within our repository.

4.1   Tendency-Based Syntactic Matching

We introduce a matching algorithm called Tendency-Based Syntactic Mathing-Levenshtein (TSM-L). This algorithm combines several naming tendencies with the Levenshtein distance (LD) (also called the *edit distance*) which is a measure of similarity between two strings. The LD is the smallest number of deletions, insertions, or substitutions required to transform a source string, s, into a target string, t. The greater the LD, the more different the strings are. For example:

- If s = "test" and t = "test", then $LD(s,t) = 0$, because no transformations are needed. The strings are already identical.
- If s = "test" and t = "tent", then $LD(s,t) = 1$, because one substitution (change "s" to "n") is required to transform s into t.

In our work, we adapted implementations of the LD algorithm from several sources [8][12]. In addition the LD algorithm, the following naming tendencies are considered:

- Part names that are not common but that are similar to the common part names tend to be supersets or subsets of the common part name (for example; endDate is similar Date).
- Exceedingly lengthy strings and strings less than 2 characters are ineffective for message management.
- Setting a threshold for similarity distance is most effective when the LD threshold is not static but some function of the strings that are being compared.

Considering the fact that the LD algorithm is an established algorithm created in 1966 [12], it is not reiterated in this paper. Instead, the TSM-L algorithm is defined as an extension of the LD algorithm. The center of TSM-L is the threshold, or the Fitz Threshold, F_T, that we use to govern the LD algorithm, L_D, when comparing a two strings, S_i and S_j. The TSM-L algorithm is defined in Figure 3. In summary, if the edit distance (LD) is less than or equal to the Fitz Threshold or if either of the strings are a subset of the other and the strings are both greater than 1 and less than 15, then the strings are considered similar.

$TSM\text{-}L(\ S_i\ ,\ S_j)$:	TSM-L Function
$L_D(\ S_i\ ,\ S_j)$:	Levenshtein Distance function
$F_T(S_i)$:	Fitz Threshold Parameter Function
$S_i\ ,\ S_j$:	two strings for comparison
$Length()$:	string length functions

$F_T(S_i)$
      $temp = [(Length(S_i) * 2) / 3] - 2$
      return *temp*

$TSM\text{-}L(S_i\ ,\ S_j)$
    if $(L_D(S_i\ ,\ S_j) <= F_T(S_i)\ )$ or
        $(\ S_i \subseteq S_j\ $ or $\ S_j \subseteq S_i\ )$ and
        $(\ S_i\ > 1\ $ and $\ S_j\ > 1)$
        return *TRUE*
    else
        return *FALSE*

Fig. 3. The TSM-L Algorithm

4.2 Repository Similarity Using TSM-L

As a first evaluation of the TSM-L algorithm we evaluated the similarity of the 30 most common part names in our repository. The results of this experiment are illustrated in Figure 4. The top 15 most common message names are ordered by the number of times they occur in the repository. Therefore, the chart shows that the number of similar matches is independent of the number of appearances of the actual value. For example, "parameters," which appeared 536 times, is the first data point on the *Ambiguous* line and it only has 1 similar match, according to the TSM-L algorithm. Whereas, the 12th highest total for Descriptive parameter names, *State*, only had 9 occurrences in the repository, yet it returned 12 similar matches using the TSM-L algorithm. The 7th highest total for Ambiguous names is *Result*, and it returned to highest number of matches in either category with 17 similar matches. The authors recognize the fact that *Result*, by definition, has different meanings for different services and sufficient matching depends on the context of the service.

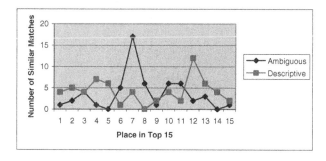

Fig. 4. Total of Unique Similar Strings by Top 30 Most Common Message Names

Table 3. Representative similarity results

String	Similar Strings (*false positives in italic*)
State	StateAbbrev, *StartDate*, state1, state2, *SQLStatement*, StateCode, USState, *StartYear, StartTime*
Identifier	id, *ie*, Identifiers, IdentifierType, IssuerIdentifier, IssuerIdentifierType
Password	*word*, phoneAlertPassword, lcPassword, password1, password2, host_password,
Country	CountryCode, CountryName, country1, country2, strCountry, *County*,

4.3 Evaluation

To evaluate the effectiveness of the TSM-L function, we chose 4 other approaches for comparison. The baseline approach, *basic equating*, simply looks for strings that completely match one another (i.e. using a string.equals method). Two other approaches consider a static number of LD transformations as threshold without considering naming tendencies. We chose 5 because that was the average string size of all message part names. We chose 11 because it was more than twice the average. Finally, we consider a dynamic threshold for LD whereas the threshold is equal to the number of characters in the message name being analyzed. The results show that the TSM-L approach consistently produces more matches than the baseline (basic equating) for both ambiguous message names (Figure 5) and descriptive names (Figure 6). The TSM-L approach produces on average 35% more matches than the baseline (this may be difficult to see in the Figure 5 and 6). The other approaches get much larger numbers of similar messages; however most of the matches are false positives as shown in Figure 7 and Figure 8. The TSM-L approach performs close to the baseline approach that by definition should not have any false positives.

Figure 9 summarizes the accuracy of the TSM-L approach with respect to the previously-defined approaches. 98% of the message names that were deemed similar accurately describe the same type of information. (i.e. ~2% were false positives). The TSM-L approach performs much better than the static approaches to string transformation which do not consider naming tendencies.

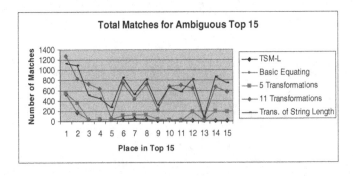

Fig. 5. Matching for Ambiguous Messages

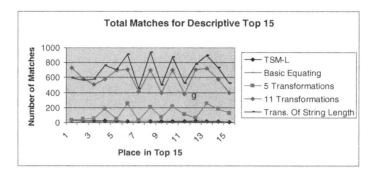

Fig. 6. Matching for Descriptive Messages

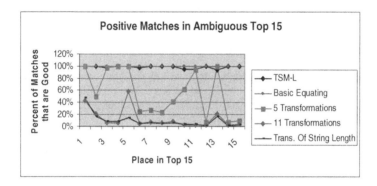

Fig. 7. Percentage of Positive Matches for Ambiguous Messages

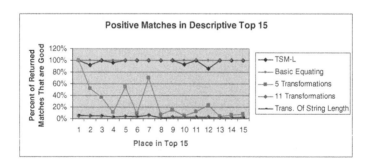

Fig. 8. Percentage of Positive Matches for Descriptive Messages

Obviously, this evaluation does not consider the context or format of the message, but relegates these lower-level issues to related semantic processing techniques. However, in a SOC scenario, the number of candidate services can be significantly decreased prior to semantic processing using our approach.

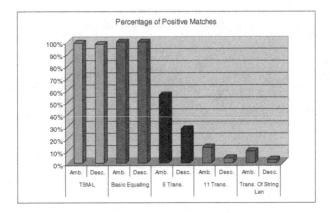

Fig. 9. Summary of Percentages of Positive Matches

5   Conclusion

In this work, we propose an approach that would facilitate semantic processing by classifying web services by their message names. We introduce a new syntactical matching algorithm, TSM-L, that extends the Levenshtein Distance algorithm by adding conditions that emulate the message naming tendencies of real-world web services developers. The true innovation of our work is this bottom-up concept of incorporating human software development tendencies into automated string process-ing techniques. TSM-L is a preliminary approach to validate that the combination of string manipulation algorithms and human concerns can be effective. Although the results show that the algorithm can make message name matches with a high degree of fidelity, there is no time-effective approach to evaluate *false negatives* (i.e. the message names that should have been discovered but were missed). In future work, we plan to investigate other analysis approaches to incorporate a false negative evaluation. We believe that such an evaluation can be used as feedback to enhance the TSM-L algorithm.

Acknowledgements

The service repository and certain parts of the service discovery software used in this work were partially funded by the National Science Foundation under award number 0548514.

References

[1]   Amazon Web Services (2006): www.amazon.com/gp/aws/landing.html
[2]   Benatallah, B., Dumas, M., and Sheng, O.Z. Facilitating the Rapid Development and Scalable Orchestration of Composite Web Services. *Distributed and Parallel Databases* 15(1):5-37, January 2005. Kluwer Academic Publishers
[3]   Blake, M.B., Kahan, D., Fado, D.H., and Mack, G.A. "SAGE: Software Agent-Based Groupware Using E-Services" *ACM GROUP 2005*, Sanibel Florida, November 2005

[4] Blake, M.B., Tsui, K.C., and Wombacher, A. "The EEE-05 Challenge: A New Web Service Discovery and Composition Competition", *Proceedings of the IEEE International Conference on E-Technology, E-Commerce, and E-Services*, Hong Kong, March 2005

[5] Bosca, A., Ferrato, A., Corno, D.., Congui, I., and Valetto, G. "Composing Web Services on the Basis of Natural Language Requests", *Proceedings of the 3rd IEEE International Conference on Web Services (ICWS 2005)*, pp 817-818, Orlando, Fl, June 2005

[6] BPEL4WS (2006): http://www.ibm.com/developerworks/library/specification/ws-bpel/

[7] DAML (2006): http://www.daml.org

[8] Koehler, J. and Srivastava, B., "Web Service Composition: Current Solutions and Open Problems" *Proceedings of the Workshop on Planning for Web Services* in conjunction with ICAPS03, 2003

[9] McIlraith, S., Son, T. and Zeng, H. Semantic web services. *IEEE Intelligent Systems*, 16(2):46{53), March/April 2001.

[10] Medjahed, B., Bouguettaya, A. and Elmagarmid, A. K. Composing Web services on the Semantic Web. *The VLDB Journal*, 12(4), November 2003.

[11] Merriam Park Software (2006): http://www.merriampark.com/ld.htm

[12] Mindreef Soapscope (2006): http://www.mindreef.com/products/soapscope/index.php

[13] NIST Levenstheim Distance (2006): http://www.nist.gov/dads/HTML/Levenshtein.html

[14] OWL-S (2006): http://www.daml.org/owl-s/

[15] Papazoglou, M. "Service-oriented computing: Concepts, characteristics and directions. *In Proceedings of WISE '03*

[16] Pu, K., Hristidis, V., and Koudas, N. "A Syntactic Rule Based Approach to Web Service Composition", *Proceedings on the International Conference on Data Engineering (ICDE'06)*, Altanta GA, USA, (to appear)

[17] Rao, J. and Su, X. "A Survey of Automated Web Service Composition Methods", *In Proceedings of the First International Workshop on Semantic Web Services and Web Process Composition, SWSWPC 2004*, San Diego, California, USA, July 6th, 2004

[18] Rocco, D, Caverlee, J., Liu, L. and Critchlow, T. ``Domain-specific Web Service Discovery with Service Class Descriptions", *Proceedings of the 3rd IEEE International* Web Services (2006): http://www.w3.org/2002/ws/desc/

[19] Sirin, E., Hendler, J., and Parsia, B. "Semi-automatic composition of Web services using semantic descriptions", *In Proceedings of Web Services: Modeling, Architecture and Infrastructure workshop in conjunction with ICEIS2003*, 2002.

[20] Williams, A.B., Padmanabhan, A., and Blake, M.B. "Experimentation with Local Consensus Ontologies with Implications to Automated Service Composition", *IEEE Transactions on Knowledge and Data Engineering*, Vol. 17, No. 7, pp 1-13, July 2005

[21] WS-Challenge (2006): http://www.ws-challenge.org/

[22] XMethods (2006): http://www.xmethods.com/

Maintaining Web Navigation Flows for Wrappers

Juan Raposo[1], Manuel Álvarez[1], José Losada[2], and Alberto Pan[1]

[1] Department of Information and Communications Technologies,
University of A Coruña. Campus de Elviña s/n. 15071 A Coruña, Spain
{jrs, mad, apan}@udc.es
[2] Denodo Technologies Inc. Real 22, 3°. 15003 A Coruña, Spain
jlosada@denodo.com

Abstract. A substantial subset of the web data follows some kind of underlying structure. In order to let software programs gain full benefit from these "semi-structured" web sources, wrapper programs are built to provide a "machine-readable" view over them. A significant problem with wrappers is that, since web sources are autonomous, they may experience changes that invalidate the current wrapper, so automatic maintenance is an important research issue. Web wrappers must perform two kinds of tasks: automatically navigating through websites and automatically extracting structured data from HTML pages. While several previous works have addressed the automatic maintenance of the components performing the data extraction task, the problem of automatically maintaining the required web navigation sequences remains unaddressed to the best of our knowledge. In this paper we propose and expirementally validate a set of novel heuristics and algorithms to fill this gap.

1 Introduction

In today's Web there are many sites which provide access to structured data contained in an underlying database. Typically these sources provide some kind of HTML form allowing issuing queries against the database, and they return the query results embedded in HTML pages conforming to a certain template.

Several approaches have been reported in the literature for building "wrappers" for this kind of sites (see for instance [4,6,14]; [8] provides a brief survey). Wrappers accept a query against the Web source and return a set of structured results to the calling application, thus enabling it to access web data in a similar manner as information from databases. Wrappers need to perform two kinds of tasks:

- Executing automated navigations sequences to access the pages containing the required data (e.g. to automatically fill in and submit the query form), and
- Extracting the structured results from the retrieved HTML pages

The vast majority of works dealing with automatic and semi-automatic wrapper generation has focused on the second task, although the problem of building automated navigation sequences (not necessarily in the context of wrappers) has been addressed in works such as [1,14].

The main problem with wrappers is that they can become invalid when the web sources change. While some previous works have addressed the problems of detecting

J. Lee et al. (Eds.): DEECS 2006, LNCS 4055, pp. 100–114, 2006.
© Springer-Verlag Berlin Heidelberg 2006

source changes that invalidate the current wrapper [5,9] and automatically maintaining the data extraction programs [9,11,12,16], the problem of automatically maintaining the navigation sequences remains unaddressed to the best of our knowledge. In this paper, we deal with this important issue.

The techniques presented here are part of a global system called ITPilot (see [15] for an overview). In [16] the techniques used in ITPilot for maintaining the data extraction programs used by the wrappers are described.

The rest of the paper is organized as follows. Section 2 provides the needed context about web navigation sequences and wrapper maintenance in ITPilot. Section 3 is the core of the paper and it describes our approach for maintaining web wrapper navigation sequences. Section 4 describes our experiments with real web sites. Section 5 discusses related work. Finally, section 6 presents our conclusions and outlines our future work.

2   Web Navigation Sequences and Wrapper Maintenance in ITPilot

A *navigation sequence* is a list of navigation steps specifying how to reach a certain web page.

ITPilot uses "lightweight" automated web browsers (built by using the APIs of most popular browser technologies) as execution environment for navigation sequences. For specifying a navigation sequence, we have created NSEQL [14], a language which allows representing a sequence as the list of interface events a user would need to produce on the web browser in order to reach the desired page. For instance, NSEQL includes commands for actions such as generating 'click' events on any element of a page (anchors, images, buttons,...), filling HTML forms, etc.

Representing navigation sequences as actions on a web browser interface lets wrapper creators forget about complexities such as client-side scripting or non-standard session mechanisms in the same way a human user of a web browser is not bothered about those issues.

2.1   Wrapper Model and Wrapper Maintenance in ITPilot

We define a *wrapper* as a component able to execute a query on the contents of a web source and return the obtained results as a set of structured data records.

We model the query results obtained by a wrapper as belonging to a *type*. Every *type* has an associated name and is composed of a list of attributes, each one having a name and a value. The value for *atomic attributes* is a character string. *Compound attributes* built by using *register* and *array* type constructors are also supported.

At wrapper generation time, the user may also optionally specify a set of *aliases* for each attribute name. The aliases represent alternative labels to name the attribute.

A query on a wrapper is a list of pairs *(attribute, value)*, where *attribute* is an atomic attribute and *value* is a string (it can be empty). We will term the attributes of a type that may appear in queries as *searchable* attributes.

In our model, wrappers require three kinds of navigation sequences to access the pages containing the data records that constitute the answer to a given query:

- Query sequence: It is in charge of obtaining the page containing the first set of results for a given query. It is typically parameterized by variables representing the query attributes (e.g. if a wrapper for a web bookshop allows queries by title and/or author, the sequence will normally include a variable for each field). Typically, this sequence navigates to some HTML form and fills it with the query input values.
- 'Next interval' sequences: Many web sources paginate their query results. This sequence (or sequences) is needed to navigate through the result intervals.
- 'More Detail' sequences: Often, the pages containing the query result listings do not show all the information about each individual result. In these cases, it is required to access one or more "detail" pages for obtaining the data of each result. For instance, accessing all information about a book in a web bookshop usually requires accessing a detail page by clicking on the anchor on the title of the book.

Now we briefly overview the global maintenance process in ITPilot and show how the tasks related with maintaining navigation sequences fit into it.

During the normal wrapper operation, the wrapper answers queries issued by a calling application. During this process, the wrapper selects some of these queries and *stores them and their results* in a database for later use in the maintenance process.

Periodically, the wrapper is examined to detect if the source has changed (the details of this process are not discussed in this paper). When a change is detected, the maintenance system performs the following steps:

1. If the query navigation sequence is not working properly then we proceed to step 2. In other case, the system tries to regenerate it having as input the previous navigation sequence and the formerly mentioned stored queries (and their results).
2. If the "Next Interval" sequence is not working properly, we need to regenerate it. Once it is done, the system can obtain all the current 'result listing' pages containing the results of a given query.
3. The following step is to regenerate the data extraction programs needed to extract the data contained in the result listing pages. As inputs to this process, we have for each stored query: 1) the former results of the query stored during wrapper operation (before the change) and 2) the set of current 'result listing' pages of the query (obtained after the change). This process is described in detail in [16].
4. The next step is regenerating the 'More Detail' pages (in case they are needed).
5. Finally, the system can regenerate the data extraction programs used for detail pages using the same method of step 3, thus completing the wrapper regeneration.

3   Maintaining Navigation Sequences

Now we proceed to describe our techniques for automatic maintenance of navigation sequences. We have the following input for this process: 1) the *type* of the extracted results (including the formerly mentioned *aliases* for the attribute names), 2) the previous navigation sequence (before the change in the source), and 3) the set of stored queries $\{q_1,...,q_n\}$ and their results. The next subsections detail the methods we use to maintain each kind of navigation sequence from section 2.1, respectively.

3.1 Maintaining the Query Sequence

Our approach for maintaining the "query sequence" relies on a crawling process that begins on the source homepage and searches for candidate query forms in the site (a maximum crawling depth may be configured).

For reaching new pages of the site, the crawling process automatically generates new *crawling steps* from the anchors of the previously reached pages and from what we will term as *bounded* forms, which are those *forms* exclusively composed of *bounded fields*. A *bounded field* is a field offering a finite list of possible query values (e.g. "checkbok" fields, "radio" buttons, "select-option" fields,...). With bounded forms, it is possible to compute every possible way of filling the form and to generate a crawling step for each one.

The pending *crawling steps* are ordered so the most "promising" ones are tried first. A crawling step is ranked by obtaining the texts visually associated to it in the page and comparing them to the texts involved in the previous navigation sequence (before the change in the source). For instance, if the previous navigation sequence contained a command for generating a 'click' event on an anchor having 'Books Search' as associated text, the anchors having associated texts such as 'Advanced Book Search' or 'Search for Books' will rank higher. We will discuss later for other purposes the techniques used to obtain the texts associated to crawling steps and to compute text similarity measures, so we will not provide further detail here.

In each page reached by the crawling process, every form (bounded or not) is examined to determine if it is a valid 'query form' for the wrapper by performing the following steps:

1. The system tries to match the "searchable" attributes of the *type* of the wrapper with the fields of the form, using visual distance and text similarity heuristics (see section 3.1.1).
2. To further check the validity of the matchings obtained at step 1, the system uses them to execute on the form some of the queries $\{q_1,...,q_n\}$, which were stored by the wrapper before the change in the source. Then, it examines the obtained response pages to determine if they are correct (we will consider them as correct if they contain a subset of the expected answers to the queries; see section 3.1.2).

If no matches are found in step 1, or the validity test in step 2 is unsuccessful, the form is discarded. If the step 1 finds a match for every searchable attribute of the type and the validity test is successful, then we will say the form is an 'exact match'. In that case, we choose it as new 'query form' and stop the crawling process.

An intermediate situation occurs when a match is found for some (but not all) the searchable attributes, and the validity test in step 2 is successful. In that case, we will consider the form as a 'partial match' and will continue with the crawling process.

If the crawling process completes without finding any 'exact match', we consider the best 'partial match' (the 'partial match' having matches for more searchable attributes) and try to add new matches to it. More precisely, for each searchable attribute *a* still not matched:

1. For each field f of the form still not assigned to any other attribute, we generate a "candidate match" between a and f.
2. For each candidate match, we issue some of the stored queries involving a and examine the obtained response pages to determine if they are correct (according to the same test used previously). If the test is successful for a candidate match, we add it to the list of valid matches.

The next sub-sections detail some aspects of the process of maintaining the query sequence: section 3.1.1 describes how we match form fields with searchable attributes while section 3.1.2 shows how we determine whether the response to a query is correct or not. Section 3.1.3 describes two special situations: executing a query involving several forms in consecutive pages and sources requiring authentication.

3.1.1 Finding Matches for "Searchable" Attributes in the Form

Given a form f located in a certain HTML page and a type t describing the schema of the expected query results, our goal at this stage is to determine if f allows executing queries for the "searchable" attributes of the type t. The method we use for determining this consists of the following steps:

1. Determining which texts are associated with each field of the form. This step is based on heuristics using visual distance measures between the form fields and the texts surrounding them.
2. Matching the fields of f with the searchable attributes of t. The system performs this step by obtaining text similarity measures between the texts associated with each form field and the name and aliases of each searchable attribute of t. If the field is *bounded* (such as a SELECT-OPTION field) then the similarity between its possible values and the input values used for the attribute in the previously stored queries is also had into account.

Measuring visual distances. At this step, we consider the texts in the page and compute its visual distance with respect to each field[1] of the form f. The visual distance between a text element t and a form field f is computed in the following way:

1. Browser APIs are used to obtain the coordinates of a rectangle enclosing f and a rectangle enclosing t.
2. We obtain the minimum distance between both rectangles. This involves finding the shortest line joining any point in one rectangle with any point in the other; the distance will be the length of this line. Distances are not computed in pixels but in more coarse-grained units to avoid making decisions on the basis of very small differences on visual distances. In our experiments we set the cell size to 15x15 pixels.
3. We also obtain the angle of the shortest line joining both rectangles. The angle is approximated to the nearest multiple of $\pi/4$.

Fig. 1a shows an example form corresponding to a web bookshop. We show the distance and angles between one field of the form and some of its surrounding texts.

---

[1] We consider the radio button and checkbox HTML elements with the same value for the *name* attribute as a single field.

Associating texts and form fields. For each form field our goal is to obtain the texts "semantically linked" with it in the page. For instance, in the Fig. 1 the strings semantically linked to the first field are *"Title"* and *"(examples: 'Jurassic Park')"*. For pre-selecting the "best texts" for a field *f*, we apply the following steps:

1. We first add to the list all the texts having the shortest distance *d* with respect to *f*.
2. Those texts having a distance lesser than *k*d* with respect to *f* are added to the list ordered by distance. This step discards those texts that are significantly further from the field than the closest ones. In our experiments we set *k*=5.
3. Texts with the same distance are ordered in function of its angle (note that since our distances are measured in more coarse-grained units than pixels it is relatively usual to have several texts at the same distance from the same field). According to the observation 3.1.1 the order privileges texts aligned with the fields (that is, angles multiples of $\pi/2$); it also privileges left with respect to right and top with respect to bottom.

As output of the previous step we have an ordered list of texts, which are probably associated to each form field. Then we post-process the lists as follows:

− We ensure that a given text is only present in the list of one field. The rationale for this is that at the following stage of the form ranking process (which consists in matching form fields and "searchable" attributes) we will need to associate a certain text with a given form field unambiguously. Note that although there may be texts in the form which are semantically related to more than one field (e.g. the text "Refine your search:" in Fig. 1a), those semantic associations will typically be irrelevant for our purposes; precisely because these texts are related to more than one field, they do not usually describe accurately any of them.
− We ensure that each field has at least one associated text. The rationale for this is that, in real pages, a given form field usually has some associated text to allow the user to identify its function.

Fig. 1b shows the process for the example form of Fig.1a. For each field[2] of the form, we show the ordered list of texts obtained by applying the visual distance and angle heuristics. The texts remaining in the lists after the post-processing steps are boldfaced in the figure. For instance, for the field F1 the final associated texts are "(example: Jurassic Park)" and "Title:".

Matching form fields and type attributes. At this step we try to detect the form fields which correspond to searchable attributes of the target type.

The basic idea to rank the "similarity" between a field *f* and a searchable attribute *a* is measuring the textual similarity between the texts associated to *f* in the page (obtained as shown in the previous step) and the texts associated to *a* in the type (attribute name and aliases specified at wrapper creation time).

---

[2] Note how the system models the *Format* 'checkbox' field as a field with three subfields. F5 refers to the whole set of checkboxes while F51, F52 and F53 refer to individual checkboxes.

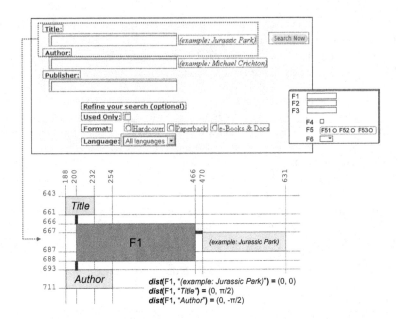

Fig. 1a. Example query form and visual distances and angles for field F1

Fields	Texts	(dist,θ)
F1	√ (example: Jurassic Park)	(0,0)
	√ Title:	(0, π/2)
	Author:	(0, -π/2)
	(example: Michael Crichton)	(1, -π/2)
	Publisher:	(3, -π/2)
F2	√ (example: Michael Crichton)	(0, 0)
	√ Author:	(0, π/2)
	Publisher:	(0, -π/2)
	(example: Jurassic Park)	(2, π/2)
	Title:	(3, π/2)
F3	√ Publisher:	(0, π/2)
	Refine your search (optional):	(1, -π/2)
	(example: Michael Crichton)	(2, π/2)
	Author:	(3, π/2)
	Used Only:	(3, -π/2)
	Format:	(4, -π/2)
	Hardcover	(4, -π/2)
	Paperback	(4, -π/2)
F4	√ Used Only:	(0, π)
	√ Refine your search (optional):	(0, π/2)
	Hardcover	(0, -π/2)
	Format:	(1, π)
	Language:	(2, -π/2)
F5	e-Books & Docs	(0, 0)
	Used Only:	(0, 3π/4)
	Language	(0, -3π/4)
	√ Format:	(1, π)
	Refine your search (optional):	(1, π/2)

Fields	Texts	(dist,θ)
F51	√ Hardcover	(0, 0)
	Used Only:	(0, 3π/4)
	Language:	(0, -3π/4)
	Format:	(1, π)
	Refine your search (optional):	(1, π/2)
F52	Hardcover	(0, π)
	√ Paperback	(0, 0)
	Refine your search (optional):	(1, π/2)
F53	Paperback	(0, π)
	√ e-Books & Docs	(0, 0)
	Refine your search (optional):	(2, 3π/4)
F6	√ Language:	(0, π)
	Hardcover	(0, π/2)
	Paperback	(0, π/2)
	Format:	(1, π)
	Used Only:	(1, π/2)
	Refine your search (optional):	(3, π/2)

F1 [(example: Jurassic Park)] [Title:];
F2 [(example: Michael Crichton)] [Author:];
F3 [Publisher:];
F4 [Used Only:] [Refine your search (optional):];
F5 [Format:];
F51 [Hardcover];
F52 [Paperback];
F53 [e-Books & Docs];
F6 [Language]

Fig. 1b. Texts associated to each field in the form of Fig. 1a

When the field is *bounded* (select-option fields, radio buttons, checkboxes...; remember the section 3.1) the system also has into account the text similarities between the possible values of f in the page[3] and the query input values used for a in the stored queries. Text similarity measures are obtained using a method proposed in [3] that combines TFIDF and the Jaro-Winkler edit-distance algorithm.

If we obtain matches for all the searchable attributes of the type then the form is an 'exact match' (as long as the validity test is also passed; see section 3.1). If we obtain matches for some (but not all) the searchable attributes, we firstly try to determine if the form is multi-step (see section 3.1.3) and, in other case, the form is a 'partial match' (as long as the validity test is also passed; see section 3.1).

3.1.2   Determining If the Response Pages Obtained Through a Form Are Valid

As seen in section 3.1, once a form has been found relevant and we have learned how to execute queries on it (or when we are considering a "candidate match"), we perform an additional test to ensure it is valid. The test consists in executing some of the queries $\{q_1,...,q_n\}$ which were stored by the wrapper before the change in the source, and analyzing the obtained response pages to determine if they are 'result listing' pages to the issued queries.

Our method to perform this test is based on the observation that, in most sources, the results to a given query are similar when that same query is repeated some time later. For instance, if we search in an Internet bookshop for the books containing the words 'java' in their title, the obtained results will be similar when we repeat the query a few hours later. Of course, the list of returned books may be slightly different and the values of some of their data fields may have also changed but a substantial subset of the data will still be present in the new response pages. Based on this observation, we perform the following steps at this stage:

1. We issue a subset of the queries $\{q_1,...,q_n\}$, using the candidate form and the previously found matches between its fields and the searchable attributes. As response we obtain $\{p_1,...,p_n\}$ where p_i is the response page obtained with q_i.

2. For each executed $q_i \in \{q_1,...,q_n\}$, we retrieve its stored results from the local database and search in p_i for the string values forming each individual result. We consider the process successful if we find at least the 10% of the expected values in the new pages. While this value may seem too low, our experiments show it is enough to achieve very high accuracy (the probability of finding result values only by chance is quite small), while still allowing the process to be successful when the sources have very high data variability with time (e.g. news sites).

3.1.3   Multi-step Forms and Login/Password Authentication

Multi-step forms. In some sources issuing a query may involve filling several forms through several consecutive pages. For dealing with these situations, when processing a form, if the system finds suitable form fields for only some of the searchable attributes, then it fills those fields and submits the form. In the page obtained, the system looks for a form with fields matching with the remaining searchable attributes.

---

[3] Obtaining these values a trivial step for SELECT-OPTION tags since their possible values appear in the HTML code enclosed into OPTION tags. For CHECKBOX and RADIO tags we apply the same visual distance techniques discussed previously.

Login-password forms. Many sources include login/password forms that must be filled before any further navigation on the site. Our approach consists in including a built-in type to deal with authentication forms. This type includes "searchable" attributes such as *LOGIN* and *PASSWORD* along with common aliases for them. Given this *type*, the system can detect and fill these forms using the same techniques we have described for query forms.

3.2 Maintaining the 'Next Interval' Sequences

Since many web sources paginate their query results, wrappers typically need sequences to browse through the successive result intervals. Our method for regenerating such sequences is based on the following observations:

– In most sources there exists some navigation step (typically an anchor) pointing to the 'next' interval of results. This navigation step is usually associated to a text such as 'Next', 'More results' or similar.
– In other sources, 'Next interval' navigation steps are presented as an *ordered* list pointing to all or some of the available intervals (e.g. '[11-20] [21-30]...', '1 2 3', '[A-B] [C-E]...').

We perform the following process for regenerating these sequences:

1. We search for navigation steps that are located visually close to strings with high textual similarity with a set of pre-defined texts such as "Next", "Next results", "More results", "Next interval", etc.
2. We also search for sets of navigation steps verifying the following requirements:
   a. The navigation steps are disposed forming a "list". This means the elements (anchors, radio buttons,...) associated to each step must be located visually close of one another and visually aligned. In the case of SELECT-OPTION HTML tags we also consider their possible values as a list.
   b. Each navigation step must contain or be located near one string that conforms to one in a set of pre-defined expressions reflecting common ways of representing intervals. For instance, the predefined expression '*[$beginInterval - $endInterval]*' matches with strings such as '*[1-2]*', '*[10-20]*' or '*[A-C]*'. *$beginInterval* and *$endInterval* represent possible ways of specifying the beginning and end of an interval (typically numbers or letters, where *$endInterval* > *$beginInterval* according to either numerical or alphabetical order).
   c. Elements in the list must be ordered. That is, the string associated to the element *n+1* in the list must specify an interval posterior to the interval specified by the string associated to the element *n* in the list.
3. We now evaluate the candidate navigation steps discovered in steps 1 and 2 (we give preference to those obtained in step 2). For this, we first use the regenerated 'query sequence' to obtain the first 'result listing' page from some of the stored queries (we select queries with a higher number of results since we are interested in queries requiring pagination). Secondly, we execute the candidate navigation steps in the pages and analyze the new obtained pages to check if they contain more stored query results different from the ones contained in the first 'result listing' page (this can be checked using the same method described in section 3.1.2). If this process is successful, we consider we have found the "Next Interval' sequence.

3.3 Maintaining the 'More Detail' Sequences

It often occurs that the pages containing the query result listings do not show all the desired data fields about each individual result and the wrapper must access one or more "detail" pages that show the complete data. The method we use to regenerate 'detail' sequences is based on the following observations:

- The navigation steps leading to detail pages are visually associated in some way with the item they refer to (e.g. an anchor on an attribute of the result, a "More information" link located in the listing besides the result,...).
- For every result, the HTML navigation element(s) used for accessing the detail pages are located in the same relative position inside each result. We say two navigation elements from two different results are in the same position if:
  - Their path in the DOM tree of the response page is the same. The tag (for instance $<a>$ or $<select>$) must be also the same for both navigation elements.
  - Both elements appear in their results in the same relative position with respect to the attributes of the result. For instance, if the first navigation element appears between the values of the attributes $a1$ and $a2$ of the result $r1$ then the second navigation step should also appear between the values of $a1$ and $a2$ in $r2$ (we only consider attributes that are present in both $r1$ and $r2$).

Based on these observations the method we use is:

1. Generating the data extraction programs for the 'result listing' pages (see [16] for detail), so we can know which HTML fragment corresponds with each result and where each attribute is located.
2. Searching the HTML fragments corresponding to each result for sets of navigation elements (each set must contain at most one navigation step from each result) verifying the previous observations.
3. For each set obtained in the previous step, we execute its navigation steps, obtaining the pages they point to and we check if they contain the values of the attributes of the result associated with the navigation step.

4 Experiments

To measure the effectiveness of our approach we performed two sets of experiments:

- We tested our system with real changes by monitoring 30 websites during four months. We selected sources from different domains such as e-commerce, patent information, news sites or databases of public sector R&D projects.
- Furthermore, we tested our system by simulating more changes in the following way: we used data collected by the wrapper of one source belonging to a specific domain (e.g. source *Amazon*, in the domain 'Internet bookshops') and used it to generate the navigation sequences needed in *another* source from the same domain (e.g. *AllBooks4Less*).

The next sub-sections detail each of these set of experiments.

4.1 Experiments Monitoring Real Changes

In this set of experiments, for every Web site, we first generated a wrapper and used it on a daily basis to execute different queries. The system automatically stored some of the queries and their results as mentioned in previous sections. When a change in the navigation sequences of the Web site was detected, the system tried to repair it. Then, we tested the wrapper with a new set of queries and checked if they were executed successfully.

Table 1 shows the web sources (14 of 30) that experimented changes during our period of study. For each source, we show the searchable attributes we defined in its wrapper, the number of changes produced (#CH), and the results of the re-generation process for each kind of navigation sequence: query sequence (QS), next interval (NS) and 'more detail' (DS). NA means the wrapper did not need that sequence.

The process was successful in every case except in the source *FreePatentsOnline* where the system incorrectly identified the query form field corresponding with the *description* attribute. Although the association between texts and form fields worked well, the text associated to the *description* field changed, and the text similarity heuristic failed for both the attribute name and its aliases. Therefore, the system tried to find a suitable field by generating "candidate assignments" as described in section 3.1. The incorrect candidate assignment matching the *description* attribute with the form field corresponding to the *claims* attribute (not used by the wrapper), passed the validity test (described in 3.1.2) because the keywords appearing on the description of some patents also appeared on its claims and, therefore, there was an overlap between the results of the queries using each attribute. To deal with these cases, we can modify how we evaluate candidate assignments: instead of choosing the first assignment passing the test, we can evaluate all possible candidate assignments for the attribute and, if several ones pass the test, we choose the one with a better score in it.

4.2 Experiments Simulating Changes

In the second set of experiments, we simulated changes on the sources as follows: we used data collected by the wrapper of one source belonging to a specific domain (e.g. source *Amazon*, in the domain 'Internet bookshops') and used it to generate the navigation sequences needed in *another* source from the same domain (e.g. *AllBooks4Less*).

We proceeded as follows. Firstly, we grouped the sources in pairs. For these tests to be possible, the sources in each pair must verify certain pre-requisites:

- The results provided to the same query by the two different sources must have substantial overlapping. For instance, in the case of two Internet bookshops, when searching for books with 'java' in its title, some books will be returned in both bookshops. This pre-requisite is needed so the validity test of section 3.1.2 still holds.
- Both sources must have a common sub-set of searchable attributes.

Table 1. Experimental Results (1)

Source	Search attribs.	#Ch	Results QS NS DS		
AllBooks4Less	Title, author, isbn, publisher, format, price_range	2	√	√	√
AmazonMusic	Category, keyword	1	√	√	√
BBC News	Keyword, section, day_from, month,_from year_from, day_until, month_until, year_until,	1	√	√	√
CDUniverse	Category, keyword	1	√	√	√
Delphion	Collection, keywords	1	√	√	√
DevJava	Category, keyword	1	√	√	√
DVDEmpire	Title, format	1	√	√	√
DVDTalk	Category, keyword	1	√	√	√
FreePatents	Patent #, inventor, title, description, assignee	1	X	√	NA
Imdb	Title	1	√	√	√
PixMania	Product, Section	1	√	√	√
Used AddAll	Title, author, isbn, minPrice, maxPrice	1	√	√	√
Yahoo Quotes	Symbol	1	√	NA	NA
ZdNet	Title, author, description, category, License	1	√	√	√
			93%	100%	100%

Once the pairs were chosen, we generated a wrapper for one of the sources (we will say this source plays the *origin* role in the process). The searchable attributes of the wrapper were the common searchable attributes in both sources.

Then, we used the wrapper to execute some queries on the *origin* source. Once we have executed a few queries, we use the information collected by the wrapper to try to generate a new wrapper for the *other* source (we will say this source plays the *destination* role in the process). The process for generating the new wrapper is the same we have explained in the previous sections: the only difference is that the 'changed' source provided as input, is actually the other source in the pair.

Finally, for each pair, we reversed the roles of the *origin* and *destination* sources and repeated the process.

Table 2 shows the pairs of sources we used, along with the considered searchable attributes and the obtained results. The third column in the table shows the results obtained for each kind of sequence when considering the first source as *origin* and the second as *destination*, while the fourth column shows the results obtained when considering the first source as *destination* and the second as *origin*.

As can be seen, the process was successful in every case except in the pair *Yahoo People/Big Book*. The reason of the failure was that the sources used different formats for representing names: while Yahoo People uses the 'Name Surname' format (e.g. 'John Doe'), BigBook uses the 'Surname, Name' format (e.g. 'Doe, John'). This made the validity test fail since the overlapping of results did not reach the threshold.

Table 2. Experimental Results (2)

Sources	Search. Attributes	Results (origin/dest)			Results (dest/origin)		
		QS	NS	DS	QS	NS	DS
Yahoo People / BigBook	name, surname	X	X	NA	X	X	NA
Barn. & Nob. / Used.addall	title, author	√	√	√	√	√	√
Amazon-book / Barn &Nob.	title, author	√	√	√	√	√	√
Amazon-dvd / TowerRecords	title, actor	√	√	√	√	√	√
Amazon-music / TowerRecords	title, artist	√	√	√	√	√	√
Amazon-book / Used.addall	title, author	√	√	√	√	√	√
FreePatentsOnline / Espacenet	title,inventor, abstract	√	√	NA	√	√	NA
CDUniverse / DiscoWeb	title	√	√	√	√	√	√
DVDEmpire / Imdb	title, year	√	√	√	X	√	√
Amazon-music / CDUniverse	title	√	√	√	√	√	√

Similar situations occurred in other sources although, in those cases, the threshold was reached anyway. For instance, the exact same difference in formatting names occurred with the *author* attribute in the pairs *Amazon/Used.addall* and *Barnes&Noble/Used.addall*. In the pair *FreePatentsOnLine/Espacenet* the patent numbers were also represented differently.

This suggests our current system may fail if the source changes the way it formats the values of some of its attributes. Although this will be rare (note that the attribute values are usually contained in a database, and changes in the visual layout of the source will not usually imply changes in the format of the database information), we are considering using text similarity measures when searching for stored values during the validity test.

5 Related Work

Wrapper generation has been an active research field for years (see for instance [4], [6], [14]; [8] provides a brief but comprehensive survey).

Some aspects of the maintenance problem have been also addressed in the literature such as wrapper verification [5], [9] and the maintenance of data extraction programs [9], [11], [12], [16]. The automatic generation of data extraction programs (without user-provided input examples) has been dealt with in works such as [2], [17]. In the cases when they are successful, these techniques greatly simplify the maintenance of data extraction programs since examples are not required and the only task to the maintenance system is to annotate the extracted results.

Nevertheless, none of these previous systems addresses the maintenance of the navigation sequences required to reach the pages containing the desired data. Thus, these efforts are complimentary to our work.

The particular problem of regenerating the 'query sequence' is similar to that of automatically learning to fill in query forms. This problem has been addressed for tasks such as accessing the hidden web [10], [13] or attaching semantic metadata to web services [7]. [13] is the work most similar to ours since they combine visual distance and text similarity measures to match HTML forms with user-defined domain types. Nevertheless, their focus is different: while they search for every form relevant to a general domain in order to index the hidden web, we try to find a particular form returning pages with the precise data used by a wrapper. In addition, they are not concerned about the remaining steps of wrapper maintenance (such as detail pages, navigation through result intervals or data extraction programs).

6 Conclusions and Future Work

In this paper, we have presented new techniques for the automatic maintenance of the navigation sequences used by wrappers for semi-structured Web sources. Our approach is based on collecting some information during wrapper creation and operation, including some of the executed queries and their results. When the source changes, this information is used as input to a crawling process that searches for a query form able to execute the previously stored queries. Once the query form has been found, the sequences for accessing the 'next interval' result pages and the 'detail' pages are also regenerated, if needed. We have experimentally tested our techniques for a variety of real-world Web sources, obtaining a high degree of effectiveness.

Regarding to our future work, when regenerating the query sequence, our system looks for forms allowing queries for the "searchable attributes" of the previous wrapper. An interesting issue is discovering new attributes that may have appeared in the source after the change, thus extending previous wrapper functionality. This is also related with the problem of automatically generating wrappers without any user-provided input. While there exist automatic methods to generate the data extraction programs used by wrappers, the problem of automatically generating the needed navigation sequences has received much less attention.

Acknowlegments. This research was partially supported by the Spanish Ministry of Education and Science under project TSI2005-07730. Alberto Pan's work was partially supported by the "Ramón y Cajal" programme of the Spanish Ministry of Education and Science.

References

1. Anupan, V., Freire, J., Kumar, B., Lieuwen, D. Automating Web Navigation with WebVCR. In Proceedings of the 9th International World Wide Web Conference. 2000.
2. Arasu, A. and Garcia-Molina, H. Extracting Structured Data from Web Pages. In Proceedings of the ACM SIGMOD International Conference on Management of data. 2003.
3. Cohen, W., Ravikumar., P., Fienberg, S. A Comparison of String Distance Metrics for Name-Matching Tasks. In *Proceedings of IJCAI-03 Workshop (IIWeb-03)*. 2003.
4. Knoblock, C.A., Lerman, K., Minton, S. and Muslea, I. Accurately and Reliably Extracting Data from the Web: A Machine Learning Approach. In Bulletin of the IEEE Computer Society Technical Committee on Data Enginnering. 1999.

5. Kushmerick, N. Regression testing for wrapper maintenance. In Proceedings of the 16th Ntl. Conf. on Artificial Intelligence and Innovative Applications of Artificial Intelligence. 1999.
6. Kushmerick, N. Wrapper induction: Efficiency and expressiveness. Artificial Intelligence, 118:15-68, 2000.
7. Kushmerick, N. Learning to invoke web forms. In Proc. Int. Conf. Ontologies, Databases and Applications of Semantics, 2003.
8. Laender, A. H. F., Ribeiro-Neto, B. A., Soares da Silva, A. and Teixeira, J. S. A Brief Survey of Web Data Extraction Tools. ACM SIGMOD Record 31(2), pp 84-93. 2002.
9. Lerman, K., Minton, S. and Knoblock, C. Wrapper Maintenance: A Machine Learning Approach. Journal of Artificial Intelligence Research 18, pp. 149-181. 2003.
10. Liddle , S., Embley , D., Scott, Del., Yau Ho, Sai. Extracting Data Behind Web Forms. Proceedings of the 28th Intl. Conference on Very Large Databases (VLDB2002). 2002.
11. Meng, X., Hu, D. and Li, C. Schema-Guided Wrapper Maintenance for Web-Data Extraction. In Proceedings of the ACM 5th Intl. Workshop on Web Information and Data Management (WIDM). 2003.
12. Mohapatra, R., Rajaraman., K., Sam Yuan, S. Efficient Wrapper Reinduction from Dynamic Web Sources. In Proceedings of the IEEE/WIC/ACM Intl. Conf. on Web Intelligence. 2004.
13. Raghavan S., Garcia-Molina, H. Crawling the hidden web. In Proceedings of the 27th Conference on Very Large DataBases (VLDB2001). ACM Press. 2001.
14. Pan , A., Raposo, J., Álvarez, M., Hidalgo, J. and Viña, A. Semi-Automatic Wrapper Generation for Commercial Web Sources. In Proceedings of IFIP WG8.1 Working Conference on Engineering Information Systems in the Internet Context (EISIC). 2002.
15. Pan , A., Raposo, J., et al. ITPilot: A Toolkit for Industrial-strength Web Data Extraction. In Proceedings of the 2005 IEEE/WIC/ACM Intl. Conf. on Web Intelligence (WI 2005).
16. Raposo, J., Pan, A., Alvarez, M., Hidalgo, J. Automatically Maintaining Wrappers for Web Sources. Proceedings of the 9th Intl. Database Engineering and Applications Symp. (IDEAS). 2005.
17. Zhai, Y., Liu, B. Web Data Extraction Based on Partial Tree Alignment. In Proceedings of the 2005 World Wide Web Conference (WWW2005). ACM Press. 2005.

Mobile P2P Automatic Content Sharing by Ontology-Based and Contextualized Integrative Negotiation

Soe-Tysr Yuan[1] and Mei-Ling Yeh[2]

[1] MIS Dept., National Chengchi University, Taipei, Taiwan
yuans@mis.nccu.edu.tw
[2] IM Dept., Fu-Jen University, Taipei, Taiwan

Abstract. The goal of enterprise computing is to achieve efficient enterprise automation and to optimize enterprise value through an understanding of external and internal status for business optimization. With the advancement in wireless technology, mobile communication has become a salient interaction media between people. Particularly, with the ad-hoc mobile networks, each peer is able to attain information and services (from the other peers) of value to the peer anywhere, any time and using a variety of different kinds of devices. However, how to empower peers to share and acquire information/services through an automated negotiation mechanism, to take into account the attributes of the context (physical and non-physical) and then to achieve social welfare is one of the ideals in exploiting a wireless Peer-to-Peer network environment in the era of enterprise computing. Accordingly, this paper presents Contextualized Integrative Negotiation Strategies (CINS) for content sharing in wireless Peer-to-Peer environments. CINS enables peers to engage proper interactions within the environment in time, to understand the needs of the other peers and to employ practices of cooperation negotiation (instead of competition ones). In CINS, peer re-learning negotiation strategies consider content-sharing ontologies employed and the reward attained from the environment for the purpose of useful sharing experience. This not only helps peers embrace a common consensus of collective benefits in content sharing but also guarantees that the negotiation results achieve win-win decisions of allocations.

1 Introduction

With the advent of wireless technologies, a broad range of information access methods enabled by mobility, small handheld devices and wireless technologies are growing rapidly. An intriguing set of questions and opportunities arise when one considers what wireless computing and ad-hoc networks can do for electronic commerce and vice versa. These prospects are now being explored under various names such as P2P, C2C, *etc.* For instance, unlike traditional information exchanged via the Internet (through a client/server model) P2P exchange of information (i.e., content sharing) refers to the creation of decentralized groups that allows for information to flow over the public Internet in an anonymous logical fashion. The individual users of these applications (e.g., KaZaA, eDonkey, WinNy) are shielded via this anonymity. The attractiveness of p2p services increases exponentially with the number of peers contributing to the services (and thus they are considered as a disruptive technology [1]).

J. Lee et al. (Eds.): DEECS 2006, LNCS 4055, pp. 115–132, 2006.
© Springer-Verlag Berlin Heidelberg 2006

Accordingly, the prospect of P2P content sharing working in wireless networks (abbreviated as WP2P Content Sharing) becomes a very interesting focus of exploration. A possible scenario of this prospect is exemplified as follows: (1) Amy (a tourist) unexpectedly arrives in a tourist city's train station (of a great number of passing-by tourists and the accessibility of wireless ad-hoc networks). (2) Presuming a lot of tourists (including Amy) carrying myriad kinds of handheld devices storing different kinds of tourist information, WP2P Content Sharing subsequently can be enabled as demanded. (3) Although the visit of the tourist city is not planned beforehand, Amy nevertheless is able to attain useful information of accommodation and transportation from the services of WP2P Content Sharing.

However, the amount of signaling traffic also increases almost exponentially with the number of participants. Over the past few years, P2P services [1, 2] have evolved to one of the most import sources of Internet traffic. Moreover, in distributed P2P models [3, 4, 5] a peer's query is sent to any peers (it is connected to) each of which subsequently propagates the query to their neighbors (i.e., a broadcast approach), further aggravating the traffic amount and deteriorating the performance of content sharing. Consequently, inefficient usage experience of these P2P services often occurs to their users. On the other hand, the essential requirement of content sharing primarily rests on if the information exchanged is what it is expected (i.e., precision of contents). *Accordingly, for success of WP2P Content Sharing specific mechanisms have to be in place for effective and quality information exchanged. Meanwhile, the mechanisms also need to take into account the characteristics of handheld devices (e.g., limited resources in computing power, storage and display) and the unreliability of wireless connection.*

In this paper, we present to the problem WP2P Content Sharing a novel solution named *Contextualized Integrative Negotiation Strategy (CINS) that enables an effective and quality usage experience of content sharing between peers in the environments of wireless ad-hoc networks. The underlying ideas are three folds: (1) Enable a stable network performance of the WP2P Content Sharing Problem. (2) Assure effective content sharing in terms of reasonable negotiation efforts and resources consumption. (3) Promise quality content sharing by means of legitimate content quality and response-reply time (given the assumption of the availability of content-sharing ontologies).*

Negotiation is a process by means of which peers communicate and compromise to reach mutually beneficial agreements [7, 8]. In the negotiation context, CINS is regarded a negotiation method characterized of the features [9] as *mediator-free* (i.e., no mediators involved to facilitate negotiation between peers), *closed* (i.e., no other pertinent external information exerted - e.g., third party's information about trust or reputation of peers - except bids), *multi-issues* (i.e., multiple attributes considered that often lead to outcomes bringing joint gains to negotiating peers), and *integrative* (i.e., win-win negotiation). These settings are sensible for the problem of WP2P Content Sharing: (1) The nature of a WP2P environment is decentralized (i.e., mediator-free). (2) The cost attempted is small (i.e., without the cost for a third party's information). (3) The outcomes intended is win-win (i.e., multi-issues and integrative). Furthermore, CINS is a many-to-many negotiation [10] in which many peers can negotiate with many other peers.

There have been a number of negotiation mechanisms proposed. They were briefly classified into three categories [11]: (1) Game-theoretic and auction-based mechanisms [12, 13]: deciding on optimal strategies of seeking equilibrium by analyzing the interactions between identical peers. (2) Heuristic-based mechanisms [14]: devising heuristics for the cases where optimal outcomes are not possible owing to limited resources, dynamic environment or incomplete uncertain information. Since heuristics are rules of thumbs that produce "good enough" outcomes, they are mainly based on empirical testing and evaluation. (3) Argumentation-based mechanisms [15]: allowing the exchange of meta information about peers (e.g., reasons of their bids, acceptance or rejection). When focusing on techniques of multi-issue negotiation, relevant research works then include the use of Multi-Attribute Utility Theory (MAUT) [16, 17], distributed constraint satisfaction [18,19], and evolutionary algorithm [20, 21] (and most of these approaches are better off when working in environments facilitated by mediators).

Nevertheless, the aforementioned mechanisms are not suitable for the problem of WP2P Content Sharing (of such features as mediator-free, no third party's information involved, win-win outcome). The reasons are three folds: (1) Game-theoretic and auction-based mechanisms violate the mediator-free constraints. (2) Win-win outcomes might not be fulfilled by heuristic-based mechanisms. (3) Argumentation-based mechanisms exert a heavy load of communications that however are not feasible in WP2P environments.

The negotiation context of CINS mainly takes on the situations of limited resources (of handheld devices carried by unequal peers), dynamic environments (of unfixed passing-by peers empowered by different handheld devices), complete information (of the needs of peers), and closed world of no argumentations. Accordingly, CINS chooses as the basis Q-Learning [22] (that can enable peers to improve their behaviors in a dynamic environment via their individual experiences and capabilities), unfolding a novel solution for an effective and quality usage experience of content sharing between peers in the environments of wireless ad-hoc networks.

The remainder of this paper is organized as follows. Section 2 presents the architecture supporting the CINS methodology (that is subsequently presented in Section 3). Section 4 provides the implementation design and the evaluation results of CINS. Finally, Section 5 concludes this paper with a discussion on CINS's contributions and limitations and the future fruitful research directions.

2   The Architecture Supporting CINS

In this section, we describe the design of the architecture that supports the operations of CINS. *Each peer of an environment is assumed to be equipped with the architecture and the CINS methodology so as to enable effective and quality WP2P Content Sharing in the environment[1].* CINS is empowered by this architecture for such features as intelligence, context awareness and engaging (that will be detailed in the delineation of the architecture design).

---

[1] This can easily be done by a provision server (e.g., servers residing at the entries of the train station of a tourist city) pushing the system to any passing-by peers in the environment.

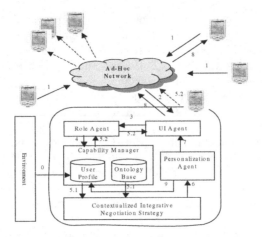

Fig. 1. The design of the CINS supporting architecture

As shown in Figure 1, the supporting architecture comprises the following components:

- *Role Agent*: Decide the role (provider or consumer) a peer plays in its situation.
- *Personalization Agent*: Learn the change in a peer's negotiation preference.
- *Capability Manager*: Assess a peer's capability in content sharing (comprise two parts - User Profile and Ontology Base).
- *User Profile*: Record a peer's surrounding environment status and its device resources allowed in content sharing service (initialized by the peer when its device is equipped with the system architecture) in terms of a number of peers that can be served simultaneously (*Participable PNumber*) and a level of device resources allowed for consumption in content sharing (*Participable RLevel*). The amount of reserved resources intended (*Reserve_Amount*) for self-use can also be defined. As follows then exhibit the definitions (Definition 1, 2, 3) of the aforementioned terms.

    For instances, '$\mathcal{M}s$ =5 'denotes the provider peer can serve up to 5 demander peers, '$\mathcal{L}s_1$=1' specifies a low percentage (say 30%) of a device resource that can be shared to those external contents-sharing services.

- *Ontology Base*: In W2P2P Content Sharing, information exchanged between peers requires a content-sharing ontology for improving communication (query and response in negotiation). In the architecture a working ontology can be embedded into the ontology base of the architecture as demanded. For the example of Amy in the train station of a tourist city (as addressed in Section 1), the provision server in the train station can push to Amy's handheld device a travel-domain ontology as demanded, presuming most passing-by peers in the train station are tourists and have a great chance of needing assistance (peer-wise or centralized) about the travel of the city.

Definition 1:

Let Ms be *the number of peers that a peer can serve once* and is called **Participable PNumbers**. When a peer acts as a provider, he may serve Ms other peers once at most. Where n is a positive number and $Ms \in [1...n]$.

Definition 2:

A set of constants $Ls = \{< Ls_1, Ls_2, Ls_3>\}$ symbolizes *the level of device resources* (that a peer can bestow) and is named **Participable RLevel**. The semantics of these symbols are *low*, *middle* and *high* respectively (represented by 1, 2, 3) (i.e., $Ls_1=1$, $Ls_1=2$, $Ls_1=3$).

Definition 3:

For a resource Rs, Reserve_Amount(Rs), *the default reserve amount*, is defined as:

$$Reserve\_Amount(Rs) \equiv TR_s - H * Ls_i + \theta$$

Where TR_s is the total amount of the resource Rs, H is a constant, L_{si} is the level of sharing resource, and θ is a positive constant used to adjust the amount of resource.

Since the ontology is employed for the purpose of Ontology-Based Search, the operations of searching and matching subsequently are considered. For simplicity, the degree of matching is named as *Goal Relevance*. For a given a query (a node Gi in the ontology tree), Goal Relevance of a possible reply (another node $Rsij$ in the ontology tree) refers to the proximity of the reply with respect to the query. A deeper reply than the query means a more complete piece of information provisioned. For the example of Figure 2, amid the 5-level ontology tree the consumer's query Gi (Hotel3) and the provider's content ($Rsij$) respectively are at the fifth level and the fourth level. Therefore, the Goal Relevance is $Dist(Gi, Rsij) = 4-5 = -1$. That is, although the demander desires a more detailed reply, the provider is only capable of offering a 80% degree of matched content for the demander.

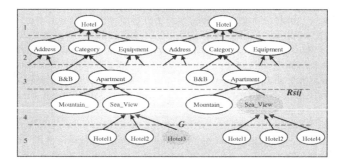

Fig. 2. An exemplar of matching between a demander's query (G) and a provider's content ($Rsii$) (*Note: The left and the right trees are for the demander and the provider respectively*).

The operational principles of the CINS supporting architecture are two-fold: (1) Upon a peer's query of specific contents, the peer broadcast the query to its neighboring peers. (2) The neighboring peers subsequently examine themselves (based on their contextualized capabilities) so as to make decisions of sharing the content or propagating the query to their neighbors. As follows are the itemized operational steps of the architecture (i.e., Figure 1's numerated steps):

(0) The device sensors of a provider peer monitor the changes of the surrounding environment and record the environment status in User Profile.
(1) Proximate demander peers emit their queries of needed contents.
(2) The queries are transmitted to the provider peer via ad-hoc mobile networks.
(3) Receiving a query by UI Agent, the provider peer confirms its providing role with Role Agent.
(4) The provider peer evaluates its own capabilities in content sharing with respect to the query.
(5) The provider peer decides actions to take:
> (5.1) Action of able to share: The peer then performs the CINS methodology for effective and quality WP2P Content Sharing.
> (5.2) Action of unable to share: The peer propagates the query to its neighboring peers via ad-hoc mobile networks.
(6) Personalization Agent learns the changes of the negotiation process.
(7) UI Agent summarizes the negotiation results.
(8) UI Agent dispatches the reply to the demander of the query via ad-hoc mobile networks.
(9) Personalization Agent updates User Profile if necessary.

3   CINS Methodology

The underlying principle of CINS methodology is to enable a peer to decide on appropriate win-win sharing actions for the problem of WP2P Content Sharing with respect to the current status of the surrounding dynamic environment (of unfixed passing-by peers empowered by different handheld devices), the changing capabilities of the peer devices (limited resources of handheld devices carried), and the sharing preferences of the peers. Accordingly, the methodology is named as *Contextualized* (i.e., environment and resources sensitive) *Integrative* (i.e., win-win) *Negotiation Strategy* (of the required intelligence - ability of automating appropriate interactions between peers regardless of the pre-set preferences or the learned experience).

In CINS, Q-Learning is a fundamental vehicle to drive the operations of CINS. However, the actions of a peer (provider or consumer) are derived based on two novel strategies - Consumer Strategy and Provider Strategy situated on this Q-Learning vehicle.

This section accordingly begins with a brief description of Q-Learning (Section 3.1), followed by the presentations of Provider Strategy (Section 3.2) and Consumer Strategy (Section 3.3).

3.1   Q-Learning

Q-Learning [22] is a form of Reinforcement Learning algorithm that does not need a model of its environment and can be used on-line. Therefore, it is very suited for repeated games against an unknown opponent. Q-Learning algorithms work by estimating the values of state-action pairs. The value $Q(s,a)$ is defined to be the expected discounted sum of future payoffs obtained by taking action a from state s and following an optimal policy thereafter. Once these values have been learned, the optimal action from any state is the one with the highest Q-value. After being initialized to arbitrary numbers, Q-values are estimated on the basis of experience as follows: (1) From the current state s, select an action a of the property of $\arg\max_a Q(s,a)$. This will cause a receipt of an immediate reward $R(s,a)$, and arrival at a next state s'. (2) Update $Q(s,a)$ based upon this experience as follows: $\Delta Q(s,a) = \psi[R(s,a) + \phi \max_a Q'(s',a') - Q(s,a)]$, where Ψ *and* ϕ are the learning rate and the discount factor. (3) Go to 1.

This algorithm is guaranteed to converge to the correct Q-values with the probability one if the environment is stationary and depends on the current state and the action taken in it.

3.2 Provider Strategy

In WP2P Content Sharing, Provider Strategy has to empower a provider peer to decide on the decision of an appropriate action (with respect to a given query) taking into account such factors as the dynamic environment, limited capabilities and preferences. This section will begin with the presentation of the strategy (Algorithm 1), followed by detailed descriptions and explanations of the strategy.

The descriptions of CINS Provider Strategy is itemized as follows:

- Upon a given query, Planning Agent calculates if there still exist vacancies for the processing of the query. A plan network P (recording the existing queries under processing) and a peer preference setting *Participle PNumber* (Definition 1) are used for this calculation of the vacancies. If there are vacancies, the query is then accepted (otherwise, it is rejected).
- When accepting the query, compute the total resources Ri required for the processing of the query with the formula: $CT_r(C_i) = \sum_{k=1}^{n} Cost\_resource_k^{Ri}$, where k indicates types of resources (e.g., CPU, RAM, HD if k=3) and $Cost\_resource_k^{Ri}$ represents the normalized amount of resource of type k required.

  (In this paper, peers are presumed to be *altruistic*, i.e., willing to share content as long as the amount of reserved resources required is not violated).
- The total cost of a bid action of a content C_i accordingly is defined as follows: $CT_b(C_i) = T_i + CTr(C_i)$, where Ti is the spent time. That is, the cost of an action of providing the content C_i arises from the device resources and the time required for the sharing of the content C_i.
- Assuming the content C_i is versioned into ones of different degrees of granularity (e.g., complete versus outlined), there are multiple bid actions associated with the provision of the content C_i accordingly. Given a set A of possible bid actions, the provider peer will select an action of the maximized utility defined as follows: $\hat{U}_{aj}(C_i) = \dfrac{1}{CT_b(C_i)}$, where $aj \in A$. In other words, the bigger the cost of an action is the smaller the utility the action partakes.

Algorithm 1

Function CINS-FOR-PROVIDER (*state, MO, TR*) **returns** *an action*
  inputs: *state*, the environment of provider
          MO, a set of result after ontology matching
          TR, total resource of device
  static: *A*, an action set
        i, a counter, initially *0*
        flag, a Boolean, initially *false*
  repeat
    Content selection:
      choose a content C_i from *MO* .
      /* Provider chooses C_i of the least i that has not yet retrieved
      before, where i means the completeness level of the content
      (i.e., C_i is more complete than C_j. when i < j). */
    Estimating the ability of service:
      if PLANNING-AGENT (*state, Ms*) = 0 **then**
        return *action* ← *reject*
      else

$$CT_r(C_i) = \sum_{k=1}^{A} Cost\_resource_k^{Ri}$$

        while $CT_r(C_i)$ < $TR - Re\text{-}serve\_Amount$ (Rs) **do**
          /* Calculate the cost of the bid of content C_i with the
          current state and the spent time T_i. Meanwhile, an action of
          presenting C_i is developed. */
          $CT_s(C_i) = (T_i + CT_r(C_i))$
          Develop the action of $a_j(C_i)$
          add $a_j(C_i)$ to A
        end
    $i ← i + 1$
  until *action* ← *reject*   or there are no suitable content
    Action selection:
      if flag = *false* **then**
        Compare the utilities of actions $\hat{U} a_j(C_i)$. j=1, ..., m,
        and choose an action that makes the highest utility

$$a_j(C_i)' \equiv \arg\max_{a_j(C_i)} (\hat{U} a_j(C_i)| j \in N)$$

        flag ← *true*

$$\Delta \hat{Q}(state, a_j(C_i)) ← \psi [Reward\_Rsi_{j} + \phi \max \hat{Q}(state', a_j(C_i)') - \hat{Q}(state, a_j(C_i))]$$

      else $a_j(C_i)' \equiv \arg\max_{a_j(C_i)} (\hat{Q}(state, a_j(C_i)| j \in N))$
  return a_j

Function PLANNING-AGENT (*state, Ms*) **returns** *vacancy*
  inputs: *state*, the environment of a provider
        Ms, Participable PNumbers (*Definition 1*)
  static: *P*, a plan network

  if *P* is empty **then**
    return *vacancy* ← *Ms*
  else
    VP ← calculate   the   count   of   *P* − *Ms*
    return *vacancy* ← *VP*

- If it is the first time the provider peer is engaged in WP2P Content Sharing (i.e., no rewards attained from the environment yet), the provider peer simply selects an action of the maximum utility (i.e., $action \equiv \arg\max_{a_j(C_i)} (\hat{U} a_j(C_i)| a_j \in A)$, followed by the updating of the Q-Value, i.e., $\Delta \hat{Q}(state, a_j(C_i)) ← \psi [Reward\_Rsij + \phi \max \hat{Q}(state', a_j(C_i)') - \hat{Q}(state, a_j(C_i))]$ as shown in Algorithm 1.

- Otherwise, there is a reward generated. The computation of the reward is as follows: $Reward\_Rsij = \dfrac{1}{\dfrac{1}{Ave\_Dist_i\,(Gi, Rsij)} + Ave\_WTime}$, where Gi and $Rsij$ are respectively defined in Definition 4 and Definition 5, $Ave\_Dist_i(Gi, Rsij) = \dfrac{\sum\limits_{j=1}^{m} Dist_i(Gi, Rsij)}{m}$,

($1 \le j \le m$), and $Ave\_WTime = Ave\_WTime = \dfrac{1}{n}\sum\limits_{i=1}^{n}\delta_i$, $\delta_i \equiv t_{i+1} - t_i$ (t_i and t_{i+1} respectively denote the time that the query is received from the demander and the time the reply is sent out to the demander).

Definition 4:
  Let Gi symbolize *the goal of demander i's will* and be called **Goal of Demander i,** where n is a positive number and $i \in [1 \dots n]$.

Definition 5:
  Let $Rsij$ symbolize the total resource Rs required in contents sharing by provider j with respect to Goal of Demander i and $Rsij$ be called **Provider j's Response to Demander i,** where m is a positive number and $j \in [1 \dots m]$.

The main ideas behind the aforementioned reward formula are three folds: (1) For the provider peer, the reward semantically specifies the feedbacks (i.e., qualities of the services rendered) from the environment (of multiple demander peers requesting information from the provider peers). (2) For simplicity, qualities of services consider two factors - average Goal Relevance ($Ave\_Dist_i\,(Gi, Rsij)$) and average service time (Ave_WTime). Bigger average Goal Relevance and smaller average service time indicates better qualities of services. (3) The reward accordingly is formulated in proportional to the average qualities of services.

- With the aforementioned reward, the optimal action of a state is then the bid with the highest Q-value. That is, $a_j(C_i)' \equiv \arg\max\limits_{a_j(C_i)} (\hat{Q}(state, a_j(C_i) | a_j \in A))$.

3.3 Demander Strategy

In WP2P Content Sharing, Demander Strategy aims to empower a demander peer to choose appropriate provider peers (with respect to a given query made the by demander) and decide if there is a need to reasonably adjust the query when the original query cannot be fulfilled by existing surrounding provider peers. This section will begin with the presentation of the strategy (Algorithm 2), followed by detailed descriptions and explanations of the strategy.

The descriptions of CINS Provider Strategy is itemized as follows:

- Given the goal of the query Gi, upon those replies $Rsij$ received from some provider peers, compute the average Goal Relevance: $Ave\_Dist_i(Gi, Rsij) = \dfrac{\sum\limits_{j=1}^{m} Dist_i(Gi, Rsij)}{m}$. Average Goal Relevance will be served as a threshold that can efficiently filter unqualified provider peers in a time-critical

manner. Moreover, average Goal Relevance also implies the overall content qualities of those provider peers.

- Filter the provider peers of the condition as follows:
$Disti(Gi, Rsij) \leq \lfloor Ave\_Disti(Gi, Rsij) \rfloor \times \beta$, where β is a user-defined parameter
(ranging from 0 to 1) denoting a speed of the selection process of the provider
candidates. After the filtering, what remains are the accepted provider candidates
proceeding subsequent negotiations.

Algorithm 2

```
Function CINS-FOR-DEMANDER (r, β ) returns action, candidates
    input: r, reward given by environment
           β , a positive constant, given by the demander
    static: CA, the count of auctions, initially 0
            TDist, total distance, initially 0
            P, a set of providers, of size CA
            Gi', the goal relevance after adjusted
            Gi_al, the level of adjustment with Gi
    candidate ←   a provider has the response first
    loop do
        Auction number count:
            if receive a response then
                add 1 to CA
        Candidate selection:
            repeat
                for each provider j do
                    TDist =  Σ   Disti  (Gi , Rsij  )
                            j=1
                    if  Disti  (Gi , Rsij  ) ≤ ⌊Ave  _ Disti  (Gi , Rsij )⌋× β
                       /* where β   is exerted to adjust the speed of
                          candidate's selection */
                        then reject
                    else
                        add provider j to P
                end
            until no provider's distance is larger than average distance
            candidates ←   P
        Goal relevance adjustment:
            if │1 – Re ward   _ Gi │ ≥ Gi _ Al    then
                Gi ←   Gi'
            else  Gi ←   Gi
            return Gi , candidates
    end
```

- Calculate the reward as follows: $Reward\_Gi = \dfrac{\sum_{j=1}^{m} Rw\_Rsij}{m}$, where

$Rw\_Rsij = \dfrac{1}{CT_r(C_i)\_P_j}$ ($CT_r(C_i)\_P_j$ denotes the total resources cost incurred to the

provider peer Pj). The reward signals the contemporary status of the device capabilities of those qualified provider peers. If the status is bad, then there is a need
for the demander peer to adjust its goal from Gi (requiring a bigger amount of
providers resources) to Gi' (requiring a smaller amount of providers resources).
Figure 3 exemplifies such a goal adjustment.

- Adjust the goal if the condition as follows is met: $|1 - Reward\_Gi| \geq Gi\_Al$,
where Gi_Al is defined in Definition 6.

The main ideas behind the above formula are as follows: (1) A big reward ($Re-ward\_Gi$) indicates a great number of positive responses attained from the provider peers, leaving no needs to adjust the goal. (2) On the contrary, a small reward implies overall poor device capabilities and thus goal adjustment is needed. (3) An adjustment threshold (Gi_Al) is exerted to decide the applicability of goal adjustment. For simplicity, Gi' refers to a node where Gi is one level deeper[2] than Gi' in the given domain ontology tree.

> **Definition 6:**
> Let Gi_Al symbolize the level of adjustment with Goal of Demander i and Gi_Al be called **the level of adjustment with** Gi, where $Gi\_Al \in [0,1]$.

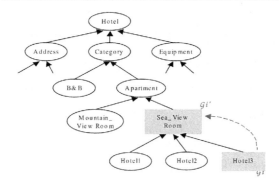

Fig. 3. An exemplar of goal adjustment

4   Implementation and Evaluations

In this section, a brief description of the system implementation is provided, followed by a thorough evaluation of the CINS methodology.

Our architecture is implemented with the technology of JXTA [24] going with Personal Java that works for handheld devices such as iPAQ. JXTA is a modular platform that provides simple and essential building blocks for developing a wide range of distributed services and applications. Both centralized and de-centralized services can be developed on top of the JXTA platform. JXTA services can be implemented to interoperate with other services giving rise to new P2P applications.

Since an ontology is utilized in the architecture for organizing and specifying myriad types of domain knowledge, in our implementation Ontology Web Language (OWL) [25] (rooted in RDF) is employed to represent the ontology in order to preserve the semantics of the information. Furthermore, RDF Query Language (RDQL) [26], a SQL-like Jena API, is exerted to search information in the ontology.

As addressed in Section 1, the CINS methodology aims at providing to WP2P Content Sharing an effective and quality solution, considering capabilities of handheld devices, user preference and quality of content services. Furthermore, due to limitation of space the evaluations of CINS are described as the following two directions of investigation:

---

[2] A node deeper in the ontology tree indicates more complete information presented.

(1) Show CINS can enable stable network performance for the WP2P Content Sharing problem (Section 4.1)
(2) Assure effective and quality content sharing in terms of reasonable negotiation efforts, device resources consumption and legitimate content provisioned (Section 4.2).

Before unfolding the investigations, we need to describe some performance metrics employed in the evaluations[3]:

- *Network Efficiency Index*: In this paper network performance refers to the stability status of successful content services rendered between peers in a WP2P environment regardless of the size of total queries posted by demander peers. In other words, good network performance indicates that large query sizes do not deteriorate the stability (as opposed to traditional broadcast-based processing of peer-to-peer communications). Accordingly, an index of network efficiency (as shown below) can be defined as the ratio of the size of accepted queries to the size of total queries, and a stable trend of this index projected over query sizes would be considered as good network efficiency for the WP2P Content Sharing Problem:

$$NE = \frac{Size\ Accepted\ Queries}{Size\ of\ Toal\ Queries}$$

- *Demander Utility index*: For a demander peer of a given WP2P Content Sharing Problem, quality of services takes into account the levels of satisfaction in the content exchanged (e.g., five levels of satisfaction where 5 and 1 denote the maximum and the minimum levels of satisfaction) and the time consumed for the demander peer waiting for the content received since its query is sent out. Accordingly, an index of demander utility is defined as follows: $U_D = \dfrac{1}{\dfrac{1}{DL}\times\varphi_1 + \dfrac{1}{AWT}\times\varphi_2}$, where DL

and AWT denote a level of content satisfaction and average waiting time, and φ_1 and φ_2 represent the weights associated with DL and AWT respectively.

- *Provider Utility Index*: For a provider peer of a given WP2P Content Sharing Problem, provider utility is regarded as the reversal to the cost of device resource consumed and the time required for processing a given query. Accordingly, an index of provider utility is defined as follows: $U_P = \dfrac{1}{\dfrac{CTr\times\lambda_1 + Ti\times\lambda_2}{100}}$, where CT_r and

T_i denote the total cost of device resources and the total cost of processing time required the provision of the content Ci in response to the given query, and λ_1 and λ_2 represent the weights associated with CT_r and T_i

respectively.

For a thorough understanding of CINS's performance, the aforementioned two focused investigation areas will be examined with different peer sizes and query sizes

---

[3] Without loss of generalization, a travel domain is presumed for the evaluations.

(Table 1 shows the experiment settings of the parameters required). Moreover, maximized social welfare is also checked against CINS to justify the win-win property of the negotiation process (i.e., allocation decisions of information, device resources and time) claimed. Social welfare refers to the overall utility state of society. It is often defined as the summation of the welfare of all the peers in the environment. Welfare in this paper is measured in terms of utilities. According to this measure of social welfare, a situation is optimal only if the sum of the utilities of the peers can be made maximized.

4.1 Investigation of Network Performance

To show the stability status of successful content services rendered between peers in a WP2P environment with respect to the size of total queries, this section presents the evaluation results with different peer sizes (N = 10, 20).

Table 1. Experiment settings

Parameter	Symbol	Values	Meaning
Peer Size	N	10 / 20	The number of peers in a given WP2P environment
Query Size	Num_Req	1 / 5 / 10 / 15 / 20 / 50 / 100	The Number of queries initiated by consumer peers.
Weight of Contents Satisfaction	φ_1	0.8	A weight used in Demander Utility Index, $0 < \varphi_1 < 1$
Weight of AWT	φ_2	0.2	A weight used in Demander Utility Index, $0 < \varphi_2 < 1$
Weight of Consumed Resources	λ_1	0.8	A weight used in Provider Utility Index, $0 < \lambda_1 < 1$
Weight of Consumed Time	λ_2	0.2	A weight used in Provider Utility Index, $0 < \lambda_2 < 1$
Provider Selection Rate	β	0.6	A parameter used in Algorithm 1 and $0 < \beta < 1$.
Location	ℓ	North area	Peer's locations (East, West, South, North)

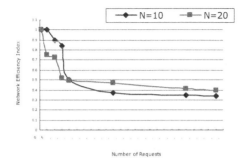

Fig. 4. Stable status of network performance after an initial learning phase

From Figure 4, stable trends of successful content services indeed are observed with N=10 or N=20 (after the initial learning phase of around 20 queries). The reasons behind these positive results are two folds: (1) Large query sizes not deteriorating network performance (as opposed to traditional broadcast-based processing of peer-to-peer communications) is contributed to a naïve approach of CINS in which the propagations of queries to neighboring peers are stopped by provider peers who are capable of rendering the requested content services (allowed by their preferences and capabilities that vary dynamically in accord with the services accepted and committed on hand in the environment).

4.2 Investigation of Social-Warfare Maximizing

To justify CINS's effective and quality content sharing (in terms of reasonable negotiation efforts, device resources consumption and legitimate content provisioned), in this section social welfare (the summation of the utilities of all the peers in the environment) is examined and aims to justify CINS ensures the property of social-warfare maximizing (i.e., CINS creates optimal allocation decisions that the sum of utilities of peers can be made maximized based on the experimental point of views).

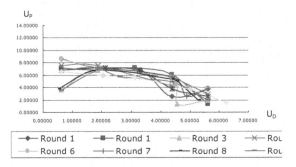

Fig. 5. Welfare distributions attained from the partially randomized version of CINS

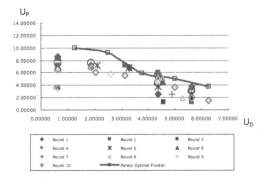

Fig. 6. Benchmark results of the partially randomized version of CINS

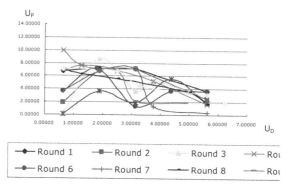

Fig. 7. Welfare distributions attained from the completely randomized version of CINS

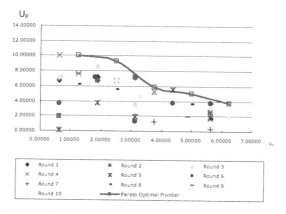

Fig. 8. Benchmark results of the completely randomized version of CINS

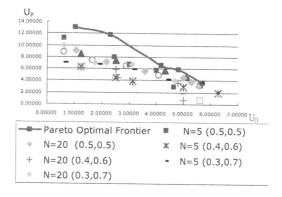

Fig. 9. Benchmark with the completely randomized version of CINS plus random settings of weights associated with utility indexes

In other words, we will show that other allocation decisions (i.e., decisions other than those determined by CINS) attained from other strategies won't beat CINS in terms of social welfare. Without loss of generalization, other strategies can be covered by the following cases of randomized[4] versions of CINS: (1) *Partially randomized CINS*: random bid actions of content provisioned for the provider strategy (while retaining the same choice actions of providers for the demander strategy). (2) *Completely randomized CINS*: random bid actions of content provisioned for the provider strategy in combination with random choice actions of provider peers for the demander strategy. (3) Completely Randomized CINS together with random settings of weights associated with Provider Utility Index and Demander Utility Index.

The evaluation results are then unfolded as follows:

- Benchmark with the partially randomized version of CINS:
    Ten rounds of the experiments (of the peer size N=10) with the partially randomized version of CINS are conducted (as shown in Figure 5) and compared to those of CINS (averaged and represented as the solid line – CINS-SW Frontier - as shown in Figure 6[5]) in terms their welfare distributions (U_p and U_D). Figure 6 shows that CINS outperforms the partially randomized versions of strategies.
- Benchmark with the completely randomized version of CINS:
    Ten rounds of the experiments (of the peer size N=10) with the completely randomized version of CINS are conducted (as shown in Figure 7) and compared to those of CINS (averaged and represented as the solid line – CINS-SW - as shown in Figure 8) in terms their welfare distributions (U_P and U_D). Figure 8 shows that CINS outperforms the completely randomized versions of strategies.

Benchmark with the completely randomized version of CINS together with random settings of weights associated with Provider Utility Index and Demander Utility Index: Exemplars of this benchmark analysis (of different peer sizes) are shown in Figure 9 (in which weights associated with Provider Utility Index are attained by randomization such as 0.3/0.7, 0.4/0.6 and 0.5/0.5). The results also show fairly satisfactory promise in CINS.

5   Conclusion

In this paper, we present to the problem WP2P Content Sharing a novel solution named Contextualized Integrative Negotiation Strategy (CINS) that enables an effective and quality usage experience of content sharing between peers in the environments of wireless ad-hoc networks. The underlying ideas of the CINS methodology

---

[4] Should the experiments be conducted repeatedly, the allocation decisions of any other strategies (other than CINS's) will be covered by the randomized versions of CINS.

[5] For a clear contrast of the results attained from the partially randomized version of CINS to those of CINS, the former are represented with dots of different shapes and colors indicating the results attained from different rounds of experiments, the latter are then averaged into a distribution named CINS-SW Frontier.

are to enable stable network performance for the WP2P Content Sharing problem and empower a peer to decide on appropriate win-win sharing actions for the problem of WP2P Content Sharing (with the aid of content-sharing ontologies employed). This win-win is with respect to the current status of the surrounding dynamic environment (of unfixed passing-by peers empowered by different devices), the changing capabilities of the peer device (limited resources of handheld devices carried), and the sharing preferences of the peer. Accordingly, the methodology is named as *Contextualized* (i.e., environment and resources sensitive) *Integrative* (i.e., win-win) *Negotiation Strategy* (of the required intelligence to automate appropriate interactions between peers - regardless of pre-set preferences or learned experience). The CINS methodology comprises two novel negotiation strategies (empowered by Q-Learning) and a supporting architecture (empowered by domain ontology). The experimental evaluation results also confirm these contributions. Moreover, the other evaluation results (not appearing in this paper) show that the Provider Selection Rate β has to be set appropriately in accord with peer sizes so as to better off the performance of CINS (a bigger β for bigger peer sizes) and that regardless of the formation[6] of domain ontology, win-win decisions are always made as long as the peers of the environment employ the same ontology during negotiation. However, the results stand valid only for the contemporary sets of experiments. Further extensive experiments are accordingly required. The future fruitful research directions include the consideration of more context attributes (e.g., time) covered in the strategies, open-world negotiation (e.g., taking into account the information of reputations of peers), distributed micro pricing, and further exploration of possible applications.

References

[1] Oram (*Edt.*), Peer-to-Peer – Harnessing the Power of Disruptive Technologies, O'Reilly, Sebastopol, CA, 2002.

[2] D. Barkei, Peer-to-Peer Computing, Intel Press, Hillsboro, OR, 2002.

[3] M. Parameswaran, A. Susarla, A. B. Whinston, P2P Networking: An Information-Sharing Alternative, IEEE Computer, Vol. 34(7), P. 31-38, 2001.

[4] The Gnutella homepage, http://gnutella.wego.com.

[5] E. Cohen and S. Shenker, Optimal Replication in Random Search Networks, Preprint, Optional 2001.

[6] Lv, P. Cao, E. Cohen, K. Li, and S. Shenker, Search and Replication in Unstructured Peer-to-Peer networks, Preprint, Optional 2001.

[7] S. Kraus, Strategic Negotiation in Multi-Agent Environments, The MIT Press, Cambridge, Massachusetts, 2001.

[8] H. Raiffa, The Art and Science of Negotiation. Harvard University Press, Cambridge, USA, 1982.

[9] T. Bosse, C. M. Jonker, J. Treur, Experiments in Human Multi-Issue Negotiation: Analysis and Support, Third International Joint Conference on Autonomous Agents and Multi-agent Systems, New York City, New York, USA, 2004

---

[6] By formation we mean the way the concepts of a domain are arranged into a domain ontology tree. Sometimes, multiples legitimate ontology trees can be arranged out of the same set of domain concepts.

[10] R. Lomuscio, M. Wooldridge, and N.R. Jennings, A classification Scheme for Negotiation in Electronic Commerce, International Journal of Group Decision and Negotiation, Vol. 12(1), P. 31-56, 2003.

[11] Rahwan, P. McBurney, and L. Sonenberg, Towards a Theory of Negotiation Strategy, in Proceedings of the Fifth Workshop on Game Theoretic and Decision Theoretic Agents (GTDT-2003), Melbourne, Australia, 2003.

[12] S. Rosenschein, and G. Zlotkin, Rules of Encounter: Conventions for Automated Negotiation among Computers, MIT Press, 1994.

[13] M. Bichler, An experimental analysis of multi-attribute auctions, Decision, Support Systems, Vol. 29(3), P. 249-268, 2000.

[14] S. S. Fatima, M. Wooldridge, and N. R. Jennings, Multi- Issue Negotiation under Time Constraints, First International Joint Conference on Autonomous Agents and Multi-agent Systems, Bologna, Italy, 2002.

[15] S. Kraus, K. Sycara, and A. Evenchik, Reaching Agreements through Argumentation: A Logical Model and Implementation, Artificial Intelligence, Vol. 104(1-2), P. 1-69, 1998.

[16] M. Barbuceanu and W.K. Lo, A Multi-Attribute Utility Theoretic Negotiation Architecture for Electronic Commerce, International Conference of Autonomous Agents, Barcelona, Spain, 2000.

[17] Sycara, The PERSUADER, In The Encyclopedia of Artificial Intelligence, D. Shapiro (ed), JohnWilley & Sons, January 1992.

[18] S. E. Conry, K. Kuwabara, V.R. Lesser, R. A. Meyer, Multistage Negotiation in Distributed Constraint Satisfaction. In IEEE Transactions on Systems, Man and Cybernetics, Vol. 21(6), P. 1462-1477, November, 1992.

[19] H. Wang, S. Liao, L. Liao, Modeling Constraint-Based Negotiating Agents, Decision Support Systems, Vol. 33(2), P. 201-217, 2002.

[20] E. H. Gerding, D.D.B. van Bragt, J.A. La Poutré, Multi-Issue Negotiation Processes by Evolutionary Simulation: Validation and Social Extensions, Computational Economics, Vol. 22(1), P. 39-63, 2003.

[21] S. T. Yuan and S. F. Chen, A Learning-Enabled Infrastructure for Electronic Contracting Agents, Expert Systems with Applications, Vol. 21(4), P. 239-256, 2001.

[22] J. Christopher, C. H. Watkins and P. Dayan, Q-learning, Machine Learning, Vol. 8(3), P,279-292, 1992.

[23] Uschold and R. Jasper, A Framework for Understanding and Classifying Ontology Applications, in Proceedings of the IJCAI99 Workshop on Ontologies, 1999.

[24] JXTA, http://www.jxta.org/

[25] W3C: OWL Ontology Web Language, http://www.w3.org/TR/owl-ref/

[26] Jena Tutorial:RDQL, http://www.hpl.hp.com/semweb/doc/tutorial/RDQL/

Integrating XML Sources into a Data Warehouse

Boris Vrdoljak, Marko Banek, and Zoran Skočir

University of Zagreb, Faculty of Electrical Engineering and Computing
Unska 3, HR-10000 Zagreb, Croatia
{boris.vrdoljak, marko.banek, zoran.skocir}@fer.hr

Abstract. Since XML has become a standard for data exchange over the Internet, especially in B2B and B2C communication, there is an increasing need of integrating XML data into data warehousing systems. In this paper we propose a methodology for data warehouse design, when data sources are XML Schemas and conforming XML documents. Particular relevance is given to the conceptual and logical multidimensional design. A prototype tool has been developed to verify and support our methodology. Because of the semi-structured nature of XML data, not all the information needed for design can be safely derived from XML Schema. In these situations, XQuery statements are generated by the tool to examine XML documents. The functionality of the tool is explained on a real-life XML Schema that describes purchase orders.

1 Introduction

A data warehousing system is a set of technologies and tools that enable managers and analysts to integrate and flexibly analyze information coming from different sources. The central part of the system is a database specialized for complex analysis of historical data, called a data warehouse. A multidimensional data model is commonly used in data warehouses in order to enable efficient data analysis and support the decision-making process.

The increasing use of XML in business-to-business (B2B) applications and e-Commerce Web sites, suggests that a lot of valuable external data sources will be available in XML format on the Internet. External XML data includes business documents like purchase orders, lists of prices or catalogs, as well as web service responses. The possibility of integrating available XML data into data warehouses plays an important role in providing enterprise managers with up-to-date and comprehensive information about their business domain.

In this paper we propose a methodology for semi-automated design of data warehouses starting from XML Schemas [16] and conforming XML documents. Many challenges, especially in conceptual multidimensional design, emerge from the fact that XML data is semi-structured. In cases when the needed information about data structure cannot be derived from XML Schema, available XML documents are examined by using XQuery [17] statements. Once a conceptual scheme is obtained as a result of the conceptual design, a *star schema* [15] can be derived. The star schema is the predominant logical multidimensional scheme, optimized for multidimensional analysis of a large amount of data.

J. Lee et al. (Eds.): DEECS 2006, LNCS 4055, pp. 133–142, 2006.

To support the methodology for data warehouse design from XML sources, a Java-based prototype tool has been developed. A conceptual scheme is derived semi-automatically by identifying and navigating relationships in XML data. The tool then creates the star schema tables and loads the data extracted from XML documents.

The paper is structured as follows. Section 2 describes the related work. Section 3 presents the main steps of the methodology for data warehouse design from XML sources. Section 4 describes our algorithm for conceptual multidimensional design from XML. Section 5 deals with logical multidimensional design. Conclusions and future work are presented in Section 6.

2   Related Work

Some approaches concerning the data warehouse design from XML sources have been proposed in the literature.

In [3], a technique for conceptual design of a data warehouse starting from DTDs is outlined. That approach is now partially outdated due to the increasing popularity of XML Schema. In [4], the initial steps of conceptual design from XML Schema, including some complex modeling situations, have been presented.

In [5] and [6], DTDs are used as a source for designing multidimensional schemas. An intermediate UML-based structure, called UML snowflake diagram, is used to represent DTDs. The unknown cardinalities of relationships are not verified against the actual XML data, but are always assumed to be -to-one. The approach described in [7] allows the external XML data to be presented along with dimensional data in OLAP query results and enables the use of the external XML data for selection and grouping. No assumptions about the existence of DTDs or XML Schemas have been made.

In [8] a framework for constructing a federated data warehouse from XML Schemas is outlined. Similarly to [5, 6], in [8] XML Schemas are first translated into a UML snowflake diagram. Since a data warehouse is subject-oriented, we argue that more attention should be given to the process of choosing a warehouse *fact* among the UML snowflake structures. The *fact* is a focus of interest for the decision making process. Furthermore, the authors state that the process of creating the UML snowflake diagram is not automated.

Papers [5], [6], [7] and [8] suggest a loosely coupled, federated, logical integration of XML data. In some cases data cannot be stored locally (and integrated physically) due to legal acts (as in the case of highly sensitive medical data) or some technical reasons. Physical storage may also not be suitable when the data is obtained from a Web service or it changes quickly and continuously, leaving no time to perform the extraction-transformation-loading process (e.g. stock market prices or air temperatures). We believe that in all other cases, when the external data is structured enough to derive a meaningful conceptual model of a warehouse, a physical integration should be achieved. When using only logically integrated (federated) data warehouse, queries must be analyzed by the federation server and then translated into a series of queries, each of them corresponding to a single component warehouse. Therefore, query execution in a federated system is slower than in case of a physical integration.

The so-called XML warehouses where all fact and dimension data is stored as XML documents are presented in [10]. XQuery language is used for processing the queries. The approach assumes that each XML document describes a single dimension or a single fact record. This may be true in some cases (the example XML documents were generated a posteriori from web data), but in most real-life cases (like examples given in our paper) dimensional and fact data are mixed within the document.

It would also be possible to translate the XML Schema into relational structures first [1, 2, 14] and then apply the existing algorithms for creating a data warehouse conceptual schema from relational sources [11, 12]. However, such a multiple format change may cause a loss of some important data. In order to avoid this, we derive a conceptual and logical schema of the warehouse directly from XML sources.

3   Methodology for Data Warehouse Design from XML Sources

A design methodology is an essential requirement to ensure the success of a complex data warehousing project. In order to address various issues and new challenges emerging from the semi-structured nature of XML data, we adapted and extended the methodology from [11] and [12]. The main steps of the methodology for data warehouse design starting from XML sources are: (1) conceptual design, (2) logical design, (3) ETL (Extraction, Transformation and Loading), and (4) physical design.

Conceptual design. A conceptual multidimensional scheme is built starting from an XML Schema (or several XML Schemas linked by their namespaces). The main problem in building the conceptual multidimensional scheme is to identify functional dependencies, which represent many-to-one relationships between attributes and enable flexible data aggregation in queries. Since XML models semi-structured data, not all the needed information about functional dependencies can be safely derived. In such cases, available XML documents have to be examined by using XQuery.

Logical design. Logical design includes a set of steps that lead to the definition of a logical scheme starting from the previously defined conceptual scheme. We use a relational logical model, particularly a star schema, consisting of one fact table, and a set of dimensional tables.

ETL design. After dimensional tables and fact tables have been created, they should be populated. Data is extracted from XML documents by using XQuery. Necessary data transformations and cleansing are provided. After the initial data loading, additional data is loaded into the data warehouse periodically.

Physical design. Physical design deals primarily with the optimal selection of indices, which plays a crucial role in the optimization of data warehouse performance.

4   Conceptual Design

4.1   Dimensional Fact Model

In order to enable efficient analysis of a large amount of data, a multidimensional data model is commonly used in the warehouse. In this paper we adopt the Dimensional

Fact Model [13], which represents a data warehouse as a set of *fact schemes*. A fact scheme is structured as a rooted graph whose root is a fact. The components of fact schemes are facts, measures, dimensions and hierarchies.

A *fact* is a focus of interest for the decision-making process. It typically corresponds to events occurring dynamically in the enterprise world (such as sales or orders, for example). *Measures* are continuously valued (typically numerical) attributes that describe the fact. Fig. 1 presents a fact scheme describing purchase orders, with *PRICE, QUANTITY* and *INCOME* as measures. *Dimensions* are discrete attributes which determine the minimum granularity adopted to represent facts. The dimensions in the purchase order example are product, partner (i.e. supplier), purchase order ID (poid) and date. *Hierarchies* are made up of discrete dimension attributes linked by -to-one relationship, and determine how facts may be aggregated. In our example, there is a hierarchy: *DATE → MONTH → YEAR*. Each hierarchy includes a set of attributes linked by functional dependences; for instance, *DATE* functionally determines *MONTH* and *MONTH* determines *YEAR*.

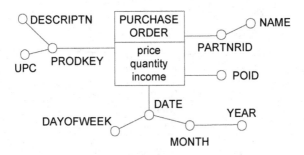

Fig. 1. Fact scheme for purchase order

4.2 Relationships in XML

The structure of XML data can be visualized by using a *schema graph* (SG) derived from the Schema describing the data. Fig. 2 shows the SG for OAGIS 7.2.1 Purchase Order XML Schema [9] (created by Open Applications Group, a non-profit organization that supports e-business and electronic exchange of data), which is used by a major grocery store company in Croatia in their B2B and B2C applications.

There are two different ways of specifying relationships in XML Schemas and the corresponding schema graphs.

First, relationships can be specified by sub-elements with different cardinalities. Cardinality of the relationships is denoted by vertices ("+", "*", "?"), which determine whether the sub-element or attribute of an element may appear one or more, zero or more, or zero or one times, respectively (taken from DTD [3, 14]). The default cardinality is exactly one (e.g. *LINEITEM→QUANTITY*) and in that case no cardinality vertex is shown. The cardinality in the opposite direction (from a child element to its parent) cannot be discovered by exploring the Schema, but only by examining the XML documents that conform to the Schema or by having some knowledge about the described domain.

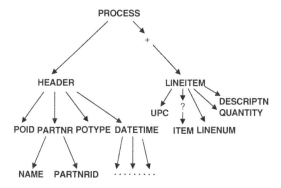

Fig. 2. Schema graph for OAGIS 7.2.1 Purchase Order

Second, the XML Schema elements *key* and *keyref* can be used in order to define keys and their references. The *key* element indicates that every attribute or element value must be unique within a certain scope and not null. If the key is an element, it should be of a simple type. Keys can be referenced by using *keyref* elements.

4.3   Conceptual Design Algorithm

The fact scheme, as a result of the conceptual design phase, is constructed by navigating the functional dependences starting from the chosen fact and by defining dimensions, measures and hierarchies. Conceptual multidimensional design from XML sources consists of the following steps:

1. Preprocessing the XML Schema.
2. Creating a schema graph.
3. Choosing facts.
4. For each fact:
     4.1 Building a dependency graph from the schema graph.
     4.2 Rearranging the dependency graph.
     4.3 Defining dimensions and measures.

All steps of conceptual design have been implemented in our Java-based prototype tool. The tool reads one or more XML Schemas (mutually related by the means of namespaces [16]) and conforming XML documents (step 1). A schema graph (SG) is created automatically from the source XML Schema(s) and shown in the graphical interface of the tool (step 2). The designer then chooses a fact among all the vertices and arcs of the SG by using a graphical interface (step 3). In order to obtain a meaningful fact schema, it is crucial that the fact is properly chosen. It is up to the designer to decide what the focus of interest in decision-making is, and which vertices or arcs represent values that are frequently updated. Applying ontologies could partially automate this process. However, for each particular domain of interest (e.g. purchase orders, web site traffic, etc.) a different ontology must be specified.

Building a dependency graph. A *dependency graph* (DG) is an intermediate structure used to provide a multidimensional representation of the data describing the fact. In particular, it is a directed rooted graph initialized with the fact vertex. The vertices of the DG are a subset of the element and attribute vertices of the SG, and its arcs represent associations between vertices. The DG is created by recursively navigating the functional dependencies between the vertices of the SG (step 4.1). In some cases the source XML documents are examined by using XQuery statements to get information about relationships. Having the SG for OAGIS 7.2.1 Purchase Order (Fig.2), the designer chooses *LINEITEM* as a fact, and the prototype tool derives the DG semi-automatically (Fig. 3). Building of a DG is a combination of four procedures, as follows. Due to the limited space, we describe the procedures only briefly (more details can be found in [4]).

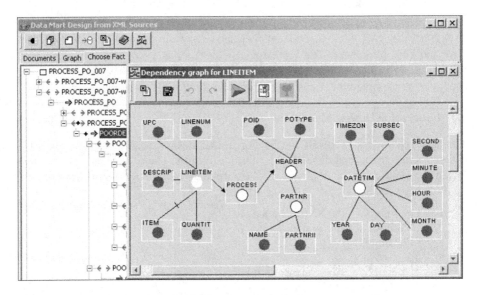

Fig. 3. DG for OAGIS Purchase Order in the prototype tool

Navigation in the "direction down". A DG is enlarged by recursively navigating parent-child relationships in the SG. After a vertex of the SG has been inserted in the DG, it should be decided which of its children will be included in the DG. When the relationship is -to-one, the child element will be included in the DG, although some exceptions exist [4].

Navigation in the "direction up". An XML schema yields no information about the relationship cardinality in the direction from the fact to its ascendants ("direction up"). In order to enlarge the dependency graph in this direction, the cardinality of child-parent relationships must be stated, which is done by examining the available XML documents using XQuery statements.

Following the key/keyref mechanism. The third part of the algorithm concerns the case when a vertex referencing a key vertex is reached in the schema graph.

Convergence and shared hierarchies. Whenever there is more than one instance of a complex type in the SG, and all of the instances have a common ancestor vertex, either a *convergence* or a *shared hierarchy* may be implied in the DG. A convergence holds if an attribute is functionally determined by another attribute along two or more distinct paths of to-one associations. For instance, there can be two paths of functional dependencies for a geographical hierarchy over the stores: *store → city → region → state* and *store → saleDistrict → state*. It is assumed that there is no inclusion relationship between the sale district and regions, and that every district makes part of only one state. Irrespective of how aggregation is done, each store always belongs to exactly one state, thus only a single description of state should exist in a dimension. On the other hand, it often happens that whole parts of hierarchies are replicated twice or more. In this case, we use a *shared hierarchy*, to emphasize that there is no convergence. In XML, all the instances of the same complex type in a specific part of XML document must always have the same content to have a convergence, otherwise a shared hierarchy is introduced. In our approach XQuery is used for examining the content of the available XML documents conforming to the given Schema.

Rearranging the dependency graph. The warehouse designer should check all vertices in the DG since the inappropriate conceptual scheme may result in storing unnecessary information in the warehouse or, worse, loosing important ones. When creating a usable and efficient conceptual scheme of a data warehouse, the designer may (step 4.2): (1) remove some existing vertices from the DG, (2) add some new vertices to the DG, (3) change the position of some existing vertices in the DG. After rearranging the initial DG (Fig. 3), the resulting DG can be seen in Fig. 4.

In the case when new vertices are added to the DG, its content may be: (1) computed using the content of other vertices (e.g. a measure is a product of other two measures), (2) obtained from an external source, different from the XML documents matching the starting XML Schema. Consider an example of the latter case: a European industry corporation sells its products in the EU and the USA, earning both a euro and a dollar income. The business analysis requires all income to be comparable. Therefore, the dollar prices have to be expressed in euros. In order to achieve this, web services operating with exchange rates can be accessed and the calculated data returned via XML documents.

Defining dimensions and measures. All vertices of the fact vertex that have its own children (in Fig. 4, the PARTNRID vertex, as well as TIMEKEY and PRODKEY added during the rearrangement process) imply a hierarchy, so the tool automatically states them as dimension keys for the partner, time, and product dimension, respectively (step 4.3). For each child of the fact without descendants the tool asks the designer whether it should be a dimension (like POID) or a measure (like PRICE, QUANTITY and INCOME). The necessary metadata for hierarchies are also created (e.g. there are four levels in the time hierarchy, represented by TIMEKEY, MONTHKEY, QTRKEY and YEAR).

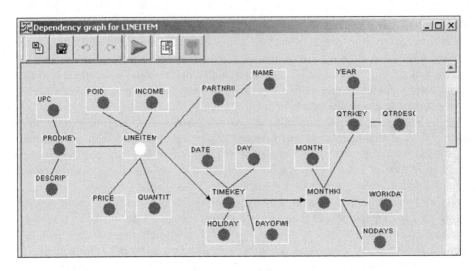

Fig. 4. The rearranged DG for OAGIS Purchase Order

5   Logical Design

Having the conceptual design completed, the tool automatically produces the logical scheme based on the star schema. The SQL statements for creating the specified tables in a database are generated and executed. As already mentioned, the star schema consists of one fact table, and a set of dimensional tables. Each dimensional table has a single-part primary key. The fact table contains all measures of the fact and a multi-part key, each part referencing a dimensional table as a foreign key. As a general rule, a logical scheme in the relational environment is obtained by translating each *n*-dimensional fact scheme into one fact table and *n* dimensional tables. However, the number of dimensional tables may in certain cases be smaller or larger than the number of dimensions in the conceptual model.

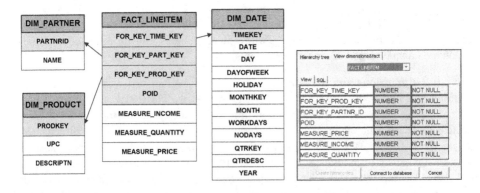

Fig. 5. Logical scheme for OAGIS Purchase Order   **Fig. 6.** Fact table in the tool

The POID dimension has a single attribute (Fig 4), so it would be space consuming to create its separate dimension table [15]. Since a partner can receive multiple orders for the same product in one day, POID becomes a part of the fact table composite key.

In the end, the logical scheme contains three dimensional tables (Fig. 5) while the corresponding conceptual scheme contains four dimensions. The fact table for OAGIS 7.2.1 Purchase Order can be seen in Fig. 6 as shown by the tool.

6 Conclusion

This paper proposes a methodology for designing and constructing a data warehouse directly from XML sources. Thus, the risk of losing relevant information is reduced, when compared to the approach of translating from XML to a general purpose relational database, and from the relational database to a data warehouse.

The conceptual design is performed by navigating the functional dependences in XML Schema and conforming documents, in order to derive a correct multidimensional presentation. In the process of logical design, the derived conceptual schema is translated into a star schema. The methodology has been implemented in a prototype tool that helps the designer in designing faster and more accurately. Many phases of the conceptual and logical design are partly or fully automated. At the end of the design process, the tool creates tables according to the derived star schema and loads data. The design methodology was tested on a real-life XML Schema that describes purchase orders, used by a large grocery store company. It has been proved that all commonly used structures of XML Schema can be successfully processed by our prototype tool, and that a wide range of different multidimensional design cases is supported.

In our future work, we will focus on developing a self-learning framework with reasoning capabilities, which will automate the process of choosing the fact as well as the rearranging of the dependency graph (as steps of the conceptual design algorithm). The framework could be particularly useful in cases when many different XML Schemas describing one domain have to be integrated. The ontology of the domain can be incrementally expanded each time a new XML Schema is joined.

References

1. Florescu, D., Kossmann, D.: Storing and Querying XML Data Using an RDBMS. *IEEE Data Engineering Bulletin, 22(3)*, 1999.
2. P. Bohannon, J. Freire, P. Roy, J. Simeon. From XML Schema to Relations: A Cost-Based Approach to XML Storage. In *Proc. of Int'l Conf. on Data Engineering (ICDE 2002)*, San Jose, USA, 2002.
3. Golfarelli, M., Rizzi, S., and Vrdoljak, B.: Data Warehouse Design from XML Sources. In: Proc. Int. Workshop on Data Warehousing and OLAP (DOLAP'01). ACM Press, New York (2001) 40-47
4. Vrdoljak, B., Banek, M., Rizzi, S.: Designing Web Warehouses from XML Schemas. In: Proc. Int. Conf. on Data Warehousing and Knowledge Discovery (DaWaK'03). Lecture Notes in Computer Science, Vol. 2737. Springer-Verlag, Berlin Heidelberg New York (2003) 89-98

5. Jensen, M.R., Møller, T.H., Pedersen T.B.: Converting XML Data to UML Diagrams for Conceptual Data Integration. In: Int. Workshop Data Integration over the Web (DIWeb'01). (2001) 17-31
6. Jensen, R.M., Møller, T.H., Pedersen T.B.: Specifying OLAP Cubes on XML Data. J. Intelligent Information Systems, Vol. 17 (2-3) (2001) 255-280
7. Pedersen, D., Riis, K., Pedersen, T.B.: XML Extended OLAP Querying. In: Proc. Int. Conf. on Scientific and Statistical Database Management (SSDBM'02), IEEE Computer Society Press. (2002) 195-206.
8. Li, Y., and An, A.: Representing UML Snowflake Diagram from Integrating XML Data Using XML Schema. In: Proc. Int. Workshop on Data Engineering Issues in E-Commerce (DEEC'05), IEEE Computer Society Press (2005) 103-111
9. Open Applications Group (OAG), "OAG Integration Specification (OAGIS), Release 7.2.1", http://www.openapplications.org/downloads/oagidownloads.htm
10. Park, B.-K., Han, H., and Song, I.-Y.: XML-OLAP: A Multidimensional Analysis Framework for XML Warehouses. Proc. Int. Conf. on Data Warehousing and Knowledge Discovery (DaWaK'05), Lecture Notes in Computer Science, Vol. 3589. Springer-Verlag, Berlin Heidelberg New York (2005) 32-42
11. Golfarelli, M., Maio, D., Rizzi, S.: Conceptual design of data warehouses from E/R schemes, In: Proc. Hawaii Int. Conf. on System Sciences (HICSS), Vol. VII (1998) 334-343
12. Golfarelli, M., Rizzi, S.: Designing the Data Warehouse: Key Steps and Crucial Issues. J. of Computer Science and Information Management, Vol. 2 (3) (1999) 1-14
13. Golfarelli, M., Maio, D., Rizzi, S.: The Dimensional Fact Model: a Conceptual Model for Data Warehouses. Int. J. of Cooperative Information Systems, Vol. 7 (2-3) (1998) 215-247
14. Shanmugasundaram, J., Tufte, K., Zhang, C., He, G., DeWitt, D.J., Naughton, J.F.: Relational Databases for Querying XML Documents: Limitations and Opportunities. In: Proc. Very Large Data Bases Conf. (VLDB'99). Morgan Kaufmann (1999) 302-314
15. Kimball, R., Ross, M.: The Data Warehouse Toolkit: The Complete Guide to Dimensional Modeling. John Wiley & Sons, New York, NY, USA (2002)
16. World Wide Web Consortium (W3C): XML Schema Part 0: Primer Second Edition (W3C Recommendation, as of 28 October 2004). http://www.w3.org/TR/2004/REC-xmlschema-0-20041028/
17. World Wide Web Consortium (W3C): XQuery 1.0: An XML Query Language (W3C Candidate Recommendation, as of 3 November 2005). http://www.w3.org/TR/2005/CR-xquery-20051103/

Remote-Specific XML Query Mobile Agents

Myung Sook Kim, Yong Hae Kong, and Chang Wan Jeon

Div. of Information Technology Engineering, Soonchunhyang University,
Asan-si, Choongnam-do, 336-745, Korea
{krhkms, yhkong, jeoncw}@sch.ac.kr

Abstract. An efficient XML query method is suggested for a distributed web environment. We develop an algorithm that promptly matches host's ontology and remote site's DTD. Then, a mobile agent system is constructed such that each agent maintains the recently matched ontology. For XML query, each agent generates remote-specific queries based on its matched ontology and returns the search results back to the host. The prompt match, remote-specific query, and autonomous mobile process can greatly reduce the search time and transmission overhead.

Keywords: XML Query, Mobile Agent, Ontology, Query Expansion.

1 Introduction

For fast query on XML web documents, we suggest a prompt ontology-DTD matching algorithm, a remote-specific XML query generation method, and a mobile agent search system. Since raw XML queries are limited in proper search of non-homogeneous documents, queries are often expanded based on ontology. This in turn makes queries to be superfluous. In order to make queries to be specific to remote documents, we develop an algorithm that matches host's ontology and remote site's DTD: [1],[2],[3]. Furthermore, the algorithm is improved to be more efficient than before, and we can promptly revise the matched ontology even though a DTD changes frequently.

Fig. 1 is the configuration of our mobile agent system and the left side of fig. 1 shows a detailed mobile agent. The mobile agent is said to be autonomous since it monitors its DTD, matches host's ontology and remote site's DTD if necessary, generates specific queries for each individual site, and sends back only the query results if any. XML information search efficiency can be improved by prompt ontology-DTD match, remote-specific query, and autonomous mobile query. We experiment the efficiency and effectiveness of this system with a set of sample XML documents.

2 Ontology and DTD Match

With raw XML queries, it is hard to search the underlying information of the documents since their structures are various. A simple query expansion with ontology will help, but superfluously generated queries will require lengthy search time: [4],[5]. Therefore, queries need to be specific to remote documents. Moreover, the

J. Lee et al. (Eds.): DEECS 2006, LNCS 4055, pp. 143–151, 2006.
© Springer-Verlag Berlin Heidelberg 2006

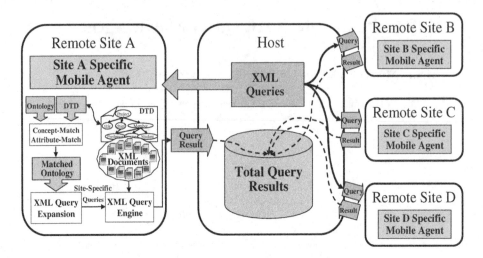

Fig. 1. Remote-Specific XML Query Mobile Agents

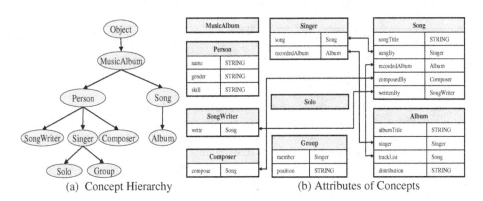

(a) Concept Hierarchy   (b) Attributes of Concepts

Fig. 2. "Music-Album" Ontology

match of host's ontology and remote site's DTD needs to be prompt because the matched ontology must reflect the current DTD. We use a sample "Music-Album" ontology in fig. 2 where its concept hierarchy is fig. 2(a) and the attributes of concept and their relations are fig. 2(b). An example DTD is fig. 3.

We first match ontology concepts and remote DTD elements. The ontology concepts that do not correspond to DTD elements are removed. Leaf concepts are removed while intermediate concepts are made inactive. Concept matching algorithm is summarized in table 1. Fig. 4 shows the concept-matched result, where the dim areas denote the inactive concepts.

A concept has its own attributes plus its ancestors, and attributes of a concept are inherited to its sub-concepts. Therefore, matching attributes needs to consider their inheritance characteristics. The concept-matched ontology is further attribute-matched to a remote DTD. The matched attributes are associated to the corresponding

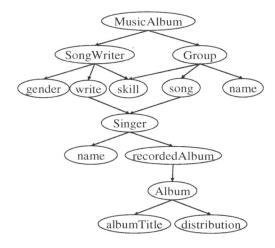

Fig. 3. A DTD Example

Table 1. Concept Match Algorithm

For all the ontology concepts,
1. Select a concept.
2. Compare the concept with elements of DTD. If the concept is not part of the DTD,
If the concept is a leaf concept,
Remove the concept and its attributes from ontology.
Otherwise, the concept is made inactive.

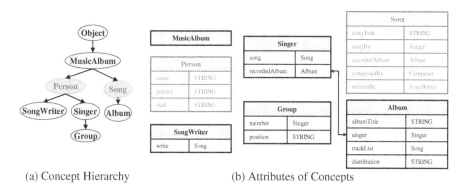

(a) Concept Hierarchy   (b) Attributes of Concepts

Fig. 4. Concept-Matched "Music-Album" Ontology

concepts, while those attributes that do not match are removed. Concept Singer has its own attributes, song and recordedAlbum, plus inherited attributes, name, gender and skill in fig. 4. But, DTD element Singer has only name and recordedAlbum in fig. 3. Therefore, removal of the unmatched attributes, skill, gender and song will prevent it from being inherited to its sub-concept Group and sibling concept SongWriter.

Attribute matching algorithm also needs to be efficient since matching all the possible attribute pairs between ontology and DTD is time-consuming: [3]. We figure out that the DTD elements that are not included in the concept-matched ontology must be the attributes of the ontology. This enables us to design an efficient algorithm of table 2. Using this algorithm, attribute matching can be accomplished by a single DTD Breadth First Search(BFS) as in fig. 5, without comparing every ontology attribute to every DTD element/attribute. The attributes that are not contained in the DTD are eliminated, while those attributes that are included in the DTD are associated with the corresponding concepts of the ontology. The attribute match result for fig. 4 is fig. 6.

Table 2. Attribute Matching Algorithm

For all the nodes in DTD, starting from the root node,
1. Select the next node in DTD by BFS.
2. If the selected node is included in concept-matched ontology, go to Step 1.
3. Otherwise(when the selected node is an attribute),
    3.1 Add all the parent nodes of the selected node to its attribute list.
    3.2 Go to Step 1.

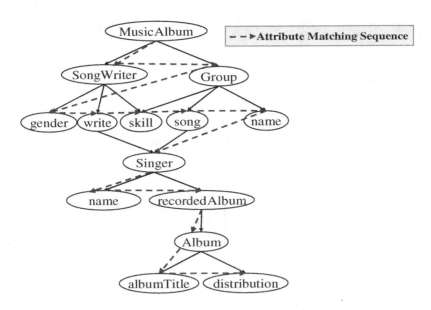

Fig. 5. Attribute Matching Sequence by DTD Breadth First Search

Attribute match further reduces the concept-matched ontology. Since the remaining attributes indicate the DTD dependency, the final ontology can produce proper queries specific to the documents having the DTD structure as in fig. 6(b).

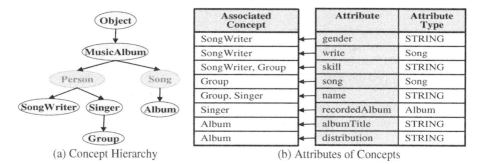

Associated Concept	Attribute	Attribute Type
SongWriter	gender	STRING
SongWriter	write	Song
SongWriter, Group	skill	STRING
Group	song	Song
Group, Singer	name	STRING
Singer	recordedAlbum	Album
Album	albumTitle	STRING
Album	distribution	STRING

(a) Concept Hierarchy   (b) Attributes of Concepts

Fig. 6. Attribute-Matched "Music-Album" Ontology

3   Remote-Specific XML Query Mobile Agents

We use the IBM aglet mobile agent and generate XMLHostAglet, an aglet instance, by executing Create command on the Tahiti menu as in fig. 7: [6],[7]. Then, XMLHostAglet dispatches XMLRemoteAglet, a mobile agent, by specifying a remote address as in fig. 8.

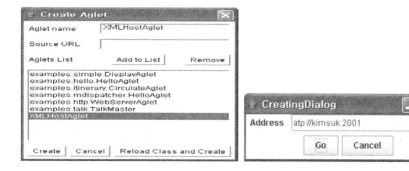

Fig. 7. Generation of Aglet Instance   **Fig. 8.** Dialog Box of XMLHostAglet

Having the matched ontology, we develop a query expansion module that considers conceptual inheritance and association. Those concepts that are associated by their attributes are inferred and stored as rules for query-expansion. In fig. 4, an association is established between concepts Singer and Album. This association generates the inference rule: Singer[recordsAlbum] <-> Album[singer]. The rule states that recordsAlbum of Singer and singer of Album is semantically identical. With the inferred rules, a query can be semantically expanded. For example, query //Singer[recordsAlbum] is expanded to concept Album and all its descendant concepts. As a result, a given query is expanded to all its sub-concepts together with the associated rules.

Fig. 9 is a diagram of XML information retrieval sequence of our mobile agent system. A mobile agent is dispatched to a remote site. It receives ontology, an ontology-DTD match module, a query expansion module, and a query engine module from a host. The remote agent is now ready to query its XML documents.

Whenever a host sends a query to the remote agent, the agent monitors its DTD status. If the DTD has been modified ever since the last match, the DTD is re-matched to the ontology and the newly matched ontology is maintained. This new one is used to generate remote-specific queries for the current documents. Finally, the query result, if any, is sent back to the host. This way of autonomous query mechanism minimizes useless queries as well as document transmission overhead.

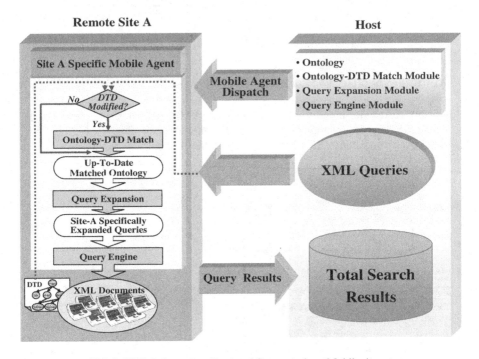

Fig. 9. XML Information Retrieval Sequence by a Mobile Agent

4   Experiments

We first experiment the effectiveness of ontology-DTD match with three remote DTDs, DTD1, DTD2 and DTD3 of fig. 10. Fig. 11 shows that each DTD yields noticeable differences among matched-ontology. These differences reflect the characteristics of the documents having individual DTDs and domain-specific queries can be generated accordingly.

Suppose that a host sends query //Person[name] to a remote site. The original query is expanded to queries, //Person[name] and //Singer[name] using the DTD1-matched ontology of the remote site. Fig. 12 shows that the two queries are applied to three XML documents there. The query results are no hit for //Person[name], two hits for //Singer[name]. Finally, the query results are sent back to the host as shown in fig. 13.

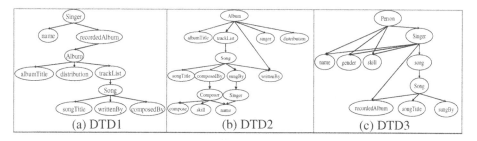

Fig. 10. Example DTDs

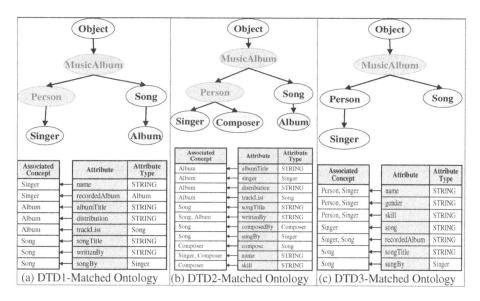

Fig. 11. Ontology-DTD Match

Fig. 12. Result of Remote Query //Person[name]   **Fig. 13.** Query Result Return to a Host

Table 3. Query Expansion Comparison between Original and Matched Ontology

Queries \ Documents	XML Document with DTD1 Structure		XML Document with DTD2 Structure		XML Document with DTD3 Structure	
	Original Ontology	DTD1-Matched Ontology	Original Ontology	DTD2-Matched Ontology	Original Ontology	DTD3-Matched Ontology
//Person[name]	//Person[name] //SongWriter[name] //Singer[name] //Composer[name] //Solo[name] //Group[name]	//Singer[name]	//Person[name] //SongWriter[name] //Singer[name] //Composer[name] //Solo[name] //Group[name]	//Singer[name] //Composer[name]	//Person[name] //SongWriter[name] //Singer[name] //Composer[name] //Solo[name] //Group[name]	//Person[name] //Singer[name]
//Song[recorded Album] *(Associated Rule, //Album[trackList] is used)*	//Song[recordedAlbum] //Album[recordedAlbum] //Album[trackList]	//Singer[recordedAlbum] //Album[trackList]	//Song[recordedAlbum] //Album[recordedAlbum] //Album[trackList]	//Album[trackList]	//Song[recordedAlbum] //Album[recordedAlbum] //Album[trackList]	//Singer[recordedAlbum] //Song[recordedAlbum]
//Composer[compose] *(Associated Rule, //Song[composedBy] is used)*	//Composer[compose] //Song[composedBy] //Album[composedBy]	//Song[composedBy]	//Composer[compose] //Song[composedBy] //Album[composedBy]	//Composer[compose] //Song[composedBy]	//Composer[compose] //Song[composedBy] //Album[composedBy]	No Query
//Song[sungBy] *(Associated Rule, //Singer[song] is used)*	//Song[sungBy] //Album[sungBy] //Singer[song] //Solo[song] //Group[song]	No Query	//Song[sungBy] //Album[sungBy] //Singer[song] //Solo[song] //Group[song]	//Song[sungBy] //Album[sungBy]	//Song[sungBy] //Album[sungBy] //Singer[song] //Solo[song] //Group[song]	//Song[sungBy] //Singer[song]

Table 4. Query Hit Comparison between Original and Matched Ontology

Queries \ DTD	Hit Ratio : No. of Queries Hit / No. of Queries Applied					
	XML Document with DTD1 Structure		XML Document with DTD2 Structure		XML Document with DTD3 Structure	
	Original Ontology	DTD1-Matched Ontology	Original Ontology	DTD2-Matched Ontology	Original Ontology	DTD3-Matched Ontology
//Person[name]	1/6	1/1	1/6	1/2	1/6	1/2
//Song[recordedAlbum]	1/3	2/2	1/3	1/1	1/3	1/2
//Composer[compose]	0/3	0/1	2/3	2/2	0/3	0/0
//Song[sungBy]	0/5	0/0	1/5	1/2	2/5	2/2
Accumulated Hit Ratio	2/17 (12%)	3/4 (75%)	5/17 (29%)	5/7 (71%)	4/17 (24%)	4/6 (67%)
Average Hit Ratio — Original Ontology	11/51 (22%)					
Average Hit Ratio — Matched Ontology	12/17 (71%)					

We then experiment the efficiency of remote-specific queries. Four queries are expanded by original ontology of fig. 2 and by matched ones of fig. 11. Query //Person[name] is expanded into 18 queries by original ontology, while the matched ontology generates only 5 queries as in the first row of table 3. Similarly, queries //Song[recordedAlbum], //Composer[compose], and //Song[sungBy] are expanded into 9, 9, and 15 queries by original ontology, compared to only 5, 3, and 4 queries respectively by the matched ontology as in the rest three rows of table 3. We then test the query hit between original and matched ontology with the XML documents having DTD1, DTD2, and DTD3 structures. As a result, the average hit ratio between the two is 22% and 71% as in table 4.

The first experiment show that ontology-DTD match results in noticeably different ontology, and these in turn generate remote-specific queries as shown in the second and third experiments. Moreover, a large amount of XML documents on many remote sites are not transmitted at all during the query process. Instead, very little amount of query results are sent back to the host.

5 Conclusions

For efficient web XML document search, we develop a prompt ontology-DTD match algorithm, a remote-specific XML query method, and an autonomous mobile search agent.

Since raw queries themselves are not sufficient to catch the underlying information in various documents and a simple ontology-based query expansion is not efficient due to superfluous query generation, we make queries to be specific to remote documents. We also make the matched ontology to be easily maintained with a single-scanning match algorithm. Therefore, a mobile agent can promptly handle the DTD change by monitoring and re-matching. This up-to-date ontology makes each agent to expand queries specifically fitted to its current documents. With these autonomous mobile agents, remote documents are searched efficiently and only a tiny amount of the query results are transmitted.

The efficiency of this system is tested with a set of sample XML documents. The proposed method properly matches host's ontology and remote site's DTD, generates specific queries to remote documents, and document transmission is minimized.

References

1. Papastavrou, S., Samaras, G., Pitoura, E.: Mobile Agents for World Wide Web Distributed Database Access. IEEE Trans Knowledge and Data Engineering, Vol. 12. No. 5. (2000) 802-820
2. Erdmann, M., Studer, R.: How to Structure and Access XML Document with Ontologies. Data & Knowledge Engineering, Vol. 36. No. 3. (2001) 317-335
3. Kim, M.S., Kong, Y. H.: Ontology-DTD Matching Algorithm for Efficient XML Query. The Second International Conference on Fuzzy Systems and Knowledge Discovery (2005) 1093 – 1102
4. Theobald, A.: An Ontology for Domain-oriented Semantic Similarity Search on XML Data. Datenbanksysteme für Business, Technologie und Web (BTW) (2003) 217-226
5. Erdmann, M., Decker, S.: Ontology-award XML queries. WebDB (2000)
6. Frabklin, S., Graesser, A.: Is it an Agent, or just a Program?: A Taxonomy for Autonomous Agents. Third International Workshop on Agent Theories, Architectures, and Languages, Springer-Verlag (1996)
7. Aglets. http://aglets.sourceforge.net/

A Process History Capture System for Analysis of Data Dependencies in Concurrent Process Execution

Yang Xiao[1], Susan D. Urban[1], and Suzanne W. Dietrich[2]

[1] Department of Computer Science and Engineering
Arizona State University
PO Box 878809 Tempe, AZ, 85287-8809 USA
[2] Department of Mathematical Sciences and Applied Computing,
Arizona State University
PO Box 37100, Phoenix, AZ, 85069-7100 USA
{yang.xiao, susan.urban, dietrich}@asu.edu

Abstract. This paper presents a Process History Capture System (PHCS) as a logging mechanism for distributed long running business processes executing over Delta-Enabled Grid Services (DEGS). A DEGS is a Grid Service with an enhanced interface to access incremental data changes, known as deltas, associated with service execution in the context of global processes. The PHCS captures process execution context and deltas from distributed DEGSs and constructs a global schedule for multiple executing processes, integrating local schedules that are extracted from deltas at distributed sites. The global schedule forms the basis for analyzing data dependencies among concurrently executing processes. The schedule can be used for rollback and also to identify data dependencies that affect the possible recovery of other concurrent processes. This paper presents the design of the PHCS and the use of the PHCS for process failure recovery. We also outline future directions for specification of user-defined semantic correctness.

1 Introduction

There is an increasing demand for integrating business services provided by different service vendors to achieve collaborative work in a distributed environment. With the adoption of Web Services and Grid Services [9], many of these collaborative activities are long-running processes based on loosely-coupled, multi-platform, service-based architectures [20]. These distributed processes pose new challenges for execution environments, especially for the semantic correctness of concurrent process execution. The concept of serializability is too strong of a correctness criterion for concurrent distributed processes since individual service invocations are autonomous and commit before the process completes. As a result, process execution does not ensure isolation of the data items accessed by individual services of the process, allowing dirty reads and dirty writes to occur. User-defined correctness of a process can be specified as in related work with advanced transaction models [6, 8] and transactional workflows [25], using concepts such as compensation to semantically undo a process. But even when one process determines that it needs to execute compensating procedures, the affect of the compensation on concurrently executing processes is

J. Lee et al. (Eds.): DEECS 2006, LNCS 4055, pp. 152–166, 2006.

difficult to determine since there is no knowledge of data dependencies among concurrently executing processes. Data dependencies are needed to determine how the data changes caused by the recovery of one process can possibly affect other processes that have read or written data modified by the failed process.

This research is investigating a process history capture system that records the execution history of distributed processes that execute over Grid Services. The research is being conducted in the context of the DeltaGrid project, which is focusing on the development of a semantically-robust execution environment for the composition of Grid Services. Distributed services in the DeltaGrid environment are extended with the capability of recording incremental data changes, known as *deltas*. These services are referred to as *Delta-Enabled Grid Services (DEGS)* [5]. The deltas generated by DEGS are forwarded to a process history capture system that organizes deltas from distributed sources into a time-sequenced schedule of data changes. Deltas can then be used to undo the effect of a service execution. This undo process is referred to as *Delta-Enabled rollback (DE-rollback)*. Deltas can also be used to analyze data dependencies among concurrently executing processes to determine how the failure and recovery of one process can potentially affect other data-dependent processes. We refer to this situation as *process interference* and are investigating how user-defined process interference rules can be used to specify how a read or write dependent process reacts to data changes caused by the failure recovery of a process on which it depends.

The focus of this paper is on the design of the process history capture system, with an illustration of how deltas are organized into a schedule that can be analyzed to reveal data dependencies. The unique aspect of the process execution history capture system is that it provides a basis for analyzing the effects that failure or recovery techniques for one process may have on other concurrently executing processes. The analysis of the process history can be used to support the recovery process at run-time or to support the testing of distributed processes, providing a means to evaluate recovery plans, or to discover the need for the specification of recovery techniques under different circumstances.

The rest of this paper is organized as follows. After outlining related work in Section 2, the paper provides an overview of the DeltaGrid system in Section 3, including the system architecture and the design of Delta-Enabled Grid Services. The design of the process history capture system is presented in Section 4, with a focus on the indexing structure for constructing the time-ordered sequence of deltas. Section 5 then illustrates how the delta schedule can be used to support rollback and analysis of dependencies, with scenarios provided from an online shopping application. The paper concludes in Section 6 with a summary and discussion of future research.

2 Related Work

Research projects in the transactional workflow area have adopted compensation as a backward recovery technique [7, 12, 23] and explored the handling of data dependencies among workflows [12, 23]. The ConTract model [23] considers the data changes caused by a workflow execution or compensation on other workflows by specifying pre- and post- condition for a step in a workflow. Exception handling is integrated with the normal flow of control, making it difficult to determine if a data change is caused by an exception handling action or the normal workflow execution. METEOR [24] handles pre-defined exceptions in a Java try-catch fashion within workflow specification. METEOR uses a hierarchical error model based on which errors can be handled at the task level, the task manager level, or the workflow engine level. In CREW [12], a static specification must be given about which data item in one workflow is equivalent to a data item in another workflow to track the dependencies among workflows. The research in transactional workflows has explored application exception handling using an embedded approach. However there is no a satisfactory solution to track process dependencies and a flexible handling mechanism separated from normal workflow control flow for the effect of failure recovery. Our research provides a logging mechanism for distributed processes execution based on which process dependencies are analyzed to support the evaluation and handling of impact of a failure recovery activity using active rules.

Exception handling in current service composition environments has been addressed through the specification of transaction semantics and through the use of rules. Transactional Attitudes (TA) [16] supports the open nested transaction over Web Services. TA provides interfaces where a service provider declares a service's transaction capabilities, and clients express transaction requirement. Services satisfying a client's requirements can form a transaction with required semantics. WS-Transactions [1] supports processes composed of Web Services as either Atomic Transactions with ACID properties or Business Activities with compensation capabilities. Web Service Composition Action (WSCA) [21] supports contingency as a forward recovery mechanism of a composite service. Rule-based approaches are also used to handle service exceptions independent of application logic, such as service availability, selection, and enactment [18, 26]. The work in [14] has experimented with providing forward recovery for a process by searching for substitute services when an application exception occurs. How to flexibly specify the handling of application exceptions and the impact of failure on other processes has not been addressed in a service composition environment. Our research is among the first to address process interference caused by backward recovery of a failed process in a service composition environment. Specifically, our research records execution history of concurrently executing processes over distributed services. The process execution history forms the basis to analyze process dependency and handle the process interference.

3   Overview of the DeltaGrid System

Before describing the manner in which the process history capture system is used to support recovery in the DeltaGrid environment, this section introduces the architectural components of the DeltaGrid system. Section 3.1 outlines the design of Delta-Enabled Grid Services as the building blocks of the DeltaGrid environment. Section 3.2 presents an abstract view of the Grid Process Modeling Language for the specification of processes. Section 3.3 then presents the architecture of the DeltaGrid system.

3.1 Delta-Enabled Grid Services (DEGS)

A DEGS is a Grid Service that has been enhanced with an interface that provides access to the incremental data changes, known as *deltas*, which are associated with service execution in the context of globally executing processes. Deltas can support DE-rollback as a backward recovery mechanism for an operation and also provide the basis for discovering data dependencies among processes.

The design of DEGS is based on our past research with capturing object deltas [19] in an object-oriented database and defining delta abstractions for the incremental, run-time debugging of active rule execution [4, 5, 22]. Whereas object deltas capture incremental state changes, delta abstractions define views over the object deltas, providing different granularity levels for examining the state changes that have occurred during the execution of active rules and update transactions.

Fig. 1 presents the architecture of the delta capture and storage subsystem of DEGS. A client application invokes operations on a DEGS. A delta event processor receives deltas back from the DEGS, which are used by the process history capture system to maintain a global log of data dependencies.

A DEGS uses an OGSA-DAI Grid Data Service [11] for database interaction. The database captures deltas using capabilities provided by most commercial database systems. Our own implementation has experimented with the use of triggers as a delta capture mechanism, as well as the Oracle Streams capability [17]. Oracle Streams is a feature that monitors database redo logs for changes and publishes these changes to a queue to be used for replication or data sharing. Deltas captured over the source database are stored in a delta repository. Deltas can also be sent to the DeltaGrid event processor after the completion of an operation execution by push mode, or be requested by the DeltaGrid system by pull mode.

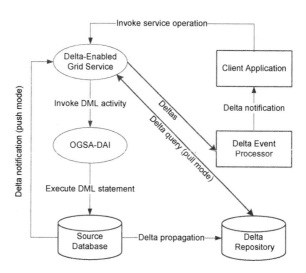

Fig. 1. Delta Capture and Storage Subsystem Architecture [5]

The DEGS uses the object delta concept [19] to create a conceptual view of relational deltas. As shown in Fig. 2, each tuple of a relation can be associated with an instance of a DeltaObject. A DeltaObject has a className indicating the name of a class (i.e., relation) that the associated object belongs to, and an objectId (i.e., primary key) to uniquely identify the associated object instance. A DeltaObject can have multiple DeltaProperty objects, which correspond to the attributes of a relation. Each DeltaProperty object has a PropertyName, and one or more PropertyValues (i.e., delta values). Each PropertyValue contains the actual delta value and is associated with a DataChange object. The DataChange object has a processId and an operationId indicating the global process and operation that has created the PropertyValue, with a timestamp to record the actual time of change. Deltas are extracted from the delta repository and communicated to the delta event processor in an XML format that captures the object structure shown in Fig. 2 [5].

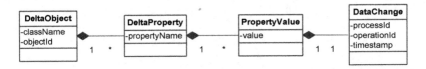

Fig. 2. The Delta Structure in DEGS

3.2 The Grid Process Modeling Language (GridPML)

A process modeling language for the composition of Grid Services, known as the GridPML [15], has been designed to define a process in the DeltaGrid system. The GridPML is an XML-based language that supports basic control flow constructs adopted from Web Service composition languages such as BPEL [3] and BPML [2] with features for invoking Grid Services. Instead of competing with languages such as BPEL, the GridPML is primarily used as a flexible implementation environment to experiment with process execution history capture in the context of our failure recovery work.

Fig. 3 presents an abstract view of a process defined using the GridPML with semantics similar to sagas [10]. The advanced features of the GridPML, such as supporting composite nested groups of service invocations [13], are not shown in this paper for the purpose of simplicity. As shown in Fig. 3, a process (p_i) contains multiple operations (op_{ij}) representing service invocations, where each operation can have an optional compensation activity (cop_{ij}). A compensation activity is used to semantically undo the effect of an operation. A process completes after the successful execution of each operation. As in the saga model [10], a process can be semantically undone by executing the compensation activity for each operation defined in the original control flow in reverse execution order. With DE-rollback supported as a backward recovery mechanism in the DeltaGrid, a process can also be semantically undone by executing DE-rollback on each executed operation as long as proper data dependency conditions are satisfied. The applicability of DE-rollback is discussed in more detail in Section 5.

process p$_i$

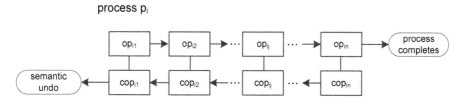

Fig. 3. An Abstract View of GridPML-defined Process

3.3 Architecture of the DeltaGrid System

Fig. 4 presents the architecture of the DeltaGrid system, providing a vision for the DeltaGrid approach to process failure recovery. As a messaging hub, the DeltaGrid event processor receives different types of events and dispatches them to appropriate handlers. Currently three types of events are considered: deltas events, system failure recovery events, and application exception events. Delta events are notifications about the arrival of deltas from DEGS. System recovery events are events that are associated with process failures as well as backward recovery actions such as compensation and DE-rollback. Application exceptions are events that are related to process execution but are outside of the normal flow of execution (i.e., a client cancels an order while the order is in progress).

The processor execution engine parses process scripts, invokes operations on DEGSs, and records process execution context into the process history capture system. The metadata manager stores process and rule metadata. The process metadata contains process schema and scripts described using the GridPML. The rule metadata stores active rules that will be used to handle application exceptions and process failure recovery interference based on user-defined correctness conditions. The rule processor evaluates rule conditions and invokes rule actions.

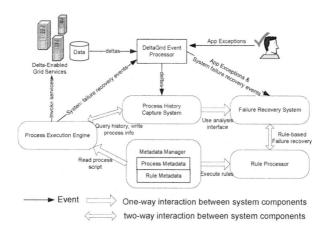

Fig. 4. The DeltaGrid Architecture

The Process History Capture System (PHCS) logs distributed process execution, integrating deltas from DEGSs and process execution context from the execution engine. More importantly, the PHCS provides analysis interfaces to determine data dependencies and evaluate process interference. The failure recovery system generates recovery scripts to resolve application exceptions and associated failure recovery interference. The failure recovery system uses the analysis interfaces provided by the PHCS to generate commands for backward recovery of a failed process and to evaluate if read or write dependent processes need to be recovered based on process interference rules.

We have implemented DEGS, the process execution engine, and the process history capture system. The design and implementation of other system components are in progress. The remainder of this paper describes the PHCS and illustrates the manner in which it is being used in our research to analyze data dependencies.

4   The Process History Capture System (PHCS) Design

This section presents the design of the PHCS. Section 4.1 describes the internal organization of the PHCS. Section 4.2 elaborates on the global delta object schedule that is created to support the analysis of data dependencies for concurrently executing processes.

4.1 Architecture of the PHCS

The PHCS is composed of three layers: the data storage layer, the data access layer, and the service layer, as shown in Fig. 5. The data storage layer stores process execution history, which includes a delta repository and a process runtime information repository. The delta repository stores deltas collected from distributed sites as Java objects organized according to the delta object model presented in Fig. 2. Additional site information is captured to indicate the source site for deltas. The process runtime information repository traces process execution context, such as the identifier, start time, end time, and execution status for each process and operation, input and output variables, and events that are associated with an operation invocation, with details described in [13, 15]. The data storage layer also contains a *global delta object schedule,* which orders DataChange objects from multiple DEGSs according to the time sequence in which they have occurred. Since DataChange objects relate global process execution activities with the delta values that they generate, the global delta object schedule serves as a logging mechanism that reveals write dependencies among processes.

The data access layer provides three components: the deltaAccess interface to read from and write to the delta repository, the processInfoAccess interface to access the process runtime information repository, and the globalScheduleAccess interface for creation and access of the global delta object schedule. The GridPML execution engine updates the process runtime information repository through the processInfoAccess interface.

The service layer receives and parses deltas sent through XML files, and provides the execution history query interface and data dependency analysis interface to other

DeltaGrid system components, such as the failure recovery system and the rule processor. The process history analyzer provides three different capabilities: 1) an execution context interface to access process runtime information, 2) a delta retrieval interface to get deltas, and 3) an analysis interface to derive data dependencies among processes and to determine the applicability of DE-rollback for a process.

Since the global delta object schedule is the primary focus of this paper, the following subsection elaborates on the internal structure of the schedule.

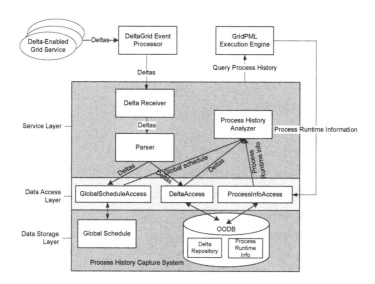

Fig. 5. The PHCS Architecture

4.2 Global Delta Object Schedule

The global delta object schedule forms a time-sequenced log of the delta objects that have been generated by concurrently executing processes. The global schedule is used to discover write dependencies, which can be further used to determine if DE-rollback is applicable as a backward recovery mechanism for a failed process, or if compensation must be invoked. More importantly, it assists in the evaluation of process failure recovery interference and serves as a monitoring mechanism for user-defined correctness.

Fig. 2 illustrates that each DataChange object associated with a delta contains a timestamp, which forms a local schedule for each DeltaProperty. When deltas are received by the PHCS, the DataChange objects provide the basis for ordering deltas. DataChange objects also serve as a link to the delta values stored in the delta repository. To assist online process failure recovery, the global schedule is built as an in-memory data structure that orders DataChange by timestamp, with a two-level index accelerating delta access through process and operation identifiers.

Fig. 6 presents a conceptual view of the global schedule and its relationship to the persistent delta repository and process runtime information repository. A global schedule contains a list of Nodes ordered by timestamp from all the active processes.

Each Node contains a className, objectId, and a propertyName, representing the data modified by a specific operation as identified by a processId and an operationId.

A time-sequence index is built to retrieve a Node through given process and operation identifiers. The index establishes a one-to-one mapping between a Node and a process-operation pair that has made the modification represented by the Node. An entry of the time-sequence index contains a processId, an operationId, and a timestamp. A time-sequence index entry also contains a sequence number (seqNum) to internally differentiate multiple objects with the same timestamp value. The Node and TimeSequenceIndex together serve as a link to the delta repository. Node can be used to access DeltaObject and DeltaProperty instances in the delta repository. The TimeSequenceIndex points to a specific DataChange object. Thus, a Node and TimeSequenceIndex can be used together to access a specific delta value.

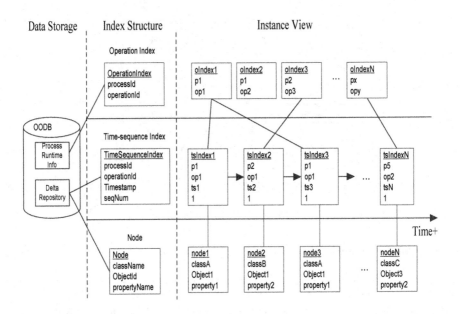

Fig. 6. A Conceptual View of the Global Schedule

When a process fails, the DeltaGrid system queries the global schedule about the processes having write dependencies on the failed process without knowing the details of the timestamp and internal sequence number. To answer this query, an operation index is built on the top of the time-sequence index. An entry of the operation index contains a processId and an operationId. From an operation index entry, all the time-sequence index entries of the same processId and operationId can be retrieved, finding all of the objects that have been modified by this given operation identified by the process-operation pair, and all the interleaved modifications made by other processes during the execution timeframe of the given operation. If only a processId is given, the PHCS can query the process runtime information repository to find all the operations that belong to this specific process. Then the process-operation pair can be used to retrieve information from the global schedule.

5 Use of PHCS

This section illustrates how the PHCS is used to analyze data dependencies. Section 5.1 defines terminology and semantic conditions for the use of DE-rollback. Section 5.2 elaborates on writes dependency scenarios, while Section 5.3 addresses read dependency scenarios.

5.1 Terminology and DE-Rollback Conditions

In a service composition environment, the act of semantically undoing the effect of completed operations within a process is referred to as *backward recovery*. The data changes introduced by backward recovery of a failed process p_f *potentially* cause a read dependent process p_r or a write dependent process p_w, to be recovered accordingly. This situation is called *process failure recovery interference*. Under certain semantic conditions, however, processes such as p_r and p_w may be able to continue running. In the DeltaGrid, we are investigating the use of process interference rules that allow users to flexibly specify how to handle p_r and p_w.

DE-rollback can be used as a backward recovery mechanism under appropriate semantic conditions based on read and write dependencies among concurrently executing processes. In a process execution environment, a *read dependency* exists if a process p_i, reads a data item x that has been written by another process p_j before p_j completes ($i \neq j$). In this case, p_i is *read dependent* on p_j with respect to x. A *write dependency* exists if a process p_i, writes a data item x that has been written by another process p_j before p_j completes ($i \neq j$). In this case, p_i is write dependent on p_j with respect to x. To address the applicability of DE-rollback, write dependency must be refined at the operation level.

An *operation-level write dependency* exists if an operation op_{ik} of process p_i writes data that has been written by another operation op_{jl} of process p_j ($i \neq j$). At the operation level, op_{ik} is write dependent on op_{jl}, thus op_{ik} is write dependent on p_j. At the process level, p_i is write dependent on p_j. When op_{ik} and op_{jl} belong to the same process ($i = j$), op_{ik} is still write dependent on op_{jl}. So operation-level write dependency might exist between two operations within the same process.

DE-rollback can be applied at either the operation level or process level. DE-rollback of an operation op_{ik} is the process of undoing the effect of op_{ik} by reversing the data values that have been modified by op_{ik} to their before images. Since a process is hierarchically composed of operations, DE-rollback of a process p_i, or *full DE-rollback* of p_i, involves the invocation of DE-rollback for every operation in p_i in reverse execution order. A *partial DE-rollback* of a process p_i can be performed if the semantic condition for a full DE-rollback of a process is not satisfied. A partial DE-rollback of a process involves the invocation of DE-rollback for those operations where DE-rollback conditions are satisfied, and compensation for other operations where DE-rollback conditions are not satisfied.

The application of DE-rollback as a backward recovery mechanism must conform to the following semantic conditions:

1) DE-rollback can be performed on an operation op_{ik}, denoted as dop_{ik}, when op_{ik} has no write dependent operations. If op_{ik} is write dependent on another operation within the same process op_{il} (k < l), DE-rollback can be performed on op_{ik} if DE-rollback will be performed on op_{il}. Otherwise compensation should be invoked.

1) A full DE-rollback can be performed on a process only when DE-rollback can be performed on every operation in reverse execution order.

2) If the condition in 2) does not hold, a partial DE-rollback can be performed on a process by invoking DE-rollback of the operations without write dependent operations, and compensation of other operations with write dependent operations. Suppose a process p_i has n executed operations as an ordered list, denoted as p_i = $[op_{i1}, op_{i2}, \dots, op_{in}]$. This list can be divided into two sets: a *DE-rollback set* denoted as DERBS = $\{op_{ik}\}$ (1<= k <= n) where op_{ik} has no write dependent operations from other processes, and a *compensation set* denoted as COMPS = $\{op_{ij}\}$ (1<= j <= n & j $\neq$ k) where op_{ij} has write dependent operations from other processes. Partial rollback of p_i invokes DE-rollback or compensation on each executed operation of p_i in reverse order of the original execution list, depending on which set an operation belongs to. If an operation is in the DE-rollback set, then DE-rollback will be performed. Otherwise compensation will be performed. Partial DE-rollback also requires that the compensation of an operation which appears later in the original execution list should not affect DE-rollback of an operation that appears earlier in the list. Suppose a process has two operations op_{ik} and op_{ij} (1 <= k < j <= n), op_{ij} requests compensation (cop_{ij}) and op_{ik} requests DE-rollback (dop_{ik}). If cop_{ij} modifies data written by op_{ik}, execution of dop_{ik} will erase the change made by cop_{ij}. So partial DE-rollback of p_i requires cop_{ij} does not modify data that have been written by op_{ik}. Otherwise compensation instead of DE-rollback should be invoked for the earlier operation op_{ik}.

3) After backward recovery (either DE-rollback or compensation), read and write dependent processes should be evaluated for possible recovery actions.

5.2 Write Dependencies

When a process p fails, the DeltaGrid system needs to determine the following information: 1) does p have any write dependent processes, and 2) can DE-rollback be fully or partially applied to p. From the global schedule, a *write dependency table* can be constructed to determine the applicability of DE-rollback on a process. A write dependency table reveals operation level write dependency on a failed process.

Fig. 7 gives a simplified view of a global schedule containing three concurrently executing processes p_1, p_2 and p_3. Each entry has a timestamp (t_x, x = 1, 2, ...), a processId (p_i, i = 1, 2, 3), an operationId (op_{ij}, j = 1, 2, ...), and an objectId (A,B,...) identifying a modified object.

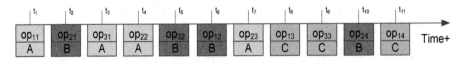

Fig. 7. A Sample Global Delta Object Schedule with Write Dependency on p_i

Suppose process p_1 fails due to execution failure of op_{14}. Table 1 is the write dependency table constructed from the global delta object schedule presented in Fig 7. We can derive the following information from Table 1:

1) p_1 has two write dependent processes: p_2 and p_3.
2) A partial DE-rollback can be performed on p_1. The DE-rollback set of p_1 is $\{op_{14}\}$. The compensation set of p_1 is $\{op_{13}, op_{12}, op_{11}\}$.
3) The backward recovery of p_1 involves the DE-rollback of op_{14} and the compensation of $op_{13}, op_{12},$ and op_{11}, denoted as a list of failure recovery activities $[dop_{14}, cop_{13}, cop_{12}, cop_{11}]$.

Table 1. Write Dependency Table for p_1

p_1 operations	Objects modified	Dependent operations	Dependent process
op_{14}	C	None	None
op_{13}	C	op_{33}, op_{14}	p_3
op_{12}	B	op_{24}	P_2
op_{11}	A	$op_{31}, op_{22}, op_{23}$	p_2, p_3

If backward recovery of p_1 causes its write dependent processes p_2 and p_3 to be backward recovered, then a write dependency table for p_2 and p_3 should also be constructed. Backward recovery of a process might cause cascading backward recovery of write dependent processes. We are investigating the development of process interference rules to minimize the recovery of processes according to application logic.

Scenario: Consider an online shopping application with processes that execute over Delta-Enabled Grid services. The process placeClientOrder is responsible for invoking services that place client orders, decrease the inventory quantity, and possibly increase a backorder quantity. The process returnClientOrder is responsible for processing client returns, and invoking services that increase the inventory quantity and possibly decrease the backorder quantity. The process replenishInventory invokes services that increase the inventory quantity when vendor orders are received and possibly decrease the backorder quantity. Furthermore, several instances of each process could be running at the same time. If anyone of these processes fail while an operation is updating the inventory quantity, DE-rollback could be used to restore the inventory value for the failed operation as well as any other completed operations of the process as long as there are no write dependent operations from other processes. If write dependencies exist, the failed process can only be restored through compensation. Furthermore, write dependent processes must be identified and *may or may not* need to be compensated. The need to perform a compensating action depends on the semantics of the situation. For example, failure of a replenishInventory process could cause a write dependent placeClientOrder process to be compensated (since the items ordered may not actually be available). However, failure and compensation of a placeClientOrder process would not affect a write dependent replenishInventory or returnClientOrder process. User-defined process interference rules are needed to define how to respond to such conditions.

5.3 Read Dependencies

The failure of a process can also affect read dependent processes. The delta repository, however, does not capture read activity from DEGS. In this case, the process runtime information component of the PHCS can be queried to identify the active processes that overlap with the execution of failed processes since the runtime information contains the start time of each process. These processes represent *potential* conflicts, but there is no explicit statement of data items that have been read. Techniques are needed to express user-defined process interference rules that define whether or not a process can continue execution or invoke compensating procedures.

Scenario: In the online shopping application, there is a placeVendorOrder process that places orders for inventory items that are below a certain threshold. Suppose the placeVendorOrder process is read dependent on a placeClientOrder process (placeVendorOrder reads the inventory quantity after placeClientOrder writes the inventory quantity). If placeClientOrder fails, placeVendorOrder will be identified as a concurrently executing process. A process interference rule could be expressed to define the conditions under which placeVendorOrder is restarted. If the quantity of the failed placeClientOrder processes is small or if there is no intersection between the items on the vendor order and the client order, then there may be no need to redo placeVendorOrder. If the quantity of the failed placeClientOrder is large, then placeVendorOrder may need to be restarted to avoid overstocking any items that the two processes may have in common. The next phase of our work is addressing how to express such process interference rules, which may require querying the delta repository.

6 Summary and Future Directions

This paper has presented the design of a process history capture system as a logging mechanism for distributed processes that are executed over Delta-Enabled Grid Services. We have implemented the PHCS to support rollback of a failed process and evaluation of process failure recovery interferences. This research contributes towards building a robust execution environment for distributed processes executing over autonomous, heterogeneous resources. A unique aspect of this research is the provision of a complete process execution history based on deltas for analyzing data dependencies among concurrently executing processes. The dependency information is not only used for failure recovery of a failed process, but also to evaluate the impact on other processes.

Our future research directions include formalization of the DeltaGrid system using an abstract process execution model, providing a theoretical foundation for building a semantically correct service composition environment. The abstract model will formally define process execution semantics, and present process failure recovery interference rule specification as the basis for user-defined correctness.

References

1. *Specification: Web Services Transaction (WS-Transaction).* (2002)   Available from: http://www-106.ibm.com/developerworks/webservices/library/ws-transpec/.
2. *Business Process Modeling Language.* (2002)   Available from: http://www.bpmi.org/specifications.esp.
3. *Specification: Business Process Execution Language for Web Services Version 1.1.* (2003)   Available from: http://www-106.ibm.com/developerworks/webservices/ library/ws-bpel/.
4. Ben Abdellatif, T.: *An Architecture for Active Database Systems Supporting Static and Dynamic Analysis of Active Rules Through Evolving Database States*,Ph.D dissertation (1999). Arizona State Univ. *Dept. of Comp. Sci. and Eng.*
5. Blake, L.: *Design and Implementation of Delta-Enabled Grid Services*,M.S. thesis (2005). Arizona State Univ. *Dept. of Comp. Sci. and Eng.*
6. de By, R., Klas, W., Veijalainen, J. , *Transaction Management Support for Cooperative Applications.* (1998): Kluwer Academic Publishers.
7. Eder, J., Liebhart, W.: *The workflow activity model WAMO*, in:*the 3rd international conference on Cooperative Information Systems (CoopIs).* (1995).
8. Elmagarmid, A., *Database Transaction Models for Advanced Applications.* (1992): Morgan Kaufmann.
9. Foster, I., *The Anatomy of the Grid: Enabling Scalable Virtual Organizations*, Int. Journal of Supercomputer Applications, (2001).
10. Garcia-Molina, H., Salem, K. : *Sagas*, in:*ACM International Conference on Management of Data (SIGMOD).* (1987). pp.249-259.
11. IBM, University of Edinburgh. *OGSA-DAI WSRF 2.1 User Guide.* (2005)   Available from: http://www.ogsadai.org.uk/docs/WSRF2.1/doc/index.html.
12. Kamath, M., Ramamritham, K.: *Failure Handling and Coordinated Execution of Concurrent Workflows*, in:*IEEE International Conference on Data Engineering.* (1998). pp.334-341.
13. Liao, N.: *The Extened GridPML Design and Implementation*,M.S. report (2005). Arizona State Univ. *Dept. of Comp. Sci. and Eng.*
14. Lin, F., Chang, H.: *B2B e-commerce and enterprise integration: The development and evaluation of exception handling mechanisms for order fulfillment process based on BPEL4WS*, in:*the 7th IEEE International Conference on Electronic commerce.* (2005). pp.478-484.
15. Ma, H., Urban, S. D., Xiao, Y., and Dietrich, S. W.: *GridPML: A Process Modeling Language and Process History Capture System for Grid Service Composition*, in:*ICEBE.* (2005). pp.433-440.
16. Mikalsen, T., Tai, S., Rouvellou, I.: *Transactional Attitudes: Reliable Composition of Autonomous Web Services*, in:*Workshop on Dependable Middleware-based Systems (WDMS 2002), part of the International Conference on Dependable Systems and Networks (DSN 2002).* (2002).
17. Oracle. *Oracle9i Streams Release 2 (9.2).* (2005)   Available from: http://download-west.oracle.com/docs/cd/B10501_01/server.920/a96571/toc.htm.
18. Shi, Y., Zhang, L., Shi. B.: *Exception handling of workflow for Web services*, in:*4th International Conference on Computer and Information Technology.* (2004). pp.273-277.
19. Sundermeir, A., Ben Abdellatif, T., Dietrich, S. W., Urban, S. D.: *Object Deltas in an Active Database Development Environment*, in:*the Deductive,Object-Oriented Database Workshop.* (1997). pp.211-229.

20. Tan, Y. *Business Service Grid: Manage Web Services and Grid Services with Service Domain technology*. (2003) Available from: http://www-128.ibm.com/developerworks/ibm/library/gr-servicegrid/.
21. Tartanoglu, F., Issarny, V., Romanovsky, A., Levy, N.: *Dependability in the Web Services Architecture*, in:*Architecting Dependable Systems, LNCS 2677*. (2003).
22. Urban, S.D., Ben Abdellatif T., Dietrich, S. W., Sundermier, A., *Delta Abstractions: A Technique for Managing Database States in Active Rule Processing*, IEEE Trans. on Knowledge and Data Eng., (2003): pp. 597-612.
23. Wachter, H., Reuter, A., *The ConTract Model*, in: *Database Transaction Models for Advanced Applications*, A. Elmagarmid, Editor. (1992). pp. 219-263.
24. Worah, D.: *Error Handling and Recovery for the ORBWork Workflow Enactment Service in METEOR*,M.S. report (1997). University of Georgia. *Computer Science Dept.*
25. Worah, D., Sheth, A., *Transactions in Transactional Workflows*, in: *Advanced Transaction Models and Architectures*, S. Jajodia, and Kershberg,L., Editor, Springer. pp. 3-34.
26. Zeng, L., Lei, H., Jeng, J., Chung, J., Benatallah, B.: *Policy-driven exception-management for composite Web services*, in:*7th IEEE International Conference on E-Commerce Technology*. (2005). pp.355-363.

Business Impact Analysis Using Time Correlations

Mehmet Sayal

Hewlett-Packard Labs, 1501 Page Mill Road
Palo Alto, CA 94043, USA
mehmet.sayal@hp.com

Abstract. A novel method for analyzing time-series data and extracting time-correlations (time-dependent relationships) among multiple time-series data streams is described. The application of time-correlation detection in business impact analysis (BIA) is explained on an example. The method described in this paper is the first one that can efficiently detect and report time-dependent relationships among multiple time-series data streams. Detected time-correlation rules explain how the changes in the values of one set of time-series data streams influence the values in another set of time-series data streams. Those rules can be stored digitally and fed into various data analysis tools, such as simulation, forecasting, impact analysis, etc., for further analysis of the data. Performance experiments showed that the described method is 95% accurate, and has a linear running time with respect to the amount of input data.

1 Introduction

This paper presents a novel method for analyzing time-series data and extracting time-correlations (time-dependent relationships) among multiple time-series data streams. The introduced method is the first one that can efficiently detect and report time-dependent relationships among multiple time-series data streams, to the best of authors' knowledge. The application of the time-correlation detection method in business impact analysis (BIA) is explained on an example. The proposed method is simpler compared to most comparative time-series analysis approaches (especially compared to similarity search methods), but it is significantly fast and generic enough to be used in many different domains in order to analyze and compare the changes in numeric variables. For example, the stock prices, sales quantities and prices of products, health status of patients who are under similar treatments, cost and profit metrics, etc., can be analyzed and compared using the described method.

A *time-series* is formally defined as a sequence of values that are recorded either at equal time intervals or at random points in time by also recording the time of measurement or recording. The method described in this paper uses the second definition in order to provide more generic algorithms that can be applied to both cases.

Time-correlations are time-dependent relationships among two or more time-series data streams such that changes in the values of one set of time-series data streams are related to the changes in the values of another set of time-series data streams. An example time-correlation may indicate a time-dependent relationship such as:

J. Lee et al. (Eds.): DEECS 2006, LNCS 4055, pp. 167–181, 2006.

A change in Response time of Database will be followed by a change with 3 times the magnitude in opposite direction in Number of Client Complaints after 30 minutes time delay.

The rest of this paper is organized as follows. Section 2 describes the time-correlation detection method. An example scenario for using the described time-correlation detection method in business impact analysis (BIA) is given in section 3. Performance evaluation is explained in Section 4. Section 5 summarizes related work in time-series analysis and mining. Finally, Section 6 contains the concluding remarks.

2 Time Correlation Detection

2.1 Summary of the Method

The method for detecting time-correlations from time-series data streams consists of the following steps, as shown in Figure 1:

- o Summarizing the data at different time granularities (e.g., seconds, minutes, hours, days, weeks, months, years)
- o Detecting change points (points at which significant changes in data values or their trends are recognized) using CUSUM (Cumulative Sum) statistical method [13] in order to convert continuous data streams into discrete data streams and reduce the search space
- o Generating time-correlation rules
  - ▪ Merging multiple time-series data to generate *Merged Time-Series Data* (note that because merged time-series data has the same data structure as regular time-series data, the term "Time-Series" will be used to refer to both regular and merged time-series data in the rest of this paper)
  - ▪ Comparing time-series data to generate time correlation rules

The input of the method is any collection of numeric data streams that are time-stamped (i.e., time-series data streams). The input data can be read from one or more database tables, XML documents, flat text files with character delimited data fields, or directly from data streams. The output is a set of time correlation rules that describe the time-dependent relationships among numeric data fields. Each time-correlation rule includes information about:

- o **Direction:** "Same" if the changes in the values of one time-series are correlated to changes in the same direction for another time-series. "Opposite" if the change direction is opposite.
- o **Sensitivity:** The magnitude and slope of changes in data values of each time-series are recorded and compared in order to measure how sensitive one time-series is to the changes in another time-series.
- o **Time Delay:** The time delay for correlated time-series data streams are recorded in order to explain how much time delay exists between related (matching) changes in the values of two or more correlated time-series data streams.

○ **Confidence:** Confidence provides an indication of how certain we are about detected time-correlations among time-series data streams. Confidence is measured as a value between zero and one. A confidence value that is close to one indicates high certainty. Similarly, a confidence value that is close to zero indicates low certainty.

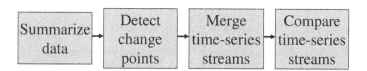

Fig. 1. Main steps of the proposed method

Figure 2 shows the overall architecture of the prototype implementation. The prototype receives time-series data streams as its input, and generates correlation rules, textual rule explanations, and stores the generated rules digitally so that those rules can be reused in other data analysis tools.

The described method applies data aggregation and change detection algorithms in order to reduce the search space. Those two algorithms are described in the following two subsections. Data mining and statistical techniques are used for various purposes, such as statistical correlation calculation for pairs or groups of data streams, data aggregation, and change detection. Sensitivity analysis is embedded inside change detection and correlation rule generation steps. Sensitivity analysis is achieved through recording the change amount and slope while detecting change points, and comparing those change amounts and slopes from different time-series data streams while generating the correlation rules.

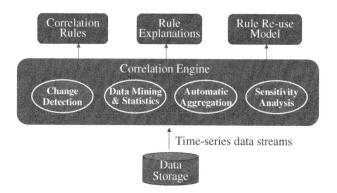

Fig. 2. Overall architecture of the prototype

Rule explanations are textual explanations of detected rules which are very important for human users to understand the findings. For example, assume that the following database table contains a simplified digital view of a time-correlation rule:

Table 1. Example database table that shows how the generated time-correlation rules can be digitally stored

COL1_NAME	COL2_NAME	TIME_DIFF	TIME_UNIT	CONFIDENCE	TYPE	SENSITIVITY
Health of Resource X	Duration of Activity Y	1	Hour	0.6	Opposite	2
Duration of Activity Y	Violations of SLA S1	0	Hour	0.7	Same	1

a textual explanation of this rule can be easily generated in the following form:

> A change in Health of Resource X will be followed by a change in Duration of Activity Y, twice the magnitude, in opposite direction, after one hour delay, with a confidence of 0.6.

Sensitivity analysis is very important because it tells us the amount of expected impact when a numeric variable (i.e., the value of a field in a time-series data stream) changes.

The digital storage of the generated time-correlation rules in this manner (i.e. in relational database tables) makes it possible to feed those rules easily into various data analysis tools, such as simulation, forecasting, etc.

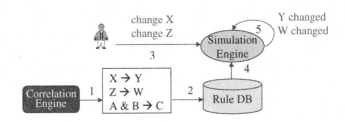

Fig. 3. Example of reusing generated time-correlation rules for simulation

As an example, Figure 3 shows how the generated time-correlation rules can be reused for simulation. The figure indicates that variables X and Z affect the variables Y and W respectively. The reuse of those rules in a simulation is carried out as follows:

1. Time-correlation rules are detected by the described method
2. The rules are written into a rule database in a digital format similar to the one shown in Table 1
3. The user of the simulation tool makes changes to the variables X and Z
4. The simulation tool retrieves the rules from the rule database in order to assess the expected impact as a result of the changes in variables X and Z
5. The simulation tool finds out from time-correlation rules that variables Y and W are going to be impacted. The time-correlation rules include information about direction, sensitivity, and time-delay so that the simulation tool can figure out exactly when, in which direction, and how much the impact is going to be observed. The confidence of time-correlation rule tells the simulator the probability of observing an impact.

2.2   Summarizing the Data at Different Time Granularities

The first step of time-correlation detection method is data aggregation. Time-stamped numeric data values (time-series data) may need to be summarized for two main reasons: 1) Volume of time-series data is usually very large. Therefore, it is more time and space efficient to summarize the data before analyzing it. 2) Time-stamps of different data streams may not match each other when recorded data is sparse, which makes it difficult to compare time-stamped data with each other.

Figure 4 shows an example of how data aggregation can be done at any particular time granularity level. The aggregation may be performed by calculating the sum, count, mean, min, max, and standard deviation of individual data values within each time unit. The figure shows the mean value calculation, which is equal to sum of values divided by the count of values in within each time unit.

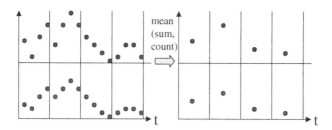

Fig. 4. Example for data aggregation at any time granularity

It is necessary to consider the cases in which the time delay among time-correlated time-series data streams may not be observed exactly the same all the time. In fact, in most cases the time delay for time-correlated data streams is likely to be shifted slightly in the time domain. The experiments showed that the time shift is not very large, and 99% of the time it is observed within one time unit difference. In order to capture those cases, the time-correlation detection method uses moving a window of three time units. For example, aggregation of data values in the "hour" granularity level involves the current hour as well as the previous and next hours. As a result, slight shifts in the time domain can be incorporated in aggregated values. Some of the existing methods use complex and costly algorithms for time-shifting or time-warping in order handle such cases [2]. The experiments showed that time-shift is very rarely larger than one unit difference; therefore, such complicated algorithms do not provide much advantage.

2.3   Detecting Change Points

The second step of time-correlation detection method is change point detection (identification of points in time where significant changes occur in data values or their trends). *CUSUM* (Cumulative Sum) [12, 13] is preferred at this step because it can be calculated incrementally, and it can detect both sharp and gradually accumulating changes. The basic CUSUM calculation is as follows at each data point:

1. Subtract the mean (or median) of the data off of each data point's value.
2. For each point, add all the mean/median-subtracted points before it.
3. The resulting values are the Cumulative Summary (CUSUM) for each point.

It is necessary to modify the basic CUSUM method in order to adapt the CUSUM and mean calculation to changing data as time-series data streams continuously flow in. Two possible approaches are sliding window and aging mechanism in which the effect of older data values in the calculations fade away or completely disappear as new data flows in. Sliding windows have the limitation that the choice of window size has a significant effect on the accuracy. Therefore, aging mechanism is preferred. Aging is achieved by combining a fraction of the new data value with a fraction of the last calculated value (i.e., last CUSUM or last mean) as follows:

$$Y(i) = p * X + (1-p) * Y(i-1) \qquad (1)$$

where $Y(i)$ is the new calculated value, $Y(i-1)$ is the last calculated value, X is the new data value from the data stream, and p is the parameter that determines the fractions of new data value and last calculated value that will be added to obtain the new calculated value. The value of p is chosen as a floating point number between zero and one. Large values of parameter p result in fading away the effect old data values quickly; whereas, small values of parameter p result in slower fade away.

Once CUSUM value for every data point is calculated, those CUSUM values are compared with upper and lower control thresholds to determine which data points can be marked as change points. The data points for which the CUSUM value is above the upper threshold or below the lower threshold are marked as change points. The best way to set thresholds is to use standard deviation (i.e. a fraction or factor of standard deviation). It is easy to calculate a moving mean or standard deviation either incrementally (e.g., using formula (1) above) or using a moving window. Therefore, the calculation of standard deviation does not introduce a large overhead in the described method. The control thresholds are usually set to three times the standard deviation in order to detect extreme changes. We use only one standard deviation to set the thresholds, because we would like to detect all significant change points, not only the extreme ones.

Detected change points are marked with labels indicating the direction of change: *Down* (trend of data values change from up or straight to down) or *Up*'(trend of data values change from down or straight to up). In addition, the amount of change is measured for each change point. The amount of change is used for sensitivity analysis.

2.4 Generating Time-Correlation Rules

Time-correlation detection method first reduces many-to-one and many-to-many time-series comparisons into pair-wise (one-to-one) time-series comparisons. Then, the problem of comparing multiple time-series data streams can be tackled efficiently using a pair-wise comparison. In order to explain the reduction and comparison steps of the method, it is first necessary to explain what is meant by one-to-one, many-to-one, and many-to-many time-series comparisons:

o **One-to-one:** comparison of two time-series data streams with each other. This is the simplest form of time-series comparison. The purpose is to find out if there exists a time correlation between two time-series. For example, if A and B identify two time-series data streams, one-to-one comparison tries to find out if changes in data values of A have any time delayed relationship with changes in data values of B. The comparison is denoted A → B.

o **Many-to-one:** comparison of a set of multiple time-series data streams with a single time-series data stream. For example, if A, B and C identify three time-series data streams, many-to-one comparison tries to find out if changes in data values of A and B collectively have a time delayed relationship with changes in data values of C. This comparison is denoted A*B→ C.

o **Many-to-many:** comparison of two sets of multiple time-series data streams. For example, if A, B, C and D identify four time-series data streams, many-to-many comparison tries to find out if changes in data values of A and B collectively have a time delayed relationship with changes in data values of C and D. This comparison is denoted A*B→ C*D.

Many-to-many comparisons do not have any practical use because they can be derived from many-to-one comparisons. The proposed time-correlation detection method can also reduce many-to-many comparisons into one-to-one comparisons.

Merging Multiple Time-Series Data Streams into One
The purpose of merging multiple time-series data streams into one is to compare multiple time-series data streams with each other in a single pass. This yields performance improvement because the merged time-series data streams can be reused, similar to the way query results can be reused in database management systems in order to provide performance improvement. For example, after merging two time-series data streams A and B, the merged time-series data stream A*B can be stored in order to generate higher order merged time-series data streams, such as A*B*C, where the symbol "*" is used for indicating the merger operation.

Time-correlation detection method uses convolution for merging multiple time-series data streams into one. Convolution is a well-known technique that can be used for merging multiple time-series data streams into a single time-series data stream. Convolution is a computational method in which an integral expresses the amount of overlap of one function $g(x)$ as it is shifted over another function $f(x)$. Convolution may therefore blend one function with another. Convolution of two functions f(x) and g(x) over a finite range is given by the equation:

$$f * g \equiv \int_0^t f(\tau) g(t - \tau) d\tau \qquad (2)$$

where $f * g$ denotes the convolution of f and g.

Since the merge operation is applied on discrete time-series data streams (after using CUSUM to detect change points), the operation can be performed much faster than merging the original time-series data streams.

Comparing Two Time-Series

Time-correlation detection method uses statistical correlation to calculate the time correlation between two time-series data streams. The time-series data streams that are compared at this step may correspond to either merged time-series or regular time-series. The statistical correlation between two time-series x and y is calculated as:

$$cor(x,y) = cov(x,y) / (\sigma(x) * \sigma(y)) \tag{3}$$

where x and y identify two time-series, and covariance is calculated as

$$cov(X, Y) = E\{[X - E(X)][Y - E(Y)]\} \tag{4}$$

and $\sigma(x)$ corresponds to the standard deviation of values in time-series x,
$\sigma(y)$ corresponds to the standard deviation of values in time-series y,
$E(X)$ and $E(Y)$ correspond to the mean values of time-series data values from x and y.

Time correlation is calculated as follows:

$$\max \{cor(x_i, y_j)\} \; \forall i,j \in t; i \neq j \tag{5}$$

where t corresponds to aggregated time span of the time-series data (e.g. minutes, hours, days, etc.). Sensitivity is calculated using the following formula:

$$sensitivity(x_i, y_j) = slope(x_i) / slope(y_j) \text{ where } i,j \in t; i \neq j, |i-j| = d \tag{6}$$

by setting the distance (d) between i and j to that of the maximum statistical correlation found, and comparing the slopes of change points from correlated time-series data streams. In other words, the statistical correlation between aggregated data points with varying time distances are calculated, and the maximum calculated correlation and the corresponding time distance (d) give us the time correlation information we need. The sensitivity is calculated by comparing the change amounts in the correlated time-series data streams using time distance (d) of the calculated maximum statistical correlation. The direction of correlation is obtained from the calculated statistical correlation. A positive correlation indicates the direction is "Same" whereas a negative correlation indicates the direction is "Opposite".

The most challenging task in this comparison step is to determine the time distance (d) for which the calculated correlation is the highest. An exhaustive search in which all possible time distances are tried and maximum correlation is determined is prohibitive due to performance reasons unless there is a known upper limit for the distance (d). Otherwise it is necessary to find the distance (d) in a faster way. The described method uses sampling in order to first determine which time distances are likely to return a high correlation between the time-series data streams that are being compared. Then, the actual correlation is calculated for a few of those candidate distances, and the one with the highest correlation is selected. The experiments with various sets of time-series data streams yielded promising results. Although the number of candidate distances has a significant effect on the accuracy of the result, the experiments showed that after sampling the data, it is enough to consider at most three or four candidate distances to find the highest correlation distance correctly for 95% of the time.

Once the time correlation is calculated, the confidence can be calculated easily by comparing the percentage of times the calculated statistical correlation with the time delay (d) of the maximum correlation is higher than a particular threshold. The confidence is calculated by measuring the percentage of the time x_i and y_j values have a statistical correlation larger than a given threshold. The threshold can be chosen by the user of this method.

It is important to note that comparing all possible combinations of time-series data streams is computationally prohibitive. If a pair or group of time-series data streams is time-correlated, they should have similar number of change points detected in the previous steps. This is an important feature of time-correlations, which can also be used for speeding up the proposed method significantly. The method described in this paper compares only those time-series data streams that have similar number of change points detected. As a result, an important performance gain is achieved without causing false dismissals (i.e., without discarding the comparison of data streams that may actually be time-correlated).

3 Example BIA Scenario

The time-correlation rules generated by the proposed method can be used in various fields. For example, BIA tries to find the impact of certain events on the operation of the business. Businesses make use of Workflow Management Systems (WfMS) [9] in order to automate the execution and monitoring of their business processes. A *business process* is a step-by-step description of activities that are carried out by humans or automated resources (e.g., databases, procurement systems, resource planning software, etc.) in order to achieve a business goal. A *workflow* is the formal definition of a business process that can be executed and monitored using a WfMS. Figure 5 shows an example workflow definition which is used for handling purchase order (PO) requests that are received from customers.

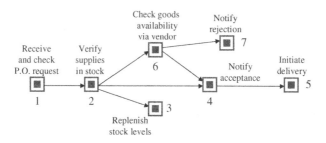

Fig. 5. Example workflow definition

The individual activities in this workflow definition are carried out by resources such as humans or automated resources. For example, "Initiate Delivery" activity may be carried out by a human who makes a phone call to internal delivery department of the business in order to initiate the delivery of the ordered products. Similarly, "Notify Acceptance" or "Notify Rejection" activities may be carried out by an e-mail messaging system that is capable of sending e-mail notifications to the customer.

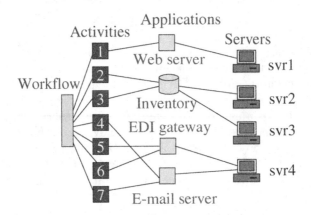

Fig. 6. Example business impact analysis scenario

The time-correlation rules are suitable for use in BIA because the time-correlation rules can tell us the impact of a change in the value of one numeric variable on the values of other numeric variables. Figure 6 shows an example BIA scenario in which time-correlation rules can be used. The activities that are number between 1 and 6 in Figure 5 are symbolized with their corresponding numbers in Figure 6. Figure 6 indicates that each one of the activities in the workflow is assigned to one or more automated resources (human resources are ignored only for simplicity of the example). It can also be observed from the figure that a resource may be in charge of handling one or more activities in the workflow. Each application runs on top of a hardware resource, which is shown as a server in the figure. Each application may run on one or more servers, and similarly each server may run one or more applications.

Business impact analysis on such a scenario requires that we know or find out the impact of a change at a lower level entity on the execution of a higher level entity. For example, if server 2 crashes or experiences performance degradation, then the Inventory application will be affected negatively. That, in turn, will affect the execution of activities 2 and 3. Eventually, that will affect the overall execution of the workflow and its execution will most probably be delayed or even become impossible.

Time-correlation rules can be used for identifying the dependencies among the performance of any entities in this scenario. A few examples dependencies in this scenario may be server performance and activity execution time, server performance and workflow execution time, application performance and activity execution time, and activity execution time and workflow execution time.

The generated time-correlation rules tell us the impact of any change at a lower level entity on the higher level entities. For example, the following rule tells us the impact of a change in the performance of a server on the execution time of an activity in the workflow:

A change in Performance of Server 1 will be followed by a change in Duration of Activity 1 twice in magnitude in opposite direction in 5 minutes.

The main advantage of using time-correlation rules in BIA is that the rules can be generated for any time-series data streams from different levels in the example scenario architecture shown in Figure 6. That means we can directly find the impact of a server crash on the overall execution time of the whole workflow without having to know about the actual dependencies or hierarchy of the existing architecture. This is an important example that shows the time-correlation detection method described in this paper is generic enough to be applied in many different problem domains without requiring domain knowledge. Similarly, the time-correlation detection method can be used in analyzing supply chain transactions, business-to-business (B2B) interactions, procurement systems, web services, etc.

4   Performance Evaluation

Performance evaluation is done using a prototype implementation and four data sets:

  o   Continuous data streams of stock quotes for 2000 NYSE stocks (i.e., 2000 data streams, each of which contains one stock quote per second).
  o   Real-time data from 2000 sensors that measure the temperature at different points of a server cluster system at Hewlett-Packard (recorded every second).
  o   Workflow execution logs for financial operations. This data set included workflow execution logs that record the start and end times of individual steps in business process executions, and various parameters related with the business processes. The data rate for this data set fluctuates depending on the time of the day, and there exist certain peak load periods. The processing delay of the proposed method was within the range that was measured for other three data sets, even during the peak load periods.
  o   Synthetic data generated using random walk model that contains 20,000 data streams, each producing one numeric data sample per second. The number of data streams in this set is much larger than those of the other three sets. The results obtained using this data set were compared with the results from the other data sets for up to 2,000 data streams. After that, this data set was used for modelling further experiments in which a larger number of data streams (i.e., 20,000) is used.

The experiments with all four data sets were repeated several times, and each run of the experiments involved at least 30,000 data records from each data stream. The experiments showed that the proposed method extracts time-dependent correlations (or temporal associations) within a small time delay while the data flows in continuously from a large number of data streams.

The accuracy of the algorithm was compared against that of exhaustive search algorithm. It has been shown that 95% of time-correlations that are detected by the exhaustive search are also detected by the proposed method using reasonable parameters.

Figure 7 shows the logarithmic value of processing delay (the time between receipt of each data record and maximum delay for completing comparative analysis for the data record, plus the total filtering and reporting time for correlation rules) compared with number of data streams, which is increased ten times at each run of the experiments. Processing delay is used as the performance measure instead of total running

Log(Delay in msec)

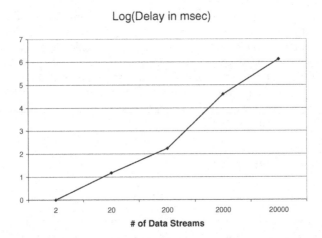

# of Data Streams

Fig. 7. Logarithmic value of processing delay compared with number of data streams (as number of data streams increase by an order of magnitude each time)

Total Delay (msec)

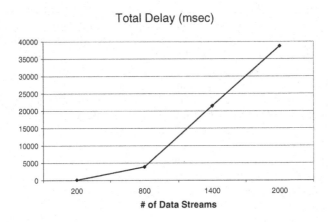

# of Data Streams

Fig. 8. Processing delay (milliseconds) with respect to number of data streams

time of the method, because data continuously flows in, and it is not practical to measure the total running time for such data stream analysis. Previous research on data stream analysis also used processing delay as the performance measure [17]. The figure shows a linear increase in logarithmic values of processing delay compared with increasing order of magnitude in number of data streams, which suggests at a first glance that the comparison of actual measurements would not yield a linear increase in processing delay. However, the x-axis values increase ten times at each data point in the figure. It can be seen that the processing delay would actually increase linearly if the number of data streams increased linearly (instead of ten times). This linear increase is demonstrated more clearly in Figure 8. The small jump between 200-2000 data stream tests in Figure 7 is due to the fact that the processing delay up to 200 data streams was hidden behind the arrival rate of the data. That means, the processing delay of each incoming data value was much shorter than the time between data value arrivals for the whole set of data streams. The proposed method can process incoming data values from up to 200 data streams in less than a second; and the time measured as the delay in Figure 7 is only due to filtering of final correlation rules based on support and confidence thresholds.

Experiments showed that the proposed method has linear running time for pairwise correlations (i.e., total execution time, not only the processing delay) with respect to the total number of data points that exist in all data streams. The running time of higher order correlations is not linear, but the method still requires only a single pass over the input data. The results of further experiments are not included here due to space limitation.

5   Related Work

Discrete event correlation has been studied extensively using different approaches, especially in network management domain. Existing approaches fall into three main groups: rule-based, model-based, and case-based. Rule-based systems do not require profound understanding of the architectural and operational principles of the underlying system and, for small systems, may provide a powerful tool for eliminating the least likely hypotheses [10, 11]. The downsides of rule-based systems include the inability to learn from experience, inability to deal with unseen problems, and difficulty in updating the system knowledge. Rule-based systems are difficult to maintain because the rules frequently contain hard-coded configuration information. Model-based approaches [6, 12] incorporate deep knowledge in the form of a model of the underlying system. Those approaches are system-specific and difficult to generalize. Case-based systems [8] make their decisions based on experience and past situations. They try to acquire relevant knowledge of past cases in order to extract new knowledge. The proposed method in this paper is a case-based approach that can dynamically update and refine the generated results as new data arrives. It does not require any domain knowledge, and is generic enough to be applied in many different domains. It has been shown that the strength of causal correlation between events may change with the length of the period of time between the events' occurrences [7, 10], which suggests that the proposed method is very suitable for causality analysis since it extracts temporal correlations automatically from data streams. The proposed method is an efficient way of performing detailed event correlation by taking event parameters into consideration.

Previous research on similarity based pattern querying may be considered as somewhat relevant to the method described in this paper. However, the existing methods in that domain can only tell us whether a given query sequence is similar enough to existing sequences stored in a database. Those methods cannot report any information about the direction, amount, or slope of changes in numeric data streams, and cannot explain how to perform detailed comparative analysis using parameters of discrete events. Most of the previous research has used Discrete Fourier Transform (DFT) in order to transform the data from time domain into frequency domain [1, 2, 3, 4, 5, 16, 17]. Those approaches have a significant limitation that similarity model is different from the data representation [14]. This limitation is the main reason why those approaches cannot be applied for time-correlation detection (detection of time-dependent relationships). Later approaches suggested the use of Discrete Wavelet Transform (DWT) in order to retain time related information, but those approaches are still limited to similarity querying applications and not suitable for detecting time-correlations among discrete events (or change points).

Based on the observation that humans can ignore small fluctuations and apply smoothing when comparing numeric data visually, Rafiei et al proposed a method based on smoothing and noise reduction using moving averages [15]. The smoothing algorithm used in our method also makes use of moving averages.

Perng et al [14] suggested a new method that first identifies landmarks, i.e., important points in time where certain events happen in numeric data streams, and then uses six transformations to compare data streams. The paper did not explain any details about how to implement those transformations, but it presented an interesting idea that detection of important points can be useful for comparative analysis. The time-correlation detection method proposed in our paper builds on top of the idea of identifying important points and using those important points to detect correlations among time-series data streams efficiently.

6 Conclusion

A novel method for detecting time-correlations in time-series data streams is described. The method consists of a few main steps in which the original time-series data is summarized using aggregation; transformed into discrete data for faster analysis using a well-known change detection technique; sampled for fast identification of candidate time distances, and scanned in linear time for confirming the correlation rules. The described method takes advantage of observations both from previous research and preliminary experiments performed using this method. The use of the time-correlation rules in business impact analysis is explained on an example scenario. Time-correlation rules generated by the described method can easily be reused for analysis of transactional or operational data in many different business environments.

References

[1] R. Agrawal, C. Faloutsos, and A. N. Swami. Efficient similarity search in sequence databases. In FODO, Evanstons, IL, October 1993.

[2] D. J. Berndt and J. Clifford. Finding patterns in time series: A dynamic programming approach. In Advances in Knowledge Discovery and Data Mining, pages 229–248. MIT Press, 1996.

[3] G. Das, D. Gunopulos, and H. Mannila. Finding similar time series. In Proceedings of Principles of Data Mining and Knowledge Discovery (PKDD), Trondheim, Norway, June 1997.

[4] C. Faloutsos, M. Ranganathan, and Y. Manolopoulos. Fast subsequence matching in time-series databases. In SIGMOD, 1994.

[5] D.Q.Goldin and P. Kanellakis. On similarity queries for time-series data: Constraint specification and implementation. In International Conference on the Principles and Practice of Constraint Programming, 1995.

[6] G. Jakobson and M. D. Weissman. Alarm correlation. IEEE Network, pp. 52–59, Nov. 1993.

[7] G. Jakobson and M. D. Weissman. Real-time telecommunication network management: Extending event correlation with temporal constraints. In Proceedings of IFIP/IEEE International Symposium on Integrated Network Management, 1995, pp. 290–302.

[8] L. Lewis. A case-based reasoning approach to the resolution of faults in communications networks. In Proceedings of IFIP/IEEE International Symposium on Integrated Network Management, 1993, pp. 671–681.

[9] F. Leymann, D. Roller, Production Workflows. Prentice-Hall, Englewood Cliffs, 2000.

[10] G. Liu, A. K. Mok, and E. J. Yang. Composite events for network event correlation. In Proceedings of IFIP/IEEE International Symposium on Integrated Network Management, 1999, pp. 247–260.

[11] K.-W. E. Lor. A network diagnostic expert system for AcculinkTM multiplexers based on a general network diagnostic scheme. In Proceedings of IFIP/IEEE International Symposium on Integrated Network Management 1993, pp. 659–669.

[12] Y. A. Nygate. Event correlation using rule and object based techniques. In Proceedings of IFIP/IEEE International Symposium on Integrated Network Management, 1995, pp. 278–289.

[13] E.S. Page, Continuous Inspection Schemes, Biometrika, 41, pp.100-114, 1954.

[14] C-S. Perng, H. Wang, S. Zhang, D. S. Parker, Landmarks: A New Model for Similarity-Based Pattern Querying in Time Series Databases. In Proceedings of the 16th International Conference of Data Engineering (ICDE), San Diego, CA, February 2000.

[15] D. Rafiei and A. O. Mendelzon. Similarity-based queries for time series data. In SIGMOD, 1997.

[16] B.-K. Yi, H. Jagadish, and C. Faloutsos. Efficient retrieval of similar time sequences under time warping. In ICDE, 1998.

[17] Y. Zhu and D. Shasha. Statstream: Statistical monitoring of thousands of data streams in real time. In Proceedings of 28th International Conference on Very Large Data Bases (VLDB), Hong Kong, China, pp. 358-369, August 20-23, 2002.

A Bottom-Up Workflow Mining Approach
for Workflow Applications Analysis

Walid Gaaloul[1], Karim Baïna[2], and Claude Godart[1]

[1] LORIA - INRIA - CNRS - UMR 7503
BP 239, F-54506 Vandœuvre-lès-Nancy Cedex, France
[2] ENSIAS, Université Mohammed V - Souissi,
BP 713 Agdal - Rabat, Morocco
gaaloul@loria.fr, baina@ensias.ma, godart@loria.fr

Abstract. Engineering workflow applications are becoming more and more complex, involving numerous interacting business objects within considerable processes. Analysing the interaction structure of those complex applications will enable them to be well understood, controlled, and redesigned. Our contribution to workflow mining is a statistical technique to discover workflow patterns from event-based log. Our approach is characterised by a "local" workflow patterns discovery that allows to cover partial results through a dynamic programming algorithm. Those local discovered workflow patterns are then composed iteratively until discovering the global workflow model. Our approach has been implemented within our prototype WorkflowMiner.

Keywords: workflow mining, workflow patterns, business process Analysis, Business process intelligence.

1 Introduction

With the technological improvements and the continuous increasing market pressures and requirements, collaborative information systems are becoming more and more complex, involving numerous interacting business objects. Analysing interactions of those complex systems will enable them to be well understood, controlled, and redesigned. Our paper is a contribution to this problem in the particular context of workflow applications analysis through workflow mining.

Our approach (a) starts by collecting log information from workflow processes instances as they took place (event collectors and adapters component). Then, (b) it builds, through statistical techniques, a graphical intermediary representation modelling elementary dependencies over workflow activities executions (events analyser component). These dependencies are then (c) refined to discover workflow patterns (patterns analyser component). Beside workflow patterns analysis, some workflow performance metrics are computed but will not be in the scope of this paper (performance analyser component).

This paper is structured as follows. Section 2 explains our workflow log model. Section 3 details our structural workflow patterns mining algorithm. Section 4 discusses related work, implementation and perspectives issues, before concluding.

J. Lee et al. (Eds.): DEECS 2006, LNCS 4055, pp. 182–197, 2006.

2   Workflow Log Model

The workflow specification might not be concerned with the details of the activities however it would have to deal, at least, with the externally visible completion events of activities (such as aborted, failed, and completed). Currently, most of WfMSs log all events
occurring during process execution. We expect the activities to be traceable, meaning that
the system should in somehow keep track of ongoing and past executions. As shown in
the UML class diagram of figure 1, WorkflowLog is composed of a set of EventStreams
(definition 1). Each EventStream traces the execution of one case (instance). It consists
of a set of events (Event) that captures the activities life cycle performed in a particular
workflow instance. An Event is described by the activity identifier that it concerns, the
current activity state (aborted, failed, completed or compensated) and the time when it
occurs (TimeStamp). A Window defines a set of Events over an EventStream. Finally,
a Partition builds a set of partially overlapping Windows partition over an EventStream.

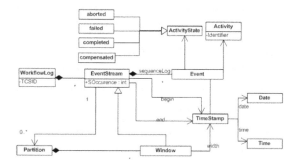

Fig. 1. Workflow Log Model

Definition 1 *(EventStream)*
An EventStream *represents the history of a workflow instance events as a tuple*
EventStream= *(begin, end, sequenceLog, SOccurrence) where:*
    ✓begin : TimeStamp *is the moment of log beginning ;*
    ✓end : TimeStamp *is the moment of log end;*
    ✓sequenceLog : Event* *is an ordered* Event *set belonging to a workflow instance;*
    ✓SOccurrence : int *is the activity instance number. A* WorkflowLog *is a set of*
EventStream*s.* WorkflowLog=*(workflowID,* {EventStream$_i$*,* $0 \leq i <$ *number of work-*
flow instances}*) where* EventStream$_i$ *is the event stream of the* i^{th} *workflow instance.*

Here is an EventStream related to an instance of workflow in figure 2. This
EventStream was filtered to take only events with completed as state.

L = EventStream$((13/5/2005, 5:42:12), (14/5/2005, 14:01:54), [$Event$("A_1"$,
      completed, $(13/5/2005, 5:42:12)),$ Event$("A_2"$, completed,
  $(13/5/2005, 11:11:12)),$ Event$("A_4"$, completed, $(13/5/2005, 14:01:54)),$
  Event$("A_3"$, completed, $(14/5/2005, 00:01:54)),$ Event$("A_5"$, completed,
    $(14/5/2005, 5:45:54)),$ Event$("A_7"$, completed, $(14/5/2005, 10:32:55)),$
            Event$("A_9"$, completed, $(14/5/2005, 14:01:54))])$

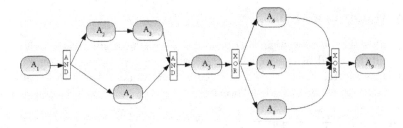

Fig. 2. Workflow running example

3   Mining Structural Workflow Patterns

As we stated before, we start by collecting WorkflowLog from workflow instances as
they took place. Then we build, through statistical techniques, a graphical intermediary representation modelling **elementary dependencies** over workflow logs (section
3.2). These dependencies are refined by **advanced structural workflow patterns** (section 3.3). An elementary dependency is an "immediate" dependency[1] linking two activities in the sense that the termination of the first causes the activation of the last.
Thus, the event of termination of the first activity is considered as the pre-condition
of the activation of the last and reciprocally the activation of the last is considered
as a post condition of the termination of the first activity. While an advanced structural workflow pattern is a set of elementary dependencies that defines an advanced
structure to express specific behaviour, in terms of control flow, linking these dependencies. A pattern is the abstraction from a concrete form which keeps recurring in
specific non arbitrary contexts. Thus, a workflow pattern [1] can be seen as an abstract description of a recurrent class of interactions based on (primitive) activation
dependency.

3.1   Overview

As illustrated in figure 3, our approach is applied in bottom up manner :

1. **Discovering activities dependencies:**   First, we specify dependencies linking
   workflow activities during execution. We divide these dependencies in two kinds :
   causal and non-causal.
   A Causal dependency between two activities expresses that the occurrence of an
   activity event involves the activation of an other activity event. While a non-causal
   dependency specifies other activities behavioural dependency.
2. **Computing statistical behavioural properties:**   Secondly, we compute the statistical behavioural properties from logs. These properties tailor the main behaviour
   features of the chosen discovered patterns. We define three types of properties :
   sequential, concurrent and choice.
   The sequential and concurrent properties inherit from causal dependency. The first
   expresses an exclusive causal dependency between two activities. While the second specifies a causal between an activity on one hand and a set of activities on

---

[1] Terms *immediate* and *direct* will be used interchangeably in the remainder of the paper.

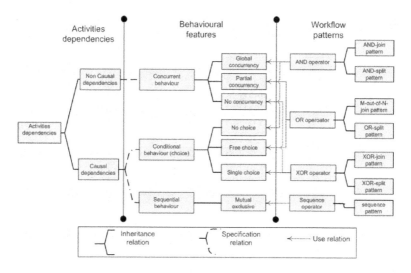

Fig. 3. Hierarchical view of workflow patterns mining approach

an other hand. The concurrent property inherits from non-causal dependency and characterises the concurrent behaviour of a set activities.

3. **Discovering workflows patterns:** Finally, we use a set of rules to discover a set of the most useful patterns. These rules are expressed using the statistical properties and specify an indicator function (could be expressed as a 1st order logic predicate, for instance) defining as a unique manner a pattern.

In this work, we have chosen to discover the most useful patterns, but the adopted approach allows to enrich this set of patterns by specifying new statistical dependencies and their associated properties or by using the existing properties in new combinations discovering new patterns.

3.2   Discovering Elementary Dependencies

The aim of this section is to explain our algorithm for discovering elementary dependencies among a WorkflowLog and build an intermediary model representing those dependencies : statistical dependency table (or SDT).

Discovering direct dependencies. In order to discover direct dependencies from a WorkflowLog, we need an intermediary representation of this WorkflowLog through a statistical analysis. We call this intermediary representation : statistical dependency table (or SDT) which is based on a notion of frequency table [2]. As workflow patterns are described only by control flow dependencies, this table captures control flow direct dependencies which are related exclusively to activities "terminated" state dependencies reporting "correct" (i.e., without "exceptions") executions. There is no need to use other EventStreams relating to failure executions containing failed or aborted or compensated states. In fact, these cases concern only transactional behaviour and dependencies which tailors the mechanisms for failures handling and recovery. These issues are out of the scope of our paper. Nevertheless, in [3, 4] we use these events to

Table 1. Initial Statistical Dependencies Table ($P(x/y)$) and activities Frequencies (#)

$P(x/y)$	A_1	A_2	A_3	A_4	A_5	A_6	A_7	A_8	A_9
A_1	0	0	0	0	0	0	0	0	0
A_2	**0.54**	0	0	0.46	0	0	0	0	0
A_3	0	**0.69**	0	0.31	0	0	0	0	0
A_4	**0.46**	0.31	0.23	0	0	0	0	0	0
A_5	0	0	**0.77**	**0.23**	0	0	0	0	0
A_6	0	0	0	0	1	0	0	0	0
A_7	0	0	0	0	1	0	0	0	0
A_8	0	0	0	0	0	0	0	0	0
A_9	0	0	0	0	0	0.38	0.62	0	0

$\#A_1 = \#A_2 = \#A_3 = \#A_4 = \#A_5 = \#A_9 = 100,$
$\#A_6 = 38, \#A_7 = 62, \#A_8 = 0$

discover and improve workflow transactional behaviour. Consequently, to mine workflow patterns, we need to filter the analysed WorkflowLog and take only EventStreams of instances executed "correctly".

Basically, SDT is built through a statistical calculus that extracts elementary dependencies between activities of a WorkflowLog that are executed without "exceptions" (*i.e.* they reached successfully their completed state). We denote by WorkflowLog$_{completed}$ this workflow log selection. Thus, the unique necessary condition to discover elementary dependencies is to have workflow logs containing at least the completed event states. These features allow to mine control flow from "poor" logs which contain only completed event states. By the way, any information system using transactional systems or workflow management systems offer this information in some form.

For each activity A, we extract from WorkflowLog$_{completed}$ the following information in the statistical dependency table (SDT): (i) The overall occurrence number of this activity (denoted $\#A$) and (ii) The elementary dependencies to previous activities B_i (denoted $P(A/B_i)$). The size of SDT is $n * n$, where n is the number of workflow activities. The (*m,n*) table entry (notation $P(A_{0 \leq i < n}/A_{0 \leq j < n})$) is the frequency of the jth activity immediately preceding the ith activity. The initial SDT in table 1 represents of the SDT of our workflow example given in figure 2. For instance, in this table P(A_3/A_2)=0.69 expresses that if A_2 occurs, then, we have 69% of chance that A_3 occurs directly after A_2 in the workflow log. As it was calculated SDT presents some problems to express correctly activities dependencies relating to concurrent behaviour. In the following, we detail these issues and propose solutions to correct them.

Discarding erroneous dependencies. If we assume that each EventStream from WorkflowLog comes from a sequential (i.e no concurrent behaviour) workflow, a zero entry in SDT represents a causal independence and a non-zero entry means a causal dependency relation (*i.e.* sequential or conditional relation). But, in case of concurrent behaviour, as we can see in workflow patterns (like and-split, and-join, etc.), the EventStreams may contain interleaved events sequences from concurrent threads. As consequence, some entries in initial SDT can indicate non-zero entries that do not correspond to dependencies. For instance, the events stream given in section 2 "suggests"

```
Input: SDT : statistical dependency Table
Output: MSDT : Marked statistical  dependency Table
Var:
    MSDT_size : int;
    Dependency : int
begin
    MSDT=SDT;
    MSDT_size = Size_tab(MSDT);
    For int i=0; i  MSDT_size; i++;
        For int j=0; j  i; j++;
            If MSDT[i][j]   0 and MSDT[j][i]   0 then
                MSDT[i][j] =-1;
                MSDT[j][i] =-1;
            endIf
        endFor
    endFor
end
```

A- Marking Concurrent behaviour in SDT Algorithm

```
Input: MSDT : Marked  statistical dependency Table
Output: ACWT : Activity Concurrent Width table
Var:
    MSDT_size : int;
begin
    MSDT_size = Size_tab(SDT);
    For int i=0; i  MSDT_size; i++;
        ACWT[i]=2;
    endFor;
    For int i=0; i  MSDT_size; i++;
        For int j=0; j  i; j++;
            If MSDT[i][j] =-1  then
                ACWT[i]++;
                ACWT[j]++;
                For int k=0; k  MSDT_size; k++;
                    If MSDT[k][i]   0 then ACWT[k]++; endIf
                endFor
            endIf
        endFor
    endFor
end
```

B- Activity Concurrent Width Algorithm

```
Inputs: Wlog : TCSLog_terminated (TCSLog) : Workflow log
        « terminated » state selection
        # : The activity occurrences table
        MSDT : Marked statistical  dependency Table
Output: FSDT : Final statistical  Dependency Table
Var:
    t_reference: int;
    t_preceded : int;
    fWin : window;
    depFreq :int[][]  /* initialized at zero*/;
    freq :int
begin
    For all win:window in partition(Wlog)
        t_reference = last_activity(win)  /* the function
        last_activity(win) returns the activityId of the
        last event in win.wLog */
        win = preceded_events(win);  /* the function
        preceded_events(win) returns win without
        the last event*/
        for all e:event in (win.wLog)
            t_preceded= e.activityId;
            If ( MSDT[t_reference, t_preceded]  0) then
                depFreq[t_referenced, t_preceded]++;
            endIf
        endFor
    endFor

    /*Final step: construction of statistical dependency table*/
    MSDT_size = Size_tab(SDT);
    For int t_ref=0; t_ref  MSDT_size;t_ref++;
        For int t_pr=0; t_pr  MSDT_size; t_prj++;
            FSDT[t_ref, t_pr]= MSDT[t_ref, t_prj] #t_ref;
        endFor
    endFor
end
```

C- Final SDT Algorithm

Fig. 4. SDT Algorithms

erroneous causal dependencies between A_2 and A_4 in one side, and between A_4 and A_3 in another side. Indeed, A_2 comes immediately before A_4 and A_4 comes immediately before A_3 in this events stream. These erroneous entries are reported by $P(A_4/A_2)$ and $P(A_3/A_4)$ in initial SDT which are different to zero. These entries are erroneous because there are no causal dependencies between these activities as suggested (i.e. noisy SDT). Underlined values in table 1 report this behaviour for other similar cases.

Formally, two activities A and B are in concurrence *iff* $P(A/B)$ and $P(B/A)$ entries in SDT are non-zero entries in SDT. Based on this definition, we propose an algorithm to discover activities parallelism and then mark the erroneous entries in SDT. Through this marking, we can eliminate the confusion caused by the concurrence behaviour producing these erroneous non-zero entries. The algorithm (A) in figure 4 scans the initial **SDT** and marks concurrent activities dependencies by changing their values to (-1). For instance, we can deduce from table 1 that A_2 and A_4 activities are in concurrence (i.e $P(A_2/A_4) \neq 0 \wedge P(A_4/A_2) \neq 0$), So after applying our algorithm $P(A_2/A_4)$ and $P(A_4/A_2)$ will be equal to -1 in the final table (see table 2).

Discovering indirect dependencies. For concurrency reasons, an activity might not depend on its immediate predecessor in the events stream, but it might depend on another "indirectly" preceding activities. As an example of this behaviour, A_4 is logged between A_2 and A_3 in the events stream given in section 2. As consequence, A_2 does not occur always immediately before A_3 in the workflow log. Thus, we have only $P(A_3/A_2) = 0.69$ that is an under estimated dependency frequency. In fact, the right value is 1 because the execution of A_3 depends exclusively on A_2. Similarly, values in bold in initial SDT report this behaviour for other cases.

Definition 2 Window
*A log window defines a log slide over an events stream S : **stream** (bStream, eStream, sLog, workflowocc). Formally, we define a log window as a triplet **window**(wLog, bWin, eWin) :*
    ○ *(bWin : TimeStamp) and (eWin : TimeStamp) are the moment of the window beginning and end (with bStream ≤ bWin and eWin ≤ eStream)*
    ○ *wLog ⊂ sLog and ∀ e: **event** ∈ S.sLog where bWin ≤ e.TimeStamp ≤ eWin ⇒ e ∈ wLog.*

To discover these indirect dependencies, we introduce the notion of *activity concurrent window* (definition 2). An *activity concurrent window* (ACW) is related to the activity of its last event covering its directly and indirectly preceding activities. Initially, the width of ACW of an activity is equal to 2. Every time, this activity is in concurrence with an other activity we add 1 to this width. If this activity is not in concurrence with other activities and has preceding concurrent activities, then we add their number to ACW width. For example, the activity A_4 is in concurrence with A_2 and A_3 the width of its ACW is equal to 4. Based on this the algorithm (B) in figure 4 calculates the activity concurrent width regrouped in the ACW table. This algorithm scans the "marked" **SDT** calculated in last section and updates the ACW table.

Definition 3 Partition
*A **partition** builds a set of partially overlapping windows over an events stream.*
Partition : WorkflowLog → (Window)*
S : EventStream(sLog, workflowocc, bStream, eStream) → {w_i :Window; $0 \le i < n$} :
    ○ *w_1.bWin = bStream and w_n.eWin = eStream,*
    ○ *∀w : window ∈ partition, e:Event= the last event in w, width(w)= ACWT[e.ActivityID],*
    ○ *∀ $0 \le i < n$; w_{i+1}.wLog - {the last e:Event in w_{i+1}.wLog} ⊂ w_i.wLog and w_{i+1}.wLog ≠ w_i.wLog.*

After that, we proceed through an EventStreams partition (definition 3) that builds a set of partially overlapping windows over the EventStreams using the ACW table. Finally, the algorithm (C) of figure 4 computes the final SDT. For each ACW, it computes for its last activity the frequencies of its preceded activities. The final SDT will be found by dividing each row entry by the frequency of the row's activity. Note that, our approach adjust **dynamically**, through the width of ACW, the process calculating activities dependencies. Indeed, this width is sensible to concurrent behaviour : it increases in case of concurrence and is "neutral" in case on concurrent behaviour absence. Thus, our algorithm that adapts its behaviour to new "concurrent" context. This strategy allows the improvement of the algorithm's complexity and runtime execution. Now by applying

Table 2. Final Statistical Dependencies Table ($P(x/y)$) and activities Frequencies (#)

$P(x/y)$	A_1	A_2	A_3	A_4	A_5	A_6	A_7	A_8	A_9
A_1	0	0	0	0	0	0	0	0	0
A_2	1	0	0	-1	0	0	0	0	0
A_3	0	1	0	-1	0	0	0	0	0
A_4	1	-1	-1	0	0	0	0	0	0
A_5	0	0	1	1	0	0	0	0	0
A_6	0	0	0	0	1	0	0	0	0
A_7	0	0	0	0	1	0	0	0	0
A_8	0	0	0	0	0	0	0	0	0
A_9	0	0	0	0	0	0.38	0.62	0	0

$$\#A_1 = \#A_2 = \#A_3 = \#A_4 = \#A_5 = \#A_9 = 100,$$
$$\#A_6 = 38, \#A_7 = 62, \#A_8 = 0$$

Fig. 5. An EventStream partition

these algorithms, we can compute the final SDT (table 2) which will be used to discover workflow patterns.

In figure 5 we applied a partition over the EventStream of the motivating example presented in section 2. For instance, the width of A_4's ACW is equal to 4 because this activity is in concurrence with two activities A_2 and A_3. And, the width of A_5's ACW is equal to 3 because this activity has two preceding activities A_3 and A_4 in concurrence. We note that for each activity in this EventStream its ACW allows it to cover all, and only all, its causal preceding activities.

3.3   Discovering Advanced Dependencies: Workflow Patterns

Patterns Statistical Properties. We have identified three kinds of statistical properties (sequential, conditional and concurrent) which describe the main behaviours of workflow patterns. Then, we have specified these properties using SDT's statistics. We use theses properties to identify separately workflow patterns from workflow log. This behaviour provides a dynamic algorithm that builds global solution (i.e. global workflow) based on local solutions (i.e. workflows patterns) iteratively. We begin with the statistical exclusive dependency property (property 1) which characterises, by the way, the sequence pattern.

Property 1 Mutual exclusive dependency property *(as* P1*)*
*A **mutual** exclusive dependency relation between an activity A_i and its immediately preceding previous activity A_j specifies that the enactment of the activity A_i depends only on the completion of activity A_j and the completion of A_j enacts only the execution of A_i. It is expressed in terms of:*

○ *activities frequencies* : $\#A_i = \#A_j$
○ *activities dependencies* : $P(A_i/A_j) = 1 \wedge 0 \le k, l < n; k \ne j; P(A_i/A_k) = 0$
$\wedge \forall l \ne i; P(A_l/A_j) = 0.$

The next two statistical properties: concurrency property (property 2) and choice property (property 3) are used to insulate statistical patterns behaviour in terms of concurrence and choice after a "fork" or before a "join" operator.

Property 2 Concurrency property *(as P2)*
A ***concurrency*** *relation between a set of activities* $\{A_i, 0 \le i < n\}$ *belonging to the same workflow specifies how, in terms of concurrency, the enactment of these activities is performed. This set of activities is commonly found after a "fork" operator or before a "join" operator. We have distinguished three activities concurrency behaviours:*

- **P2.1: Global concurrency** *where in the same instantiation the whole activities are performed simultaneously :* $\forall 0 \le i \ne j < n; \#A_i = \#A_j \wedge P(A_i/A_j) = -1$
- **P2.2: Partial concurrency** *where in the same instantiation we have at least a partial concurrent execution of activities :* $(\exists 0 \le i \ne j < n; P(A_i/A_j) = -1)$
- **P2.3: No concurrency** *where there is no concurrency between activities:* $\forall (0 \le i \ne j < n; \wedge P(A_i/A_j) \ne -1)$

Property 3 Choice property *(as P3)*
A ***choice*** *is a relation between the two operands before and after the "join" and the "fork" operator. It specifies, in terms of control flow, how the workflow instance performs the choice of activities' operands activations (i.e. which activities are executed after a "fork" operator or before a "join" operator). The two operands of the "fork" operator (respectively the "join" operator) performing this relation are : (operand 1) an activity A from which comes (respectively to which) a single thread of control which splits (respectively converges) into (respectively from) (operand 2) multiple activities* $\{A_i, 0 \le i < n\}$. *We have distinguished three activities choice behaviours :*

- **P3.1: Free choice** *where a part of activities from the second operand are chosen. We have in terms of activities frequencies* $(\#A \le \Sigma_{i=0}^{n-1}(\#A_i)) \wedge (\#A_i \le \#A)$ *and in terms of activities dependencies we have :*
   ○ *In "fork" operator* (A_i *occurs certainly after A occurrence):* $\forall 0 \le i < n; P(A_i/A) = 1$
   ○ *In "join" operator* (A *occurs certainly after some* A_i *occurrences "$1 <$", but not always after all* A_i "$< n$") $: 1 < \Sigma_{i=0}^{n-1} P(A/A_i) < n$
- **P3.2: Single choice** *where only one activity is chosen from the second operand. We have in terms of activities frequencies* $(\#A = \Sigma_{i=0}^{n-1}(\#A_i))$ *and in terms of activities dependencies we have :*
   ○ *In "fork" operator* (A_i *occurs certainly after A occurrence):* $\forall 0 \le i < n; P(A_i/A) = 1$
   ○ *In "join" operator* (A *occurs certainly after only one of* A_i *occurrences):* $\Sigma_{i=0}^{n-1} P(A/A_i) = 1$
- **P3.3: No choice** *where all activities in the second operand are executed. We have in terms of activities frequencies* $\forall 0 \le i < n$, $\#A = \#A_i$ *and in terms of activities dependencies we have :*

○ *In "fork" operator (A_i occurs certainly after A occurrence):* $\forall 0 \leq i < n; P(A_i/A) = 1$

○ *In "join" operator (A occurs certainly after all A_i occurrences):* $\forall 0 \leq i < n; P(A/A_i) = 1$

Using statistical properties 1, 2 and 3, the last step is the identification of workflow patterns through a set of rules. In fact, each pattern has its own statistical rules which abstract statistically its causal dependencies, and identify it in a unique manner. These rules allow, if workflow log is complete, the discovery of the whole workflow patterns included in the mined workflow. To be complete, workflow log should cover all possible cases (i.e. if a specific routing element can appear in the mined workflow model, the log should contain an example of this behaviour in at least one case).

Our control flow mining rules are characterised by a "local" workflow patterns discovery. We propose a different approach that follows **dynamic programming** technique that deals with concurrency and dynamic programming algorithm and mines iteratively the global workflow application by composing local patterns mining techniques. Indeed, these rules proceed through a **local log analysing** that allows to **recover partial results** of mining workflow patterns. In fact, to discover a particular workflow pattern we need only events relating to pattern's elements. Thus, even using only fractions of workflow log, we can discover correctly corresponding workflow patterns (which their events belong to these fractions).

We divided the workflows patterns in three categories (c.f figure 6) : sequence, split and join patterns. In the following, we present rules to discover the most useful workflow patterns belonging to these three categories.

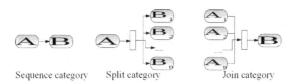

Sequence category   Split category   Join category

Fig. 6. Workflow patterns categories

Discovering sequence pattern. In this category, we find out only the sequence pattern (table 3). In this pattern, the enactment of the activity B depends only on the completion of activity A. So we have used the statistical exclusive dependency property to ensure this relation linking B to A.

Table 3. Rules of sequence workflow pattern

sequence	Rules
	$(\#B = \#A) \wedge$ $(P(B/A) = 1) \wedge \forall A_{0 \leq i < n} \neq A; P(B/A_i) = 0 \wedge \forall B_{0 \leq j < n} \neq B; P(B_j/A) = 0$

For instance, by applying the rules on this pattern over the Final Statistical Dependency Table FSDT (*i.e.* table 2), we discover a sequence pattern linking A_2 and A_3. Indeed, $(\#A_2 = \#A_3)$ and $(P(A_2/A_3) = 1)$ and $\forall A_{0 \leq i < n} \neq A_2; P(A_3/A_i) = 0$ and $\forall A_{0 \leq j < n} \neq A_2; P(A_j/A_3) = 0$.

Discovering fork **patterns.** This category (table 4) has a "fork" operator where a single thread of control splits into multiple threads of control which can be, according to the used pattern, executed or not.

The dependency between the activities A and B_i before and after "fork" operator differs in the three patterns of this category: xor-split, and-split, or-split. These dependencies are characterised by the statistical choice properties. The xor-split pattern, where one of several branches is chosen after "fork" operator, adopts the single choice property (P3.2). and-split and xor-split patterns differentiate themselves through the no choice (P3.3) and free choice (P3.1) properties. Effectively, only a part of activities are executed in the or-split pattern after a "fork" operator, while all the B_i activities are executed in the and-split pattern. The non-parallelism between B_i, in the xor-split pattern are ensured by the no concurrency property while the partial and the global parallelism in or-split and and-split is identified through the application of the statistical partial and global concurrency properties. For instance, the FSDT table (*i.e.* table 2), indicates that we have an and-split pattern linking A_1, A_2 and A_4. In fact,there is a global parallelism between A_2 and A_4 and these activities depend exclusively on A_1.

Discovering join **patterns.** This category (table 4) has a "join" operator where multiple threads of control merge in a single thread of control. The number of necessary branches for the activation of the activity B after the "join" operator depends on the used pattern. To identify the three patterns of this category: xor-join pattern, and-join pattern and M-out-of-N-Join pattern we have analysed dependencies between the activities A_i and B before and after "join". Thus, the single choice (P3.2) and the no concurrency (P2.3) properties are used to identify the xor-join pattern where two or more alternative branches come together without synchronisation and none of the alternative branches is ever executed in parallel. As for the and-join pattern where multiple parallel activities converge into one single thread of control, the no choice (P3.3) and the global concurrency (P2.3) are both used to discover this pattern. In contrary of the M-out-of-N-Join pattern, where we need only the termination of M activities from the incoming n parallel paths to enact the B activity, The concurrency between A_i would be partial (P2.2) and the choice is free (P3.1). For instance, using FSDT table we mine an xor-join pattern linking A_6, A_7 and A_9. In fact, the FSDT's entries of these activities indicate non concurrent behaviour between A_6 and A_7 and the execution of A_9 depend on the termination of all these last activities.

3.4   Composing Discovered Workflow Patterns: Towards Global Workflow

After the discovery of all workflow patterns, the construction of the complete graph of the global workflow will be done following by linking one by one the discovered workflow patterns (figure 7). Discovering a pattern-oriented model ensures a sound and well-formed mined workflow. Therefore, by using this kind of model we are sure that the extracted workflow models do not contain any deadlocks or other anomalies. Furthermore, comparing the initial workflow (figure 2), the activity A_8 is missed in the discovered workflow. This indicates that this activity is never executed and can be removed from the designed model because it does not reprensent a "real" choice after the termination of A_5. If our structural workflow mining approach is important for business

Table 4. Rules of split and join workflow patterns

split	Rules	join	Rules
(xor)	$(\Sigma_{i=0}^{n-1} (\#B_i)=\#A) \wedge$ $(\forall 0 \leq i < n; P(B_i/A) = 1) \wedge$ $(\forall 0 \leq i \neq j < n; P(B_i/B_j) = 0)$	(xor)	$(\Sigma_{i=0}^{n-1} (\#A_i)=\#B) \wedge$ $\Sigma_{i=0}^{n-1} P(B/A_i)=1) \wedge$ $\forall 0 \leq i \neq j < n; P(A_i/A_j) = 0$
(and)	$((\forall 0 \leq i < n; \#B_i=\#A) \wedge$ $(\forall 0 \leq i < n; P(B_i/A) = 1) \wedge$ $(\forall 0 \leq i \neq j < n\ P(B_i/B_j) = -1)$	(and)	$(\forall 0 \leq i < n; \#A_i=\#B) \wedge$ $(\forall 0 \leq i < n; P(B/A_i) = 1) \wedge$ $(\forall 0 \leq i \neq j < n\ P(A_i/A_j) = -1)$
(or)	$\#A \leq \Sigma_{i=0}^{n-1} (\#B_i)) \wedge$ $(\forall 0 \leq i < n; \#B_i \leq \#A)$ $(\forall 0 \leq i < n; P(B_i/A) = 1) \wedge$ $(\exists 0 \leq i \neq j < n; P(B_i/B_j) = -1)$	(M-out -of-N)	$(m * \#B \leq \Sigma_{i=0}^{n-1} (\#A_i))$ $\wedge (\forall 0 \leq i < n; \#A_i \leq \#B)$ $(m \leq \Sigma_{i=0}^{n-1} P(B/A_i) \leq n)$ $\wedge (\exists 0 \leq i \neq j < n; P(A_i/A_j) = -1)$

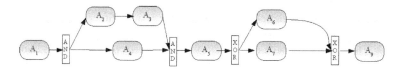

Fig. 7. Workflow discovered example

process intelligence, other techniques are needed in order to discover more than structural aspects of business processes (e.g. performance key indicators and behavioural
process mining [5]).

4   Discussion

In this paper, we discussed issues related to patterns workflow mining from event-based
Log. Obvious applications of workflow patterns mining exist in model driven business
process software engineering, both for bottom up approaches used in business process
alignement [6, 7], and for top down approaches used in workflow generation [8]. The
idea of applying process mining in the context of workflow management was first introduced in [9]. This work proposes methods for automatically deriving a formal model
of a process from a log of events related to its executions and is based on workflow
graphs. Cook and Wolf [10] investigated similar issues in the context of software engineering processes. They extended their work limited initially to sequential processes,
to concurrent processes [11]. Herbst [12, 13] presents an inductive learning component
used to support the acquisition and adaptation of sequential process models, generalis-
ing execution traces from different workflow instances to a workflow model covering
all traces. Starting from the same kind of process logs, van der Aalst et al. propose
techniques to discover workflow models based on Petri nets. Beside analysing process
structure, there exist related works dealing with process behaviour reporting, such as
[14, 15] that describe a tool that provides several features, such as analysing deadline
expirations, predicting exceptions, process instances monitoring.

   Our contribution proposes a new approach characterised by a **partial discovery** of
workflow patterns. This approach recovers partial results from log fractions. It discov-

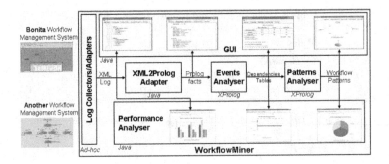

Fig. 8. WorkflowMiner Pipes and Filters mining process

ers **more complex features** with a better specification of "fork" operator (and-split, or-split, xor-split patterns) and "join" operator (and-join, M-out-of-N-Join, and M-out-of-N-Join patterns). It deals better with concurrency through the introduction "*concurrent window*" that deals **dynamically** with concurrence. It seems to be more simple in computing. This simplicity will not affect its efficiency in processing the concurrent aspect of workflow.

We have implemented our presented workflow patterns mining algorithms within our prototype WorkflowMiner [16]. WorkflowMiner, as seen in figure 8, is composed of (a) Events Analyser component dealing with causal dependency analysis (producing different SDT tables), (b) Patterns Analyser component using causal dependencies to discover partial workflow patterns and compose them iteratively into a global workflow model, and (c) Performance Analyser exploiting brute event-based log, discovered causal dependencies, and discovered partial and global workflow patterns to measure performance metrics (see paper [5] for more details on adopted performance measurement approach). WorkflowMiner is written in Java and based on Bonita Workflow Management System[2] and XProlog Java Prolog API[3].

Starting from executions of a workflow, (1) event streams are gathered into an XML log. In order to be processed, (2) these workflow log events are wrapped into a 1st order logic format, compliant with UML class diagrams shown in figure 1. (3) Mining rules are applied on resulted 1st order log events to discover workflow patterns. We use a Prolog-based presentation for log events, and mining rules. (4) Discovered patterns are given to the workflow designer so he/she will have a look on the analysis of his/her deployed workflow to restructure or redesign it either manually or semi-automatically.

To illustrate the logical aspects of the two components (events analyser and patterns analyser) implementing step (3), we illustrate the example of sequence workflow pattern 1st order logical rules (of table 3) mapped to a Prolog predicate sequence. The predicate sequence(A, B, Log) returns True if there exists a sequence pattern between the activities A and B within the event stream Log, else it returns False. The predicate occurrence(A, Log, NA) return the number of occurrence NA of an activity A within the event stream Log. The predicate sdt_frequence(B, A, F) computes

[2] Bonita, bonita.objectweb.org
[3] XProlog, www.iro.umontreal.ca/∼vaucher/XProlog/

in F the value of $P(B/A)$. Thus, sdt_frequence(B, A, 1) means $P(B/A) = 1$. The predicate delete_from(Log, A, LAi) computes in a list LA_i all activities different from A within Log. Thus $LA_i = (Log \setminus A)$. The predicate sdt_frequence_right_iterator(B, LAi, F) ensures that $\forall A_i \in LA_i$, $P(B/A_i) = F$. Thus, sdt_frequence_right_iterator(B, LAi, 0) means $\forall A_i \in (Log \setminus A)$, $P(B/A_i) = 0$. Similarly, the predicate sdt_frequence_left_iterator(LBj, A, F) ensures that $\forall B_j \in LB_j$, $P(B_j/A) = F$. Thus, sdt_frequence_left_iterator(LBj, A, 0) means $\forall B_j \in (Log \setminus B)$, $P(B_j/A) = 0$.

```
sequence(A, B, Log) :-
        occurrence(A, Log, NA), occurrence(B, Log, NB), NA = NB,
        sdt_frequence(B, A, 1),
        delete_from(Log, A, LAi), delete_from(Log, B, LBj),
        sdt_frequence_right_iterator(B, LAi, 0),
        sdt_frequence_left_iterator(LBj, A, 0).
```

Table 5 compares our WorkflowMiner prototype to workflow mining tools representing previous studied approaches. We focus on seven aspects: **structure** of the target discovering language, **local discovery** dealing with incomplete parts of logs (opposed to global and complete log analysis), **parallelism** (a fork path beginning with and-split and ending with and-join), **non-free choice** (NFC processes mix synchronisation and choice in one construct), **loops** (basics cyclic workflow transitions, or paths),**Short loops** (mono- or bi- activity(ies) loops), **noise** (situation where log is incomplete or contains errors or non-representative exceptional instances), and **time** (event time stamp information used to calculate performance indicators such as waiting/synchronisation times, flow times, load/utilisation rate, etc.). There are others process mining tools (concerning for instance, Social network mining, workflow analysis frameworks), but they are out of the scope of this paper.

Table 5. Comparing Process Mining Tools

Process Mining Tools	EMiT [17]	Little Thumb [18]	InWoLvE [19]	Process Miner [20]	WorkflowMiner [16]
Structure	Graph	Graph	Graph	Block	**Patterns**
Local discovery	No	No	No	No	**Yes**
Parallelism	Yes	Yes	Yes	Yes	**Yes**
Non-free choice	No	No	No	No	**Yes**
Basic Loops	Yes	Yes	Yes	Yes	**Yes**
Short Loops	Yes	Yes	No	No	**No**
Noise	No	Yes	Yes	No	**No**
Time	Yes	No	No	No	**No**

WorkflowMiner can be distinguished by supporting **local discovery** through a set of control flow ming rules that are characterised by a "local" workflow patterns discovery enabling **partial results** to be discovered correctly. Morevoer, even if non-free choice (NFC) construct is mentioned as an example of a workflow pattern that is difficult to mine, WorkflowMiner discovers M-out-of-N-Join pattern which can be seen as a generalisation of the useful Discriminator pattern that were proven to be inherently non free-choice. None of related works can deal with such constructs. Our current work is about discovering complex patterns by using more metrics (*e.g.* entropy, periodicity, etc.) and by enriching the workflow log. We are also interested in discovering more complex transactional characteristics of cooperative workflows [3, 4].

References

1. W. M. P. Van Der Aalst, A. H. M. Ter Hofstede, B. Kiepuszewski, and A. P. Barros. Workflow patterns. *Distrib. Parallel Databases*, 14(1):5–51, 2003.
2. J. E. Cook and A. L. Wolf. Event-based detection of concurrency. In *6th ACM SIGSOFT international symposium on Foundations of software engineering*. ACM Press, 1998.
3. W. Gaaloul, S. Bhiri, and C. Godart.   Discovering workflow transactional behaviour event-based log. In *12th International Conference on Cooperative Information Systems (CoopIS'04)*, LNCS, Larnaca, Cyprus, October 25-29, 2004. Springer-Verlag.
4. W. Gaaloul and C. Godart. Mining workflow recovery from event based logs. In *Business Process Management*, volume 3649, pages 169–185, 2005.
5. K. Baïna, I. Berrada, and L. Kjiri. A Balanced Scoreboard Experiment for Business Process Performance Monitoring : Case study. In *1st International E-Business Conference (IEBC'05)*, Tunis, Tunisia, June 24-25 2005.
6. W. M. P. van der Aalst. Business alignment: Using process mining as a tool for delta analysis. In *CAiSE Workshops (2)*, pages 138–145, 2004.
7. B. Benatallah, F. Casati, and F. Toumani. Analysis and management of web service protocols. In *ER*, pages 524–541, 2004.
8. K. Baïna, B. Benatallah, F. Casati, and F. Toumani. Model-driven web service development. In *CAiSE*, pages 290–306, 2004.
9. R. Agrawal, D. Gunopulos, and F. Leymann. Mining process models from workflow logs. *Lecture Notes in Computer Science*, 1377:469–498, 1998.
10. J. E. Cook and A. L. Wolf. Discovering models of software processes from event-based data. *ACM Transactions on Software Engineering and Methodology (TOSEM)*, 7(3):215–249, 1998.
11. J. E. Cook and A. L. Wolf. Event-based detection of concurrency. In *Proceedings of the 6th ACM SIGSOFT international symposium on Foundations of software engineering*, pages 35–45. ACM Press, 1998.
12. J. Herbst. A machine learning approach to workflow management. In *Machine Learning: ECML 2000, 11th European Conference on Machine Learning, Barcelona, Catalonia, Spain*, volume 1810, pages 183–194. Springer, May 2000.
13. J. Herbst and D. Karagiannis. Integrating machine learning and workflow management to support acquisition and adaptation of workflow models. In *9th International Workshop on DEXA*, page 745. IEEE Computer Society, 1998.
14. M. Sayal, F. Casati, M.C. Shan, and U. Dayal. Business process cockpit. *Proceedings of 28th International Conference on Very Large Data Bases (VLDB'02)*, pages 880–883, 2002.
15. D. Grigori, F. Casati, M. Castellanos, U. Dayal, M. Sayal, and M-C. Shan. Business process intelligence. *Comput. Ind.*, 53(3):321–343, 2004.
16. W. Gaaloul, K. Baïna, and C. Godart. Towards mining structural workflow patterns. In Kim Viborg Andersen, John K. Debenham, and Roland Wagner, editors, *DEXA*, volume 3588 of *LNCS*, pages 24–33. Springer, 2005.

17. Wil M. P. van der Aalst and B. F. van Dongen. Discovering workflow performance models from timed logs. In *1st International Conference on Engineering and Deployment of Cooperative Information Systems*, pages 45–63. Springer-Verlag, 2002.
18. A. J. M. M. Weijters and W. M. P. van der Aalst. Workflow mining: Discovering workflow models from event-based data. In *ECAI Workshop on Knowledge Discovery and Spatial Data*, pages 78–84, 2002.
19. J. Herbst and D. Karagiannis. Workflow mining with inwolve. *Comput. Ind.*, 53(3):245–264, 2004.
20. G. Schimm. Process Miner - A Tool for Mining Process Schemes from Event-Based Data. In *European Conference on Logics in AI*, pages 525–528. Springer-Verlag, 2002.

BestChoice: A Decision Support System
for Supplier Selection in e-Marketplaces*

Dongjoo Lee, Taehee Lee, Sue-kyung Lee, Ok-ran Jeong, Hyeonsang Eom,
and Sang-goo Lee

School of Computer Science and Engineering, Seoul National University,
Seoul 151-742, Republic of Korea
{therocks, thlee, sklee, orjeong, sglee}@europa.snu.ac.kr,
hseom@cse.snu.ac.kr

Abstract. A growing number of companies are outsourcing their purchasing
processes to independent purchasing agencies. These agencies now have to
process an ever increasing number of purchase requests each day. The conventional methods of selecting the right suppliers for the purchase requests incur
heavy human and time costs. We have designed and implemented *BestChoice*, a
decision support system for supplier selection. It allows the evaluator to create
rules for supplier evaluation based on the Multi Attribute Utility Theory, a theory for evaluating the utility of alternatives. BestChoice provides rule structures
that can be saved and reused for similar selection cases. The architecture and
selection rules of BestChoice are presented. Performance of BestChoice at one
of the largest procurement agencies is analyzed.

1 Introduction

Purchasing is one of the most important operations of a company that greatly affects
the competence of the company in the current highly competitive market. For effective purchasing, some companies invest large amounts of money and effort to build a
purchase management system. Others outsource the operation to purchasing agencies
for cost and quality. Purchasing agencies make profit from the service fees for the
purchase transactions and from sharing the cost savings they can bring. Computerized
online process is a necessary condition to achieve the required efficiency and effectiveness. Multiple suppliers are maintained for each of the product classes and clients
and their purchase requests are managed online, forming a virtual market place controlled by the agency.

In finding the best supplier for the products requested, the purchasing agency must
satisfy the purchasing objectives of the customer companies such as price, delivery
constraints, and quality of service. The supplier selection problem has been a long-
standing area of research. Multi Attribute Utility Theory [1], Analytic Hierarchy Process [2] and OutRanking Method [3] are the representative selection methods, and
many variations of these have been proposed. The human cost and time used in evaluating candidate suppliers and analyzing the evaluation results to select the suppliers

---

* This work was supported by the Ministry of Information & Communications, Korea, under
the Information Technology Research Center (ITRC) Support Program.

J. Lee et al. (Eds.): DEECS 2006, LNCS 4055, pp. 198–208, 2006.

that satisfy the purchasing objectives of the purchasing companies are major cost factors that directly affect an agency's profit. Most of the supplier selection methods focus on selecting the optimal suppliers, and leave the human cost and time aspects of supplier selection largely unaddressed.

We believe that one way to address this problem is to use a decision support system which supports the selection of optimal suppliers. We have designed and implemented BestChoice, a decision support system for the selection of optimal suppliers by incorporating a supplier rating method based on Multi Attribute Utility Theory (MAUT) and Analytic Hierarchy Process (AHP). Further, it organizes and stores various key elements needed for supplier evaluation as Supplier Evaluation Policy (SEP) rules. The use of rules, which capture the domain expertise of experienced evaluators, is responsible for the time and cost reduction in supplier evaluation. We have validated the effectiveness of BestChoice by running it at iMarketKorea, Inc. [4], the largest e-marketplace purchasing agency in Korea. The results of running BestChoice for six months show that the average time for selecting candidate suppliers is reduced by 50%, and the average time for selecting the optimal suppliers is also reduced by 50%.

In this paper we will describe the theoretical underpinnings of BestChoice, and the validation of BestChoice based on actual design, implementation, and deployment in a commercial setting. In Section 2, we review the related work on the supplier selection problem. In Section 3, we discuss the supplier selection problem in purchasing agencies. In Section 4, we present elements of BestChoice. In Section 5, we describe application of BestChoice at a commercial purchasing agency and analyze the results there. Section 6 concludes the paper.

2   Related Work

The supplier selection problem is a complex problem that requires consideration of many criteria. Since the 1960s it has been a subject of great interest to researchers and practioners. In 1966 Dickson extracted from the then-existing literature over fifty factors for evaluating suppliers and their respective characteristics [5]. [6] provides a review of 74 papers after Dickson's publication. Most supplier selection methods are focused on methodologies for evaluating suppliers, and fall into three categories, Elimination, Optimization and Probabilistic [7].

Recently with the advance of the Internet, the process of purchasing has been automated on the e-marketplace by iMarketKorea [4], Ariba [8], Commerce One [9], etc. Such e-marketplace purchasing agencies mainly deal with MRO. MRO requires fast processing of optimal supplier selection, and it has become a subject of recent research. One supplier-selection system is DEALMAKER, a rule based automatic supplier selection system for the Defense Logistics Agency in the US [10]. It makes use of rules for filtering suppliers and selecting optimal suppliers. Another supplier selection system, ES3 - Electronic Supplier selection system, more advanced than [10] was implemented and presented in [11]. It is a 3-tired client server based system that makes use of a multi-objective decision algorithm. It relies heavily on human efforts to organize the information for evaluating suppliers and does not offer analysis methods. [12] presents CBES (Cost – Benefit Evaluation Server) based on CBDM (Cost Benefit Decision Model). Because the CBDM is based on a hierarchal aggregation of attributes, it is hard to simplify the evaluation process.

3   Supplier Selection Problem in Purchasing Agency

The steps that purchasing agencies take to process purchasing requests are shown in Fig. 1.

Fig. 1. When a customer requests purchasing, a purchasing agency begins by assigning it to a purchasing agent. First he finds supplier candidates who are able to supply the requested product. Then he requests quotes for the product from them. When he receives the quotes, he selects a supplier to supply the product using the quotes and his own experience. Then a supply contract for the product between the purchasing agency and the supplier is made. The purchasing agency supplies it to the customer.

For each processing request, the supplier selection problem occurs twice. First is the selection of candidate suppliers to whom a Request for Quotes is to be sent. Usually purchasing agents use only their prior experience of processing similar requests in selecting candidates. Second is the selection of an optimal supplier, that is, a supplier with whom the purchasing agent will contract. Purchasing agents use quotes received from the candidate suppliers and various other types of information they have at their disposal, including their experiences, to select the optimal supplier. This is a more critical than the first. A typical purchasing agent goes through this purchasing process many ten times a day.

A purchasing agency organizes agents into groups, called Sourcing Group (SG) [13], on the basis of the types of products to purchase. There are both experienced and inexperienced purchasing agents in an SG, but in reality, there are more inexperienced agents than experienced.

Decision support systems for supplier selection by purchasing agencies have to take into account two other facts besides the selection of an optimal supplier. First, there are many purchasing requests to process. Second, there are not enough experienced agents to process purchasing requests.

4   BestChoice

We designed BestChoice to solve the two problems mentioned at the end of Section 3. It is a framework for evaluating suppliers; the result is a numeral value called *Utility*. It supports the five-step supplier evaluation process that we have defined. The first step is the establishment of an evaluation goal. The second is the determination of the evaluation *Factors* sufficing the goal. In the third step, *Utility Functions* are used to convert the *Factor*'s values to normalized values. In the fourth step, the importance of each *Factor* is calculated as a numeral value called *Weight*. In the fifth step, total utilities of suppliers are calculated, using supplier information retrieved from a data warehouse. The definitions of components for evaluating suppliers, such as Factors, Utility Functions and Weights, are based on MAUT. Details of these are presented in Section 4.1.

The supplier evaluation process outlined above is a little time-consuming. But information gathered through this process can be stored in a database in the form of Supplier Evaluation Policy (*SEP*). Purchasing agents can reuse SEP for similar purchasing requests. This speeds up the process of selecting the right suppliers. The database storing the SEP plays the role of a knowledgebase from which inexperienced purchasing agents can obtain domain expertise.

Because evaluation results are expressed simply in normalized numeral values, analysis methods are needed to make the evaluation process easily understandable. Using the analysis methods, purchasing agents can simulate the various factors and grasp the current evaluation results. In Section 4.4 three analysis methods are presented.

4.1 Supplier Evaluation

Factors for Supplier Evaluation

Factors for evaluating suppliers and their importance have been studied for a long time. In [5], 23 important factors are summarized. Composition of factors to evaluate suppliers and their importance can vary according to the products. [5] lists quality, delivery, performance history, warranties, claim policies and price as the most important factors. Factor may be qualitative or quantitative. Raw values for qualitative factors can be collected from human activities such as a survey. But quantitative factors can be aggregated from historical transaction data such as contract records or past quotes stored in databases. The construction of a data warehouse is very important. However, its discussion is beyond the scope of this paper.

Multi Attribute Utility Theory

The utility theory approach is an attempt to rigorously apply objective measurement to decision making. The value of an alternative is assumed to consist of measures over the criteria that contribute to worth, all converted to a common scale of util. The basic hypothesis of MAUT is that in any decision problem, there exists a real valued function U defined on the set of feasible alternatives which the decision maker wishes, consciously or not, to maximize[1]. MAUT can be applied to supplier evaluation. So the total utility of a supplier is expressed as the weighted sum of the utilities of the attributes as Equation (1).

When we use MAUT to solve real world problems, utility calculation of each attribute is an important issue. Because the characteristics of each attribute are different, a different utility calculation scheme must be applied to each attribute. However, determining the calculation scheme is not simple, and to simplify the problem, we organize the pool of utility functions used for various attributes. The next subsection deals with the details of this problem. Another issue when using MAUT is the calculation of the influencing power of each attribute in supplier evaluation. AHP is used for weighting each attribute. More details of AHP are presented in the section "*Weighting of Factor.*" Hereforth, *Factor* is used on the same line as *Attribute*.

$$U(s) = \sum wifi(xi) \qquad (1)$$

$s = (x_1, x_2, x_3, ..., x_k)$: supplier

x_i : Attribute (same as Factor)

f_i : Utility function applied to attribute x_i

w_i : Importance of attribute x_i represented as numerical value

Calculation and Normalization of Utility

To express the utility of a factor, its raw value is calculated to the normalized numeral value through *Utility Function*. According to the property of the factor, a different utility function can be used. For example, the Log type function leads to a low penalty being applied to a low valued supplier. In the case of selecting suppliers of pens or similar products, it can be applied to the factor having relatively low importance such as After Service. Besides these, there are Linear, Exponential, Step and Redistributing type utility functions. These are summarized in Table 1.

Table 1. Utility Functions

Function Type	Basic Formula	Shape	Effect
linear	$u = ax + b$		base function
logarithm	$u = a \log x + b$		low penalty to a low ranked supplier
exponential	$u = ae^{bx} + c$		high penalty to a low ranked supplier
step	$u = \begin{cases} u_1 & 0 \le x < r_1 \\ u_2 & r_1 \le x < r_2 \\ ... \\ u_k & r_{k-1} \le x \le r_k \end{cases}$		step function
redistribution	$u = \ln\left(\dfrac{xi}{1 - xi}\right)/10 + 0.5$		low penalty to a low ranked supplier and low benefit to a high ranked supplier

What kind of utility function was applied to the factor is very important knowledge, because the inexperienced can not easily determine the proper utility function. But decisions of experts are stored in the SEP and it can be easily delivered to the inexperienced. Normalization of the factor's raw value as well as the determination of the type of utility function is very important. Raw values of various factors may be in different ranges according to their properties. Different ranges of factors have to be converted to fit in one common range. In particular, because BestChoice uses the range (0, 1), each raw value is converted to the value between 0 and 1. If the purchasing agent knows the minimum value ($\min_i$) and the maximum value ($\max_i$) of the factor, the raw value (x_i) can be easily converted to the normalized value (x_{in}) using Equation (2).

$$x_{in} = \frac{x_i - \min_i}{\max_i - \min_i} \tag{2}$$

To use this naïve method, the purchasing agent has to know both the minimum and maximum values. But it is hard to know them before seeing all possible values. To solve this problem, the minimum and maximum values are determined automatically when calculating utility.

At the time of utility calculation, BestChoice reads all raw values of the factor. Then the original minimum and maximum values can be determined. Using these values, the minimum and maximum values are always converted to 0 and 1. But in practice exact 0 and 1 are not possible. So those original values are converted using Equation (3) and Equation (4).

$$\min_i = \min_{si} - (\max_{si} - \min_{si}) \times \alpha \tag{3}$$

$$\max_i = \max_{si} + (\max_{si} - \min_{si}) \times \alpha \tag{4}$$

α is the normalization factor, which usually is the value between 0.1 and 0.2. Once the minimum and maximum values are calculated in this way, later process is same as the naïve method.

Weighting of Factor
The AHP is a technique for converting subjective assessments of relative importance into a set of weights. AHP has been used to develop linear utility functions reflecting the relative importance of decision objectives or problem features that have been used for mathematical programming, as well as for ranking things [2]. In practice, most agents face difficulty in expressing the importance or the influencing power of factor. But using AHP, through simple Pairwise comparison, importance is calculated and expressed as a numeral value called *Weight*. Due to its simplicity, it is very useful in practice. Also its usefulness and reliability have been proven in previous research [14] [15]. BestChoice offers a graphical user interface for the Pairwise comparison of factors, as well as for the manual setting of weights.

4.2 Constraints

By searching past contract histories for products having equal class with requested products, supplier candidates can be determined. And purchasing agents may think that some of the suppliers who have a lower or upper value than certain specific limits can be ignored. We call these up-limit and low-limit *Constraint*, which is the knowledge of the experienced. It can be delivered to the inexperienced through the SEP. And it also can be used to increase the speed of utility calculation of suppliers. For utility calculation, many aggregations and arithmetic calculations are needed. These are processed using a DBMS and are time-consuming. If the number of target suppliers decreases, the calculation time also decreases. When Constraint is applied, usually the number of target suppliers decreases.

4.3 Supplier Evaluation Policy (SEP)

The SEP consists of components for supplier evaluation based on MAUT. These are Factor, Utility Function and Weight presented in Section 4.1. Constraint presented in Section 4.2 is another component. Supplier evaluations are done differently according to the products suppliers supply. This supplier evaluation method is determined by the requested product. If this condition is added to the SEP, the SEP can be a kind of a rule interpreted as "if requested product is p then evaluate by this evaluation method". Because products belonging to the same class have similar properties, evaluation methods for them can be the same. Purchasing requests for products having similar properties are processed by SG, the sourcing group. So the SG also can be the condition determining the scope of the application. That is, the SEP is the rule defined in Equation (5). Because making the SEP for all products is impossible, as the number of products reaches hundreds and thousands, SG or class is proper to express the scope.

The SEP stored in a database can dramatically speed up the processing of a purchasing request. When a purchasing request for product is received, specific SEP is determined. Then BestChoice find the supplier candidates and filter them according to Constraints in the SEP. After which, the Utilities of the suppliers are calculated and the suppliers are listed in descending order of Utility. All these processes are done automatically. But it is possible only when the SEP exists. Also if there is more than one SEP satisfying the given condition, the selection of SEP is still the problem.

$$SEP = (S, \{(x_i, u_i, w_i)\}, \{(x_j, C_j)\}) \tag{5}$$

S : Scope (sourcing group or class or product)

x_i, x_j : Factor

w_i : Weight

u_i : Utility Function

C_j : Constraints

Determination of Factors, Utility Functions, Weights and Constraints is not easy for the inexperienced. So it is very hard for the inexperienced to do this. Once the experienced makes the SEP with various simulations and analyses, the inexperienced can reuse it for similar purchasing requests. Owing to SEP, it is possible to deliver knowledge of the experienced to the inexperienced.

4.4 Analysis Methods for Supplier Evaluation Results

To make sense of the evaluation results, analysis methods are needed. The inexperienced can acquire experience more easily using these analysis methods, and information obtained by them can be used during negotiations with suppliers. Though there are various analysis methods, the most useful methods we selected are *What if Analysis*, *Similarity Analysis* and *Sensitivity Analysis*.

What if Analysis

'What if Analysis' method enables the evaluator to simulate the evaluation condition. We implemented line and bar graphs to show the evaluation result. The evaluator can change the Factor, Weight, Utility Function and even the raw values of suppliers and then he can observe the changes of the results that are presented in graphs.

Similarity Analysis

'Similarity Analysis' method is a method for extracting the most similar supplier that the evaluator wants to find. If the evaluator wants to find a specific supplier that has certain values, he inputs the values of Factors. Then BestChoice evaluates the similarity through the calculation of the difference between the values of supplier and what the evaluator wants, and it shows the results.

Sensitivity Analysis

When the evaluator wants to know the Factor's range where the order of suppliers does not change, 'Sensitivity Analysis' method can be used. Because it is within the bounds of possibility that some supplier is strong in some Factor while some other supplier is better in other Factor, a change in the Weight of some Factor can change the order of suppliers. The evaluator can specify the Factor whose weight is changed or fixed. He can comprehend why Weight had been determined like that.

5   Implementation

5.1   Architecture

Fig.3 illustrates the architecture of BestChoice. It is a 3-tier system which consists of a database layer, a logic layer and an interface layer.

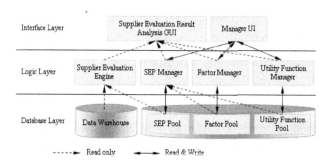

Fig. 2. Architecture of BestChoice

To manage Factors, Utility Functions, and SEP in the pool, they are stored in a relational database. *Managers* in the logic layer manage business logic to process the SEP and its components. *Supplier Evaluation Engine* calculates utilities of suppliers by reading the suppliers information from a data warehouse (i.e., the relational database) and the SEP from the *SEP Pool*. There are analysis interface and management interface for the SEP, Factor and Utility Function in the interface layer.

5.2 Application

BestChoice was installed at a real purchasing agency, *iMarketKorea* [4], which is one
of the major purchasing agencies in Korea. For integration with an existing purchasing system, it was implemented as a *Java* based application following the *J2EE* architecture. The logic layer was implemented as a *Session Bean* and the interface layer as
JSP and *Java Applet*.

Fig.3 is the captured screen which is processing a purchasing request.

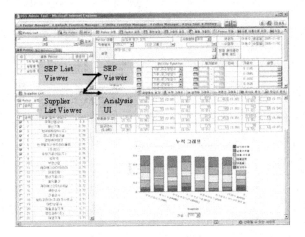

Fig. 3. Implemented Application

If a requested product is provided, applicable SEPs are listed on the upper-left *SEP
List Viewer*. If a specific SEP is selected, it is shown in the upper-right *SEP Viewer*. It
provides the interface that is able to change the components of the SEP. When the
SEP is applied, suppliers are listed in the lower-left *Supplier List Viewer* in a descending order of Utility. And selected suppliers in it can be analyzed in the lower-right
Analysis UI. Because iMarketKorea is a Korean company, the user interface of the
application is shown in Korean.

5.3 Validation of BestChoice

We have validated the effectiveness of BestChoice in terms of two intuitive aspects:
the decrease in the average time spent in selecting suppliers in steps 2 and 5 in Fig.1
and the accuracy of supplier evaluation.

Average time for supplier selection for six months before and after the application
of BestChoice is compared in Table 2.

Table 2. Changes in average time spent to select suppliers

Average time	Step 2	Step 5
Before 6 months	10 minutes	60 minutes
After 6 months	5 minutes	30 minutes
Ratio of changes	50% decrease	50 % decrease

The total number of purchase requests measured is the proprietary information of iMarketKorea and thus cannot be made public. Suffice it to say that the number if more than statistically significant to render the results of our validation meaningful. Average time for selecting suppliers to request quotes decreases by 50% from 10 to 5 minutes. Average time for selecting an optimal supplier to contract decreases 50% from 60 to 30 minutes.

In order to calculate the accuracy of supplier evaluation, we collected data relevant to determine if purchasing agents used the evaluation results in practice. We selected 5 SGs who used BestChoice most actively and averaged the ratio. The average usage ratio is presented in Table. 3.

Table 3. Usage ratio of the evaluation results

Step	Step 2		Step 5	
Supplier rank in order	In rank 1	In rank 3	In rank 1	In rank 3
Average usage ratio (%)	67.72	81.34	90.42	95.65

In step 5, which is for contracting average usage ratio is over 90%. This result shows that BestChoice can store the experiences of the experienced in SEP very well.

After the application of BestChoice, the profit at iMarketKorea increased by about US$3.5 million. This increase is considered to be caused by a decrease in processing time and an increase in the rationality of the selection via the SEP. The ROI – Return on Investment, relative to the cost of installing BestChoice and training the agents on its use, for six months is 4670%.

These results show that BestChoice is a practical decision support system for supplier selection in e-marketplace.

6 Conclusion

The current methods of selecting the right suppliers largely do not address the time and human cost. We believe that one way to reduce this cost is to use an automated decision support system that will make use of domain expertise of evaluators and historical data for suppliers. To validate our idea, we have designed and implemented BestChoice. In this paper, we described the theoretical underpinnings of BestChoice, and experimental validation of our idea. We have deployed BestChoice in a commercial e-marketplace purchasing agency and analyzed the data collected over a period of six months. The result confirms the effectiveness of our system. One challenging topic for future research is to evaluate suppliers with no historical data. The use of segmentation data obtained by mining the representative collections of suppliers may be a basis for addressing the challenge.

References

1. David L. Olson., Decision Aids for Selection Problems, Springer (1996) 19-33
2. David L. Olson., Decision Aids for Selection Problems, Springer (1996) 49-68
3. de Boer L., van der Wegen L., Telgen J., Outranking methods in support of supplier selection. European Journal of Purchasing and Supply Management 4 (1998) 109-118

4. iMarketKorea, http://www.imarketkorea.co.kr
5. Dickson, G.W., An Analysis of Vendor Selection Systems and Decisions, Journal of Purchasing, Vol. 2 No. 1 (1966) 28-41.
6. Weber, C.A., Current, J.R. and Benton, W.C., Vendor Selection Criteria and Methods, European Journal of Operations Research, Vol. 50 No. 1 (1991) 2-18.
7. Ding H., Benyoucef L., Xie X., A Simulation-Optimization Approach Using Genetic Search for Supplier Selection, Proceedings of the 2003 Winter Simulation Conference (2003) 1260-1267
8. Ariba, http://www.ariba.com
9. Commerce One, http://www.commerceone.com
10. Szekely P., Neches B., Benjamin D. P., Chen J., Rogers C. M., Controlling Supplier Selection in an Automated Purchasing System, In AAAI-99 Workshop on Artificial Intelligence in Electronic Commerce (AIEC-99), Menlo Park, CA, USA. (1999)
11. Senthil K. R., Dan L.S, Mark R.H., ES3 -Electronic Supplier Selection System, AMSMA 2000, (2000)
12. Liu Y., Yu F., Stanley Y. W. Su, Lam H., A Cost-Benefit Evaluation Server for Decision Support in e-Business, Decision Support Systems, Vol. 36 , Issue 1 (2002) 81 - 97
13. UNSPSC, http://www.unspsc.org
14. Zahedi, F. The Analytic Hierarchy Process: A Survey of the Method and Its Applications. Interfaces 16:4 (1986) 96-108
15. Shim, J.P. Bibliographical Research on the Analytic Hierarchy Process (AHP). Socio-Economic Planning Sciences Vol. 23:3 (1989) 161-167

Semantic Web Services Enabled B2B Integration

Paavo Kotinurmi[1,2], Tomas Vitvar[1], Armin Haller[1], Ray Richardson[3],
and Aidan Boran[3]

[1] Digital Enterprise Research Institute(DERI), Ireland
`firstname.lastname@deri.org`
[2] Helsinki University of Technology, Finland
`firstname.lastname@tkk.fi`
[3] Bell Labs Ireland, Lucent
`firstnamelastname@lucent.com`

Abstract. The use of Semantic Web Service (SWS) technologies have been suggested to enable more dynamic B2B integration of heterogeneous systems and partners. We present our approach to accomplish dynamic B2B integrations based on the WSMX SWS environment. We particularly show how WSMX can be made to support the RosettaNet e-business framework and how it can add dynamics to B2B interactions by automating mediation of heterogeneous messages. This is illustrated through a purchasing scenario. The benefits of applying SWS technologies include more flexibility in accepting heterogeneity in B2B integrations and easing back-end integrations. This allows for example to introduce more competition into the purchasing process within e-business frameworks.

1 Introduction

To integrate heterogeneous enterprise information systems, such as Enterprise Resource Planning (ERP), several e-business frameworks have been developed [10]. The e-business frameworks address B2B integration on business process, message and communication levels [5, 6]. As e-business frameworks define B2B integration interfaces between the partners, they can change their internal processes and information systems without a need to change the B2B integration interface. Electronic Data Interchange (EDI) standards, such as EDI X12[1], have been around since the 1970's and are still widely used for B2B integrations. RosettaNet[2] is a widely used XML-based e-business framework.

Companies have invested considerable amounts of money and resources to implement the B2B integrations based on these e-business frameworks and they have the supporting infrastructure largely in place. Back-end integration requires ensuring that internal systems can produce and consume the pre-agreed messages in the collaborative processes. Due to the flexibility of these e-business frameworks regarding message details and message ordering, considerable effort is required to ensure that the B2B integration details of two partners match

---

[1] http://www.x12.org/
[2] http://www.rosettanet.org/

J. Lee et al. (Eds.): DEECS 2006, LNCS 4055, pp. 209–223, 2006.

[13]. Therefore, B2B integrations suffer from long setup times and high costs [7]. This leads to a business models with simple processes, in which long term rigid partnerships are established between organisations. There is, for example, no competition for getting multiple quotes as the default partner is always selected directly for purchasing. This is because there is too much overhead to manage multiple partner specific quoting and purchasing integrations from back-end applications directly.

Semantic technologies and Semantic Web Services (SWS) have been proposed to achieve more dynamic partnerships [1]. The SWS approach based on, for example, OWL-S [4] or the Web Service Modeling Ontology (WSMO) [8] enables annotation of the B2B integration interfaces with semantic information. This allows automated or semi-automated mediation. In addition, SWS enables powerful discovery, composition, and selection capabilities of services. This paper presents a scenario for B2B integration, where a buyer organisation's internal use of SWS technologies enables it to integrate with heterogeneous suppliers that support different e-business frameworks.

The scenario assumes that SWS technologies are introduced to B2B integration stepwise rather than all at once. Instead of designing scenarios of partners using only SWS in the communication, we combine the security, reliability, and scalability strengths of existing e-business frameworks with the SWS's benefits of a more flexible integration with powerful discovery, composition, and selection capabilities.

The SWS solution in this paper is based on the Web Service Modelling eXecution environment (WSMX) [3]. WSMX is a reference implementation of the WSMO and operates using the Web Service Modeling Language (WSML).

The rest of this paper is structured as follows: Section 2 describes a scenario of B2B interactions. Section 3 presents how SWS technologies address the requirements identified in the scenario. Section 4 discusses expected benefits of SWS technologies. Section 5 presents related work and section 6 concludes our solution and discusses topics for further research.

2   Use Case Scenario

We consider an *organisation A* that manufactures electronic devices. For a particular device, organisation A needs specific components that can be delivered by approved suppliers, referred here as *partners B* and *C*. Organisation A needs *X-type of display unit* components that can be delivered by partners B and C. In the current situation, the B2B integration only covers purchasing activities as shown in figure 1 and there is no competition for purchasing per delivery basis. In this proposed scenario, organisation A first submits *Requests For Quotes* (RFQ) to all its suppliers for the components. After the responses, it selects the best quote and initiates the *Purchase Order* (PO) process with the selected partner.

Considering the integrations, the following heterogeneities exist with partners according to general B2B integration levels [5, 6]:

Communication level interoperation is needed to understand different languages used to describe the messages exchanged and how the message exchange happens. *Partner B* uses the RosettaNet Implementation Framework (RNIF) 2.0 over HTTP(S) for secure communication and the message contents are in XML. RNIF guides how the messages are sent and acknowledged and how digital signatures are used. With *partner C* the communication is achieved via a Value Added Network (VAN) operator, which takes care of the communication between the partners. EDI X12 format messages are put to a file system folder, where the VAN operator collects the messages and ensures the secure delivery of the messages to the partners.

Message level interoperation is the ability to understand exchanged messages (sometimes referred as business documents or payload). RosettaNet defines *Partner Interface Processes* (PIPs) that define standard inter-company process choreographies and the related schemas for the XML messages exchanged. *Partner B* uses the PIP *3A1 Request for Quote* and *3A4 Request Purchase order* messages [3] according to the message guidelines provided by RosettaNet. Both PIPs contain request and response messages. *Partner C* uses EDI X12 messages and expects the *840 Request for Quotation* for quotes and *850 Purchase Order* for orders [4]. The quotes are responded with *879 Price Information* message and the purchase orders by *855 Purchase Order Acknowledgment* message. These PIP and EDI X12 messages use different terms and identifiers in referring to the same concepts. In addition, for example the product identifiers used differ among the companies.

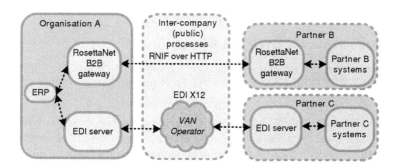

Fig. 1. Overall scenario

Business Process level interoperation is the ability of companies to exchange messages in the right sequence and timing. *Partner B* complies with PIP 3A1 and 3A4 standard choreographies. That means the partner's response arrives within 24 hours of sending the requests. For every PIP message sent, there is a receipt acknowledgment for delivery. *Partner C* with EDI X12 has not such fixed response times between different messages as it is not dictated by EDI

---

[3] http://www.rosettanet.org/pipdirectory
[4] http://www.disa.org/x12workbook/ts/

X12. In this case the partner C has agreed to answer the quotes and purchase orders in the same 24 hours. Hence, the choreography differs since the receipt acknowledgment message is not always used with EDI.

3   B2B Integration with SWS Technologies

This section introduces a WSMX enabled architecture to address the requirements of the scenario. We show how SWS technologies can help to mediate the communication, message and process level heterogeneities. We outline some prerequisites for a SWS enabled solution, describe the integration set-up phase using the WSMX and then describe the run-time behaviour. For brevity, we concentrate on presenting the scenario with *Partner B*, who utilises RosettaNet e-business framework.

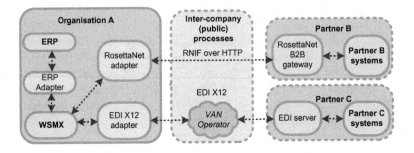

Fig. 2. Use Case Scenario with WSMX

3.1   Prerequisites for SWS Infrastructure

In this section we analyse the prerequisites organisation A has to address when it sets up the WSMX environment for the B2B integration described above.

Message Ontologies

Based on its requirements, organisation A has to create or ideally reuse *domain ontologies*. In our example these ontologies are used for a formal description of the RFQ and PO process messages. Creating these domain ontologies requires an expert who first understands specific e-business scenarios and second has knowledge about ontology languages to be able to capture information in messages *semantically*. However, since we are still far from an industry wide recognised formal ontology, organisation A in our example needs to define the ontology itself. We assume that organisation A is not in a position to dictate its proprietary ontology to its partners. It is further realistic to assume that it bases its ontology on an existing e-business framework, in our case RosettaNet. This for two reasons, first that organisation A minimises the effort of lifting the RosettaNet PIP XML messages most of its partners still use to the ontological level and second to further minimise the mapping requirements to its internal ERP system, which still operates on syntactic messages. Figure 3 outlines how the ontology is applied by organisation A and where the lifting/lowering of messages is performed.

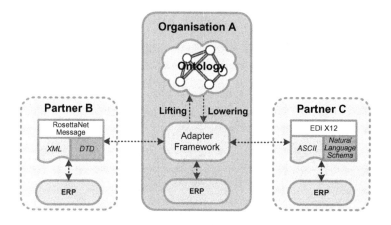

Fig. 3. Lifting/Lowering to/from Domain Ontology

The ontology in our scenario ultimately represents simply a different serialisation of the information in the RosettaNet framework with the advantages that it explicitly states logical relationships between elements which can not be expressed in the RosettaNet PIP XML Schemas and DTDs. In RosettaNet this information is included in a natural language document explaining the respective PIP. One of these advantages of the higher expressivity in the WSML ontology language is depicted in the following example.

The DTD versions of PIP 3A1 and PIP 3A4 support two different kind of product identifiers; the Global Trade Identification Number (GTIN), which is recommended by RosettaNet, and company-specific identifiers. The extract in listing 1.1 shows the definition of product identifiers in the PIP 3A1 (and 3A4). The PIP3A1 DTD is very long so only the relevant lines (291-304) are shown.

```
291    <!ELEMENT ProductIdentification
292      (GlobalProductIdentifier?,
293       PartnerProductIdentification*)>
294
295    <!ELEMENT GlobalProductIdentifier
296      (#PCDATA)>
297
298    <!ELEMENT PartnerProductIdentification
299      (GlobalPartnerClassificationCode,
300       ProprietaryProductIdentifier,
301       revisionIdentifier?)>
302
303    <!ELEMENT ProprietaryProductIdentifier
304      (#PCDATA)>
```

Listing 1.1. PIP 3A1 DTD extract

RosettaNet message guidelines for PIP 3A1 add a *natural language constraint* for ProductIdentification that the DTD's expressive power does not capture: *Constraint: One instance of either "GlobalProductIdentifier" or "PartnerPro-*

ductIdentification" is mandatory. Without this constraint, a valid ProductIdentification could be without any identifiers as both identifications are optional.

Some of the RosettaNet PIPs have also an XML Schema definitions that can present cardinality constraints for the elements. Listing 1.2 shows an extract of the PIP 3A4 XML schema, where namespaces and annotations are dropped for brevity. The XML Schema has different element names than the ones in DTDs. It also allows arbitrary authorities to specify the identification schemes, which introduces another mapping challenge.

```
<xs:element name="ProductIdentification" type="ProductIdentificationType" />
<xs:complexType name="ProductIdentificationType">
 <xs:complexContent><xs:sequence>
   <xs:element name="ProductName" type="xs:string" minOccurs="0" />
   <xs:element name="Revision" type="xs:string" minOccurs="0" />
   <xs:choice><xs:element ref="AlternativeIdentifier" maxOccurs="unbounded" />
   <xs:element ref="GTIN" /></xs:choice>
 </xs:sequence></xs:complexContent>
</xs:complexType>
<xs:element name="AlternativeIdentifier" type="AlternativeIdentifierType" />
<xs:complexType name="AlternativeIdentifierType">
 <xs:sequence><xs:element name="Authority" type="xs:string" />
 <xs:element name="Identifier" type="xs:string" /></xs:sequence>
</xs:complexType>
```

Listing 1.2. PIP 3A4 XML Schema extract

The product identifier information in the WSML domain ontology is presented in listing 1.3. In this, the GTIN is handled as any other identification authority/qualifier (*qualificationAgency*) and the RosettaNet DTD, XML Schema, and EDI X12 product identification information can be presented in this ontology including the natural language constraints. The qualification agency can be for example the *buyer's, seller's or manufacturer's identifier* or any other identification scheme provider. The axiom in listing 1.3 makes sure that the value of *qualificationAgency* is among those supported for organisation A. Thus, the benefit from applying a more expressive language such as WSML is that it allows the description of logical relationships between the elements. This information can subsequently be applied for better validation of the message contents.

```
244   concept productIdentification
245        nonFunctionalProperties
246            dc#description hasValue "Collection of business properties describing identifiers."
247        endNonFunctionalProperties
248        productIdentifier ofType (1 1) _string
249        qualificationAgency ofType (1 1) _string
250        revision ofType (0 1) _string
251   axiom qualificationAgencyConstraint
252        nonFunctionalProperties
253            dc#description hasValue "The valid list of agencies who have defined product identifiers."
254        endNonFunctionalProperties
255        definedBy !- ?x[qualificationAgency hasValue ?type]
256            and (?type = "GTIN" or ?type = "Manufacturer" or ?type = "Buyer"
257                or ?type = "Seller" or ?type = "EN" or ?type = "BP").
```

Listing 1.3. Product ontology extract in WSML

Adapters to the Back-End Applications

For the integration of back-end systems, the messages used within the ERP system have to be mapped to/from the domain ontology. The ERP adapter is required to perform the lifting/lowering of the internally used messages in the ERP system (e.g. Intermediate Documents (IDocs) in the case of SAP) to the logical framework, i.e. WSML, required by WSMX.

Registration

In current e-business frameworks, a prior agreement between business partners determines with whom the partners do business. For RosettaNet, this includes the specification on the set of PIPs used by the partner in the communication and the *role* for the partner in a certain PIP (e.g. *seller* or *buyer*). In addition, the partners need to provide the *endpoint* information of the *IP address* and the *port*, as well as the public *certificate* used by the partner to sign the messages.

In a SWS enabled integration process a *registration interface* allows a partner to register this information to the SWS environment of organisation A. The registration interface can be accessed by a partner through a web portal or an API of organisation A. By invoking this registration interface, a service description based on a set of PIPs and roles is created and described in WSML. The semantic service description provides all information including the endpoint information necessary to invoke the service.

Adapter Framework to External Partners

The adapter framework is required to provide a communication interface to partners, who are not able to directly provide WSML compliant messages to WSMX. The adapter framework receives every non-WSML message and acts for WSMX as the actual service. Thus, essentially the adapter functionality is registered as a service with the system. Further, WSMX only operates on the choreography of the adapter (c.f. left part of figure 4), which maps between the choreography of the partner's (c.f. right part of figure 4) e-business environment and the choreography registered with WSMX. The choreography definition is part of the WSMO description of a service and specifies the input and output operations as well as transition rules and constraints on the states in the communication.

Figure 4 shows the RosettaNet adapter execution flow in a PIP process of RFQ request and response messages:

- WSMX first sends the WSML message to the RosettaNet adapter as a WSML RFQ message.
- The adapter receives the RFQ and translates it to a RosettaNet RFQ XML message.
- The adapter creates a RNIF envelope for this message and signs the message using certificates and sends it to the endpoint of partner B (certificate as well as endpoint are implemented in the adapter). As a result, a confirmation that the message has been received is sent back to WSMX.
- WSMX subsequently expects an acknowledgment message by partner B as an RNIF 2.0 signal message.

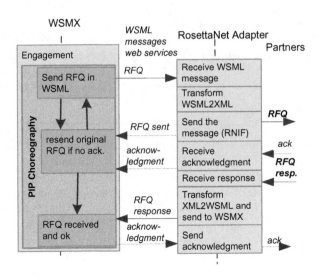

Fig. 4. RosettaNet Adapter

- After receiving the acknowledgment, WSMX waits for the RFQ response from partner B.
- The adapter receives the RFQ response and translates it using an XSLT script to WSML and sends it to WSMX to check that the response does not violate the axioms of the ontology. This response is processed in WSMX and sent to the back-end applications. WSMX also forwards an acknowledgment signal indicating that their RFQ response was received to the adapter which itself translates it to the message schema expected by the partners.

3.2   Integration Set-Up Phase

In the integration set-up phase, the B2B integration for a specific partner is built. The integration set-up phase also includes the registration of the partner's service description with the SWS system of organisation A. Hence, in case a new partner that uses RosettaNet wants to register a service, he needs to provide his endpoint information and choreography details. Partners need to provide this information using the *Registration Interface* described in the previous section. In addition, the information what components they supply is required for discovery.

In case that the new partner uses some other standard or a proprietary format for his messages appropriate adapters and mapping rules might need to be defined.

Creating the Adapter to the Partners e-Business Frameworks

The integration of the organisation A and the e-business frameworks of each partner needs specific *RosettaNet* and *EDI X12 adapters*. The role of the adapters is to translate the RosettaNet XML and EDI X12 data formats to WSML and taking care of e.g. RosettaNet-specific RNIF protocol details. For example, the E-business framework message translation based on the mapping rules happens in the WSMX adapter.

- **The communication interface with a partner** is used to send and receive e-business framework-specific messages. It acts as a wrapper for RosettaNet communication with the partner.

Other basic functionality of the RosettaNet adapter involves the functionality related to enveloping, encrypting and decrypting and validation of RosettaNet messages. Here, the existing B2B gateway functionality can be used if the
organisation already has a product for RNIF communication. The RosettaNet
adapter needs to have roughly similar functionality to the system presented in
[12] with the additional step of XML2WSML and WSML2XML translations.
Similarly the ERP and EDI X12 adapters need analogical functionality.

```
<xsl:for−each select="ProductIdentification/GlobalPartnerClassificationCode">
  instance localUID memberOf productIdentification
    productIdentifier hasValue <xsl:value−of select="."/>
    qualificationAgency hasValue GTIN
</xsl:for−each>

<xsl:for−each select="ProductIdentification/PartnerProductIdentification/">
  instance localUID memberOf productIdentification
    <xsl:for−each select="ProprietaryProductIdentifier">
    productIdentifier hasValue <xsl:value−of select="."/>
    </xsl:for−each>
    <xsl:for−each select="GlobalPartnerClassificationCode">
    qualificationAgency hasValue <xsl:value−of select="."/>
    </xsl:for−each>
</xsl:for−each>
```

Listing 1.4. DTD-based PIP instance mapping extract

- **Creating Data Mapping Rules from RosettaNet Messages to Domain Ontologies**
The mapping rules need to be defined for the run-time phase to lift RosettaNet
instance messages to the ontology applied by organisation A and lower it back
to the XML level respectively. In the scenario mapping rules for PIPs 3A1 and
3A4 are required. There are two options to do that, either to lift the messages
from XML Schemas to WSML and then use a data mediation tool such as the
one included in the Web Services Modeling Toolkit [5] to perform the mappings
on the ontological level or to directly lift the messages to the domain ontology
and essentially implement the mediation in the adapter. In our case, we have
chosen the latter option and we perform the using XSLT stylesheets. Listing
1.4 contains such an example mapping from a PIP DTD to WSML. Listing
1.5 does the same for XML Schema version PIPs. The mapping lifts the GTIN
number to the uniform identification scheme in the ontology. Similarly with
EDI X12 the information is lifted to our domain ontology. In the lowering of
messages, by knowing that a GTIN identifier and company-specific identifiers
point to the same product, the mapping can provide an identifier needed by the
given partner. The mapping rules need to be registered in the WSMX ontology
repository for run-time mappings. As the product information definitions in all
DTD and XML Schema based PIPs are similar, these mapping templates can

---

[5] http://sourceforge.net/projects/wsmt

be reused with all the PIPs. With small modification it is easy to create templates for other e-business frameworks as well.

```
<xsl:for−each select=" ProductIdentification/GTIN" >
  instance localUID memberOf productIdentification
    productIdentifier hasValue <xsl:value−of select="." />
    qualificationAgency hasValue GTIN
</xsl:for−each>

<xsl:for−each select=" ProductIdentification/AlternativeIdentifier/" >
  instance localUID memberOf productIdentification
    <xsl:for−each select=" Identifier" >
      productIdentifier hasValue <xsl:value−of select="." />
    </xsl:for−each>
    <xsl:for−each select=" Authority" >
      qualificationAgency hasValue <xsl:value−of select="." />
    </xsl:for−each>
</xsl:for−each>
```

Listing 1.5. XML-Schema-based PIP instance mapping extract

3.3 Integration Run-Time Phase

After the set-up phase is completed, WSMX is ready for running the processes. We describe here the whole execution process and interactions in WSMX according to the scenario: (1) *Converting back-end message to a WSMX goal*, (2) *Discovery* of the possible suppliers capable of fulfilling this request, (3) *Engagement* to negotiate and contract with the discovered suppliers to get the price and condition information, (4) *Selection* of the best supplier, (5) *Invocation* of the PO process with the selected supplier and finally (6) *Returning the answer* to the ERP. The sequence diagram for the run-time behaviour is depicted in figure 5.

- **Converting back-end message to WSMX goal.** Organisation A's ERP system sends out a request in its proprietary format to the back-end adapter. The request is *to get 10 display units X delivered to the plant in Galway, Ireland within 8 days.* The adapter translates this to WSML and converts it to a *goal* in WSML and sends it to WSMX.
- **Discovery.** The execution process starts by invoking the WSMX discovery component. All services in the repository matching the request are found. In our case the services of partners B and C are discovered as potential suppliers. During the discovery, data mediation rules could be executed to resolve differences in the ontologies used for the goal and the service descriptions. However, in our example we only deal with one ontology and all the mediation is done in the lifting and lowering of the XML messages.
- **Engagement.** As discovery operates on abstract description of services, the next step is to find out whether each discovered service can deliver the required product within the given time and give a price for that. In our example, engagement is performed for partners B and C by sending RFQ documents and the partners answer those with the RFQ responses. Data and process mapping rules are implemented in the adapters, which handle

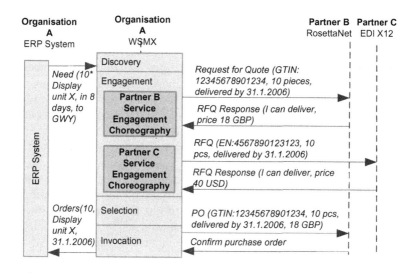

Fig. 5. WSMX Process interactions

differences between the RosettaNet and the X12 message exchange patterns (choreographies). Responses coming in RosettaNet PIP 3A1 and EDI X12 879 messages are translated to WSML and sent to WSMX.

- **Selection.** Based on the information provided from engagement, the best service is selected. In this scenario, this is done simply according to the cheapest price. To do this a conversion of different currencies used in quotes is done in WSMX by invoking an appropriate currency transformation service. In our scenario, the partner B has a cheaper quote and is selected.
- **Invocation.** The PO process starts with the partner B using PIP3A4. The concrete interactions between WSMX and partner B happens analogically to the case of the engagement choreography, just the messages exchanged are different.
- **Returning answer.** After the invocation returns the PO response, the necessary data mediation for the product identifiers and currencies expected by the organisation A's ERP is done. Then the result is sent back to ERP adapter as expected by the ERP system.

4 Expected Business Benefits and Related Work

This section first discusses the scenario and the expected benefits of applying SWS to e-business frameworks and then we discuss WSMX and RosettaNet specific issues.

4.1 Scenario and Expected Benefits

Our scenario discussed throughout the paper is still simplified and considered only two suppliers. In practice, the number of companies and e.g. proprietary data formats for integration can be larger and that means more mappings to the ontology. However, still the number of required mappings is reduced from n^2 to $2n$. Further the valid suppliers for the given part would need to be checked against the approved manufacturer lists in the product data management systems. In addition, the selection might involve more variables than price, such as history data on supplier quality concerning defects and delivery accuracy. Furthermore, the required service might be something that needs to be configured from a set of services. For example the product manufacturing and transportation could be separated and the different valid combinations should be discovered in a service composition.

As WSML is a more expressive language than the schema languages used currently, the lifting of PIPs to ontologies can represent more information. As a simple example, we provided the mapping of product information to ontologies that captured the natural language constraints and made the "GlobalProductIdentifier" RosettaNet meaning of GTIN number more explicit. The use of formal ontologies enables using common conversion functions to mediate some differences with logical dependencies. RosettaNet currently defines more than 300 *GlobalProductUnitOfMeasureCode*s as a list without any relations to each other. With help of logical relationships, automatic transformations between e.g. "*25 Kilogram Bulk Bag*" and "*50 Pound Bag*" can be done. Currently matching all the details related to PIP messages takes time and only small differences can cause additional system development and testing work. SWS techniques can be applied to describe how companies use the PIPs and automate message compatibility matching, thus making the B2B integration process faster. The resulting integration is more flexible to slightly varying use of messages. For example, different measurement units can be supported easily if they are specified. Adding new partners should be a lot quicker, as a new partner using a domain ontology in describing his services would only need to register the needed details to WSMX before participating in the RFQ processes. Furthermore all this does not require changes to the ERP interfaces. As a result, organisation A would get more quotes to select from.

4.2 WSMX and RosettaNet Specific Issues

This work utilises existing/planned WSMX components such as data and process mediation. Our contribution is the concept to integrate WSMX with RosettaNet and pointing out how SWS can help to support RosettaNet and EDI X12. As security of communication is not tackled by the current version of WSMX, the use of RNIF for secure communication addresses the security aspects.

There are many challenges related to ontologising RosettaNet specifications. RosettaNet evolves over time. The introduction of XML Schema PIPs have brought some major changes to RosettaNet specifications. The element naming has changed and supporting the same PIP in DTD and XML Schema formats requires own mappings. This involves additional work in defining the necessary mapping rules for different message versions. Having RosettaNet specifications in current non-ontology language means that developers currently need to do this lifting to ontologies. We hope that RosettaNet will adopt an ontology language to formally specify PIP messages as others have also suggested [14].

Our approach requires a lot of work in setting up the SWS infrastructure. However, developing adapters is needed for every e-business framework. The domain ontologies and the mappings are needed with different messages used. After ontologising one PIP process, adding support for other PIPs is easy and exploits in the reuse of mapping rules already one of the benefits of applying an ontology. Furthermore, the RosettaNet adapter behaviour concerning RNIF is identical in all RosettaNet PIPs and thus needs to be defined just once. So far, we have defined the conversations in valid RosettaNet messages and created the domain ontology representing the concepts in the example scenario. The current ontology contains the information carried in those messages rather than all concepts in the RosettaNet PIPs.

5   Related Work

Preist, Trastour, et al. have presented multiple papers on SWS and B2B integration [7, 14, 13] as research toward similar benefits for B2B integration using semantic web languages. *Preist et al.* [7] presented a scenario and an agent architecture of B2B integration with SWS technologies. In their approach, the partner discovery used service descriptions in the Web Ontology Language (OWL). They also provided a concept of lowering ontology messages and presented ideas of mediating between EDI (EDIFACT) and RosettaNet messages. *Trastour et al.* [14] augment RosettaNet PIPs with partner-specific DAML+OIL constraints to overcome the shortfalls of RosettaNet. They want to determine if parties have compatible processes and messages, and automatically propose modifications if not. *Trastour et al.* [13] use agent communication to help in negotiation and contract forming (engagement) processes for making B2B integration faster. Common to all these three papers is that they expect the participating companies to at least partly use semantic web languages in the inter-company communication. Furthermore, neither the non-functional security properties nor integration to back-end systems are addressed in the papers. Our work goes a step further in defining details how the B2B integration with RosettaNet using a SWS environment can be achieved and how to integrate existing back-end systems with it.

Many papers present B2B integration solutions that do not use any SWS technologies, but still have more similarities to our work. *Dogaz et al.* [2] present an implementation where an ebXML infrastructure is developed by exploiting the UDDI registries and RosettaNet PIPs. The UDDI registry is used to store ebXML documents and process descriptions that correspond to WSMX registries described here. They also provide a solution for secure communication. *Sundaram and Shim* [11] present an infrastructure for B2B exchanges with RosettaNet. They have a three-tier client-server prototype that allows customers to send PIP messages using a browser. *Sayal et al.* [9] present a tool, that supports RosettaNet PIPs and allows generating complete processes from PIPs by taking internal integration needs into account. These approaches are more static and lack both the mediation capabilities enabled by SWS and secure communication. Common to all these related works is a lack of the concept for integrating with existing back-end systems.

6   Conclusions and Future Work

We presented a scenario and a supporting WSMX Semantic Web Service (SWS) architecture for B2B integration, where a buyer organisation communicates with partners using RosettaNet and EDI X12. We showed how the interoperation aspects are handled from the buyer organisation's point of view and how the use of SWS technologies enables communication with its heterogeneous partners. We demonstrated parts of the ontologising process of existing messages and how they can be used to mediate the differences in B2B integrations. We particularly showed how the product identification information can be captured in WSML ontology language covering current RosettaNet and EDI X12 definitions. We also presented the functionality of a RosettaNet adapter that is needed to adapt the WSML ontology language and web services used in WSMX to RosettaNet communication requirements.

As future work, we plan to show more benefits of using formal ontologies for B2B integration and extend the examples to include more complex product data and axioms related to valid product individuals. This scenario had rather static choreography descriptions, but we plan to extend this to more complex choreographies and to apply process mediation rules to non-matching choreography descriptions.

Acknowledgments

This material is based upon works supported by the Science Foundation Ireland under Grant No. SFI/02/CE1/I131 and the EU funded Knowledge Web project (FP6 - 507482). This work is also partly supported by the Finnish Funding Agency for Technology and Innovation (Tekes) and the Graduate School for Electronic Business and Software Industry.

References

1. C. Bussler, D. Fensel, and A. Maedche. A Conceptual Architecture for Semantic Web Enabled Web Services. *SIGMOD Record*, 31(4):24 – 29, 2002.
2. A. Dogac, Y. Tambag, P. Pembecioglu, S. Pektas, G. Laleci, G. Kurt, S. Toprak, and Y. Kabak. An ebXML infrastructure implementation through UDDI registries and RosettaNet PIPs. In *Proceedings of the 2002 ACM SIGMOD International Conference on Management of Data*, pages 512–523, 2002.
3. A. Haller, E. Cimpian, A. Mocan, E. Oren, and C. Bussler. WSMX – A Semantic Service-Oriented Architecture. In *Proceedings of the 3rd International Conference on Web Services*, pages 321 – 328, Orlando, Florida, USA, 2005. IEEE Computer Society.

4. D. Martin et al. Owl-s: Semantic markup for web services. Member submission, W3C, 2004. Available from: `http://www.w3.org/Submission/OWL-S/`.

5. B. Medjahed, B. Benatallah, A. Bouguettaya, A. H. H. Ngu, and A. K. Elmagarmid. Business-to-business interactions: issues and enabling technologies. *VLDB Journal*, 12(1):59–85, 2003.

6. J.-M. Nurmilaakso and P. Kotinurmi. A Review of XML-based Supply-Chain Integration. *Production Planning and Control*, 15(6):608–621, 2004.

7. C. Preist, J. E. Cuadrado, S. Battle, S. Williams, and S. Grimm. Automated Business-to-Business Integration of a Logistics Supply Chain using Semantic Web Services Technology. In *ISWC '05: Proceedings of 4th International Semantic Web Conference*, 2005.

8. D. Roman, U. Keller, H. Lausen, J. de Bruijn, R. Lara, M. Stollberg, A. Polleres, C. Feier, C. Bussler, and D. Fensel. Web Service Modeling Ontology. *Applied Ontologies*, 1(1):77 – 106, 2005.

9. M. Sayal, F. Casati, U. Dayal, and M.-C. Shan. Integrating Workflow Management Systems with Business-to-Business Interaction Standard. In *Proceedings of the 18th International Conference on Data Engineering*.

10. S. S. Y. Shim, V. S. Pendyala, M. Sundaram, and J. Z. Gao. Business-to-Business E-Commerce Frameworks. *IEEE Computer*, 33(10):40–47, 2000.

11. M. Sundaram and S. S. Y. Shim. Infrastructure for B2B Exchanges with RosettaNet. In *Proceedings of the Third International Workshop on Advanced Issues of E-Commerce and Web-Based Information Systems*, pages 110–119, 2001.

12. J. Tikkala, P. Kotinurmi, and T. Soininen. Implementing a RosettaNet Business-to-Business Integration Platform Using J2EE and Web Services. In *7th IEEE International Conference on E-Commerce Technology*, pages 553–558. IEEE Computer Society, 2005.

13. D. Trastour, C. Bartolini, and C. Preist. Semantic Web support for the business-to-business e-commerce pre-contractual lifecycle. *Computer Networks*, 42(5):661–673, 2003.

14. D. Trastour, C. Preist, and D. Coleman. Using Semantic Web Technology to Enhance Current Business-to-Business Integration Approaches. In *Proceedings of the 7th International Enterprise Distributed Object Computing Conference*, pages 222–231. IEEE Computer Society, 2003.

A Novel Genetic Algorithm for QoS-Aware Web Services Selection*

Chengwen Zhang, Sen Su, and Junliang Chen

State Key Lab of Networking and Switching Technology
Beijing University of Posts & Telecommunications (BUPT),
187# 10 Xi Tu Cheng Rd., Beijing 100876, China
zwjcbj2007@gmail.com, {susen, chjl}@bupt.edu.cn

Abstract. A novel genetic algorithm characterized by improved fitness value is presented for Quality of Service (QoS)-aware web services selection. The genetic algorithm includes a special relation matrix coding scheme of chromosomes, an initial population policy and a mutation policy. The relation matrix coding scheme suits with QoS-aware web service composition more than the one dimension coding scheme. By running only once, the proposed genetic algorithm can construct the composite service plan according with the QoS requirement from many services compositions. Meanwhile, the adoption of the initial population policy and the mutation policy promotes the fitness of genetic algorithm. Experiments on QoS-aware web services selection show that the genetic algorithm with this matrix can get more excellent composite service plan than the genetic algorithm with the one dimension coding scheme, and that the two policies play an important role at the improvement of the fitness of genetic algorithm.

1 Introduction

Web service is software application identified by URI. Some interoperation mechanisms [1], like service description, service discovery, service binding, are enabled in a service-oriented architecture.

The framework of Web services creates new possibilities to assemble distributed Web services. How to create robust service compositions becomes the next step work in web services [15] and has attracted a lot of researches [8], [9], [16], [17]. At the same time, since web services with same functions and different QoS are increasing with the proliferation of web services, and web services requesters always express their functional requirements as well as their QoS constraints set, a decision needs to be made to select which services are used in a given composite service on the basis of multiple QoS attributes in order to maximize user satisfaction. Hence, QoS-aware web services selection plays an important role in web services composition [2-3]. In

---

* The work presented in this paper was supported by the National Basic Research and Development Program (973 program) of China under Grant No. 2003CB314806; the National Natural Science Foundation project of China under Grant No. 90204007; the Program for New Century Excellent Talents in University of China under Grant No. NCET-05-0114; the program for Changjiang Scholars and Innovative Research Team in University (PCSIRT).

J. Lee et al. (Eds.): DEECS 2006, LNCS 4055, pp. 224–235, 2006.

the past years, the researches about web services selection have gained considerable momentums [4-11].

To figure out QoS-aware web services selection, some approaches are made with the help of semantic web [4-6], and the others are based on the QoS attributes computation [7-11]. But it is obvious that the latter approaches are more suitable solutions to satisfy the global QoS requirements. It is a combinatorial optimization issue that the best combination of web services is selected in order to accord with the global constraints. Some traditional optimization techniques are proposed in [7-9], and since finding a solution for quality driven web services selection is NP-hard [11], different strategies based on Genetic Algorithm (GA) are adopted in [10], [11].

Genetic Algorithm is a powerful tool to solve combinatorial optimizing problems [13]. The design of a genetic algorithm has the greatest influence on its behavior and performance [12], especially the coding scheme of chromosomes and the evolution operators will effect directly on the efficiency and the global astringency of genetic algorithm. The special coding scheme of chromosomes should accord with different problems, such as the coding scheme for QoS-aware web service selection should express not only the services composition but also the information of composition paths. It is only according with the characters of web services selection that genetic algorithm can get the global convergence. In the literatures, a suitable genetic algorithm for QoS-aware web services selection has not been taken into account from the character of web services selection, although the presented genetic algorithms can attain service composition supporting QoS to some extent. They always adopted the one dimension coding scheme that can not express all paths of assemble service at one time, so they did not suit effectively web services selection with many paths. Clearly, a new coding scheme should be designed for web services selection. We propose a relation matrix coding scheme on the basis of the characters of web services selection. By means of the particular definition, the relation matrix coding scheme can represent simultaneously all paths of services selection. In the end, the simulated results show that the relation matrix coding scheme excels the one dimension coding scheme in composite service plan. Furthermore, Web service composition has many scenarios [3], such as probabilistic invocation, parallel invocation, sequential activation and so on. The relation matrix coding scheme can denote simultaneously many web service scenarios that the one dimension coding scheme can not express at one time. Additionally, an initial population policy and a mutation policy are proposed to promote the fitness of genetic algorithm.

The remainder of this paper is organized as follows. After a review of the literature of the QoS-aware web services selection using QoS computation in section 2, Section 3 presents the genetic algorithm with the relation matrix coding scheme, special crossover operator, special mutation operator, the initial population policy and the mutation policy. Section 4 describes the simulations of the proposed algorithm and discusses results aiming to support the work. Finally, section 5 is our conclusions.

2   Quality Computation-Based Selection of Web Services

According to Std. ISO 8402 [18] and ITU E.800 [19], QoS may include a number of nonfunctional properties such as price, response time, availability, reputation. Thus, the QoS value of a composition service can be achieved by the fair computation of QoS of every component web services. Clearly, the QoS model of web services composition should be discussed firstly. On the basis of the QoS model, there are some techniques in the literatures, including some traditional optimization techniques [7, 8, 9] and strategies based on Genetic Algorithm (GA) [10, 11].

The QoS computation based on the QoS matrix is a representative solution. In order to rank web services, [7] normalized the QoS matrix. However, it was only a local optimization algorithm but not a global one for services selection.

Other works in the area of QoS computation include [8], [9], which proposed local optimization and global planning. The local optimization approach could not take the global selection constraints into consideration. In contrast, the global planning method would bring a perceivable overhead in a dynamic environment. So, both had limitation to some extent.

Since finding a solution for quality driven web services selection is NP-hard [11], genetic algorithm is well suitable for the QoS-aware services selection belonging to the class of NP-hard [13]. In [10], the author proposed binary strings of chromosome for service selection. Every gene in the chromosome represented a concrete service with values of 0 and 1. So the more service candidates or web services clusters were, the longer the chromosome was. Since at most only single service candidate could be selected from each web services cluster, only one gene was 1 in all of genes of every cluster and others were 0. This kind of manner resulted in poor readability. In [11], genetic algorithm was also used to tackle the service selection problem. The one dimension coding way of chromosome was proposed to express services composition, and each gene represented one abstract service of composite service. The value of abstract service was one of concrete services matching that abstract service. The length of genome was shorter obviously than the one in [10]. The change of the number of concrete services could not influence the length of the genome. So the stability of the length of the genome was better than [10].

Since the one dimension coding schemes can not express all paths of assemble service at one time, the selection of the optimal path is finished only after all paths are coded and selected respectively. Moreover, the crossover and mutation operator based on these schemes and schemes themselves are not able to express other web service scenarios, such as probabilistic invocation, parallel invocation, etc.

3   Genetic Algorithm Based on Relation Matrix Coding Scheme

As stated in the section 2, the proposed approaches using genetic algorithm used the one dimension coding scheme of chromosome for the selection issue. In this section, we present a novel genetic algorithm in order to resolve quality-driven selection, including the design of a special relation matrix coding scheme of chromosomes as well as an initial population policy and a mutation policy. The foundation of the two policies is the relation matrix coding scheme.

3.1 Relation Matrix Coding Scheme

During web service is composed of other service components, there may be a lot of abstract composition processes that accord with users' functional requirements. In order to process simply service composition, these abstract processes should be built into an abstract composition graph. In the graph, the same abstract services in the different processes are represented by one node. If there is not the unique starting node or the unique ending node in the graph, a starting node or an ending node will be constructed in order to build up a directed-graph with the unique starting node and the unique ending node. In the paper, an abstract service is signified by task and an abstract composition process is signified by path.

At run-time, a great deal of concrete services with the same function and different QoS attributes are discovered for every abstract service. So, there are various composite ways for each path to correspond to the specific function of the composite service. Therefore, an ideal approach should be able to select the best way from all available candidate paths in order to meet the consumers' constraints set.

From the above analysis, web services composition is characterized by the following: all of tasks are invoked on the basis of special order, different composition for same function will be made up of different tasks, every task has many concrete services with same function and different QoS attributes, the dynamic changes in QoS attributes and services themselves are always done in dynamic environments.

According to the characteristic of the services composition, it is possible to adopt a novel relation matrix coding scheme using neighboring matrix. The coding scheme has the function to express not only the relation among tasks but also paths information. Figure 1 is the structure of the relation matrix coding scheme.

$$\begin{pmatrix} g_{11} & g_{12} & g_{13} & \cdots & g_{1n} \\ g_{21} & g_{22} & g_{23} & \cdots & g_{2n} \\ g_{31} & g_{32} & g_{33} & \cdots & g_{3n} \\ \vdots & \vdots & \vdots & \vdots & \vdots \\ g_{n1} & g_{n2} & g_{n3} & \cdots & g_{nn} \end{pmatrix}$$

Fig. 1. Relation matrix coding scheme

In figure 1, "n" is the number of all tasks included in services composition. The relation matrix is built as follows: The abstract composition directed-graph is searched on the basis of breadth-first search rule from the starting node of the graph and the node is coded simultaneously one by one until all of nodes in the graph are coded. The coding rule ensures that the nodes in the graph are ordered from the starting node to the ending node. Then, the elements along the main diagonal of the matrix express all of the abstract service nodes one by one and are arranged from the node with the smallest code number to the node with the largest code number.

The following is the definition of the relation matrix coding scheme.

(1) The g_{ii} is located at the main diagonal of the matrix for the ith locus of the chromosome and presents a task. The possible values of g_{ii} are the following:

a) The number "0" that represents that the pointed task is not included in the special services composition.

b) The number "-1" that represents that the pointed task is in the running status while the composite service re-planning.

c) The number "-2" that represents that the pointed task is in the invalid status while the composite service re-planning, such as all of concrete services of the pointed task become invalid or the pointed task is canceled for some reasons.

d) The number "-3" that represents that the selected service of the pointed task has some changes while the composite service re-planning, such as the selected service becomes invalid or some QoS constraints of the selected service have some changes.

e) Other values that represent that the pointed task is included in the special services composition and a special web service is selected.

(2) The g_{ij} represents the direct relation between the ith task and the jth task. Here, $i \neq j$.

Before g_{ij} is defined, four values of k1, k2, k3 and k4 should be defined firstly. The four values are adjustable and represent the different situations of parallel invocations. The following is the definition of g_{ij}:

a) The number "0" represents that the ith task is not the immediate predecessors of the jth task.

b) The number "p" represents that the ith task is the immediate predecessors of the jth task and the ith task invokes the jth task with probability "p". Here, $0 < p \leq 1$.

c) The number "m" represents that the ith task is the immediate predecessors of the jth task and the ith task invokes the jth task with "m" times. Here, $1 \leq m < \text{Min}\{k1, k2, k3, k4\}$.

d) The number "k1" represents that all of parallel invocations of immediate predecessors of the jth task belong to same group. The ith task is one of the immediate predecessors.

e) The number "k2" represents that all of parallel invocations of immediate successors of the ith task belong to same group. The jth task is one of the immediate successors.

f) The number "k3" represents that all of parallel invocations of immediate predecessors of the jth task belong to the different groups. The ith task is one of the immediate predecessors.

g) The number "k4" represents that all of parallel invocations of immediate successors of the ith task belong to the different groups. The jth task is one of the immediate successors.

Obviously, in the case of k3 and k4, it is necessary to seek a table of parallel invocations to find out which parallel invocations belong same group.

By means of the combination of values of m, p, k1, k2, k3, k4, many web service scenarios, such as probabilistic invocation, parallel invocation, sequential activation, etc, can be represented by the relation matrix. Additionally, values of m, k1, k2, k3, k4 should not influence the decomposition of the value of g_{ij}.

Following the definition of the relation matrix, the objects of the evolution operators are all of elements along the main diagonal of the matrix. The chromosome is made up of these elements. The other elements in the matrix are to be used to check whether the created new chromosomes by the crossover and mutation operators are available and to calculate the QoS values of chromosomes.

As stated in the above, the functions of the relation matrix are the following:

(1) The ability to seek simultaneously all of paths: since every locus of the chromosome can randomly be set to value "0", the chromosome has the ability to express all of paths of services composition.

(2) The abilities of the path re-planning and the task re-planning thanks to the introduction of values of "-1/-2/-3" to g_{ii}.

(3) The ability to resolve the cyclic paths thanks to the introduction of values of "m" to g_{ij}.

(4) The ability to represent simultaneously many web service scenarios, such as probabilistic invocation, parallel invocation, sequential activation, etc.

3.2 Design of Crossover Operator and Mutation Operator

Since it is possible that crossover operator or mutation operator creates invalid paths if the relation matrix coding scheme is used, the check operation is necessary after the invocations of the two evolution operators. There are two occasions to check whether the new chromosome is valid: One is during the running of the two evolution operators, and the other is after the running of the two operators. The former need to modify the two operators and the later need not.

(1) The check operations of the crossover operator: if the values of the crossover loci in two crossover chromosomes are all for the selected web services, the new chromosomes are valid. Or else, the new chromosomes need to be checked on the basis of the g_{ij} of the relation matrix.

(2) The check operations of the mutation operator:

a) While the value of the mutated task is changed from selected web service to "0": if the immediate predecessor of the mutated one has the parallel invocations of immediate successors including the mutated one or the mutated task has the parallel invocations of immediate predecessors, the mutation operation fails and runs again. Or else, if the immediate predecessor of the mutated task has other immediate successors excluding the mutated task, the new chromosome is valid. If has not, the mutation operation runs again.

b) While the value of the mutated task is changed from "0" to a selected web service, the new chromosome should be checked whether valid or invalid based on the g_{ij} of the relation matrix. Further, the mutated chromosome has embranchments due to the increase of the new task after the mutation operation. The chromosome should be divided into many chromosomes that represent different paths respectively.

c) While the value of the mutated task is changed from one web service to another web service, the check operation is not necessary.

d) While the mutated task is not changed with the value of "0", the check operation is not necessary.

3.3 Mechanism to Improve the Fitness

An initial population policy and a mutation policy are proposed to improve the fitness of GA in this section. The characteristic of randomicity ensures that genetic algorithm has the ability to search all of paths of web services composition, but it also introduces the situation of "prematurity" that the local optimal value is always the final result. Aiming at solving the problem, the two policies based on the characteristic of services composition are proposed in order to direct the evolution of genetic algorithm.

3.3.1 Initial Population Policy

During the evolution, the initial population is the predecessor of all successor populations. So, it is the basis for genetic algorithm to obtain better fitness. It has an important influence on the final fitness. Hence, an optimized initial population can effectively overcome the situation of "prematurity". The following is the proposed policy.

First of all, it is necessary to confirm the proportion of chromosomes for every path to the size of the population. The method is to calculate the proportion of compositions of every path to the sum of all compositions of all paths. The more the number of compositions of one path is, the more chromosomes for the path are in the population.

Secondly, the value of every task in every chromosome is confirmed according to a local optimized method. The larger the value of QoS of a concrete service is, the larger the probability to be selected for the task is. The QoS model in [9] is used to calculate the value of QoS of every concrete service. The probability of one concrete service to be selected is the result of the value of QoS of itself divided by the sum of QoS of all concrete services for same task. The "roulette wheel selection" is the mechanism to select concrete services for every task.

The result of the above policy is that every chromosome has so high fitness that the entire population has very high fitness. The special initial population becomes the basis to get higher fitness during the later evolution.

3.3.2 Mutation Policy

In the standard genetic algorithm, the probability of mutation is for the locus of the chromosome. Here, in order to promote the probability to create different paths from the mutated path, the probability of mutation is for the chromosome instead of the locus. The concrete policy is as follows: before mutation operation of every chromosome, the probability of mutation is used to confirm whether the chromosome mutates or not. If mutation, the object path will be confirmed firstly whether it is the same as the current path expressed by the current chromosome. If difference, the object path will be selected from all available paths except the current one. If the object is itself, the new chromosome will be checked whether the new chromosome is the same as the old chromosome. Same chromosome will result in the mutation operation again. If the objects are different paths from the current path, a new chromosome will be created on the basis of the object path. Obviously, it is not necessary to check whether new and old chromosomes are same.

4 Experiments

To verify the excellence of the GA we have proposed, numerous simulation comparisons between itself and the standard GA had been performed on QoS-aware web services selection. All the experiments were taken on same software and hardware, which were Pentium 1.6GHz processor, 512MB of RAM, Windows XP Pro, development language JAVA, IDE Eclipse 3.1. Same data were adopted for two compared GAs, including workflows of different sizes, 15-50 concrete web services for each task and 5 QoS data for each web service. A simplified representation of web service was used, including an ID number, some QoS data that were retrieved randomly in the range of defined values.

The compared two GAs were set up with same population size, crossover operation and probability, mutation probability. QoS model in [9] and fitness function in [11] were used for both of them. The penalty technique is used for constrained optimization problems in both algorithms. The two algorithms have same selection mechanism of individuals, that is the "roulette wheel selection".

The coding scheme, the initial population policy and the mutation policy are the different points between the two GAs. The data of the experiments were collected with two methods: statistic data and process data.

4.1 Experiments on Coding Scheme

The capital letter "N" represented the GA with the relation matrix coding scheme and the capital letter "O" for the standard GA with the one dimension coding scheme. The coding scheme is the only different point between the two GAs. The following is the experiments between "N" and "O". The one dimension coding scheme in [11] was adopted in the standard GA. A fair way to create the initial population was introduced: during every period of two algorithms running, the "N" algorithm created firstly an initial population in which the chromosomes for every path must exist. Then the standard algorithm would use the chromosomes for every path in the initial population created by "N" as its initial population one by one. The final fitness of the standard GA was obtained after the standard algorithm finished all of calculates of all paths and compared all of fitness values among paths. The object is to create a fair environment where the coding scheme is the only different point between the two GAs.

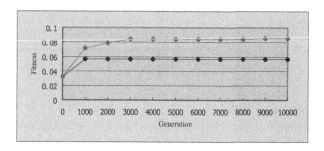

Fig. 2. Fitness comparison

Figure 2 plotted the fitness function evolution across GA generation. Figure 2 was the population size 400, crossover probability 0.7, mutation probability 0.1, number of tasks 30. The upper curve stood for the "N" and the lower one stood for the standard GA in figure 2. This means the GA with the relation matrix coding scheme has better fitness than the standard GA.

As shown in table 1, the statistic data of the average fitness and time for the maximal fitness were collected after the two GAs running for 50 times with the population size 400, iterations 500, crossover probability 0.7 and mutation probability 0.1. The unit of the time is ms.

Table 1. Fitness and time (N:O)

Tasks Num	Average Fitness	Time
10	0.198:0.197	278: 768
25	0.084:0.062	5078: 2716
30	0.066:0.052	7355: 3161

As described above, it is the introduction of the relation matrix coding scheme that ensures that the "N" can get more optimal solution than the standard GA, and to some extent overcomes the premature phenomenon of the standard GA. The service composed by the "N" is better than the one composed by the standard GA. The enlarged probability to create different paths corresponds with the enlarged searching domain. It is the main reason that the relation matrix coding scheme is better than the one dimension coding scheme. From the above figure and table, the more the number of services composition is, the better the effect of the relation matrix coding scheme is.

However, it can be seen that the execution time of the "N" GA is longer than the standard GA at the cost of the check operation. The general indication given by the simulations is that the weaknesses are including the long running time and slow convergence. These would require refining the convergence and shrinking the running time in the future work.

4.2   Experiments on Initial Population and Mutation Policies

The initial population policy and the mutation policy are the different points between the compared two GAs. Clearly, the compared two GAs should adopt the relation matrix coding scheme. Some same parameters are the population size 200, crossover probability 0.7, mutation probability 0.1, iterations 500, running times 50. The unit of the time is ms.

4.2.1   Initial Population Policy
In table 2, the capital letter "A" represented the GA with the initial population policy and the capital letter "B" for the standard GA that created randomly the initial population. The initial population policy is the only different point between "A" and "B".

Table 2. Fitness (A:B)

Tasks Num	Average Fitness
10	0.197:0.197
25	0.193:0.092
30	0.155:0.071

As shown in table 2, it is obvious for the initial population policy to promote the fitness. The more the number of the tasks is, the better the effect to improve the fitness is. The reason is that the A creates an initial population with better fitness.

4.2.2 Mutation Policy

In the experiments, the capital letter "C" represented the GA with the proposed mutation policy. There are two other policies were compared with "C". The first one is "D": it is similar to "C". The different point is that the object path of the current path will be selected directly from all of available paths including the current path. The second one is "E": the probability of mutation is for the locus. During the mutation of one task, the selection probability of every concrete service and the "0" value is equal. The mutation policy is the only different point among "C", "D" and "E".

The table 3 is the results of experiments among "C", "D" and "E".

Table 3. Fitness (C:D:E)

Tasks Num	Average Fitness
10	0.191: 0.191:0.196
25	0.165: 0.141:0.089
30	0.132: 0.108:0.069

In table 3, the largest fitness value is from "C" and the more the number of the tasks is, the better the effect to improve the fitness is. These mean that the proposed mutation policy is effective. "C" and "D" increasing the probability to create the different paths from the mutated path is the reason that "C" and "D" are better than "E". If mutation, the probability to hold the mutated path in "C" is 0.5, but the probability to hold the mutated path in "D" is the value of 1 divided by the number of all paths. So, "D" has higher probability to lose the good genetic information from the predecessor populations than "C". This is why "C" has better fitness than "D".

4.2.3 Integration of Initial Population Policy and Mutation Policy

In table 4, the capital letter "F" represented the GA with the two proposed policies and the capital letter "G" for the standard GA that creates randomly the initial population and adopts the mutation policy of the above "E". The initial population policy and the mutation policy are the different points between "F" and "G".

As expressed from the table 4, the effect of the integration of the initial population policy and the mutation policy is very obvious. After comparing among the table 2, 3 and 4, it is the fact that the integration excels the two single policies in fitness value. The combination of the relation matrix coding, the initial population with good fitness foundation and the mutation policy to direct the evolution should bring better fitness.

Tasks Num	Average fitness
10	0.197:0.197
25	0.216:0.091
30	0.189:0.068

5 Conclusions

The QoS-aware web services selection is an active research area. In this paper, we present a genetic algorithm characterized by a special relation matrix coding scheme of chromosomes, an initial population policy and a mutation policy. The situation of prematurity is overcome effectively through the integration of the relation matrix coding scheme, the initial population policy and the mutation policy.

The relation matrix has the ability to represent simultaneously the composite service re-planning, cyclic paths and many web service scenarios, such as probabilistic invocation, parallel invocation, sequential activation, etc. It also improves the fitness of GA. We also verify the two policies that we use in genetic algorithm through experiments and the results show that the genetic algorithm with the two policies can get more excellent composite service plan than the standard genetic algorithm.

To provide adaptive capability of genetic algorithms is an active research area [14]. Therefore, how to design a self-adaptive genetic algorithm for QoS-aware selection is one of our future works. Work-in-process is devoted to better extend the approach as follows: accelerating the convergence of GA, supplying the self-adaption.

References

1. W3C.Web Services Architecture. http://www.w3.org/TR/2004/NOTE-ws-arch-20040211/ (2004)
2. D. A. Menascé: QoS Issues in Web Services. IEEE Internet Computing, 6(6) (2002) 72–75
3. D. A. Menascé: Composing Web Services: A QoS View. IEEE Internet Computing (2004) 88-90
4. M. Tian, A. Gramm, H. Ritter, J. Schiller: Efficient Selection and Monitoring of QoS-Aware Web Services with the WS-QoS Framework. IEEE/WIC/ACM International Conference on Web Intelligence (WI'04) (2004)
5. A. Soydan Bilgin, Munindar P. Singh: A DAML-Based Repository for QoS-Aware Semantic Web Service Selection. Proceedings of the IEEE International Conference on Web Services (ICWS'04) (2004)
6. Chen Zhou, Liang-Tien Chia, Bu-Sung Lee: DAML-QoS Ontology for Web Services. IEEE International Conference on Web Services (ICWS'04) (2004)
7. Y. Liu, A. H. Ngu, L. Zeng: QoS Computation and Policing in Dynamic Web Service Selection. In Proceedings of the 13th International Conference on World Wide Web (WWW), ACM Press (2004) 66-73
8. L. Zeng, B. Benatallah, M. Dumas, J. Kalagnanam, Q. Z. Sheng: Quality Driven Web Services Composition. Proc. 12th Int'l Conf. World Wide Web (WWW) (2003)

 9. Liangzhao Zeng, Boualem Benatallah, Anne H. H. Ngu, etc.: QoS-Aware Middleware for Web Services Composition. IEEE Transactions on Software Engineering, 30(5) (2004) 311-327
10. LiangJie Zhang, Bing Li, Tian Chao, etc.: On Demand Web Services-Based Business Process Composition. IEEE (2003) 4057-4064
11. G. Canfora, M. Di Penta, R. Esposito, M. L. Villani: A Lightweight Approach for QoS–Aware Service Composition. ICSOC (2004)
12. R. Ignacio, G. Jesús, P. Héctor, etc.: Statistical Analysis of the Main Parameters Involved in the Design of a Genetic Algorithm. IEEE Transactions on Systems, Man, and Cybernetics—Part C: Applications and Reviews, 32(1) (2002) 31-37
13. M. Srinivas, L. M. Patnaik: Genetic Algorithm: a Survey. IEEE (1994) 17-26
14. R. Hinterding, Z. Michalewicz, A. E. Eiben: Adaptation in Evolutionary Computation: a Survey. IEEE EC (1997) 65-69
15. F. Curbera, R. Khalaf, N. Mukhi, etc.: The Next Step in Web Services. Communication of the ACM, 46(10) (2003) 29-34
16. Nikola Milanovic, Miroslaw Malek: Current Solutions for Web Service Composition. IEEE Internet Computing (2004) 51-59
17. B. Orriens, J. Yang, M P Papazoglou: Model Driven Service Composition. In the First International Conference on Service Oriented Computing (ICSOC'03) (2003)
18. ISO 8402, Quality Vocabulary
19. ITU-T Recommendation E.800 (1994), Terms and Definitions Related to Quality of Service and Network Performance Including Dependability

Analysis of Web Services Composition and Substitution Via CCS*

Fangfang Liu[1], Yuliang Shi[2], Liang Zhang[1,**], Lili Lin[1], and Baile Shi[1]

[1] Department of Computing and Information Technology, FUDAN University,
Shanghai, China, 200433
{041021055, zhang1, 042021020, bsh}@fudan.edu.cn
[2] School of Computer Science and Technology, Shandong University, Jinan, China
lingyus@163.com

Abstract. Web services composition is a key issue in web service research area. Substitution of service is closely related with composition and important to robustness of service composition. In this paper, we use process algebra as formalism foundation modeling and specifying web services and reasoning on behavioral features of web services composition. We analyze some cases that have effects on design and implementation of composition. Upon that, and based on definition of composition, we study substitution. As to the problem of how to substitute a component web service, we present a relation. Any new selected web services can substitute old component service independent of context and take part in composition successfully in the case that they satisfy criteria of this relation.

1 Introduction

As a basic building block of Service Oriented Computing (SOC [1]), web services are promoted as a promising way to develop distributed applications through the internet. One of the challenging and attractive issues of web service is service composition [2]. When user's request cannot be satisfied by single web service, it is needed to make different web services work together to fulfill the request. That is the case composition addresses. Substitution of service is important for robustness of service composition. Substitution and composition are the two flip sides of the interoperability coin [15]. Component service in composition may become unavailable for reasons like hardware or software crash. A new service would substitute it and correctness of composition needs to be preserved after substitution.

Current standards WSDL [3], UDDI [4] and SOAP [5] build a foundation for web service architecture, which support definition, advertisement and bindings of web services for invocation purposes respectively. In this architecture, web services are autonomous, heterogeneous and loosely coupled. Communications among services are asynchronous. Therefore, composition of different web services is complex.

---

* This work is partially supported by the National Basic Research Program (973) under grant No. 2005CB321905, the Chinese Hi-tech (863) Projects under the grant No. 2002AA4Z3430, and No. 2002AA231041 To whom correspondence should be addressed.
** Corresponding author.

J. Lee et al. (Eds.): DEECS 2006, LNCS 4055, pp. 236–245, 2006.
© Springer-Verlag Berlin Heidelberg 2006

Emerging standards for web service composition, such as BPEL4WS [6], WSCI [7], WSFL [8] and WS-CDL [10], focus on the implementation or description aspect of composition and say little about behavior aspects of composition, such as whether interactions of services can run correctly to terminate and all messages exchanged among services have been processed etc.. Formal methods have been used by many researchers [11-19] to model web services and address issues like describing, reasoning and verifying correctness of composition. Substitution of service is based on composition. Though at the WSDL level, it is just a matter of checking that the interface of a new web service contains all the operations of the original service. However, things are different at the behavior level [15]. It is needed to check that all exchanged messages are handled correctly and order of messages is guaranteed etc.. That means, substitution should be treated at behavior level.

It is known that cost of verification of web service composition increases rapidly when number of component services becomes large [24]. Thus, verification of correctness would have effect on efficiency of execution of composition when substitution appears frequently. To avoid it, context-independent substitution is preferred. Context here represents other component service in composition.

In this paper, aiming at autonomous, heterogeneous and asynchronous features of web service we extend works in [11, 15]. Inspired by [21, 22], we define a kind of conformance relation between original service and new service. When a new service substitutes the old service, and given that their specifications meet constraints of the relation, correctness of new composition can be preserved after substitution.

The remainder of this paper is organized as follows. Section 2 is related work. Section 3 introduce preliminary about CCS (Communication and Concurrency System), and analyze service composition using it. Then our preliminary results on substitution is presented. And conclusions and future work is in section 4.

2 Related Work

Many works have been done on web service composition. T. Bultan et al [17] proposes conversation specification for design and analysis of web services composition, which is a top-down approach. Conversation is a sequence of messages. Web services are modeled as mealy machines. Services communicate by sending asynchronous messages. Understanding local behavior of constituent services and global behavior of composite service is important for verifying correctness of web services composition. R. Hamadi and B. Benatallah [16] propose a Petri net-based algebra, to modeling control flows, a necessary constituent of reliable web service composition process. D. Berardi et al [23] present a framework Colombo. Using Colombo, they mainly devise a sound, complete and terminating algorithm for building a composite web service. G. Meredith and S. Bjorg [12] consider trying to take pi-calculus and types of pi-calculus to solve automate discovery, composition and verification of web services. CCS (Communication and Concurrency Systme) is taken in [13, 15, 19] to describe and reason on web service. G Salaun et al [13] offer a case study of efficient verifying conformance between the design requirements and composite web service composed of selected web services. M. Koshkina and F. Breugel [19] introduce a verification tool CWB for model checking, preorder checking and equivalence checking relevant to web service composition. CWB modified to support a small language based on BPEL4WS. Another kind of process algebra LOTOS has been used in [14, 18]. A. Ferrara [14] defines a two-way mapping between abstract specifications written using LOTOS and executable web services written in BPEL4WS. This approach offers two choices web service composition. L. Bordeaux and G. Slalun [18] provide a summary for researches made on web service using process algebra and present features of different process algebra like CCS, pi-calculus and LOTOS, etc.. But, researches above didn't deal with substitution.

Representative of researches on substitution of web service include [9, 11, 15]. M. Mecella et al [9] present one kind of definition for compatibility of web service composition and an algorithm to check the compatibility. They prescribe web services and their composition in a clearly formal way and discuss about "contract" of services which is a target specification selected web service taking part in composition should satisfy. When a new service replaces the old one of component web service, it has to be consistent with the "contract". Their proposals are in synchronous environment. Context-independent substitution is not mentioned. In [11], labeled transition system has been used to describe web services behavior and to define the notions of compatibility of different levels. According to compatibility definitions, it shows how these notions can also be used to tackle substitutability issues. A set of formal definitions for substitutability has been defined to clarify context-dependent and context-independent substitution of component web services. But it doesn't consider asynchronous factor and offer no specific conditions for substitution. A. Brogi et al [15] present formalization of web services choreography proposal based on WSCI using CCS. It distinguishes global and internal choices and provides reasoning mechanism and tools to check compatibility of web services. Context-independent substitution is also taken into account. A subtype relation is presented. When web services are not compatible, it generates specification of adaptors to enable communication of incompatible web services. But because of asynchronous communication, description of successful composition in [15] is not suitable in some cases. And as to subtype relation, authors say little about that it is sufficient for context-independent substitution. In our paper, we complement model of web service in [15] and also distinguish global/local choices, which we call external/internal choices, to make it suitable for asynchronous environment. Upon that, we offer a kind of relation between new selected service and original component service for substitution and prove that it is sufficient for context-independent.

3   Substitution of Web Service Composition

3.1   Preliminary About CCS

In [15], authors formalize web service composition described by WSCI using CCS. Here, we firstly give a brief introduction to syntax of CCS process. A process (ranged over by P, Q, R, M etc.) in CCS is defined by:

$$P ::= 0 \mid \alpha.Q \mid P + Q \mid P \parallel Q \mid P \setminus sm$$

$$\alpha ::= a\,?(x) \mid a!(x) \mid \tau$$

α is either to receive (denoted by a?) or send a message (denoted by a!) through a channel a. A process which is terminated is written as 0. Generally, a CCS process executes a sequence of the form $\alpha.P$. A process can perform a choice $P + Q$, which means executes P or Q but not both. A process can be a parallel composition of sub-processes: $P\|Q$. A process may have restriction, which denoted by $P \setminus sm$. P is a process and sm is a set of channel names, imposing that sending of a message through channel $m \in sm$ by one sub-process of P can occur only if another sub-process of P does a reception through the same message channel m. The sending and reception of local channel are called hidden action. Additionally, we need a symbol τ denoting hidden actions performed by two sub-processes or by a non-determinate choice.

We focus on behavioral aspects of web services and data type and value offer no more information for behavioral features, so specific data arguments of a channel is omitted. Furthermore, restriction of processes can also be neglected because we assume that channels are only used for composition purpose.

Some axiomatic and operation semantics of CCS adapted from [20] are defined by a transition system as below. They describe the possible derivations of a process.

$$\text{Rule\_1 } \overline{a.P \xrightarrow{a} P} \qquad \text{Rule\_2 } \frac{P \xrightarrow{a} P'}{P+Q \xrightarrow{a} P'} \qquad \text{Rule\_3 } \frac{P \xrightarrow{a} P'}{P \| Q \xrightarrow{a} P'\| Q}$$

$$\text{Rule\_4 } \frac{Q \xrightarrow{a} Q'}{P \| Q \xrightarrow{a} P \| Q'} \qquad \text{Rule\_5 } \frac{P \xrightarrow{a?(y)} P', Q \xrightarrow{a!(x)} Q'}{P \| Q \xrightarrow{\tau} P'\| Q'\{x/y\}}$$

Rule_1 states a process $a.P$ can evolve to the process P after taking action a and Rule_2 states a process involving a choice can evolve following one of the processes of the choice after taking action a. Rule_3, Rule_4 and Rule_5 rules state that parallel processes evolve through synchronization on action a or an internal τ action. Rule_3 and Rule_4 are symmetrical rules. Here, structure congruence rules are not given. Given that process P and Q are alpha-convertible, then P is structure congruence with Q, i.e. $P \equiv Q$. In this paper, we think that P represents all the processes that can be alpha-convertible to P. 0.

A web service described by WSCI can be translated into CCS process. Consider a simple *BookingTrip* service: a *Traveler* sends message to *bookingRequest*, and *BookingTrip* acknowledge that it receives the message. When service is not available the request is refused. Otherwise, *BookingTrip* receives request. Service is represented using process:

$$BookingTrip = booking\,Request?.ack!.(\tau.refusal!.0 + \tau.confirm!.0)$$

3.2 Analysis of Asynchronous Web Service Composition

Now we can consider composition of web services. Each service wanted to be composed has an interface of WSCI, which can be represented by CCS processes. Composition of services is described using parallel construct of CCS. In [15], authors consider that generally, composition is successful when derivation of composition terminates. That is, composite web service performs a finite number of τ silent actions, finally leading to the inaction 0. In some cases, web services may not terminate even if they can be composed, because they may run in an infinite loop. This is a general case in client/server architecture. Hence, in [15], authors start from a negative notion for correct composition. That is state of *failure* in the case that composition doesn't lead to inaction 0 or a repeated state but can't proceed any more. When composition is not a failure, it is successful, or put it another way, services can be composed.

However, sometimes even if composition of services does not lead to *failure* in design phase, services still can not be composed together in practice. That is because messages exchanges among web services are asynchronous.

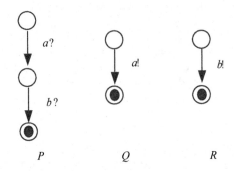

Fig. 1. An example for message queues of web services

For example, in Fig. 1, three web services Ws_1, Ws_2, Ws_3 represented by three processes P, Q and R respectively, want to be composed together. We see that after derivation, $P \parallel Q \parallel R = a?.b? \parallel a! \parallel b!$ can lead to inaction. But in asynchronous case, error may happen. When message b sent by service Ws_3 arrives earlier than message a sent by service Ws_2, no service can receive it and composition will fail. Even if service Ws_1 does have a queue for all types of incoming messages, message b has to be abandoned in case b arrives before a.

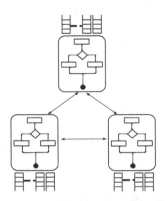

Fig. 2. Model for web services interaction

Thus, inspired by asynchronous message-based software system in [21, 22], we assume that each service has queues for each type of incoming messages and model for web services interaction is in Fig.2. Then in the same situation, message b will be buffered in the queue of its type. After a arrives and is processed, b will be fetched from the queue. The composite service can continue to successfully terminate.

In [15], authors distinguish global/local choices for analyzing services composition and avoid appearance of deadlock for execution composition. In fact, that is also because of asynchronous environment. For example in Fig. 2, two web services Ws_1, Ws_2 represented by processes P and Q respectively. Composition of Ws_1 and Ws_2, $P \parallel Q = (a?.b!+\tau.b!) \parallel (b?+\tau.a!.Q)$, can lead to inaction in both execution branches. Ws_1 can make an internal decision such that a message is sent through channel b and Ws_2 receives it and both services terminate. Ws_2 also can make an internal decision sending message through channel a, Ws_1 receives it and then sends message through b back to Ws_2, now Ws_2 sets a new execution to receive message on b. Finally both services finish. But in the latter case, Ws_2 has performed two different tasks. That is not consistent with users' request. Then, in this example two services cannot be composed together. To avoid problem of Fig.3, global/local, or external choice and internal choice in our paper, should be differentiated.

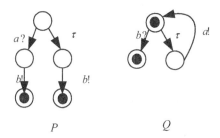

Fig. 3. Example for internal and external choices

External choice means that a choice is influenced by its environment and made depending on environmental situations or factors. Internal choice is determined by the service itself. In WSCI, choice construct is modeled as external choice and conditional construct like switch, is modeled as internal choice. Internal choice is represented by hidden action τ. In asynchronous environment, web services located at different organizations are autonomous and heterogeneous, to achieving successful interactions requires that the exchanging sequence of messages among these web services should be under control. The internal choice represents that the process chooses to transition to one of the branches, whereas the external choice represents that the environment controls whether the process move to a branch. Hence, we allow internal choices and external choices but not the construct that have both of them.

Based on restrictions above, according to descriptions in [15], we give definitions about composition below.

Definition 1 [failure]. Web services $Ws_1, Ws_2, ...Ws_l$, specified using CCS processes $M_1, M_2, ...M_l$. Composition of $Ws_1, Ws_2, ...Ws_l$, denoted by $P = M_1 \parallel M_2 \parallel ... \parallel M_l$ is called a failure, if P is not leading to inaction or a repeated state and can't proceed any more.

Definition 2 [Composition]. Web services $Ws_1, Ws_2, ...Ws_n$, specified using CCS processes $M_1, M_2, ...M_l$ respectively. Composition of $Ws_1, Ws_2, ...Ws_l$, denoted by $P = M_1 \parallel M_2 \parallel ... \parallel M_l$ is correct, if P is not a **failure**.

Then composition can be checked using definitions above. For example, *BookingTrip* service and *Traveler* denoted by CCS processes are defined as follows.

BookingTrip = booking Re *quest* ?.*ack*!.(τ.*refusal*!.0 + τ.*confirm*!.0)
Traveler = booking Re *quest*!.*ack* ?.(*refusal*!.0 + *confirm*!.0)

According to the Def. 2, *BookingTrip* $\parallel$ *Traveler* is correct.

3.3   Substitution of Web Service Composition

Substitution of web service composition is based on correct composition. In [15], authors present a subtype relation for substitution which requires that if any global (external) choice offered by original service is also offered by new service; new service does not extend original service; and new service terminates when original one does also terminate. This subtype relation doesn't consider critical actions in original service like internal choice for service substitution. And that may not guarantee context-independent substitution.

We define a kind of conformance relation solving these problems and prove that it can assure context-independent substitution.

Composition of web services $Ws_1, Ws_2, ...Ws_l$, specified using processes $M_1, M_2, ...M_l$, is $P = M_1 \parallel M_2 \parallel ... \parallel M_l$. We use R represents the environment, i.e. $M_2, M_3, ...M_l$, of web service M_1 . Composition can be expressed by $P = M_1 \parallel R$. To achieve the purpose that substitution can assure correct composition, we analyze the relation of design requirement and selected web service.

Definition 3 [conformance]. Two web services Ws_1, Ws_2 specifying using P and Q respectively, Q conforms to P, denotes by $Q \triangleright P$, if the conditions followed are satisfied.

C1.if $Q \xrightarrow{\tau^* a} Q'$ then there exists P' such that $P \xrightarrow{\tau^* a} P'$, and $Q' \triangleright P'$.

C2.if P has external choices $a_1?.P_1 + a_2?.P_2 + ...a_n?.P_n$, then for all $1 \le i \le n$, there exists Q_i , such that $Q \to Q'$ and $Q' \xrightarrow{\tau^* a_i?} Q_i$

C3.if P has internal choices $\tau.b_1!.P_1 + \tau.b_2!.P_2 + ...\tau.b_n!.P_n$, then there exist $1 \le i \le n$, such that $Q \to Q'$ and $Q' \xrightarrow{\tau^* b_i!} Q_i$

C4.if P terminates then Q terminates.

Then, we prove that when selected service and desired part have the relation mentioned above, the composition after substitution can be guaranteed.

Theorem 1. Web services Ws_1 and Ws_1', specified using CCS processes M_1 and M_sub_1, R represents context of composition of M_1. If $M_1 \parallel R$ is correct and $M\_sub_1 \rhd M_1$, then $M\_sub_1 \parallel R$ is correct.

Proof. Assuming that $M\_sub_1 \parallel R$ is not correct, then from Def.1and 2, there exist M_sub_1' and R' such that $M\_sub_1 \parallel R \xrightarrow{\tau^*} M\_sub_1' \parallel R'$ and $M\_sub_1' \parallel R'$ is failed.

Let $\alpha = a_1 a_2 ... a_n$, $a_i, 1 \leq i \leq n$ denotes sending or receiving action, and $M\_sub_1 \xrightarrow{a_1 a_2 ... a_n} M\_sub_1'$, then for $\bar{\alpha} = \bar{a}_1 \bar{a}_2 ... \bar{a}_n$, $\bar{a}_i, 1 \leq i \leq n$ denotes inverted action of $a_i, 1 \leq i \leq n$, we have $R \xrightarrow{\bar{a}_1 \bar{a}_2 ... \bar{a}_n} R'$.

$M\_sub_1 \rhd M_1$ and from Def. 3, condition C1, then there is M_1' such that $M_1 \xrightarrow{\tau^* a_1 \tau^* a_2 ... a_n} M_1'$ and $M\_sub_1' \rhd M_1'$. Thus, $M_1 \parallel R \xrightarrow{\tau^*} M_1' \parallel R'$.

Now, we get $M_1' \parallel R'$ is correct and $M\_sub_1' \rhd M_1'$,

If M_sub_1' terminates and R' not, from C1 and C4 of Def.3, M_1' also terminates. And for $M_1' \parallel R'$ is correct, R' is inaction which is inconsistent with assumption. Then the case that M_sub_1' terminates but R' not doesn't exist.

If M_sub_1' is waiting for receiving a message b and other component services of R' can't send message b to it, then M_1' also can receive b. If b is one of the external choice of M_1', according to Def. 1 and 2, surely R' will send b. If reception of b is the only action of M_1', from C1 of Def.3, R' will also send b. Therefore, the case that M_sub_1' waiting for b and R' can't send b doesn't exist.

If M_sub_1' sends a message c and R' can't receive c, then M_1' also can send c. For the reason that $M_1' \parallel R'$ is correct, R' can receive c in any case. Thus assumption that M_sub_1' sends a message c and R' can't receive c is not true.

From discussion above, we get conclusion that when $M_1' \parallel R'$ is correct and $M\_sub_1' \rhd M_1'$, $M\_sub_1' \parallel R'$ is also correct. Hence, $M\_sub_1 \parallel R$ is correct   □

Utilizing theorem 1 we can substitute services context-independently. We illustrate this still using the *BookingTrip* example. If web service *BookingTrip'* is defined as follows.

BookingTrip'= booking Re *quest* ?.*ack*!.*confirm*!.0

From Def. 3, *BookingTrip'* $\rhd$ *BookingTrip* , then *BookingTrip'* can substitute *Booking-Trip* and *BookingTrip'* $\parallel$ *Traveler* is correct.

4 Conclusion and Future Work

The autonomous and heterogeneous characteristics of web service make web service composition complex. Substitution of service makes services composition more reliable. We analyze some effects on services composition caused by asynchronous environment and define a kind of subtype relation to restrict constituent web services that can be used to substitute the original part. The substitution is context-independent. A number of questions have been left for future work. When services are not compatible, it is natural to do something to correct the flaws in their interaction. CCS needs to be extended to include transactions, compensations and other properties that are also important in web services composition.

References

1. G. Alonso, F. Casati, H. Kuno, V. Machiraju. "Web Services: Concepts. Architectures and Applications", Springer Verlag, 2004
2. C. Peltz. "Web Service Orchestration and Choreography", www.wsj2.com, July 2003
3. W3C, "Web Service Description Language (WSDL) 1.1",World Wide Web Consortium (2001), available at http://www.w3.org/TR/wsdl
4. OASIS, Universal Description, Discovery and Integration of Web Services (UDDI), http://www.oasis-open.org/committees/uddi-spec/tcspecs.shtml#uddiv3, 2002
5. W3C, Simple Object Access Protocol (SOAP)1.1 http://www.w3.org/TR/2000/NOTE-SOAP-20000508/# Toc478383487, 2000
6. IBM, "Business Process Execution Language for Web Services (BPEL4WS)", http://www.ibm.com/developworkers/library/ws-bpel, 2002
7. W3C, "Web Service Choreography Interface (WSCI)",World W3C (2002), http://www.w3.org/TR/wsci
8. F. Leymann. "Web Services Flow Language (WSFL 1.0)", May 2001
9. M. Mecella, B. Pernici, P. Craca. "Compatibility of e-services in a cooperative multi-platform environment". *TES 2001*, Springer 2001, LNCS 2193, pp. 44–57.
10. W#C, "Web Service Choreography Description Language (WS-CDL.)" http://www.w3.org/TR/2004/WD-ws-cdl-10-20041012
11. L. Bordeaux, G. Salun, D. Berardi, and M. Mecella. "When are Two Web Services Compatible?" *TES 2004*, Springer, 2005, pp.15-28
12. G. Meredith and S. Bjorg. "Contracts and types". *Communications of the ACM*, 2003. 46(10):41–47
13. G. Sala¨un, L. Bordeaux and M. Scharef. "Describing and reasoning on web services using process algebra". *ICWS'04*, IEEE Computer Society Press, 2004. pp. 43–51
14. A. Rerrara. "Web Services: a Process Algebra Approach". *ISCOC'04*, New York, USA, 2004
15. A. Brogi, et al. "Formalizing web services Choreographies". *WS-FM*, 2004..
16. R.Hamadi and B. Benatallah. "A Petri Net-based Model for Web service Composition". *ADC 2003*
17. T. Bultan, X. Fu, R. Hull, and J. Su. "Conversation Specification: A New Approach to Design and Analysis of E-Service Composition", Proc. *WWW2003*. ACM Press, 2003, pp. 403-410
18. L. Bordeaux and G. Slaun. "Using Process Algebra for Web Services: Early Results and Perspetives", *TES 2004*,. Springer 2005, LNCS 3324, pp. 54-68

19. M. Koshkina and F. van Breugel. "Modelling and Verifying Web Service Orchestration by means of the Concurrency Workbench", TAV-WEB Proceedings/ACM SIGSOFT SEN, Sep. 2004 Volume 29 Number 5
20. R. Milner. "Communication and Concurrency". Prentice Hall, 1989.
21. C. Fournet, T. Hoare, S.K. Rajamani, and J. Rehof. "Stuck-Free Conformance Theory for CCS", Microsoft Technical Report, MSR-TR-2004-69
22. S. K. Rajamani and J. Rehof. "Conformance Checking for Models of Asynchronous Message passing Software", CAV2002, Springer 2002, LNCS 2402, pp.166-179.
23. D. Berardi, et al. "Automatic Composition of Transition-based Semantic Web Services with Messageing". Proceedings of the 31st VLDB Conference, Trondheim, Norway, 2005
24. N. Milanovic and M. Malek. "Current Solutions for Web Service Composition". IEEE Internet Computing, November. December, 2004, pp. 51-59

Modified Naïve Bayes Classifier for E-Catalog Classification*

Young-gon Kim[1], Taehee Lee[1], Jonghoon Chun[2], and Sang-goo Lee[1]

[1] School of Computer Science and Engineering / Center for E-Business Research
Seoul National University, Seoul 151-742, Republic of Korea
{gumory, thlee, sglee}@europa.snu.ac.kr
[2] Department of Computer Engineering
Myongji University,
449-728, Yongin, Kyunggi-Do, Republic of Korea
jchun@mju.ac.kr

Abstract. As the wide use of online business transactions, the volume of product information that needs to be managed in a system has become drastically large, and the classification task of such data has become highly complex. The heterogeneity among competing standard classification schemes makes the problem only harder. However, the classification task is an indispensable part for successful e-commerce applications. In this paper, we present an automated approach for e-catalog classification. We extend the Naïve Bayes Classifier to make use of the structural characteristics of e-catalogs. We show how we can improve the accuracy of classification when appropriate characteristics of e-catalogs are utilized. Effectiveness of the proposed methods is validated through experiments.

1 Introduction

E-catalog (Electronic catalog) hold information of products and services in an e-commerce system. E-catalog classification is the task of assigning an input catalog to one of the predefined categories (or classes). The categories are defined according to a specific classification scheme which usually has a hierarchical structure and thousands of leaf nodes. Correct classification is essential not only for data alignment and synchronization among business partners but also to keep the rapidly increasing product data maintainable and accessible. However, product data classification is a highly time-consuming task when it is done manually because of the increased scale of product information and the inherent complexity of the classification schemes. A number of competing standard classification schemes, such as UNSPSC[1] and eCl@ss, do exist nowadays. Since none of them has yet been accepted universally, we need to reclas-

---

* This work was supported by the Ministry of Information & Communications, Korea, under the Information Technology Research Center (ITRC) Support Program.
[1] http://www.unspsc.org

sify the product data for mapping between different classification schemes as a part of business operations [1]. The reclassification task increases the need for an automated approach for product data classification.

E-catalogs are text intensive documents, so text classification techniques can be applied to e-catalog classification. Works in [2] applied several techniques from information retrieval and machine learning to product data classification. Among the well known algorithms such as Vector Space Model, k-Nearest Neighbor, and Naïve Bayes Classifier, they report that the Naïve Bayes Classifier shows the best accuracy. Although there is no single standard form of the e-catalog, conceptually it is a set of attribute-value pairs which, in turn, can be viewed as a structured document. Motivated by the intuition that the structural nature can be utilized, we shift our attention to making a structure-aware Naïve Bayes Classifier.

When the Naïve Bayes Classifier is used for flat text classification, each word position is defined to be an attribute of the Naïve Bayes Classifier [3, 4]. Our approach differs from [3, 4] since our objective is to classify a set of attribute-value pairs instead. We start from the conventional Naïve Bayes Classifier rather than the text-oriented model in order to make use of the attribute-wise distribution of the terms. Furthermore, noticing that each attribute has different discriminative power, we treat individual attributes differently by assigning weights according to their importance. In order to assign weights to the attributes in a reasonable way, we normalize attributes before weighting. We further improve the classification accuracy by utilizing the 'category name' attribute which is available in the training data. Our classifier shows improved accuracy compared to the Naïve Bayes Text Classifier especially in the real data which possibly have noisy attributes.

The remainder of this paper is organized as follows. In section 2, we investigate the related work. In section 3, we describe how we modify conventional Naïve Bayes Classifier to make it applicable for e-catalog classification. In section 4, we present the implementation of our classifier and in section 5, we present experimental results. Finally in section 6, we conclude this paper.

2   Related Work

Recently, with the rapid growth of semi-structured documents their classification issue has attracted an increasing attention. The common motivation is that the structure of documents may contain useful information for classification. In [5], terms in a document are augmented with tags. For example, in an XML document *<resume><name>John Doe</name>...</resume>*, the term 'John' is augmented to yield 'resume.name.John'. Using these augmented terms, the Naive Bayes Classifier shows fairly improved accuracy. The classifier in [6] is based on the Bayesian networks. For each document in the training set, it constructs a Bayesian network whose structure is the same as that of the document itself (a hierarchically structured document can be modeled as a tree). The conditional probabilities collected from these Bayesian networks are used to infer the category of an input document which is also represented as a Bayesian network. Works in [7] present a way of building a rule based classifier for

XML documents and [8] suggests a Bayesian network based classifier which classifies structured multimedia documents. [9], which has just been published online, presents similar model to ours. It splits a semi-structured document into parts according to the structure of the document and builds a separate classifier, level-0 classifier, for each part. Then the result of each level-0 classifier serves as an input to the meta-classifier which combines the inputs to finally determine the category. In comparison, our work takes simpler approach where the entire process is done in a single classifier by using a predetermined weighting policy to assign normalized weights for different attributes. By designing an efficient weight determining method, we expect that our model can be effectively used for general structured document classification.

3 Customized Naïve Bayes Classifier for E-Catalog Classification

The Naïve Bayes Classifier has a long successful application history in the field of text classification due to its favorable space and speed complexity and relatively good performance. In this section, we illustrate the process of customizing the Naïve Bayes Classifier for e-catalog classification.

3.1 Naïve Bayes Classifier

To classify an instance d, the Naïve Bayes Classifier calculates the posterior probability $P(c|d)$ based on the Bayes Theorem and the independence assumption. Given a set of classes C, the attributes $< a_1, a_2, \cdots, a_n >$ and the values $< v_1, v_2, \cdots, v_n >$ that describe an input instance, the Naïve Bayes Classifier assigns the most probable category according to the following formula.

$$c_{NB} = \arg\max_{c_j \in C} P(c_j) \prod_i P(a_i = v_i \mid c_j) \tag{1}$$

Conceptually, this model classifies an instance which consists of a set of attribute-value pairs. If we try to use this classifier to diagnose a disease, proper attributes may be age, sex, blood pressure, etc. and the domains of the attributes must be totally different. When this model is applied to text classification, each word position is defined as an attribute. Given a list of words $< w_1, w_2, \cdots, w_n >$ that constitutes an input document,

$$c_{NB} = \arg\max_{c_j \in C} P(c_j) \prod_i P(a_i = w_i \mid c_j) \tag{2}$$

In this formula, the domain of each attribute is assumed to be the same. To reduce the computation cost, we can make an additional assumption that the attributes are identically distributed, which means that the probability of encountering a specific word is independent of the specific word position [4]. This is quite reasonable for flat text classification but clearly wrong for structured document classification. Most of the adaptations of Naïve Bayes Classifier for text classification are based on this formula. The classifiers introduced in Sect. 2, [5] and [6], also start from this model although they use their own techniques to take advantage of the structural information. In contrast, we start from the model described by Eq. (1), the original Naïve Bayes Classifier. The attributes are those of e-catalog. (Fig. 1) In Sect. 3.2 and Sect. 3.3, we present how we made it possible.

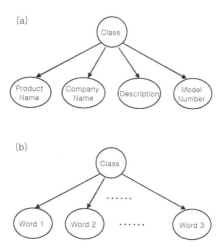

Fig. 1. (a) represents the structure of our classifier and (b) represents that of the Naïve Bayes Classifier for flat-text classification

3.2 Extending Attributes

The main problem of our approach is about matching the attribute values. Since the values are texts composed of many words and are often noisy, accepting only the exact matches is misleading. It is clearly wrong to distinguish between 'Desktop' and 'Desktop Computer'. The problem becomes worse when we try to use an attribute like 'product description' which is sometimes composed of full sentences. So, with a parser we have implemented, we made use of partial matches between attribute values. The parser which successfully manages Korean language extracts terms from a string by a set of heuristics including stemming and removing stop-words. In this model, each extracted term is treated as an independent attribute. In Fig. 2, (a) represents the original Naïve Bayes Classifier when an instance catalog is assigned and (b) represents our model extended according to the result of the parser. To cope with this model, we redefine the value of an attribute as a set of terms.

$$v_i = \{t_{i1}, t_{i2}, \ldots, t_{im}\} \tag{3}$$

where t_{ik} is a term produced from v_i by the parser. Then we can reasonably assume that

$$P(a_i = v_i \mid c_j) = \prod_k P(t_{ik} \text{ appears in } a_i \mid c_j) = \prod_k \frac{n(c_j, a_i, t_{ik})}{n(c_j, a_i)} \tag{4}$$

where $n(c_j, a_i, t_{ik})$ denotes the number of occurrences of t_{ik} in a_i of the catalogs that belong to class c_j. Similarly, $n(c_j, a_i)$ denotes the sum of frequencies of all terms in a_i of the catalogs that belong to class c_j. $n(a_i)$ denotes the total number of terms appearing in attribute a_i. When none of the terms in training data matches t_{ik}, $1/n(a_i)$ is used as $P(t_{ik}$ appears in $a_i \mid c_j)$. Using Eq. (4), the classifier is reformulated as follows.

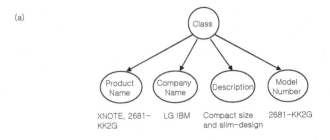

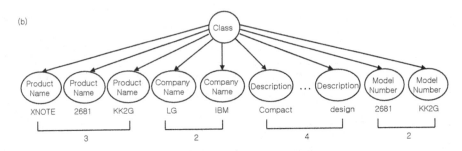

Fig. 2. The structure of two Naïve Bayes Classifiers. The texts below the nodes represent values of an input catalog. (a) is the structure before extension and (b) is the structure after extension. In (b), 3, 2, 4, 2 terms are generated from each attribute.

$$c_{NB} = \arg \max_{c_j \in C} P(c_j) \prod_{i,k} P(t_{ik} \text{ appears } in \ a_i \mid c_j)$$

$$= \arg \max_{c_j \in C} \{ |c_j| \prod_{i,k} \frac{n(c_j, a_i, t_{ik})}{n(c_j, a_i)} \} \tag{5}$$

Using the training data, we count all the parameters, $n(c_j, a_i, t_{ik})$ and $n(c_j, a_i)$. They are stored in RDB tables and retrieved when the classification is performed.

3.3 Normalizing and Weighting Attributes

Our model in the previous section is structure aware in that it calculates the conditional probability based on attribute-wise distribution of terms. But one problem arises in this model, that is, longer attributes which generate more terms are likely to dominate the classification. In our data, the attribute 'product description' generates the most terms although its effect on the classification is proven to be relatively low(Sect. 5). So we use normalized attributes. Since normalizing the product of probabilities rather than the sum of probabilities, we use geometric mean($\sqrt[n]{t_1 \dots t_n}$) for normalization.

$$
\begin{aligned}
c_{NB} &= \arg \max_{c_j \in C} P(c_j) \prod_i \left(\prod_k P(t_{ik} \ appears \ in \ a_i \mid c_j) \right)^{\frac{1}{|v_i|}} \\
&= \arg \max_{c_j \in C} \{ | c_j | \prod_i \left(\prod_k \frac{n(c_j, a_i, t_{ik})}{n(c_j, a_i)} \right)^{\frac{1}{|v_i|}} \}
\end{aligned}
\tag{6}
$$

Normalization enables us to weight the attributes. As we mentioned above, attributes have different effect on the classification although they are equally treated due to the independence assumption. Therefore giving more weights to more informative attributes can enhance the classification accuracy. It is impossible to reasonably weight the attributes without normalization because they are implicitly and arbitrarily weighted by the number of terms produced by the parser. In our model, weights are given as exponents for the same reason as we use geometric mean for normalizing attributes. Eq. (7) is our final formula where w_i denotes the weight for attribute a_i.

$$
\begin{aligned}
c_{NB} &= \arg \max_{c_j \in C} P(c_j) \prod_i \left(\prod_k P(t_{ik} \ appears \ in \ a_i \mid c_j) \right)^{\frac{w_i}{|v_i|}} \\
&= \arg \max_{c_j \in C} \{ | c_j | \prod_i \left(\prod_k \frac{n(c_j, a_i, t_{ik})}{n(c_j, a_i)} \right)^{\frac{w_i}{|v_i|}} \}
\end{aligned}
\tag{7}
$$

To find out which attribute has greater effect on the classification, we classify a set of catalogs using only one attribute at a time(Sect. 5). We determine the weighting policy based on the result of this experiment.

3.4 Utilizing Category Names

The target attribute of e-catalog classification is the class code. In most cases, a class code is represented as a string of digits and each has a corresponding name, which we call category name. For instance, in UNSPSC, the category name for the class code '43171801' is 'Notebook Computers'. Since the category name which is also an attribute of catalogs has one-to-one correspondence with the class code, it is intuitive that using this information can help the classification. Input catalogs cannot have category names because their categories are not decided. But the catalogs in the training set do have category names. As a way to utilize this valuable information, we use the product names of input catalogs instead of the category names. This is possible because the domains of the two attributes, category names and product names, have considerable amount of intersection. In our data, 57% of the terms in category names also appear in product names although the opposite is low because the domain of product names is much larger. We show the validity of this method in Sect. 5, through experiments.

4   Implementation

4.1   Training

In the training phase, catalogs in the training set are parsed and the term frequencies are counted to build the 'frequency table' and 'total frequency table' which are relational database tables. There is an example frequency table in Fig. 4. The column 'Class_Code' is for the class code, the target attribute, and 'Term' stores the terms parsed. In 'Attr', digits which denote specific attributes of catalogs are stored. 1 is for product name, 2 is for category name and 3 indicates company name. 'Freq' corresponds to $n(c_j, a_i, t_{ik})$ (See Sect. 3.2). The total frequency table is for storing $n(c_j, a_i)$ and its structure is straightforward. Fig. 3 shows an example of the training data and Fig. 4 depicts the resulting frequency table and total frequency table. In the frequency table in Fig. 4, since each of 'LCD SyncMaster100' and 'Flatron LCD171' in Fig. 3 produces one 'lcd', the 'Freq' of the term 'lcd' which corresponds to $n(c_{43172410}, a_1, 'lcd')$ is 2. In the same manner, the 'Freq' of 'syncmaster' and 'flatron' is 1. In the example total frequency table, 'Total_Freq' of attribute 1 which corresponds to $n(c_{43172410}, a_1)$ is 6, 2+1+1+1+1.

<Training Data>

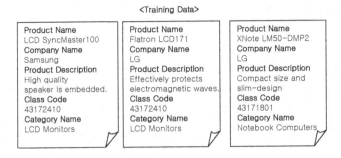

Fig. 3. Three catalogs as training data. Two are from '43172410' and one is from '43171801'.

<Frequency Table>

Class_Code	Attr	Term	Freq
43172410	1	lcd	2
43172410	1	syncmaster	1
43172410	1	100	1
43172410	1	flatron	1
43172410	1	171	1
43172410	2	lcd	2
43172410	2	monitors	2
43172410	3	samsung	1
43172410	3	lg	1
43172410	4	high	1
43172410	4	...	...
43171801	1	xnote	1
43171801	1	lm50	1
43171801	1	dmp2	1
43171801	2	notebook	1
43171801	2	computers	1
43171801	3	lg	1
43171801	4	compact	1
43171801	4	...	...

<Total Frequency Table>

Class_Code	Attr	Total_Freq
43172410	1	6
43172410	2	4
43172410	3	2
43172410	4	8
43171801	1	3
43171801	2	2
43171801	3	1
43171801	4	4

Fig. 4. Frequency table and total frequency table generated from training the catalogs in Fig. 3

4.2 Classification

An example classification process of a simple input catalog is depicted in Fig. 5. The posterior probabilities of two categories, $c_{43172410}$ and $c_{43171801}$, are calculated according to Eq. 7 and the data in Fig. 4. Both $n(a_1)$ and $n(a_4)$ (See Sect 3.2) which are used for the probability estimation of the mismatching terms are assumed to be

Product Name
Flatron LCD180
Product Description
Compact size and slim-design
Class Code
?

$$P(c_{43172410} \mid d) = P(c) \times P(a_1 = v_1 \mid c_{43172410}) \times P(a_4 = v_4 \mid c_{43172410})$$

$$= 750 \times (\frac{1}{6} \times \frac{2}{6} \times \frac{1}{50000})^{\frac{5}{3}} \times (\frac{1}{50000} \times \frac{1}{50000} \times \frac{1}{50000} \times \frac{1}{50000})^{\frac{1}{4}}$$

$$= 750 \times (1.19 \times 10^{-10}) \times (2 \times 10^{-5}) = 2.60 \times 10^{-18}$$

$$P(c_{43171801} \mid d) = P(c) \times P(a_1 = v_1 \mid c_{43171801}) \times P(a_4 = v_4 \mid c_{43171801})$$

$$= 1100 \times (\frac{1}{50000} \times \frac{1}{50000} \times \frac{1}{50000})^{\frac{5}{3}} \times (\frac{1}{4} \times \frac{1}{4} \times \frac{1}{4} \times \frac{1}{4})^{\frac{1}{4}}$$

$$= 1100 \times (3.20 \times 10^{-24}) \times (2.5 \times 10^{-1}) = 8.88 \times 10^{-22}$$

Fig. 5. An input catalog and the probability calculation. For simplicity, the input catalog contains only two attributes.

50000. The weight for a_1, product name, is 5 and 1 is assigned to a_4, product description. The final posterior probability of $c_{43172410}$ is much higher although its probability from a_4 is much lower than that of $c_{43171801}$. Without normalization and weighting, the result would have been the opposite.

The pseudo code in Table 1 describes our classification algorithm.

Table 1. Classification Algorithm

Input : A catalog to be classified, Frequency Table, Total Frequency Table
Output : Top-k most probable categories
(1) Parse the values of the input catalog :
$\{ v_1 , \ldots , v_n \} \rightarrow \{ (t_{11} , t_{12} , \ldots), \ldots , (t_{n1} , t_{n2} , \ldots) \}$
(2) for each class_code c_j in frequency_table {
(3) $score(j) = 1$;
(4)   for each attribute a_i {
(5) $terms(j,i)$ = set of terms in a_i of c_j;
(6) $score(j,i) = 1$;
(7)   for each input term t_{ik} from a_i {
(8)   if (t_{ik} is in $terms(j,i)$)
(9) $score(j,i) = score(j,i) \times (n(c_j , a_i , t_{ik}) / n(c_j , a_i))$;
(10)   else
(11) $score(j,i) = score(j,i) \times (1 / n(a_i))$;
(12)   }
(13) $score(j,i) = \sqrt[|v_i|]{score(j,i)}$
(14) $score(j) = score(j) \times score(j,i)^{w_i}$;
(15)   }
(16) $score(j) = score(j) \times |c_j|$
(17) }
(18) return Top-k class_code according to $score(j)$

The first step should be parsing the values of the input catalog. Then the scores of categories are computed and according to the scores, top-k categories are returned. This algorithm computes our final formula, Eq. (7), step by step. Lines (8) through (11) show how we calculate the probabilities. In lines (13) and (14), normalization and weighting is applied respectively and the statement in line (16) makes the final score of c_j by multiplying the class size part of our formula. Lines (2) through (17) are implemented as an SQL query with 2 GROUP BY clauses. In the query, a product of probabilities is computed as a sum of logarithms of the probabilities.

Due to the three loops and the keyword search in line (8), the time required by our algorithm is $O(|c| \times |a| \times \log t \times i)$ where $|c|$ and $|a|$ is the number of classes and attributes, t is the average size of $terms(j,i)$ in line (5) and i is the average number of input terms from one attribute. t is taken in logarithm because the keyword search is done on the index. Selecting top-k is performed at $O(|c| \times k)$ so it does not affect the entire complexity. Regarding $|a|$ as constant, which is 5 in our data since we use five attributes, the time complexity can be rewritten as $O(|c| \times \log t \times i)$. In the next section, we present the result of our experiment which measured the classification time with varying $|c|$.

5 Experimental Results

The e-catalogs used for our experiment are from a practical product database of Public Procurement Services (PPS) of Korea. PPS is responsible for procurement for government and public agencies [10] and the database currently contains 495,653 product catalogs under *G2B* classification system. The *G2B* classification system is made based on UNSPSC classification system and consists of 7960 leaf classes. From the dataset, we measured the time for classifying a catalog and the accuracy of the algorithm. Since Naïve Bayes classifier is a *lazy classifier* which is known to require a relatively short training time, we did not compare the time for training with other classifiers. We ran our tests on Intel Pentium4 2.4Ghz machine which has 2GB of RAM. Database server we used is Oracle 9i and the interface including parsing and selecting top-k was implemented with JDK1.4.1.

Fig. 6 shows the result of measuring classification time with varying number of categories in the training data. The set of training categories in the experiment was selected randomly from the test dataset. As the figure shows, the classification time increases linearly as the number of target categories increases. Under the assumption that the average number of terms contained in a category is almost same over the whole categories, this result follows the time complexity we estimated in the previous section. In our experiments, a classification was performed within a second even in a case of more than 7,000 target categories and 256 terms in a category on average.

Prior to applying our classifying algorithm, the weight of each attribute has to be decided. For taking a hint as to the weight of each attribute, we classified a set of catalogs by utilizing one attribute at a time and disregarding the others. Since meaningful attributes in our consideration are *product name*, *company name*, *product description*, *model number* and *category name*, the experiments were done for the five attributes and the result is given in Fig. 7. The result shows that the discriminative power of *product name* far surpasses those of the other attributes. But the weight of each attribute can not be determined proportionally to the accuracy of each attribute because the attributes are not completely independent of one another. Since the final result is not very sensitive to the weights, after performing more experiments, we concluded that weighting 5 on *product name* and 1 on the others gives the best result in our dataset.

To examine the accuracy of our classification algorithm, we have generated 2 datasets, Data1 and Data2. In Data1, we divided the catalogs into a training set and a test set which are 70% and 30% of the whole respectively. In Data2, the whole product data is used as a training set and 10,000 randomly sampled product data from the user request

$\log^2$ were used as a test set. The product data in user request log are raw descriptions containing many noisy terms whereas those of Data1 are standardized, structured and cleansed by manual efforts of domain experts. From the experimental result of using Data2, we could estimate the performance of our algorithm in a real environment. The result of the accuracy test is shown in Fig. 8. (a) is the result from Data1 and (b) is from Data2. In each of them, the accuracy is measured in 4 different settings.

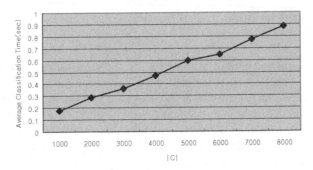

Fig. 6. Average Classification Time

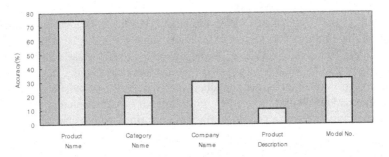

Fig. 7. Classification accuracy with only one attribute

- **Flat:** Naive Bayes Classifier for flat text classification
- **Structured:** After extending and normalizing attributes
- **Weighted:** Weighting 5 for *product name* and 1 for the others
- **Category Name:** Utilizing category names in addition to the **Weighted**

We considered the accuracy of only the first ranked category though our classifier returns top-k categories. As expected the overall accuracy is much higher in Data1 than in Data2 since Data2 has more noise. But normalizing and weighting considerably increase the accuracy of Data2 up to 81%. Normalizing and weighting have the effect of reducing noise and improving the accuracy. Utilizing *category names* slightly improved the accuracy in both Data 1 and Data 2.

---

[2] The user request log contains product descriptions in a raw format that customers submit for cataloging or purchasing.

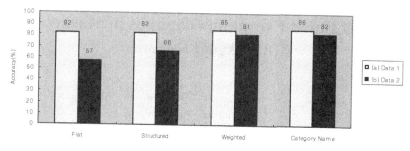

Fig. 8. The result of the accuracy test

6   Conclusion

In this paper, we propose a modified Naïve Bayes Classifier which effectively classifies e-catalogs. Our model presents a way of implementing a structure-aware classifier based on the Naïve Bayes Classifier. It deals with attribute-wise distribution of terms to cope with the structured nature of e-catalogs. By normalizing attributes, it is possible to assign weight irrespective of the different length of the attributes. By weighting attributes according to their discriminative power, we could achieve improved accuracy. As the experimental results show, our classifier successfully manages the real data which possibly have noisy attributes. Since many of the characteristics of our model can be applied to other types of structured documents, we expect that our classifier can be adapted to XML or HTML document classification.

References

1. D. Fensel, Y. Ding, E. Schulten, B. Omelayenko, G. Botquin, M. Brown, and A. Flett: Product Data Integeration in B2B E-commerce. IEEE Intelligent System, Vol 16/3, pp 54-59, 2001.
2. Y. Ding, M. Korotkiy, B. Omelayenko, V. Kartseva, V. Zykov, M. Klein, E. Schulten, D. Fensel: GoldenBullet: Automated Classification of Product Data in E-commerce. Business Information System 2002, 2002.
3. F. Sebastiani: Machine Learning in Automated Text Categorization. ACM Computing Surveys Vol 34/1, pp 1-47, 2002.
4. T. Mitchell: Machine Learning, McGraw-Hill, 1997.
5. J. Yi, N. Sundaresan: A classifier for semi-structured documents. 6th ACM SIGKDD, pp 340-344, 2000.
6. L. Denoyer, P. Gallinari: Bayesian Network Model for Semi-structured Document Classification. Information Processing & Management, Vol 40/5, pp 807-827, Elsevier, 2004.
7. M. J. Zaki, C. C. Aggarwal: XRules: An Effective Structural Classifier for XML Data. 9th ACM SIGKDD, pp 316-325, 2003.
8. L. Denoyer, J. Vittaut, P. Gallinari, S. Brunessaux, S. Brunessaux: Structured Multimedia Document Classification. ACM DOCENG 2003, pp 153-160, 2003.
9. A. Bratko, B. Filipic: Exploiting Structural Information for Semi-structured Document Categorization. Information Processing & Management, Vol 42/3, pp 679-694, Elsevier, 2006.
10. KOCIS (Korea Ontology-based e-Catalog Information System), http://www.g2b.go.kr:8100/index.jsp. Accessed on Feb, 2006.

A Sentinel Based Exception Diagnosis in Market Based Multi-Agent Systems

Nazaraf Shah[1], Kuo-Ming Chao[1], Nick Godwin[1], Anne James[1],
and Chun-Lung Huang[2]

[1] DSM Research Group, Department of Computer and Network Systems
Coventry University, Coventry UK
{n.shah, k.chao, a.n.godwin, a.james}@coventry.ac.uk
[2] Institute of Information Management, National Chiao Tung University, Taiwan
clhuang@iim.nctu.edu.tw

Abstract. Market based Multi-agent systems (MAS) operate in an open and dynamic environment where agents enter and leave the system unpredictably. The dynamism and unpredictable nature of an open environment gives rise to unpredictable exceptions. It becomes essential to have some exception diagnosis mechanisms in these systems to effectively manage their exception diagnose processes. The defining characteristic of mechanisms is their ability to provide a uniform exception diagnosis capability to independently developed agents. In this paper we present a brief discussion of our proposed sentinel based approach to exception diagnosis in an open MAS and discuss the accuracy and performance overhead of our approach when applying in a market based MAS.

1 Introduction

MAS's operate in open and dynamic environment. The issue of openness and dynamism is addressed by standardising efforts such as FIPA standards [1]. These standards address the issues of communication and interaction in an open MAS.

Open MAS's evolve dynamically from the interactions of independently developed agents. These independently developed agents cannot be assumed to be benevolent, unlike agents in closed systems. The members of an open MAS are often unrelated, may have no experience of prior interactions, and may have no information about each other's reputation [2]. Agents in such environments are prone to a variety of types of failure such as missed deadlines, communication channel failures, agent death, or agents deviating from their contracted behaviours, either intentionally or unintentionally. If agents have no mechanism, or no intention, to handle such unexpected behaviours, then exceptions will occur. Such exceptions could occur at any point during an interaction.

The detailed description of the architectural components and their functionalities can be found in our work [3], [4]. The proposed architecture is realised in terms of agents known as sentinel agents. Our proposed architecture enables the real time exception detection and diagnosis in an MAS operating in a complex and dynamic environment, by monitoring the agents' interactions. A sentinel agent can also start a

J. Lee et al. (Eds.): DEECS 2006, LNCS 4055, pp. 258–267, 2006.

diagnostic process on receiving a complaint from its associated problem solving agent or from another sentinel agent regarding a disputed contract.

When an agent joins an MAS, a sentinel agent with default functions is created and assigned to it. Agent developers need to provide their agents with the ability to inform the sentinel agent about their goals, plans, and also the ability to report on their mental state. The sentinel agent is used as a delegate of the problem solving agent, and all further communication with the problem solving agent takes place via its associated sentinel. When a problem solving agent plans to interact with another agent, it sends an ACL [5] message via its associated sentinel. Such an arrangement enables agents' runtime interaction monitoring and abnormality detection in these interactions.

The architecture is implemented using the JACK™ [6] agent framework using FIPA standards add on for FIPA standards compliance and use JADE [7] ontology support for implementing an exception ontology. The MAS used in evaluation is an implementation of the FIPA Travel Assistant [8] application case study.

The paper is organized as follows: In Section 2 we describe existing mechanisms for exception diagnosis and resolution. In section 3 we briefly provide the discussion of our proposed architecture. In section 4 we discuss the detail of fault tree. Section 5 briefly describes the case study. Section 6 provides a discussion of the accuracy and the performance overhead of our proposed mechanism. Finally section 7 concludes the paper.

2   Related Work

Exception handling (e.g., detection, diagnosis and resolution) is not well addressed area in open MAS research, much of the work has been done in closed and reliable environment without taking into account the challenges of an open environment. In our proposed architecture we address the monitoring and diagnostic aspects of the exception handling process. A few well known approaches have been proposed by MAS researchers in order to address the issue of exception handling. These approaches generally falls into two categories, those using external agents called sentinel agents that monitor agents' interactions and those that are based on introspection and provide an agent with the ability to monitor its own runtime behaviour and detect failures. Each of these approaches uses some form of redundancy. These proposals can also be categorised as either domain dependent or domain independent approaches.

The ARCHON project [9] involves the diagnosis of several real world distributed applications. ARCHON enables the integration of several independently operating systems into a cooperating MAS. It is an application driven approach and focuses on problems of global coordination and coherence. Exception diagnosis is treated as a part of managing global coordination not as a problem in its own right.

Ross et al. [10], [11] presented an approach and distributed protocol to diagnose faults using spatially distributed knowledge of the system. This approach is realised by an MAS of diagnostic agents, where each agent has a model of its associated subsystem. The behaviour of each subsystem is considered as dependent on other subsystems. Once abnormal behaviour is detected agents get involved in a diagnosis process.

In doing so agents must take into consideration the correctness of the inputs to their subsystems provided by the other subsystems. Each agent produces a local minimal diagnosis so that these are consistent with a global diagnosis made by a single agent combining the knowledge of all agents. The protocol reduces the complexity of establishing global minimal diagnosis by ensuring that each agent produces a local minimal diagnosis consistent with the global diagnosis. This approach assumes that the system to be diagnosed can be decomposed in subsystems and subsystems are related via data input relationships.

Mishra et al. [12] present fault-tolerant protocols for detecting communication or node failure and for recovery of lost mobile agents. Every mobile agent is associated with an agent watchdog, which monitors the functioning of the agent and manages the agent migration. The watchdog agent uses checkpointing and rollback recovery [13] for recovering the lost agent's state. The approach targets the mobile agent's mobility failure related issues only.

Wang et al. [14] proposed an intelligent agent based approach to monitoring financial transactions. A society of agents monitors a vast volume of dynamic information in a distributed manner. Each agent in the society is capable of performing its function autonomously. The agents are able to detect financial fraud and other risks using their monitored information and they do not involve diagnosis or remedial actions.

Fedoruk et al. [15] introduce a technique for fault tolerance in MAS's by replicating individual agents within the system. This approach uses proxy-like structures to manage agents in a replicate group. A group proxy acts as an interface between replicates in a group and the rest of the MAS. This arrangement makes the replicate group appear as a single entity. When an active agent fails, its proxy will detect the failure, activate a new replicate and transfer the current state to the new replicate. In this approach proxy agents only detect the exception in an agent and select the alternative replicate agent in order to deal with the exception. It does not diagnose the underlying cause of an agent failure.

Venkatraman et al. [16] present a generic approach to detecting the non-compliance of agents to coordination protocols in an open MAS. It uses model checking to determine whether the present execution satisfies the specifications of the underlying coordination protocol. This approach is limited to one class of exceptions and its does not include its diagnosis and resolution methods

Hägg [17] proposes the use of sentinel agents that build the models of interacting agents by monitoring their interaction and intervene on detection of an exception according to given guidelines. The sentinel agents copy the world model of problem solving agents, thus giving sentinel agent access to the problem solving agent's mind. Such mind reading has serious consequences for the autonomy of an agent.

Kaminka and Tambe [18] propose an approach called 'social attentive monitoring' to diagnose and resolve exceptions in a team of problem solving agents. This approach involves the monitoring of peers, during execution of their team and individual plans and the detection, and diagnosis of failures by comparing their own state with the state of their monitored team-mates. The monitoring of agents is external to them, but there is no sentinel agent involved in this monitoring, the responsibility of monitoring is delegated to one or more of the team-mate agents. This approach is applicable only to the teamcore protocol.

Kumar and Cohen [19] propose the use of redundant agents in order to deal with broker agent failure. This approach only deals with failure detection of agents in a team of agents.

Horling et al. [20] suggest the use of a domain independent technique to diagnose and resolve inter-agent dependencies. Their work is concerned with the issue of performance using situation specific coordination strategies. In contrast our approach deals with abstract action failure diagnosis in plans.

Klein et al's effort [21], [22] is the first step towards open MAS exception detection, diagnosis and resolution. They argue that domain independent sentinel agents can be used to monitor the interactions among problem solving agents in an open MAS. Their sentinel agents deal with protocol related exceptions only, without any regard to the application domain. Their approach has the following limitations.

Firstly their approach lacks a well defined structure for a sentinel agent; neither have they addressed the issue of interoperability. Secondly their approach does not classify the exceptions according to the level at which the exception occurs, and the approach is also silent on how to diagnose and resolve agents' belief inconsistencies. Thirdly this approach is unable to diagnose plan action failure exceptions using plan abstract knowledge. Fourthly the approach claims to be suitable for open system, but it does not propose the use an ontology to give uniform meanings to concepts, actions and predicates involved in the interactions during a diagnosis process.

3 Proposed Approach

Our proposed mechanism addresses some of the limitations of the current approaches and provides a detailed framework within which knowledge of different kinds of exception and their diagnosis can be organised and utilised effectively. None of the previous sentinel based approaches provide such a comprehensive framework for representing and utilising the exception diagnosis knowledge to facilitate reasoning about runtime exceptions and their underlying causes.

In this paper we will briefly mention our proposed architecture, the details discussion of the architecture can be seen in our previous work [3], [4]. The purpose of the architecture is to provide a structure for the detection and diagnosis of runtime exceptions in an open MAS. In order to offload the burden from agents, implementing the complex exception diagnosis capabilities, the proposed architecture is realised as a sentinel agent and each problem solving agent is assigned a sentinel agent. This results in an MAS composed of problem solving agents and sentinel agents. The sentinel agents are provided by the MAS infrastructure owner and treated as trusted agents, which are assumed to be truthful. The sentinel agents require the problem solving agents to provide information cooperatively regarding their mental attitudes, whenever requested to during the exception detection and diagnosis process.

This enables the sentinel agents to diagnose exceptions interactively and heuristically by asking questions from effected agents through ACL messages. This means that the sentinels do not have direct access to the mental states of problem solving agents. The sentinels also reason using the knowledge that an agent can possibly violate its role's responsibilities in a given coordination protocol.

4 Fault Tree

We have arranged exceptions and their underlying causes hierarchically into a taxon-omy. The resultant fault tree is shown in Figure 1. The fault tree represents the rela-tionship among different exceptions and their causes. The root elements represent the underlying cause of the exception and the non root elements represent the exceptions at different levels. The main advantage of arranging exceptions in a hierarchy is that such an arrangement facilitates the search of the exceptions and their cause in a sys-tematic way. When an exceptions occurs the sentinel agent could follow one of the six paths emanating from the root of the fault tree. This reduces the search space and increases efficiency of the diagnosis process. All causes have their associated tests which are encoded in terms of the sentinel agent's diagnostic plans. These plans are executed by the sentinel in order to confirm or refute a hypothesis.

All exceptions in the hierarchy apart from *action failure* and *wrong result* excep-tions are domain independent; they can occur in any FIPA compliant MAS regardless of the problem domain. The proposed sentinel agent has capability of diagnosing these exceptions in a domain independent way.

In our implementation we treat a plan's action failure exceptions in form of ab-stract representations rather than using the stack trace of the exceptions. These ab-stract exceptions are defined as predicates in our proposed *ExceptionOntology* object

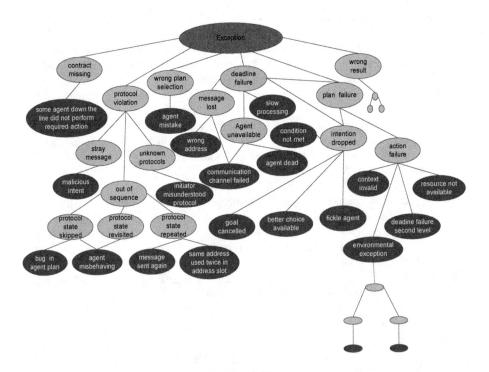

Fig. 1. Fault Tree

[23]. A plan implemented according to abstract specifications has associated abstract exceptions that are used to represent the failure of different actions in a plan [24]. A low level exception representation may be used by the individual agents when dealing with their environmental exceptions. If an abstract action is not recovered from an environmental failure, that action is marked by the agent as a failed action with a reason representing the environmental exception at abstract level.

As shown in Figure 1 the environmental exceptions can have deep hierarchy depending upon the types of exception. We are not concerned with this level of information; such information is not of any use outside the plan where the exceptions occurred. Similarly a domain related exception can be represented in a hierarchy of exceptions, based on the structure of the domain and the possible exceptions in that domain.

We do not have such domain related hierarchy to deal with *wrong result* exception automatically. The implementation of such a hierarchy requires a knowledge acquisition process in order to accumulate exception knowledge from domain experts. The current implementation classifies such exceptions as disputed contracts and brings them to the attention of the system operator.

5   Case Study

To evaluate the capability of our proposed exception diagnosis agents, we have applied them to a Personal Travel Assistant (PTA) System [8]. The PTA system is a case study provided by FIPA as an example to show the benefits of applying agent technology in an open, dynamic and diverse electronic travel domain. The PTA system is composed of different types of roles represented by different agents, and their main goal is to provide a user with the best travel package available in current circumstances.

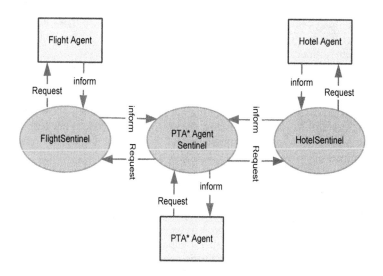

Fig. 2. System Structure

This case study involves different scenarios in which different kinds of agents interact with each other in order to plan a trip for a user. The PTA electronic market is a multi-agent system based on an existing travel domain, which incorporates the electronic equivalents of travel agents, a user assistant, and service providers. There are three main types of agent in the PTA domain that collaborate to fulfil travel requirements for a human user.

We assign each agent in a PTA domain an associated sentinel agent, which monitors and mediates its associated agent's interactions with other agents in the PTA domain in order to demonstrate the exception diagnosis capability of our proposal. All problem solving agents and sentinel agents are FIPA compliant. We will also provide a comparison of performance trade offs between a system using sentinel agents and a system without sentinel agents. The over all system structure is shown in figure 2.

6 Diagnosis Performance and Accuracy

It is essential to demonstrate the applicability of the proposed architecture by showing how accurately and efficiently it is able to diagnosis runtime exceptions. We introduce into the system the causes shown as leaves of the fault tree in order to check the accuracy of the diagnosis mechanism. The sentinel agents diagnose the cause correctly in all cases, apart from two cases where the sentinel agent settles for a more general cause rather than a specific cause.

We have injected faults in the system one by one and in order to verify the diagnostic accuracy of the proposed architecture. In the case of *abstract action failure*, a fault was injected in an abstract action. The sentinel was able to find the underlying cause of this exception through interaction between problem solving agent and sentinel agent.

In the case of the *Protocol Violation Exception* the sentinel was able to make diagnosis correctly in all cases apart from a *protocol state skipped* case. It is hard for a sentinel agent to distinguish between *bugs in agent code* and *misbehaving agent*. The sentinel agent always takes this as a *misbehaving agent,* because there is no way for a sentinel agent to run a test on the agent's plan to confirm or refute the presence of bugs in an agent's plan.

In the case of the *contract missing* exception the sentinel agent is always able to diagnose the cause of the exception. The sentinel seeks help from other sentinel agents when it is unable to make the diagnosis itself.

We injected deadline failures by making an agent's plan: sleep for a specified period of time to simulate slow processing; by disconnecting the agent from platform; by inserting a wrong address in a message, and, by making the agent drop its intention. The sentinel agent was unable to distinguish between agent communication link failure and agent death. This case is treated by the sentinel agent as agent unavailable. The only way a sentinel can distinguish between the two cases is if the sentinel agent and its associated agent are on same machine. In all other cases the sentinel agents diagnose the deadline failure causes correctly.

The *wrong plan* selection exception was injected by introducing a mismatch between the descriptions of an agent's stated capability and its actual capability. It is easy to detect and the sentinel infers that the agent made the mistake, but the sentinel is unable to interrogate more deeply in order to find why the agent has made a mistake in selecting the right plan. The sentinel agent informs the agent of this mistake.

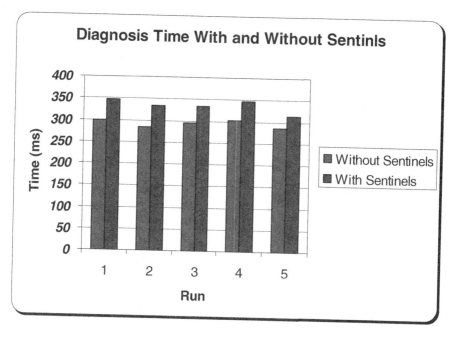

Fig. 3. Exception Diagnosis Comparison

Figure 3 shows the comparison of time taken to diagnosis a plan action failure with and without using sentinel agents. As expected the use of a sentinel takes more time due to the extra communication involved between sentinel agents and their processing. On average the diagnosis using sentinel agents took 14% more time than diagnosis using no sentinels. Of the total 14%, 8% of the time was taken due to extra communication involved between sentinels and 6% was taken by the sentinels for their internal processing.

Although the use of sentinel agents cost time, the use of sentinel based approach brings extra advantages as mentioned [17], [21], [22]. Such advantages include the provision of a global view of a distributed transaction, separation of problem solving knowledge and exception handling knowledge, uniform representation of exceptions and their semantics, flexibility in incorporating new exception types and dealing with system operation strategies in a dynamic environment.

7 Conclusions

We have provided the performance analysis and accuracy of the proposed approach for different runs. The variations in task completion time depend on variation in the level of traffic flow in the communication channels. It is found that the percentage overhead of the proposed approach also varies with the choice of problem solving load. Larger problems have been shown to give a smaller percentage of overhead as compared to smaller problems. In none of the previous reports related to a sentinel based approach has there been such performance analysis. We also provide a discussion about exception diagnosis accuracy of the proposed sentinel agent and the diagnostic overhead incurred by the use of sentinel agents. This also provides insight into some situations where a sentinel agent settles on a more general cause in the fault tree, rather than finding the more specific cause. We have also shown the overheads of using sentinel based approach to exception diagnosis in an open MAS are within reasonable limits.

References

1. Foundation for Intelligent Physical Agents (FIPA), www.fipa.org.
2. Zacharia, G., Moukas, A., Maes, P., Collaborative Reputation Mechanisms in Electronic. In proceedings of the 23rd Hawaii International conference on System Marketplaces, (1999).
3. Shah, N., Chao K-M., Godwin, N., Younas, M., Laing, C., Exception Diagnosis in Agent-Based Grid Computing. In IEEE International Conference on Systems Man and Cybernetics, (2004) 3213-3219.
4. N. Shah, K-M Chao, Nick Godwin, and Anne James, Exception Diagnosis in Open Multi-Agent Systems. In IEEE/WIC/ACM Intelligent Agent Technology Conference (2005).
5. Foundation for Intelligent Physical Agents, FIPA Communication Act Library, http://www.fipa.org/specs/fipa00037
6. JACK™ Intelligent Agents, Agent Oriented Software, http://www.agent-software.com/shared/home/
7. JADE, TILAB, http://jade.tilab.com/
8. FIPA Personal Travel Assistance Specification. Foundation for Intelligent Physical Agents, (2000) http://www.fipa.org/specs/fipa00080/
9. Jennings N. R., Cora J. M., Laresgoiti I., Mandani, E. H., Perriollat F., Skarek P., Varga L. Z., Using Archon to Develop Real-World DAI Applications, Part 1, IEEE Expert: Intelligent Systems and Their Applications, (1996) 64-70.
10. Roos N., Teiji, A., Bos A., Multi-Agent Diagnosis with Spatially Distributed Knowledge. In 14th Belgian-Dutch Conference on Artificial Intelligence (BNAIC'02), (2002) 275-282.
11. Roos N., Teije A., Witteveen C., A Protocol for Multi-Agent Diagnosis with Spatially Distributed Knowledge. In AAMAS'03, Melbourne, Australia, (2003) 655-661.
12. Mishra S., Huang Y., Fault Tolerance in Agent-Based Computing. In proceedings of the 13th ISCA International Conference on Parallel and Distributed Computing Systems, Las Vegas, NV (2000)
13. Elnozahy E. N., Zwaenepoel W., Manetho: Transparent Rollback Recovery with Low Overhead, Limited Rollback and fast Output Commit. In IEEE Transactions on Computers, Special Issue on Fault Tolerance Computing, (1992) 526-531.
14. Wang H., Mylopoulos J., Liao S., Intelligent Agents and Financial Risk Monitoring Systems, Communications of the ACM, (2002) 83-88.
15. Fedoruk, A., and Deters, R., Improving Fault-Tolerance by Replicating Agents. In proceedings of the First International Conference on Autonomous Agents and Multi-agent Systems Bologna Italy, (2002) 337-344
16. Venkatraman, M., Singh M. P. Verifying Compliance with Commitment Protocols: Enabling Web-Based Multi-agent Systems, Autonomous Agents and Multi-Agent Systems, volume 2, (1999) 217-236.

17. Hägg, S., A Sentinel Approach to Fault Handling in Multi-Agent Systems. In proceedings of Second Australian Workshop on Distributed AI, Carnis Australia, Verlog-Springer, (1997) 181-195.
18. Kaminka, G. A., Tambe, M., What is Wrong with Us? Improving Robustness Through Social Diagnosis. In proceedings of the 15th National conference on Artificial Intelligence, (1998) 97-104
19. Kumar S., Cohen P. R., Levesque H. J., The Adoptive Agent Architecture: Achieving Fault Tolerance Using Persistent Broker Teams. In proceedings of the Fourth International Conference on MultiAgent Systems (ICMAS-2000), USA, (2000)159-166.
20. Horling, B., Lesser V., Vincent, R., Bazzan, A., Xuan, P., Diagnosis as an Integral Part of Multi-Agent Adaptability, In Proceedings of DARPA Information Survivability Conference and Exposition, (2000) 211-219.
21. Dellarocas, C., Klein, M., Juan, A. R., An Exception-Handling Architecture for Open Electronic Marketplaces of Contract Net Software Agents, In Proceedings of the Second ACM Conference on Electronic Commerce, Minneapolis Minnesota USA, (2000) 225-232.
22. Klein, M., Dellarocas C., Exception Handling in Agent Systems. In proceedings of the Third Annual Conference on Autonomous Agents, (1999) 62-68.
23. N Shah, Exception Diagnosis in Multi-Agent Systems, PhD Thesis Coventry University UK, (2006).
24. N. Shah, K-M. Chao, N. Godwin, A. James, Diagnosing Plan Failures in Multi-Agent Systems Using Abstract Knowledge, In proceedings of the 9th International Conference on Computer Supported Cooperative Work in Design, IEEE, (2005) 46-451.

Dynamical E-Commerce System for Shopping Mall Site Through Mobile Devices*

Sanggil Kang[1], Wonik Park[2], and Young-Kuk Kim[2]

[1] Department of Computer Science, University of Suwon,
San 2-2, Wau-ri, Bongdam-eup, Hwaseong, Gyeonggi-do 445-743, South Korea
sgkang@suwon.ac.kr
[2] Division of Information & Communication Engineering, Chungnam National Univeristy
220 Gung-dong, Yeoseong-Gu, Daejeon 305-764, South Korea
{wonik78, ykim}@cnu.ac.kr

Abstract. We introduce a novel personalized E-commerce system through mobile devices. By providing mobile clients' preferred service category or items in a shopping mall website, the problem of the limitation of resource of mobile devices can be solved. In this paper, the preferred service items are inferred by analyzing customers' statistical preference transactions and consumption behaviors in the website. In computing the statistical preference transactions, we consider the ratio of the length of each service page and customers' staying time on it. Also, our system dynamically provides the personalized E-commerce service according to the three different cases such as the beginning stage, the positive response, and the negative response. In the experimental section, we demonstrate our personalized E-commerce service system and show how much the resource of mobile devices can be saved.

1 Introduction

The E-commerce services through Internet have already become an essential tool of the on-line business. Because of development and popularization of mobile devices characterized with mobility and ubiquity, the existing wire internet service is rapidly expanding to the wireless internet service through the mobile devices. In order to enable to provide E-commerce services to mobile devices, it is needed to transfer the shopping mall web pages serviced through computers to a suitable format for the mobile devices. However, it is challenge because of the limitation of the monitor size of mobile devices and their resources. As the try to solve the problems, many researchers render a web page on a small display with various techniques such as four-way scrolling [1], web-clipping [2], and miniaturization of web pages [3, 4]. However, those techniques can not overcome the limitation of resources of mobile devices because all contents of a web site have to be delivered to mobile customers once the customers request the web service.

---

* This research was supported by the Ministry of Information and Communication, Korea, under the College Information Technology Research Center Support Program, grant number IITA-2005-C1090-0502-0016.

J. Lee et al. (Eds.): DEECS 2006, LNCS 4055, pp. 268–277, 2006.

In order to solve the problem, we provide a personalized shopping mall web service according to customers' preference of each web page. The preference of the web pages can be obtained from the history of the customers' navigation and consumption behaviors who visited the shopping mall website through computers. By providing the customers' preferred web pages or items, the problem of the resource limitation can be solved to some extent. In this paper, the preferred web pages in a shopping mall site are provided by analyzing the customers' statistical preference transactions among web pages and consumption behaviors for each web page. In computing the statistical preference of each web page, we consider the ratio of the length of each web page to customers' staying time on it. Also, we provide the weight to the preference of each web page according to the customers' three different consumption behaviors for each item, such as "buying" and "adding to shopping cart without buying". In addition, our system dynamically provides the personalized E-commerce service according to the different three cases such as the beginning stage, the positive response, and the negative response. In the experimental section, we demonstrate our personalized E-commerce service system and show how much the resource of mobile devices can be saved.

The remainder of this paper is organized as follows. Section 2 describes related works of methods of adaptation of web contents to mobile devices and various personalization techniques in E-commerce systems. Section 3 defines fundamental terms related to our work. In Section 4, we describe our personalized E-commerce service system through mobile devices. Section 5 describes the architecture of our system. In Section 6, we show the experimental result of our system and its analysis. We then conclude our paper in Section 7.

2 Related Work

Many studies have been done about how to present web contents effectively on mobile devices in order to overcome the limitation of their monitor size. Researchers in Palm Inc. [2] made information in smaller chunks and compiled them into a compact format that can be decoded on the Palm VII. The Wireless Access Protocol's Markup Language (WMA) [5] replaces HTML to its own markup language to lay out each page for optimal viewing on small screen. The technique is effective, but it has to prepare the same information for both standard web browsers and PDAs. Another popular technique is to miniaturize standard Web pages by the ProxiWeb browser [4]. This technique is also effective, but it needs the large amount of necessary scrolling action.

Even though the techniques above can solve the problem on providing the standard web pages to the small mobile devices, they can not overcome the limitation of resources of mobile devices. In order to solve the problem, many researchers employed the personalization techniques for E-commerce systems.

Various personalization techniques for E-commerce systems can be classified into two possible categories such as the rule-based and collaborative filtering. The rule-based recommendation is usually implemented by a predetermined rule, for instance, if -then rule. Kim et al. [5] proposed a marketing rule extraction technique for personalized recommendation on internet storefronts using tree induction method [6]. Jain el al. [7] and Yarger [8] used fuzzy logic rule for modeling market structure because of its ability to handle the uncertainty associated with customer choice.

The collaborative filtering techniques can also be classified into two groups: one is the item-to-item collaborative filtering (IICF) and the other is people-to-people collaborative filtering (PPCF). The IICF technique recommends items to customers based on a small set of items the customers have expressed interest in. Linden et al. [9] introduced an online recommendation at Amazon.com website using the IICF technique. Their method is independent of the number of customers and number of items in the catalog. Lemire and McGrath [10] proposed the rating-based IICF which ask customers to rate items so that they can help each other find better items. The PPCF technique recommends items to the target customer based on the correlation between that customer and other customers who have bought items. Resnick et al. [11] and Konstan et al. [12] used group opinions to recommend information items to individuals in the Usenet news website.

In this paper, we utilize the PPCF technique for inferring the customers' preferred items in the shopping mall website, with the collected customers' navigation and consumption behaviors. Then, the preferred items are provided or recommended to the mobile users when they request the shopping mall website through their mobile devices.

3　Tree Structured Shopping Mall Website and Page Segment

To provide the personalized E-commerce service to mobile devices, the shopping mall web server needs to collect the log information of the customers visited to the web site by personal computers. In general, a shopping mall website is the hierarchical tree structure with four level segments such as the home page, service page, service category, and service item as seen in Fig. 1.

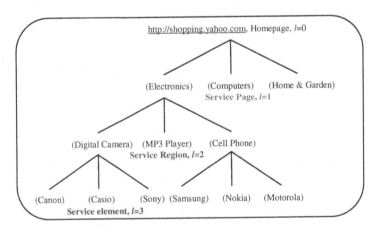

Fig. 1. The tree structure of the yahoo shopping mall website

Using the collected customers' log information, we can infer the preference of those segments using only the implicit log information, i.e., customers' web page navigation and consumption behaviors. The web page navigation behavior is defined as the customers' transactions among the segments during a session. The session means the period from visiting to leaving the shopping mall website. Using the method explained in [13], the segments can be automatically obtained as follows: Each web fragment engine in a web server extracts <HTML><HEAD>~</HEAD> <BODY> from the proxy server and generates a new page with basic frame. Then, in order to segment the new page into sections, we find the position of the <TABLE> tag and classify the content of the page.

From the following section, we explained the method to infer customers' preference of each segment based on the tree structure of shopping mall website.

4 Proposed Personalized E-Commerce Service

4.1 Probabilistic Preference of the Webpage Segments

From Fig. 1, each service page is linked to the different number of service categories which are also connected to the different number of service items. For the convenience, we denote the homepage, the service page, the service category, and the service item as level $l=0$, $l=1$, $l=2$, and $l=3$, respectively. Also, the entry of each level is viewed as the node in the figure.

Usually, the preference of each node can be expressed as the frequency of visit to the node using personal computers. The shopping mall web server computes the frequency from customers' navigation history collected for a predetermined period. Thus, the more frequently visited is a node, the node is considered more preferred by the customers. The behavior of visiting from a node at a level to another node at the next level is called preference transaction. The probabilistic preference transaction from a node at higher level to nodes at its lower level can be computed as follows:

$$p_{l,l+1}(i,j) = \frac{n_{l,l+1}(i,j)}{\sum_j n_{l,l+1}(i,j)} \qquad (1)$$

where, $p_{l,l+1}(i,j)$ is the statistical preference transaction from node i at level l to node j at level $l+1$ and $n_{l,l+1}(i,j)$ is the frequency of the transactions from node i at level l to node j at level $l+1$. In Equation (1), the frequency of visiting the nodes is the absolute count of the visit regardless of customers' staying time on the node. However, the staying time can be a critical factor for estimating the preference of the node. For instance, if a customer stays a node shortly, it can not be meant that the customer is interested in the node. To compensate the problem, we need to count the frequency of the visit in a relative manner, with taking into the consideration of the staying time. Also, the length of each node is various according to the amount of its contents. Thus, the staying time needs to be measured in a relative manner, too. In other words, the more is the amount of contents in a node, customers need the longer the staying time to review it. According to the ratio of staying time to the amount of the contents in a node, we provide the weight to the computation of the frequency as seen in Equation (2).

$$w_j = \begin{cases} \dfrac{s_j}{t_j}, & \text{for } s_j < t_j \\ 1, & \text{for } s_j \geq t_j \end{cases} \tag{2}$$

where s_j is the staying time duration at node j and t_j is the standard reviewing time duration of node j estimated by expert or by transferring the amount of content to the time length. The probabilistic preference transaction with the weight can be expressed as Equation (3).

$$p_{l,l+1}(i,j) = \frac{\overline{w}_j n_{l,l+1}(i,j)}{\sum\limits_j \overline{w}_j n_{l,l+1}(i,j)} \tag{3}$$

where $\overline{w}_j$ is the average weight to the frequency $n_{l,l+1}(i,j)$ of the transaction node i at level l to node j at level $l+1$.

Equation (3) is the preference computed using customers' navigation behaviors only. However, the users' consumption behaviors such as "buying" and "adding service items to cart" can be a useful clue for inferring the preference of each segment. We provide the behavior weight to the visiting frequency of each segment according to the customers' consumption behavior for every visit. Equation (3) can be modified as seen in Equation (4).

$$p_{l,l+1}(i,j) = \frac{b\overline{w}_{b,j} n_{b,l,l+1}(i,j) + a\overline{w}_{a,j} n_{a,l,l+1}(i,j) + \overline{w}_j n_{l,l+1}(i,j)}{\sum\limits_j b\overline{w}_{b,j} n_{b,l,l+1}(i,j) + a\overline{w}_{a,j} n_{a,l,l+1}(i,j) + \overline{w}_j n_{l,l+1}(i,j)} \tag{4}$$

where the subscript b and a of each term implies the action "buy" and the action "adding service items to cart" for each service segment, respectively. The b and a are the corresponding weights for the actions. Obviously, the value of the weight for action "buy" is bigger than that for action "adding service items to cart."

4.2 Dynamical E-Commerce Service Scenario

We can provide dynamically personalized E-commerce service according to three different scenarios such as the beginning stage, the positive response, and the negative response. The beginning stage means the service pattern at the initial, when a mobile user requests a shopping mall site. The positive response implies that the user purchased serviced item at the previously stage, while the negative response is the case the user did not. For example, at the beginning stage, we provide the service pattern composed with the highest preference service segment at each level as follows: $x_{0,1_{r1}} \rightarrow x_{1_{r1},2_{r1}} \rightarrow x_{2_{r1},3_{r1}}$, here $x_{0,1_{r1}}, x_{1_{r1},2_{r1}}$, and $x_{2_{r1},3_{r1}}$ are the first ranked preference transaction at each level, i.e., from homepage at level 0 to service page at level 1, from service page to service category at level 2, and service category to service item at level 3, respectively. If the user responds positively for the beginning stage, we provide the next ranked service item $x_{2_{r1},3_{r2}}$ in the same service category served at the previous service pattern. For the negative response case, the service category is moved to the next ranked service category from the previously served service category. The service pattern can be expressed as follows: $x_{0,1_{r1}} \rightarrow x_{1_{r1},2_{r2}} \rightarrow x_{2_{r2},3_{r1}}$, here $x_{1_{r1}.2_{r2}}$ is the preference transaction from first ranked service page at level 1 to the second ranked service category at level 2.

As explained above, our method can dynamically provide the personalized E-commerce service by adapting the various cases of users' responses. Thus, our method can compensate the resource limitation of mobile devices because we do not need to provide too low ranked or no ranked service patterns.

5 System Architecture

Fig. 2 shows the system architecture of personalized E-commerce service based on mobile gateway. The architecture is composed of main five modules such as Web Collection, Page Reconstruction, Recommendation, Document Conversion, and Protocol Confirmation. The Web Collection module collects the HTML of web-pages from shopping mall web-server. The Page Reconstruction module partitions the collected HTML into service categories and service items as explained in Section 3. The service categories and service items are stored in the Page Reconstruction Cache for re-usage. The Recommendation module provides or recommends the users' preferred fragments from the service items stored in the Page Reconstruction Cache as using our preference algorithm. The Document Conversion module converts the preferred service items to the format suitable for the user's mobile device. In order to do document conversion, we need to know the information of the user's mobile device. It can be done by analyzing HTTP header of shopping mall web-pages in the Protocol Confirmation module.

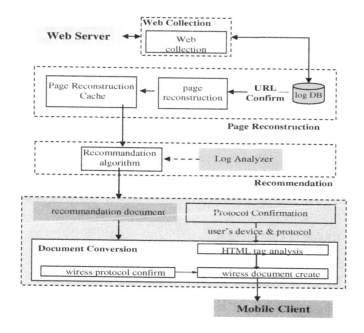

Fig. 2. The architecture of mobile gateway system

5.1 Experimental Environment

Fig. 3 shows the experimental environment of our personalized E-commerce service. We implemented our system by the TCP/IP socket network with the mobile gateway in the Linux environment. The access to simulator is enabled by binding a specific port. In order to allow the connections of multiple users to the gateway server at the same time, the POSIX pthread, which is the Linux standard thread, is used. In order to test our personalized E-commerce service, SDK 6.22 of WML browser produced by Openwave Corp. is used. Also, we made a sample shopping mall web site by modifying shopping.yahoo.com. To allow users to connect to the sample pages in the sample web site, the apache was used in the gateway server. To analyze users' log information, the Squid [14] is used. The Squid is very flexible for adapting it to a specific experimental environment, as an open source web proxy cache driven in UNIX.

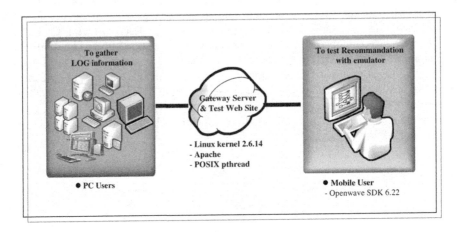

Fig. 3. The experimental environment

We collected the navigation information of the sample shopping.yahoo.com for 160 students enrolled in the Chungnam National University in Korea. The sample shopping.yahoo.com has 120 service items. The navigation information had been collected from the log data recorded for 20 days. Also, the weights of consumption behaviors for computing the preference of each segment, as seen in Equation (4), was set to $a= 2$ and $b= 4$.

5.2 Demonstration of Our Method

In this section, we show the demonstration of our personalized E-commerce service according to the three different scenarios. Using the equations in Chapter 5, we computed the preference of each service page, service category, and the corresponding service items. From the result, the order of preference of the service pages was Electronics, Computers, Home&Garden, etc. In the service page of Electronics, the order of the preference of service categories was Digital Camera, Digital mp3, TVs, etc. In the service category of Digital Camera, the order was Canon, Casio, Samsung, etc. In the service page of Computer, the category of Laptop was the best preference. In the category of Laptop, the order was Apple, IBM, Sony, etc.

Fig. 4(a) shows the service pattern provided at the initial stage when a mobile user requests the shopping.yahoo.com site. As explained in the figure, the service pattern is Electronics → Digital Camera → Canon, according to the order of segments at each level. If the mobile user purchased the provided service item Canon then the service item Casio is served with corresponding the service pattern Electronics → Digital Camera → Casio as seen in Fig. 4(b). If the user does not interested (not buying or not reading) in the service item Casio then the next service pattern is Electronics → Digital mp3 → Apple as seen in Fig. 4(c). As demonstrated above, the dynamical personalized E-commerce service continues until the user disconnects the yahoo shopping mall site.

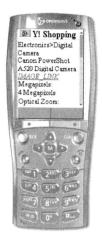  

(a) The beginning stage   (b) The positive response   (c) The negative response

Fig. 4. The example of dynamical E-commerce for each scenario

5.3 Performance Evaluation

In this section, we show how much the resource of mobile devices can be saved by applying our personalized E-commerce service. Also, we compare the accuracy of our method when the staying time is applied with that of when not.

From the result of the computation of the preference of each service item from the students' shopping mall navigation history and consumption behaviors collected for 20 days, only 68 service items out of the 120 sample service items have been visited by 160 students so 52 service items do not need to be served to the mobile devices. Thus, the resource of the mobile devices can be saved as much as the amount of 52 items and can be utilized by any other services.

We also examined the accuracy of the personalized E-commerce service for both when the staying time is applied and not applied in computing the preference of each item. The 120 students are used for training our system out of 160 students and 40 students are used for testing the accuracy of our system. The accuracy evaluation was repeated by varying the collection period of the users' log information.

Table. The comparison of the performances for both the staying time is considered and not considered in computing the preference of the service items

Collection Period (day)	Accuracy(%)	
	No staying Time	**Staying Time**
4	55.24	**65.50**
8	61.41	**72.42**
12	70.11	**78.85**
16	72.58	**84.21**
20	73.61	**84.44**

As seen in Table, the accuracy is better when the staying time is applied than that of when not applied, regardless of the collection period. As seen in the table, the accuracy increases as the collection period increases. However, the increase is very gentle from day 16.

6   Conclusion

In this paper, we proposed a novel personalized E-commerce service system through mobile devices. The experimental results in the previous section show that the limitation of mobile devices can be compensated by utilizing our system. Also, it was shown that we can have better performance by considering the staying time for estimating the preference of each segment than not.

However, the 160 students might not be enough for verifying that our system is excellent. It is needed to collect more users' shopping mall web navigation information. Also, we need to do further study for developing an automatic algorithm to segment various shopping mall website into smaller segments suitable for being viewed on various types of mobile devices. It is because each mobile device can have different size of screen.

References

1. Jones, M., Marsden, G., Mohd-Nasir, N., Boone, K & Buchanan G, " Improving Web Interaction on Small Displays. Proc. WWW8. Vol 1, pp. 51-59, 1999.
2. Palm, Inc., Web Clipping Development. http://www.palmos.com/dev/tech/webclipping/.
3. Fox, A., Goldberg, I., Gribble, S.D., Lee, D.C, Polito, A.. & Brewer, E.A.: A Experience With Top Gun Wingman: A Proxy-Based Graphical Web Browser for the 3Com PalmPilot. Conference Repots of Middleware, 1998.
4. ProxiNet, Inc., ProxiWeb: http://www.proxinet.com/.
5. Kim, J.W., Lee, B.H., Shaw, M.J., Chang, H.L., Nelson, M.: Application of Decision-Tree Induction Techniques to Personalized Advertisements on Internet Storefronts," International Journal of Electronic Commerce, vol. 5, no. 3, pp. 45-62, 2001

6. Quinlan, J.R., Induction of Decision Trees, "Machine Learning," vol. 1, no. 1, pp. 81-106, 1986
7. Jain, V., Krishnapuram, R., "Applications of Fuzzy Sets in Personalization for e-Commerce," Proc. IFSA-NAFIPS 2001 Conference, pp. 263-268 , 2001
8. Yager, R.,"Fuzzy Methods in E-Commerce," Annual Conference of North American Fuzzy Information Processing Society, pp. 5-11, 1999
9. Linden, G., Smith B., York, J., "Amazon.com Recommendations: Item-to-Item Collaborative Filtering," IEEE Internet Computing, pp. 76-80, 2003
10. Lemire, D., McGrath, S., "Implementing a Rating-Based Item-to-Item Recommender System in PHP/SQL," Technical Report D-01, 2005
11. Resnick, P., Iacovou, N., Suchak, M., Bergstrom, P., Riedl, J., "Grouplens: An Open Architecture for Collaborative Filtering of Netnews," Proc. ACM CSCW'94 Conference on Computer Supported Cooperative Work, pp. 175-186, 1994
12. Konstan, J.A., Miller, B.N., Maltz, D., Herlocker, J.L., Gordon, L.R., Riedl, J., "GroupLens: Applying Collaborative Filtering to Usenet news," Communications of the ACM, Vol. 40, No. 3, pp. 77-87, 1997
13. Jeon, Y., Hwang, E., "Automatically Customizing Service Pages on the Web for Mobile Devices," Lecture Notes in Computer Science, vol. 2822, pp. 53-65, 2003
14. Squid Web Proxy Cache- http://www.squid-cache.org/

PROMOD: A Modeling Tool for Product Ontology

Kyunghwa Kim[1], Moonhee Tark[1,*], Hyunja Lee[1], Junho Shim[1], Junsoo Lee[1],
and Seungjin Lee[2]

[1] Department of Computer Science, Sookmyung Women's University, Seoul, Korea
{kamza81, mhtark, hyunjalee, jshim, jslee}@sookmyung.ac.kr
[2] Department of Software Engineering,
SungKongHoe University, Seoul, Korea
lsj@skhu.ac.kr

Abstract. Product ontology is often constructed by explicating the domain ontology in a formal ontology language. The OWL Web Ontology Language has been positioned as a standard language. It requires technical expertise to directly represent the domain in OWL. An alternative way is to let a domain expert provide a conceptual representation of the domain, and to mechanically translate it into the corresponding OWL codes. We have developed a modeling tool called PROMOD to achieve this process in the product domain. We employ an Extended Entity-Relationship for conceptual model, enriched with modeling elements specialized for the product domain. We present how each element may be technically represented in OWL. We also provide a modeling scenario to demonstrate the practical feasibility of the tool in the field.

1 Introduction

Growing e-Commerce is one of the areas that would benefit from the product ontology because how to clearly define product information is a key for an e-Commerce system. Product information includes various types of information such as pricing, features, or terms about the goods and services. This information are related each other, and should be searched and navigated efficiently by a customer or an application program. Recent application of ontology to product information brings these features used in reality. Product ontology specifies a conceptualization of product information in terms of classes, relationships and constraints. Product ontology not only can play an important role in the formalization of product information but also it enables us to search necessary information quickly and correctly by grasping essential words that define relationships between distributive information composing products [4,7,5,3].

Product ontology has been often constructed by explicating the domain ontology in a formal ontology language [10]. Although the OWL Web Ontology Language has been positioned as a standard language, it requires technical expertise to directly represent the domain in OWL. An alternative approach is to let a domain expert provide a conceptual representation of the domain and mechanically translate it into the corresponding OWL codes.

---

* Her current affiliation is with Samsung SDS Co Ltd, Seoul, Korea.

J. Lee et al. (Eds.): DEECS 2006, LNCS 4055, pp. 278–287, 2006.

In this paper we have developed a modeling tool called PROMOD (MODeling tool for PRoduct Ontology) to achieve an automatic generation of OWL code for the product domain. We employ an Extended Entity-Relationship for a conceptual model, enriched with modeling elements specialized for the product domain. Then we illustrate how each element of EER can be technically represented by OWL. In addition, we showcase a modeling scenario to demonstrate the practical feasibility of the PROMOD tool.

Among previous researches, a dominant and well-known modeling approach for building an ontology application is to directly employ a formal ontology language such as OWL [9] to represent domain knowledge. However, an ontological modeling is not technically easy for a domain expert if she or he is not familiar with the formal language. To solve this problem, recently, visual ontology modeling tools have been proposed such as Protégé [8] developed by SMI(Stanford Medical Informatics) and i*com proposed by I*COM [1] may be regarded as representative tools.

Our contributions in this paper compared with other existing ontology modeling tools such as Protégé or by I*COM are summarized as follows. First, PROMOD includes specialized modeling features for the product domain. There are fundamental set of concepts and relationships that are frequently used in the domain. Among these relationships, those that are not included in a traditional Entity-Relationship are added as specific modeling constructs. These newly added constructs in PROMOD can play a useful role particularly in product ontology modeling.

In addition, automatic translation from an EER model to an OWL code is possible in PROMOD. PROMOD adopts an Extended Entity-Relationship conceptual data model to conceptually and pictorially represent the semantic information. Entities, attributes and relationships created by a user are encoded to OWL code automatically. Detailer description can also be added by modifying created OWL code directly in a built-in text editor. Protégé-OWL, an extension of Protégé, may also enable to edit classes and import/export OWL codes. However, its modeling approach is not based on EER and limited to edit or visualize a model with regard to the OWL syntactic structure.

Finally, PROMOD is loosely-coupled and therefore compatible with any OWL reasoning engine. It produces OWL code as a modeling result. Compared to this, i*com seems to perform tightly-coupled with a specific reasoning server.

The rest of this paper is organized as follows. Section 2 provides an overview of product ontology. Section 3 summarizes our translation scheme from EER model to OWL. In Section 4, we present the design and implementation of PROMOD. Section 5 shows a scenario to demonstrate the usage of the tool. Finally, conclusions are drawn and future work is outlined in Section 6.

2 Modeling of Product Ontology

Product ontology involves a conceptualization of the product information with regard to classes (or concepts) and relationships. From a project to building a product ontology database for an e-procurement system, we learned that products, classification scheme, attributes, and unit-of-measures may be regarded as the key concepts of product ontology [4]. The semantic relationships include ones from general domain [11]; such as class inclusion (isa), meronymic inclusion (component, substance, and member), attribution, and synonym. In addition, product domain specific relationships such as substitute, complement, purchase-set, and mapped-to are also considered.

A feature of our modeling tool is to adopt those domain specific relationships as the modeling elements. We extend the EER modeling elements to accommodate component, substance, member, substitute, complement, purchase-set, and mapped-to; and the tool provides icons for each of them (Figure 1).

In the figure, products such as computers monitors, printers, mouse, and keyboards form a purchase-set relationship as they may be purchased together. A complement relationship represents that one may be added to another in order to complete something. For example, a toner may be complement to a laser printer. A substitute relationship means that one may serve as a replacement of the other. For example, a LCD monitor is a substitute of a CRT monitor. And the mapped-to relationship is to assign a product into a specific class code within a classification scheme, or to map a class code from one classification scheme to the other scheme.

We regard CC(component/composed), SM(substance/made), and MC(member/collection) as the most frequently observed meronymic inclusions in product domain. For example, a spindle motor is a component of a hard disk, or a hard-disk is composed of a spindle motor. Aluminium is a substance of a hard-disk, or a hard-disk is made of aluminium. Similarly, a LCD monitor is a member of monitor products.

Note that those relationships mentioned herein may not cover the whole product domain, and users may project different perspectives to one domain. Consequently the tool should be easily modifiable to include new types of modeling constructs. The EER methodology featuring the meta-modeling approach may benefit in this sense.

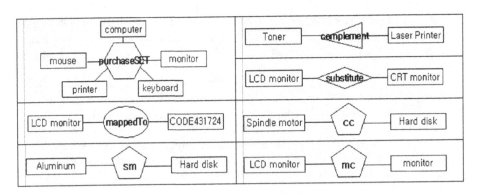

Fig. 1. Extended ER modeling constructs for the product domain

3   Modeling Element and OWL Representation

A core feature of PROMOD is to automatically generate the corresponding OWL codes to the EER modeling elements drawn by a user. We analyze the OWL language with regard to its expressiveness and complexity, and employ OWL-DL to represent our product ontology model [7]. This section summarizes the mapping procedure from the EER modeling elements to their OWL representations. More detail on this procedure may be found in [6].

Entity concept corresponds to the class concept in OWL, and it provides abstract mechanism to group objects which have similar characteristics. Basically, entities can be represented by using <owl:Class>, and the name of a entity has the same value as the OWL class name.

In order to represent the class inclusion relationship, <rdfs:subClassOf> expression is employed. There are two types of properties in OWL; owl:DatatypeProperty and owl:ObjectProperty. The datatype property is used for relationship which exists between a class instance and a data value, while the object property is used for relationships between instances. An attribution may be represented using owl:DatatypeProperty in accordance with the xml schema datatypes. Type of an attribute (e.g., string or integer) can be represented by the corresponding <rdf:datatype>. Object property describes a relationship between the instances of classes, and this corresponds to the relationship in EER. Relationships may have additional property restrictions, which should be selectively added to each object property to convey precise semantics. Those restrictions include <owl:TransitiveProperty>, <owl:SymmetricProperty>, <owl:inverseOf>, and <owl:FunctionalProperty>, and <owl:someValuesFrom> and <owl:allValuesFrom> to further constrain the range of a property in specific contexts as well as domain and range of property.

In terms of the semantics, a PurchaseSet is a relationship of arbitrary arity, i.e., it could be n-ary where n>2 in EER while in traditional DL and OWL-DL as well only unary and binary relationships are considered. Therefore, a Purchase Set denoted as n-ary in EER should be represented as fully pair-wised multiple number of OWL object properties. PurchaseSet may have the symmetric property. In this case, <owl:SymmetricProperty> is added to denote the symmetric property. For example, the computerPurchaseSET is a subproperty of purchaseSET property. Computers are often purchased with OS such as Windows XP, vice versa. Computers may be also purchased with mouse or monitor, etc. Thus, Computers may be defined through computerPurchaseSET with the local range restriction <owl:someValuesFrom>.

Complement may have two interpretations. It may have functional characteristic, i.e., one unique value for each instance. For example, cell phone and battery are complement if every cell phone requires different type of battery so that only one type of battery can be used for each type of cell phone. In this case, we use <owl:FunctionalProperty>. The other case of complement does not require unique value for each instance. For example, consider a relationship between anti glare filter and monitor. Any anti glare filter can be used and therefore complement to any monitor. This can be represented by assigning monitor as the range of the complement property.

Substitute has the symmetric property, and it may also have the transitive characteristic depending on the context, i.e., if A is a substitute of B, and B is a substitute of C, then A becomes a substitute of C. In OWL, it is represented as <owl:TransitiveProperty>. For instance, if sugarSubstitute is a subproperty of substitute property with transitive characteristic and sugar is substitute aspartame, aspartame is substitute saccharin, then sugar is substitute saccharin.

CC(component/composed), SM(substance/made), and MC(member/collection) are the meronymic inclusion relationships. Similarly, they can be expressed in two different ways depending on the inclusion of transitive characteristic.

4 Design and Implementation of PROMOD

Figure 2 shows the overall structure and interactions between components of PROMOD. First, a user develops a EER model with Graphical User Interface. At this time, a user can utilize newly added modeling diagrams for semantic relationships on product ontology. When a user develops a EER model, Analyzer receives and reports events. Analyzer is composed of Event Handler and Modeling Verifier. Event Handler processes events that occur when a user draws a diagram and then calls Modeling Verifier to analyze the syntactic structure of the composed entity or relationship. Modeling Verifier verifies the feasibility of EER model.

Predefined Classes with Functions are a collection of library used to generate the instances for each modeling element entity. These libraries are classes and functions of JAVA instances, with which the result of EER modeling is converted to OWL code. Generator consists of Instance Generator and OWL Code Generator. Whenever a user draws an entity, Instance Generator generates instance and maintains the status and relationship of the composed entity. Then OWL Code Generator actually generates OWL code upon receiving a code generation event.

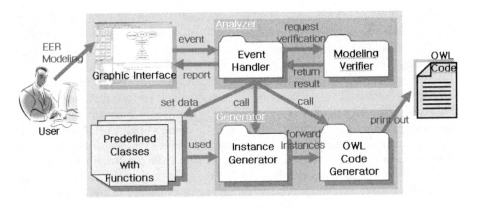

Fig. 2. Architectural components in PROMOD

Our development environment is under Windows 2000 Professional Operating System with Java 2 Platform Standard Edition 5.0 and JBuilder. To implement Graphical User Interface, Java Awt, Swing and library (commons-beanutils-1.6.1, commons-collections-3.1, commons-logging-api) are utilized.

5 Experimental Modeling Scenario

This section illustrates a scenario how PROMOD may be utilized in product domain. We showcase a consumer-electronic appliance company that utilizes the relationships between product classes to promote the Internet sales by employing product ontology database. Relationships such as Inclusion, Substitute, Complement, and PurchaseSet, are employed to model their ontology. We illustrate a partial model for camera-related products of this company in Figure 3. Because the knowledge base is named PromodProduct, all the products are subclass of PromodProduct, and all domain and range of relationship are within PromodProduct class.

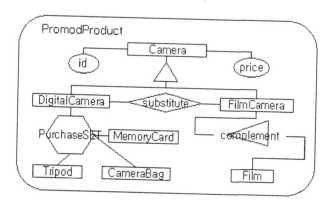

Fig. 3. Relationships in camera-related products

Suppose that a consumer visits this company's web site to buy a film camera, and he/she tries to find a product in Film Camera under the Camera category. However, he/she finds oneself not to like any of film cameras in this web site, but eventually to show interests in its substitute product. In this case digital camera's substitute information might be useful since Digital Camera has a substitute relationship with Film Camera. Note that some people may not consider Film Camera as a substitute of Digital Camera. Here in this scenario we just assume it just for illustration purpose. In addition, when he/she selects and orders a digital camera, this web site may recommend other products (e.g., Memory card, Tripod, Camera bag) which may be purchased together with a digital camera.

Figure 4 shows a snapshot of modeling the above scenario on PROMOD. As shown in the figure, the PROMOD screen layout consists of Palette, Canvas, OWL Output, Menus and Shortcuts. Palette contains the icons for each modeling element that the tool provides. A user may select, drag and drop the icons on Canvas to draw an EER diagram for product ontology. Note that there are icons in Palette for purchase-set, complement, member, and etc, which are product domain specific relationships. The OWL Output shows OWL code corresponding to the diagram drawn in Canvas. And Menus and Shortcuts contain commands and macros that are required to develop a diagram.

After developing a EER diagram, a user may press 'To OWL' button to generate the corresponding OWL code. Then the translated code appears in OWL Output located on the down part of the screen. If necessary, a user may modify or add additional constraints to the generated code by directly editing the code. We have the OWL Output window as an editable Java text class to allow this.

Finally, when a user presses 'To RacerPro' button a java application is called. The application allows a user to type and issue a query to RacerPro [2], a ontology inference engine, and then it prints the query results returned from RacerPro in a same window. In Figure 4, it appears on the right down part of the screen. By using this application, we may verify OWL code's consistency through testing various queries. Note that as mentioned in Introduction PROMOD produces OWL code as a modeling result and may be compatible with any OWL reasoning engine, as Protégé is with Jena. Although we currently employ RacerPro, any other inference engine with a feature to support OWL could be linked with PROMOD.

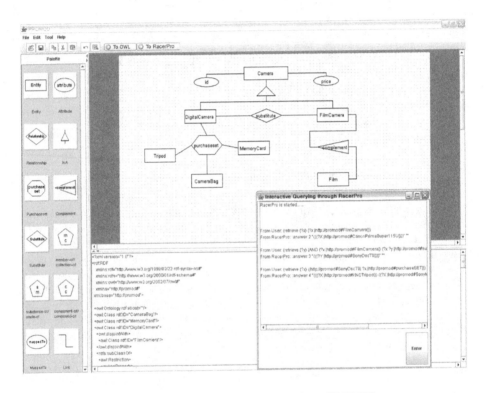

Fig. 4. A snapshot of modeling a scenario on PROMOD

Figure 5 shows a part of OWL code generated from the modeling scenario shown in Figure 4. Then we provided some actual individuals for a realistic testing of the scenario. Let us say that the individuals of FilmCamera, DigitalCamera, MemoryCard, Tripod, and CameraBag class are CanonPrimaSuper115U, SonyDscT9, SonyMsxM1gst, KNCTripod, and JPBag01, respectively.

Figure 6 shows the results of some queries tested in the above scenario as they appear in Figure 4. A customer searches for all FilmCamera instances on the web site and as a result CanonPrimaSuper115U is returned. However, suppose the customer does not want to buy this product and try to find another instance that may substitute film

```
......
<owl:Class rdf:ID="CameraBag"/>
<owl:Class rdf:ID="MemoryCard"/>
<owl:Class rdf:ID="DigitalCamera">
  <owl:disjointWith>
    <owl:Class rdf:ID="FilmCamera"/>
  </owl:disjointWith>
  <rdfs:subClassOf>
    <owl:Restriction>
      <owl:onProperty>
        <owl:ObjectProperty
rdf:ID="purchaseSET"/>
      ......
  <rdfs:subClassOf>
    <owl:Restriction> <owl:someValuesFrom>
      <owl:Class rdf:about="#FilmCamera"/>
      ......
    <owl:onProperty>
      <owl:ObjectProperty
rdf:ID="substitute"/>
      ......
  <rdfs:subClassOf>
    <owl:Class rdf:ID="Camera"/>
  </rdfs:subClassOf>
</owl:Class>
<owl:Class rdf:about="#FilmCamera">
<owl:disjointWith
rdf:resource="#DigitalCamera"/>
  <rdfs:subClassOf rdf:resource="#Camera"/>
  <rdfs:subClassOf>
    <owl:Restriction>
      <owl:someValuesFrom
rdf:resource="#DigitalCamera"/>
```

```
    <owl:onProperty>
      <owl:ObjectProperty rdf:about="#substitute"/>
    </owl:onProperty> ......
</owl:Class>
<owl:ObjectProperty rdf:about="#purchaseSET">
......
<owl:ObjectProperty rdf:about="#substitute">
  <rdfs:domain
rdf:resource="#PromodProduct"/>
  <rdf:type
rdf:resource="http://www.w3.org/2002/07/owl#S
ymmetricProperty"/>
  <owl:inverseOf rdf:resource="#substitute"/>
<rdfs:range rdf:resource="#PromodProduct"/>
  <rdf:type
rdf:resource="http://www.w3.org/2002/07/owl#Tr
ansitiveProperty"/>
</owl:ObjectProperty>
<owl:DatatypeProperty rdf:ID="price">
  <rdfs:domain rdf:resource="#Camera"/>
  <rdfs:range
rdf:resource="http://www.w3.org/2001/XMLSche
ma#string"/>
</owl:DatatypeProperty>
<owl:DatatypeProperty rdf:ID="id">......
<MemoryCard rdf:ID="SonyMsxM1gst">
......
<DigitalCamera rdf:ID="SonyDscT9">
......
<CameraBag rdf:ID="JPBag01">
......
<FilmCamera rdf:ID="CanonPrimaSuper115U">
......
<CameraTripod rdf:ID="KNCTripod"> ......
```

Fig. 5. OWL code generated for the scenario

camera. So the customer searches for instances that have substitute relationship with FilmCamera and receives SonyDscT9 as a result. The customer also wants to buy accessory products together with the camera. In this case, he/she can search for products which have purchaseSET relationship with SonyDscT9. In this example, SonyMsxM1gst, JPBag01, and KNCTripod are recommended, which are the individual product of MemoryCard, Tripod, and CameraBag, respectively.

```
From User: (retrieve (?x) (?x |http://promod#FilmCamera|))
From RacerPro: (((?X |http://promod#CanonPrimaSuper115U|)))
From User: (retrieve (?y) (AND (?x |http://promod#FilmCamera|)
           (?x ?y |http://promod#substitute|)))
From RacerPro: (((?Y |http://promod#SonyDscT9|)))
From User: (retrieve (?x) (|http://promod#SonyDscT9| ?x |http://promod#purchaseSET|))
From RacerPro: (((?X |http://promod#KNCTripod|)) ((?X |http://promod#SonyMsxM1gst|))
           ((?X |http://promod#JPBag01|)))
```

Fig. 6. Searching for individual products in our scenario

6 Conclusion

We have developed a modeling tool to generate OWL code for a pictorial and conceptual model drawn by a user. We employ an Extended Entity-Relationship for conceptual model and enrich it with modeling elements specialized for the product domain. The tool helps a user to decrease the time to develop a ontology, although the user is not deeply aware with the OWL language. The product domain specific modeling elements are especially helpful to conceptualize the key concepts and relationships that are frequently observed in the domain.

Our translation scheme from EER to OWL may not be the only way. In [3], they focus on OWL derivation for industry standard taxonomy and classify concepts to capture the semantics of those standards. There would be other ways that might convey the proper semantics but employ different syntax. Readers should note that it is beyond the scope of the paper to formally prove the correctness of each translation in perspective of logics. Instead we translated each modeling element into a formal representation in description logics and checked its consistency. The OWL-DL language is a XML-based ontology language of which syntax and semantics has correspondence to description logics. The corresponding DL and OWL representations are tested its consistency on a reasoning tool. Readers who are interested in more detail on this process should be referred to [7,6].

The current design of the tool does not allow any update in the OWL output window to be propagated into a EER diagram. This needs complete parsing the OWL language. We are planning to implement this feature so that OWL code and EER diagram are synchronized in both directions. The tool is also limited in a sense that instances (individuals) are not handled in a EER diagram. To add or edit the instances of a class requires much higher complicated design of database capabilities such as storage structures for instances and query processing for instance retrieval. At the same time, the tool should be coupled to a publicly available and robust OWL inference engine to effectively handle a large scale of instances. These are the future works that we shall deal with.

Acknowledgement

This research was supported partly by the Ministry of Information and Communication, Korea, under the College Information Technology Research Center Support Program, grant number IITA-2005-C1090-0502-0016.

References

1. E. Franconi and G. Ng, "The i•com Tool for Intelligent Conceptual Modeling," 7th International Workshop on Knowledge Representation meets Databases (KRDB'00), 2000.
2. V. Haarslev and R. Möller, "Description Logic Systems with Concrete Domains: Applications for the Semantic Web", 10th International Workshop on Knowledge Representation meets Databases (KRDB'03), 2003.
3. M. Hepp, "A Methodology for Deriving OWL Ontologies from Products and Services Categorization Standards", 13th European Conference on Information Systems (ECIS), 2005.

4. I. Lee, S. Lee, T. Lee, S.-g. Lee, D. Kim, J. Chun, H. Lee, and J. Shim, "Practical Issues for Building a Product Ontology System," International Workshop on Data Engineering Issues in E-Commerce (DEEC2005), IEEE Society, 2005.
5. J. Lee and R. Goodwin, Ontology Management for Large-Scale E-Commerce Applications, Electronic Commerce Research and Applications, Elsevier, 2006.
6. H. Lee and J. Shim, "Product Ontology and OWL Correspondence", IEEE Pacific Rim International Workshop on Electronic Commerce (IEEE-PRIWEC2006), 2006
7. H. Lee, J. Shim, and D. Kim, "Ontological Modeling of e-Catalogs using EER and Description Logic", International Workshop on Data Engineering Issues in E-Commerce (DEEC2005), IEEE Society, 2005.
8. Protégé, http://protégé.stanford.edu.
9. M.K. Smith, C. Welty, and D.L. McGuinness, "OWL Web Ontology Language Guide – W3C Recommendation", http://www.w3c.org/TR/owl-guide/, 2004.
10. S. Staab and R. Studer (Eds.), Handbook on Ontologies. International Handbooks on Information Systems, Springer-Verlag, 2004.
11. V. C. Storey, "Understanding Semantic Relationships", VLDB Journal, Vol. 2, VLDB Endowment, 1993.

Author Index

Lecture Notes in Computer Science

For information about Vols. 1–3960

please contact your bookseller or Springer

Vol. 4005: G. Lugosi, H.U. Simon (Eds.), Learning Theory. XI, 656 pages. 2006. (Sublibrary LNAI).

Vol. 4004: S. Vaudenay (Ed.), Advances in Cryptology - EUROCRYPT 2006. XIV, 613 pages. 2006.

Vol. 4003: Y. Koucheryavy, J. Harju, V.B. Iversen (Eds.), Next Generation Teletraffic and Wired/Wireless Advanced Networking. XVI, 582 pages. 2006.

Vol. 4001: E. Dubois, K. Pohl (Eds.), Advanced Information Systems Engineering. XVI, 560 pages. 2006.

Vol. 3999: C. Kop, G. Fliedl, H.C. Mayr, E. Métais (Eds.), Natural Language Processing and Information Systems. XIII, 227 pages. 2006.

Vol. 3998: T. Calamoneri, I. Finocchi, G.F. Italiano (Eds.), Algorithms and Complexity. XII, 394 pages. 2006.

Vol. 3997: W. Grieskamp, C. Weise (Eds.), Formal Approaches to Software Testing. XII, 219 pages. 2006.

Vol. 3996: A. Keller, J.-P. Martin-Flatin (Eds.), Self-Managed Networks, Systems, and Services. X, 185 pages. 2006.

Vol. 3995: G. Müller (Ed.), Emerging Trends in Information and Communication Security. XX, 524 pages. 2006.

Vol. 3994: V.N. Alexandrov, G.D. van Albada, P.M.A. Sloot, J. Dongarra (Eds.), Computational Science – ICCS 2006, Part IV. XXXV, 1096 pages. 2006.

Vol. 3993: V.N. Alexandrov, G.D. van Albada, P.M.A. Sloot, J. Dongarra (Eds.), Computational Science – ICCS 2006, Part III. XXXVI, 1136 pages. 2006.

Vol. 3992: V.N. Alexandrov, G.D. van Albada, P.M.A. Sloot, J. Dongarra (Eds.), Computational Science – ICCS 2006, Part II. XXXV, 1122 pages. 2006.

Vol. 3991: V.N. Alexandrov, G.D. van Albada, P.M.A. Sloot, J. Dongarra (Eds.), Computational Science – ICCS 2006, Part I. LXXXI, 1096 pages. 2006.

Vol. 3990: J. C. Beck, B.M. Smith (Eds.), Integration of AI and OR Techniques in Constraint Programming for Combinatorial Optimization Problems. X, 301 pages. 2006.

Vol. 3989: J. Zhou, M. Yung, F. Bao, Applied Cryptography and Network Security. XIV, 488 pages. 2006.

Vol. 3987: M. Hazas, J. Krumm, T. Strang (Eds.), Location- and Context-Awareness. X, 289 pages. 2006.

Vol. 3986: K. Stølen, W.H. Winsborough, F. Martinelli, F. Massacci (Eds.), Trust Management. XIV, 474 pages. 2006.

Vol. 3984: M. Gavrilova, O. Gervasi, V. Kumar, C.J. K. Tan, D. Taniar, A. Laganà, Y. Mun, H. Choo (Eds.), Computational Science and Its Applications - ICCSA 2006, Part V. XXV, 1045 pages. 2006.

Vol. 3983: M. Gavrilova, O. Gervasi, V. Kumar, C.J. K. Tan, D. Taniar, A. Laganà, Y. Mun, H. Choo (Eds.), Computational Science and Its Applications - ICCSA 2006, Part IV. XXVI, 1191 pages. 2006.

Vol. 3982: M. Gavrilova, O. Gervasi, V. Kumar, C.J. K. Tan, D. Taniar, A. Laganà, Y. Mun, H. Choo (Eds.), Computational Science and Its Applications - ICCSA 2006, Part III. XXV, 1243 pages. 2006.

Vol. 3981: M. Gavrilova, O. Gervasi, V. Kumar, C.J. K. Tan, D. Taniar, A. Laganà, Y. Mun, H. Choo (Eds.), Computational Science and Its Applications - ICCSA 2006, Part II. XXVI, 1255 pages. 2006.

Vol. 3980: M. Gavrilova, O. Gervasi, V. Kumar, C.J. K. Tan, D. Taniar, A. Laganà, Y. Mun, H. Choo (Eds.), Computational Science and Its Applications - ICCSA 2006, Part I. LXXV, 1199 pages. 2006.

Vol. 3979: T.S. Huang, N. Sebe, M.S. Lew, V. Pavlović, M. Kölsch, A. Galata, B. Kisačanin (Eds.), Computer Vision in Human-Computer Interaction. XII, 121 pages. 2006.

Vol. 3978: B. Hnich, M. Carlsson, F. Fages, F. Rossi (Eds.), Recent Advances in Constraints. VIII, 179 pages. 2006. (Sublibrary LNAI).

Vol. 3977: N. Fuhr, M. Lalmas, S. Malik, G. Kazai (Eds.), Advances in XML Information Retrieval and Evaluation. XII, 556 pages. 2006.

Vol. 3976: F. Boavida, T. Plagemann, B. Stiller, C. Westphal, E. Monteiro (Eds.), Networking 2006. Networking Technologies, Services, and Protocols; Performance of Computer and Communication Networks; Mobile and Wireless Communications Systems. XXVI, 1276 pages. 2006.

Vol. 3975: S. Mehrotra, D.D. Zeng, H. Chen, B. Thuraisingham, F.-Y. Wang (Eds.), Intelligence and Security Informatics. XXII, 772 pages. 2006.

Vol. 3973: J. Wang, Z. Yi, J.M. Zurada, B.-L. Lu, H. Yin (Eds.), Advances in Neural Networks - ISNN 2006, Part III. XXIX, 1402 pages. 2006.

Vol. 3972: J. Wang, Z. Yi, J.M. Zurada, B.-L. Lu, H. Yin (Eds.), Advances in Neural Networks - ISNN 2006, Part II. XXVII, 1444 pages. 2006.

Vol. 3971: J. Wang, Z. Yi, J.M. Zurada, B.-L. Lu, H. Yin (Eds.), Advances in Neural Networks - ISNN 2006, Part I. LXVII, 1442 pages. 2006.

Vol. 3970: T. Braun, G. Carle, S. Fahmy, Y. Koucheryavy (Eds.), Wired/Wireless Internet Communications. XIV, 350 pages. 2006.

Vol. 3969: Ø. Ytrehus (Ed.), Coding and Cryptography. XI, 443 pages. 2006.

Vol. 3968: K.P. Fishkin, B. Schiele, P. Nixon, A. Quigley (Eds.), Pervasive Computing. XV, 402 pages. 2006.

Vol. 3967: D. Grigoriev, J. Harrison, E.A. Hirsch (Eds.), Computer Science – Theory and Applications. XVI, 684 pages. 2006.

Vol. 3966: Q. Wang, D. Pfahl, D.M. Raffo, P. Wernick (Eds.), Software Process Change. XIV, 356 pages. 2006.

Vol. 3965: M. Bernardo, A. Cimatti (Eds.), Formal Methods for Hardware Verification. VII, 243 pages. 2006.

Vol. 3964: M. Ü. Uyar, A.Y. Duale, M.A. Fecko (Eds.), Testing of Communicating Systems. XI, 373 pages. 2006.

Vol. 3963: O. Dikenelli, M.-P. Gleizes, A. Ricci (Eds.), Engineering Societies in the Agents World VI. XII, 303 pages. 2006. (Sublibrary LNAI).

Vol. 3962: W. IJsselsteijn, Y. de Kort, C. Midden, B. Eggen, E. van den Hoven (Eds.), Persuasive Technology. XII, 216 pages. 2006.